www.wadsworth.com

www.wadsworth.com is the World Wide Web site for Wadsworth and is your direct source to dozens of online resources.

At *www.wadsworth.com* you can find out about supplements, demonstration software, and student resources. You can also send email to many of our authors and preview new publications and exciting new technologies.

www.wadsworth.com
Changing the way the world learns®

Digital Design Basics

Amy E. Arntson

EMERITA

University of Wisconsin–Whitewater

THOMSON
WADSWORTH

Australia • Brazil • Canada • Mexico • Singapore • Spain • United Kingdom • United States

THOMSON
WADSWORTH™

Digital Design Basics
Amy E. Arntson

Publisher: Clark Baxter
Executive Editor: David Tatom
Art Editor: John R. Swanson
Development Editor: Cynthia L. Henthorn
Assistant Editor: Anne Gittinger
Technology Project Manager: David Lionetti
Marketing Manager: Mark Orr
Marketing Communications Manager: Kelley McAllister
Project Manager, Editorial Production: Trudy Brown
Creative Director: Rob Hugel
Executive Art Director: Maria Epes
Print Buyer: Rebecca Cross
Permissions Editor: Kiely Sisk

Production Service: Lachina Publishing Services
Text Designer: Jerry Wilke
Photo Researcher: Linda Sykes
Copy Editor: Carolyn Crabtree
Cover Designer: Bartay
Cover Image: Large image: A. E. Arntson. Small images, left to right: *Dream Narrative*, Casey Swanson; *Digital Lace*, A. E. Arntson; *Jasper Johns*, Jorel Tingesdahl; *Wisconsin Stamp*, Casey Swanson; *"O" Alphabet*, Seth VandeLeest; *Scissor Fragments*, A. E. Arntson
Cover Printer: Phoenix Color Corp
Compositor: Lachina Publishing Services
Printer: Courier Corporation/Kendallville

Printed in the United States of America
1 2 3 4 5 6 7 09 08 07 06 05

Library of Congress Control Number: 2005921589

ISBN 0-15-505958-0

Thomson Higher Education
10 Davis Drive
Belmont, CA 94002-3098
USA

For more information about our products, contact us at:
Thomson Learning Academic Resource Center
1-800-423-0563

For permission to use material from this text or product, submit a request online at **http://www.thomsonrights.com.** Any additional questions about permissions can be submitted by e-mail to **thomsonrights@thomson.com.**

Dedicated to the Homefront: Kipper, Cameo, and Paul

and

To the many talented, sincere people I've had the opportunity to meet as students

Brief Contents

Preface xv

Acknowledgments xviii

About the Author xix

1 **A New History for A New Medium** 2

2 **Old Tools, New Tools** 22

3 **Digital Imaging** 46

4 **Mastering Color** 78

5 **Intermediate Raster Graphics** 102

6 **Intermediate Vector Graphics** 132

7 **Web Design** 152

8 **Multimedia Design** 170

Glossary 189

Selected Bibliography 197

Picture Credits 201

Index 205

Contents

Preface xv

Acknowledgments xviii

About the Author xix

1 **A New History for a New Medium** 2

Terminology 2

- **Conceptual Beginnings** 4
  - Modernism and Postmodernism 4
  - Concept and Innovation 5
- **Early Innovations in Computer Graphics** 11
  - The Moving Dot 11
  - Realism in Computer Graphics 11
  - Desktop Development 13
- **Hallmarks in Electronic Artwork** 13
  - Painting and Drawing 13
  - Illustration and Graphic Design 15
  - Layered Communication 18
- **CHAPTER SUMMARY** 20

  IN THE STUDIO 20
  - *Art and Design Research* 20
- **MOVING ON** 21

2 **Old Tools, New Tools** 22

Terminology 22

- **Visual Communication Tools** 24
  - Moveable Type 24
  - The Photographic Image 27
- **Analog and Digital Data** 30
  - Altering Our Senses 32

Focus On Concept 32
The Digital Image 32
Analog to Digital Conversions 32
Focus On Concept 35
Visual Literacy 36
Visual Language 38
How To Basics 38
File Formats 38
Visual Perception 39
Hands On Practice 39
Scanning 39
Warming Up 42
In The Studio 42
Exploring Similarity and Variety 42
How To Basics 42
Creating Variety 42
SUMMARY CRITIQUE 44
Gallery Profile—April Greiman 45
MOVING ON 45

3 Digital Imaging 46
Terminology 46
Drawing and Painting 48
Object-Oriented and Bitmapped Graphics 48
Vector Graphics 49
Vector Image Creation 50
Focus On Concept 50
How To Basics 50
Beginning Vectors 50
Hands On Practice 53
Visual Language 56
Warming Up 58
In The Studio 58
Stable 58
Reversible 58
Ambiguous 62
Raster Graphics 62
Gallery Profile—René Magritte 63
Size and Resolution 64
Raster Image Development 64
How To Basics 65
Resizing Exercise 65
Image Correction 65

Warming Up 68

Image Creation 68

Hands On Practice 68

Warming Up 72

In The Studio 72

Visual Perception 73

Gallery Profile—Diane Fenster 76

- **SUMMARY CRITIQUE** 77
- **MOVING ON** 77

4 Mastering Color 78

Terminology 78

- **Understanding Color** 79
  - The Physics of Color 80
  - Eye and Brain 80
- **Color Theory** 81
  - Properties of Color 81
  - Color Schemes 82
  - The Psychology of Color 83

Focus On Concept 83

The Relativity of Color 83

Gallery Profile—Josef Albers 84

- **Electronic Color** 85
  - Color Models 85
  - More about Modes and Models 86

Visual Perception 87

Accessing Color Options 88

- **Output** 88

Gallery Profile—Leslie Bellavance 89

- **Color Manipulations** 90
- **Creating with Color** 91

How To Basics 92

Illustrator 92

Hands On Practice 93

Illustrator 93

How To Basics 95

Photoshop 95

Hands On Practice 99

Photoshop 99

Warming Up 100

In The Studio 100

- **SUMMARY CRITIQUE** 101
- **MOVING ON** 101

5

Intermediate Raster Graphics 102

Terminology 102

- The Photographic Image 104
- Applying Design Principles 105
  - Gallery Profile—Man Ray 106
- Creative Imaging in Photoshop 108
  - How To Basics 109
  - More How To Basics 113
  - Hands On Practice 115
- Concept Development 115
  - Warming Up 116
  - Visual Perception 117
  - In The Studio 118
- SUMMARY CRITIQUE 118
  - Focus On Concept 118
- MOVING ON 118
- Creative Imaging in Painter 118
  - How To Basics 120
  - Hands On Practice 127
  - Warming Up 127
  - In The Studio 127
- SUMMARY CRITIQUE 128
  - Gallery Profile—Joan Truckenbrod 129
- MOVING ON 129

6

Intermediate Vector Graphics 132

Terminology 132

- Applying the Vector Image 133
- Applying Design Principles 136
- Creative Imaging in Illustrator 136
  - How To Basics 138
  - Visual Perception 142
  - Hands On Practice 142
  - More How To Basics 142
  - More How To Basics 143
  - Hands On Practice 146
  - Gallery Profile—David McLimans 147
  - How To Basics 148
  - Hands On Practice 149
- Gestalt Principles 149
  - Focus On Concept 149
  - Warming Up 149

In The Studio 150
- SUMMARY CRITIQUE 151
- MOVING ON 151

7

Web Design 152

Terminology 152
- **An Introduction** 153
  Gallery Profile—Jessica Helfand 154
- **Origins** 154
- **New Media** 155
  Focus On Concept 156
- **How Does the Web Work?** 156
  - Methodology 157
  - Design and Production 158
  - What Are the Rules? 161
  Visual Perception 165
- **Web Components** 165
  - Pages and Sites 165
  - Interactivity 165
  - Tables and Frames 166
  - Animation and Sound 166
  - Video 168
  - Web Publishing 168
  Hands On Practice 168
  Warming Up 169
  In The Studio 169
- MOVING ON 169

8

Multimedia Design 170

Terminology 170
- **Interactivity** 171
- **How Does Multimedia Work?** 174
  - Methodology 175
  - Design and Production 176
  Visual Perception 176
- **Authoring Software** 176
- **Animation** 176
  Focus On Concept 177
  How To Basics 178
  - *Animation Packages* 179
  How To Basics 179
  - *Creating a Basic Flash Animation* 180
  Hands On Practice 184
  Warming Up 184

- **Advertising and Entertainment** 184
- **Video Editing** 184

  In The Studio 186

  A Public Service Announcement 186

  A Personal Narrative 186

  Gallery Profile—Nam June Paik 186
- **SUMMARY CRITIQUE** 188
- **MOVING ON** 188

Glossary 189

Selected Bibliography 197

Picture Credits 201

Index 205

Preface

Digital Design Basics bridges two overlapping and merging areas: art and communications technology. By relating core aesthetic concepts to computer graphics software instruction, the book addresses how to build and integrate strong design technique with the development of computer skill sets. *Digital Design Basics* introduces essential software techniques in Illustrator, Photoshop, and other raster and vector programs, and uniquely harmonizes technical instruction with fundamental design concepts, design theory, and art/design history. The process of constructing a strong aesthetic base is enabled in *Digital Design Basics* with an inspiring combination of images from the history of art and design, contemporary computer graphics, digital student portfolio examples, and step-by-step diagrams.

The book is designed for students learning the basics of computer graphics. It is appropriate for any major or minor in fine art, advertising, marketing, communications, graphic design, or multimedia.

Major Features in the Text and Accompanying CD-ROM

There is currently no textbook that attempts to integrate the instruction of digital imaging skills with design principles and art/design history. *Digital Design Basics* answers that need with aplomb by offering a unique combination of concept, theory, technique, and design instruction. This integrated approach makes *Digital Design Basics* a useful contribution to a field that is well supplied with information related to "How." Students and instructors will benefit from a book also presenting discussion about "Why."

Step-by-Step The step-by-step features contribute to the book's unique combination of concept, technique, and design instruction:

How To Basics provide the instructor a base for software lecture/demonstration with step-by-step images. Instructors may elect to study the software as presented or follow the raster instruction, returning later to study the vector software.

The CD provides access to *trial software* and *freeware*.

Step-by-step illustrated *How To Basics* for software appear on the CD.

Hands On Practice gives the student practice in the techniques presented in *How To Basics*. Step-by-step diagrams enhance the instruction.

Warming Up gives a practice exercise related to the chapter.

In The Studio presents an assignment that incorporates both software techniques and elements of visual perception presented in the chapter.

Hands On, Minds On *Digital Design Basics* emphasizes the creative partnership between computer tools and the eye, mind, and hand of the artist/designer. Each chapter is enriched by a discussion of the relationship between design concepts and software tools and techniques:

Visual Perception adds to the design concepts introduced in the chapter, which are incorporated in the *In The Studio* assignments.

Focus On Concept introduces topics for discussion related to the more theoretical or philosophical material introduced in the chapter.

Visual Sources and References Artists learn by example and emulation. An indispensable part of this learning process involves exposure to the best work in the field. The full-color art and design examples showcased in this text and the accompanying CD provide a rich venue for students' visual instruction:

Gallery Profiles present an artist or designer whose work is exemplary of a design concept and/or technique. The book includes many full-color samples of art and design that make excellent use of design principles and concepts related to a variety of fields in fine art, illustration, and design, both past and present. Examples include student and professional work.

Artist Portfolios on the CD consist of electronic files of prints illustrated in the chapters and created by students. On the CD, layers will be available for examination.

The CD includes free *scans* of objects, *clip art*, and *digital photographic imagery* intended for the chapter assignments.

Terminology lists provide a summary of new terms introduced at the opening of *each* chapter. These terms, which appear boldfaced in the chapter, are also defined in the book's *Glossary*, consisting of accessible extended definitions.

The *Selected Bibliography* provides references for further study in art and design history, theory, and practice. The standard bibliography is enhanced by the CD's "webliography" links to related art and design sites rich in imagery and reference materials.

Tools and Techniques: Design Topics and Software Instruction

The design elements and principles that form the underpinning of all art and design also give structure to successful computer graphics. As in any art medium, there are specific tools and techniques that must be mastered:

Students learn the basics of scanning and perform various manipulations to the scans based on readings about unity and variety in design.

The difference between vector and raster graphics is covered. Students are introduced to image creation and manipulation in both areas using Photoshop, Illustrator, and related programs. Figure/ground concepts are introduced, illustrated, and assigned as *In The Studio* work. Students are also introduced to more advanced levels of raster and vector applications through masking and various collage and pen tool techniques. The principles of balance and focal point are covered and assigned in this context.

Color theory is taught as a fundamental part of visual perception. Both pigment-based and electronic work are presented. Students learn gradients and color modes in Photoshop and gradients and building color swatches in Illustrator. Archival inkjet and Iris prints are profiled. *Warming Up* exercises are based on simultaneous contrast in design practice.

Students are introduced to fundamental web design using illustrations in Dreamweaver. The importance of a careful plan for site navigation is discussed. *In The Studio* work emphasizes the similarities and differences between design principles in print and on the web.

Forms of multimedia design and animation are discussed, including Flash and Photoshop's ImageReady. Instructors may choose to focus on teaching software applications, or to discuss the concepts behind interaction and time-based animation. Understanding time-based rhythm concludes the book's emphasis on design principles applied in the creation of digital media.

Acknowledgments

Thanks are due to a great many people who worked on this book. It is a complex undertaking that requires much more than just the author's input. The people at Thomson Wadsworth have been excellent to work with. Thanks to everyone from John Swanson, who decided to publish this book, to Cynthia Henthorn for many, many excellent suggestions as the text developed, to Trudy Brown and Maria Epes who helped shape the finished product. The text design is by Jerry Wilke. The accompanying CD was created with organizing help and suggestions from Dave Lionetti, with design and production by an excellent staff at CowTown. The freelancers and staff at Lachina Publishing provided invaluable services including page layout by Carol Kurila, final copyediting by Carolyn Crabtree, permissions assistance by Linda Sykes. Ronn Jost was my communications contact person.

Thanks to my colleague Assistant Professor Daniel Kim for creating the initial design concept for the textbook. It got everything off to a great start. Heartfelt thanks to the talented student designers who allowed me to reproduce their artwork.

Special appreciation is given to Tammy Roemer and Seth VandeLeest. These two students (now beginning their professional careers) created the majority of the freelance technical illustrations with consistent creativity, speed, and cheerfulness.

The following colleagues reviewed this book in its early draft stage, and provided valuable comments and insights.

Rhonda Levy, School of Visual Arts
Mary R. Scott, Academy of Art University
Al Wasco, Cuyahoga Community College
Jim Watson, University of Central Oklahoma
Ronald J. York, Fashion Institute of Technology

About the Author

Amy E. Arntson is a Professor Emerita at the University of Wisconsin–Whitewater where she taught art, design, and computer graphics for over twenty years. Her artwork is exhibited nationally and internationally. Her presentations on the nature of design and perception have been given in Europe, Scandinavia, Central and South America, China, and the United States. Currently a full-time artist, Professor Arntson is also the author of *Graphic Design Basics*.

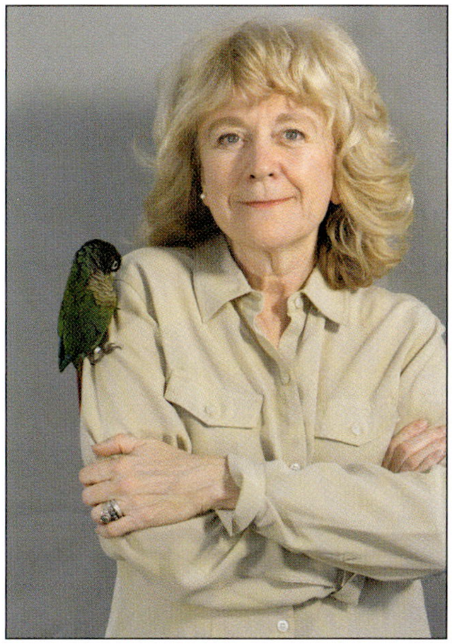

Digital Design

Basics

TERMINOLOGY

CHAPTER 1

See Glossary for definitions

Computer Graphics

New Media

Modernism

Postmodernism

Analytic Cubism

Synthetic Cubism

Collage

Dada

Photomontage

Photogram

Bauhaus

International Style

Fluxus

Hidden Line Elimination

Wire Frame Drawing

Tweening

Depth Cueing

Paint Systems

1 A New History for a New Medium

The computer is our active, creative partner, an extension of our mind, as well as our hand and eye. As artists and designers, we are working in partnership with a powerful digital tool that possesses a voice of its own. The relationship between the computer and the work created on it is as fundamental as oil is to a painting, or clay is to a ceramic vessel. The artist's and designer's hands, eyes, and intent play a vital role in this partnership to create digital design. An integral member of this partnership is the tool itself.

New ways of thinking and doing are born in response to a new medium. Our tools have always had an important role in shaping our society. Consider the importance to civilization of the invention of the wheel and of the gradual development of hand tools. Our tools of visual communication have also contributed to building our world. From cave drawings to today's varied personal computers we learn, grow, and build the world around us with communication tools as much as with physical ones.

In philosopher and media theorist Marshall McLuhan's words, "Societies have always been shaped more by the nature of the media by which men communicate than by the content of the communication." He was especially interested in the pervasive role of television, but certainly predicted the vital role of the new computer-based digital media. Now it's hard to imagine living without a computer in the house.

The general "umbrella" term **computer graphics** refers to the entire field of hardware and software that evolved in the 20th century, enabling us to create an image on and with the computer. The term **New Media** is often used to describe digital creations that can combine various forms of communication such as visuals, sound, motion graphics, or interactivity. As artists and designers, we use computer graphics to design and create digital images for a vast array of applications. The doors to new frontiers are opening up as this technology continues to develop new, powerful combinations.

Computer graphics is extending our senses by showing us things we have never seen before in geology, space, medicine, and a host of other areas. The translation of numerical data into visual digital information allows us to see inside storms and along chains of molecules. Computer-generated graphics are now recognized as carrying as much or more information than the linear, printed word. For those who have access to computer equipment, and to the Internet, computer-generated graphics are revolutionizing the way we communicate with one another around the globe. New technology and new ways of seeing are inseparable.

The intent of this chapter is to introduce a sense of the evolution of computer graphics and the digital image and to show computer graphics' relationship to various modes of art and design. Understanding the development of computer graphics and the role it plays in today's world is important to students of art and design. Throughout this text, we'll present the creative partnership between computer tools and the eye and mind of the artist and designer.

Conceptual Beginnings

We will begin by examining the tie between computer graphics and other art forms in art and design history. Science, engineering, and the disciplines of art and design intertwine throughout the brief history of the development of computer graphics. Our new digital media do not exist in isolation, but were born into and carry on the standards of our long visual history. In particular, certain 20th-century art and design movements influenced the design concepts of the electronic (computer-based) age. This chapter and later ones will present those relationships.

Modernism and Postmodernism

Before progressing, we need to introduce two key conceptual and stylistic periods. **Modernism** and **postmodernism** provide the backdrop for understanding the 20th-century art movements whose principles influenced the New Media design concepts of the electronic age. Whole semesters are devoted to modernism and postmodernism. Perhaps as students you will soon encounter an in-depth study of them in your program. Why does having a grasp of modernism and postmodernism matter? Because understanding these two periods and the artistic ideas they fostered can help you identify and choose among the myriad of approaches to take in your own creative work. It will also help you to understand and utilize what you see in contemporary art and design.

Modernism was the major artistic force of the late 19th and early 20th centuries in the Western world. During its first decades, modernism was an exclusively European phenomenon. After World War II the United States became the focal point of new modernist artistic developments. The term *modernism* refers to a period roughly dating from the 1860s through the 1970s and is used to describe the dominant style and ideology of art, architecture, and design produced during that era. Modernism refers to an approach to art beginning in the mid-19th-century when it was no longer important to literally represent a subject (photography captured it so well) or show that subject in an allegorical or story-telling narrative.

In architecture and design, this same approach translated into the rejection of extraneous ornament that had nothing to do with an object's or a building's function. Instead, artists started experimenting with new ways of structuring two-dimensional and three-dimensional space, often moving toward abstraction. This emphasis on the importance of the formal qualities of objects and spaces led modernists in architecture and design to focus on the utilitarian structure of the buildings, products, or graphics they were creating. They no longer applied decorative, ornamental details often derived from historical periods such as the Greco-Roman or Gothic. Instead, they came to believe that the formal elements should reinforce the function of the design. The modernist precept of "form follows function" will be discussed at greater length in the following section along with the relationship between abstract formal design elements and function. Despite the rise of postmodernism in the 1970s, modernist design principles continue to be powerful organizing forces, particularly in the design field.

The term *postmodernism* expresses what happens in art "after" modernism. The term came into use in the 1970s. Postmodernism is characterized by a simultaneous combination of media, genres, and styles and often flagrantly rejects the modernist insistence on clarity and reduction of form. Postmodernism is more a state of mind than an emphasis on strict adherence to particular formal rules, like modernism. Postmodernism embraces a variety of "value positions" about art, and many of these positions are likely to be in conflict. It is an attitude of openness, questioning, and inclusiveness. Topics can be examined from multiple points of view with multiple techniques. The artwork from previous centuries is often referenced and incorporated as postmodern artists adopt, alter, and reinvent artwork from a variety of cultural resources across time and across geographic borders. Deliberately taking elements out of their original context and bringing them together somewhat arbitrarily are common postmodern strategies for creation.

With its ability to combine various techniques and images, the computer became an important tool in the continuing development of contemporary postmodern art and design. You'll soon see the relevance among modernism, postmodernism, and the computer as a tool. But first let's visit some important 20th-century developments in art that influenced the New Media design concepts of the electronic age.

Concept and Innovation

A variety of technological and artistic innovations occurring during the late 19th and early 20th centuries contributed to the eventual aesthetic development of digital imaging. These innovations included the development of moving pictures. But even before motion picture technology became the cinema as we know it today, Eadeward Muybridge (1830–1904) studied movement by capturing it in photographs. These sequential images are the ancestor of motion graphics in film and animation. **Figure 1-1** shows a photographic study by Muybridge of a moving horse. The series documented for the first time the actual placement of a running horse's legs, thus giving us information we never before could see with the unassisted eye. Later, the computer would make this kind

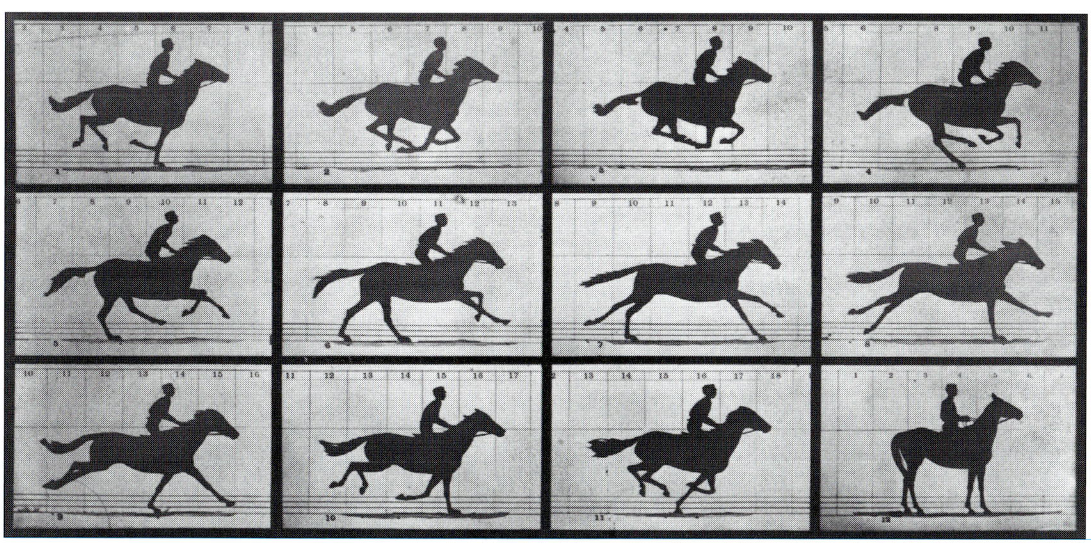

1-1 *Eadeward Muybridge.* Galloping Horse. *1878. Silverprint.* Corbis.

of assistance to our vision an almost commonplace occurrence.

We can trace the aesthetic roots of contemporary digital imaging to early-20th-century modernist movements like Cubism. Cubism had two phases, and Pablo Picasso (1881–1973) and Georges Braque (1882–1963) were leading practitioners of both. The first phase dates from around 1907 to 1912 and is called **Analytic Cubism**. Analytic Cubists took apart and flattened natural forms into geometric shapes. Different angles and viewpoints are interwoven through a series of overlapping, intersecting planes, creating a sense of ambiguous space as shown in **Figure 1-2**, an oil painting by Picasso. Despite its highly abstract character, this painting still contains naturalistic elements like a wave of hair and a tie knot that suggest the form of a seated man.

In Analytic Cubism, the three-dimensional object became part of the two-dimensional picture plane, a common modernist practice which attempted to show that a painting was an object itself and not necessarily an illusion or a window looking onto a scene (see the Gallery Profile on René Magritte in Chapter 3). This technique was also a way of representing an object without relying on the traditional rules of modeling and perspective drawing developed during the Renaissance. A great deal of contemporary digital imaging uses these freeing concepts.

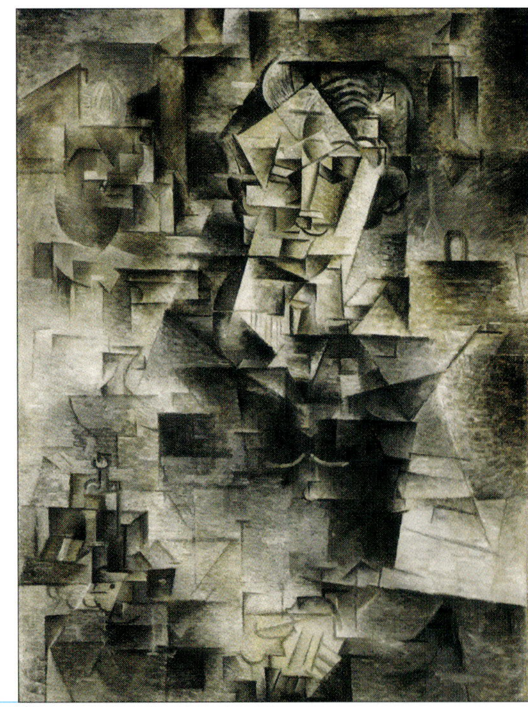

1-2 *Pablo Picasso.* Daniel-Henry Kahnweiler. *1910. Oil on canvas, 40" × 29".* Art Institute of Chicago. Gift of Mrs. Gilbert W. Chapman, in memory of Charles B. Goodspeed, 1948.561. © 2005 Estate of Pablo Picasso/Artists Rights Society (ARS), New York.

The second phase of Cubism is called **Synthetic Cubism**. The visual language developed in Analytic Cubism can still be seen in this next phase. But during the second phase, Picasso introduced the technique of **collage** to modernism, combining (synthesizing) objects in this new manner. The term *collage* comes from the French word *coller*, which means "to glue." Picasso and Braque pasted cutout shapes to the canvas surface. Synthetic Cubist artworks were created with bits of "non-art" materials such as newspapers, advertisements, cloth, or wallpaper. In this way, Synthetic Cubism, with its layers of "ordinary" machine-printed typography and textures, linked itself to the mass media–dominated culture whose development would accelerate after World War I. **Figure 1-3** by Picasso is a collage of pasted and drawn elements on newspaper, supported by cardboard.

Dada is a European-born artistic and literary movement that came into being in reaction to the horrors of World War I, but the spirit of Dada lasted in Germany to protest Hitler's rise to power in the 1930s. Dadaists embraced the irrational as a way to emphasize how the "rationality" of Western society had given rise to the brutality of World War I. Challenging conventional Western aesthetic and cultural values, Dadaists produced artworks marked by nonsense and incongruity. Members of the Dada movement often celebrated the socially unacceptable with intentional bad taste. Base, mass-produced consumer items, like a urinal presented as art, were selected for their ability to shock. These "found objects" were placed on pedestals in galleries as a way to question the limitations of what constituted art. In this respect, Dada was considered an anti-aesthetic. Yet artists identified with Dada created artworks that visually and conceptually inspire us today.

Many Dada artists borrowed from the vast array of mass media images available to create a new form of artwork: **photomontage**. This appropriation of imagery is the hallmark of later postmodern art. Photomontage is a collage of cut-and-pasted items, often combining machine-printed typography and photographic images. **Figure 1-4** shows such a montage created by Dada artist Hannah Höch (1889–1978) that collages type and image.

Following the Dada rejection of traditional art, some photographers of the time experimented with **photograms**, a type of photograph created in the darkroom when objects are laid directly on the paper and exposed to a light source. **Figure 1-5**, created by Man Ray (1890–1976), shows the subtle tones recording the passing of light through and around "found objects" laid on photographic paper. The relationship between the image and the object is interesting to consider. Which is more real? Photograms are a shadow of an existing object. These experiments from Höch and Ray, inspired by the Dadaist movement, evoke today's Photoshop effects where anything is possible with a photographic image, whether it is scanned or shot with a camera.

Cubism and Dadaism had a great influence on 20th-century art, and their influences are felt in contemporary digital imaging where artists and designers are free to collage many different planes, angles, and viewpoints as well as to incorporate "found objects" selected from consumer culture and the mass media. We are free to create a realistic digital image, but are also encouraged by the medium to explore variations. Figure 3-25 is a good example of a computer-generated collage that combines different planes and mass media images reminiscent of the Cubist and Dadaist movements (see Chapter 3).

Another highly important 20th-century art and design movement, the **Bauhaus**, takes its name from an educational institution that existed in Europe from 1919 to 1933. Bauhaus faculty members espoused the modernist concept of an integration of form and function. The modernist maxim, "form follows function," describes a fundamental modernist belief that the form of an object (its physical structure and appearance) should be descriptive of how the object is used. Utility, style (that is, the look), and an object's or image's role should be related. In graphic design, "form follows function" came to mean that the image, or the layout on the page, should reinforce the message by its physical appearance.

In the Bauhaus philosophy, fine and applied art (craft, design, and architecture) were embraced as related complementary disciplines. They were not divided into categories of "high" (fine art) or "low" (applied art). In integrating the arts, various Bauhaus designers and architects also embraced the idea that art and industry (machine production) could be harmoniously balanced. Bauhaus practitioners hoped to breathe new aesthetic life into ordinary factory-made consumer products. This functionalist philosophy contributed to the modernist belief in the importance of abstract form to reinforce a message. We can see this emphasis on form

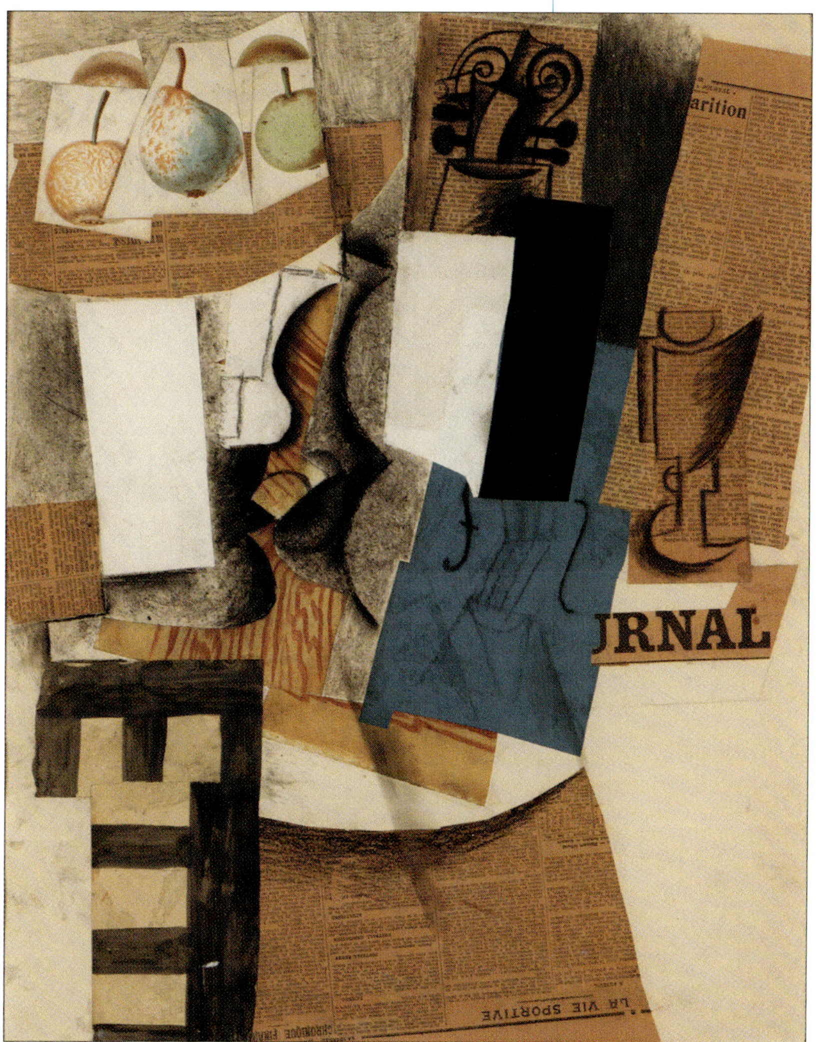

1-3 *Pablo Picasso.* Still Life with Violin and Fruit. *1912. Charcoal, black chalk, watercolor, oil paint, coarse charcoal or black pigment in binding medium, on newspaper. 25" × 19½".* Philadelphia Museum of Art: A. E. Gallatin Collection, 1952/© 2005 Estate of Pablo Picasso/Artists Rights Society (ARS), New York.

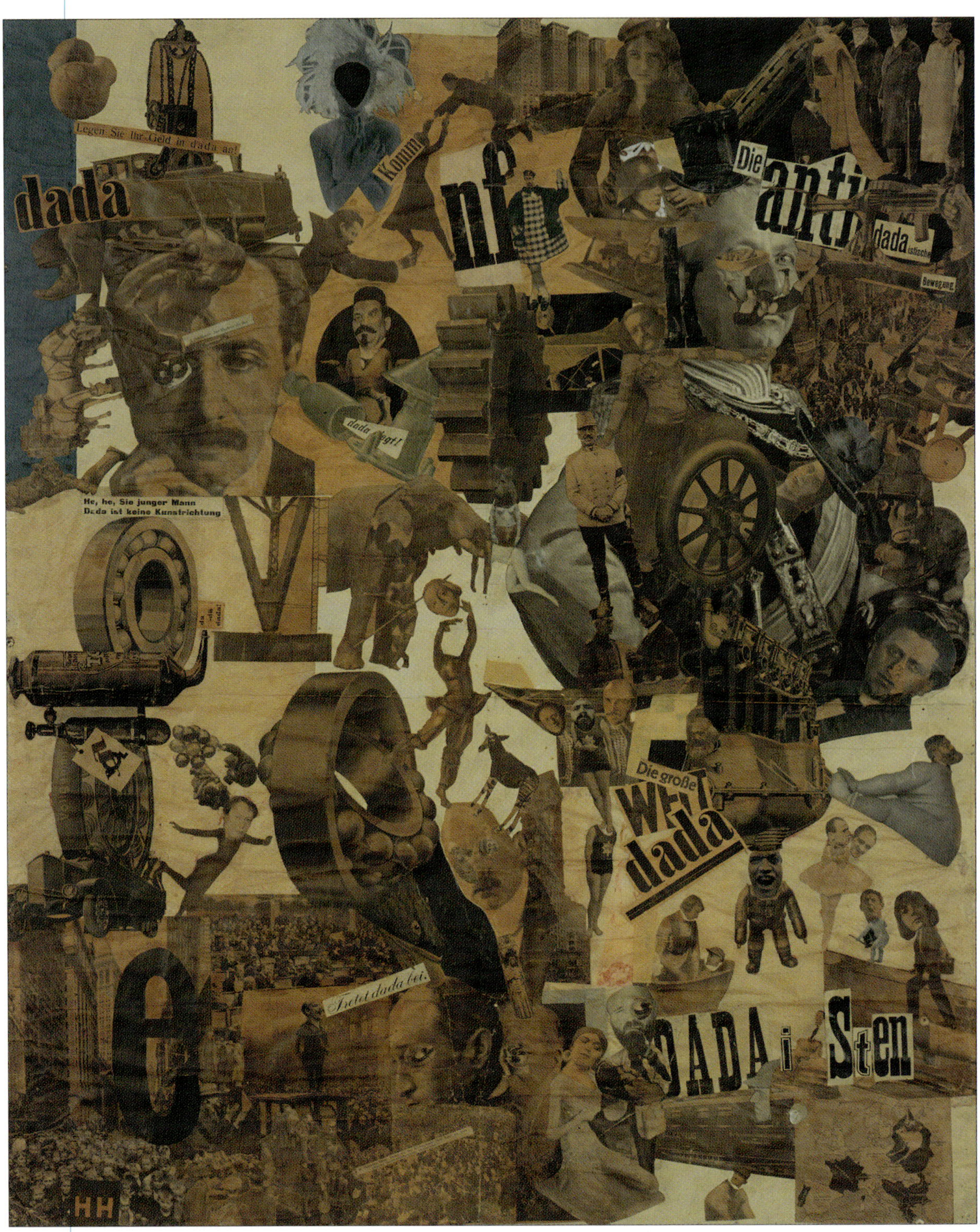

◆ **1-4** *Hannah Höch.* Cut with the Kitchen Knife (through the Last Beer-Swilling Cultural Epoch of the Weimar Republic). *1919. Collage.*

Nationalgalerie, Staaliche Museen, Berlin/Bildarchiv Preussischer Kulturbesitz/Art Resource, NY © 2005 Artists Rights Society (ARS)/VG Bild-Kunst, Bonn.

applied in graphic design in **Figure 1-6**. Bauhaus student and instructor Herbert Bayer (1900–1985) designed this cover for the Bauhaus magazine, created in 1928. Bayer's layout emphasizes the inter-relationship between typography and image, between the designer's tools and the basic two-dimensional triangle, circle, and square and the three-dimensional volume of the 3-D pyramid, sphere, and cube. The functionalist ideals followed by Bauhaus faculty and students became highly influential in the contemporary fields of design and architecture, which readily acquire and integrate new computer technology. The modernist beliefs of the Bauhaus continue to guide graphic designers today.

Another modernist movement that continues to have significant influence in contemporary graphic design is the **International Style**, sometimes called Swiss design. Visual standards on which the International Style is based have their roots in Bauhaus philosophy, and many Bauhaus instructors and students became the forerunners of the post–World War II International Style in

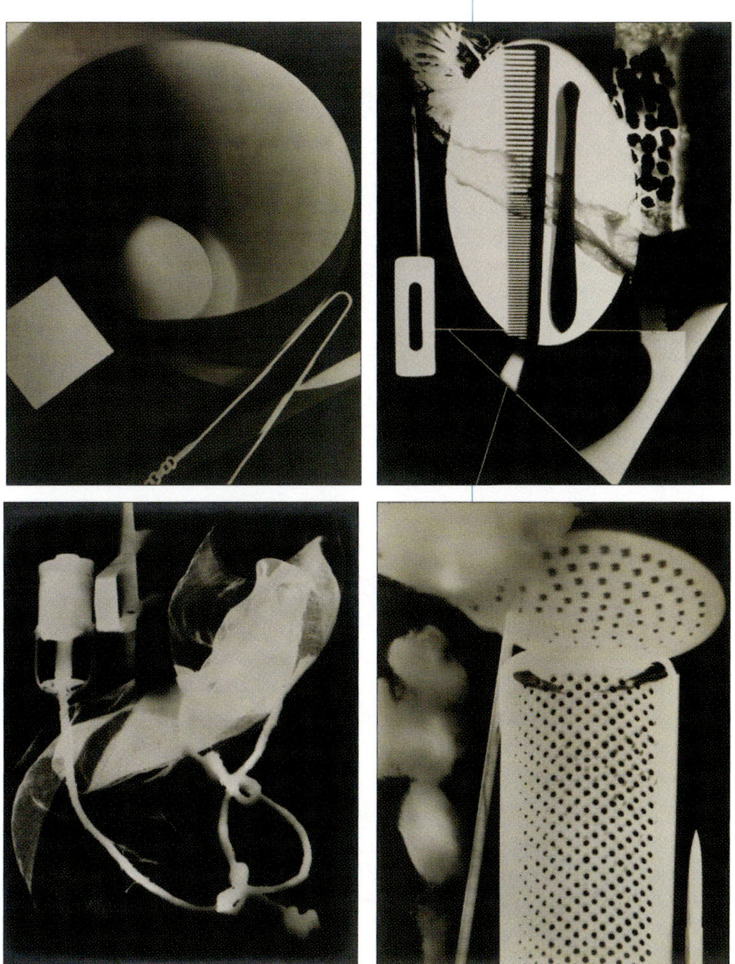

1-5 [a–d] *Man Ray.* Champs delicieux. *1922. Rayogram.*
Musée National d'Art Moderne, Centre Georges Pompidou, Paris/Art Resource, NY/© 2005 Man Ray Trust/Artists Rights Society (ARS), NY/ADAGP, Paris.

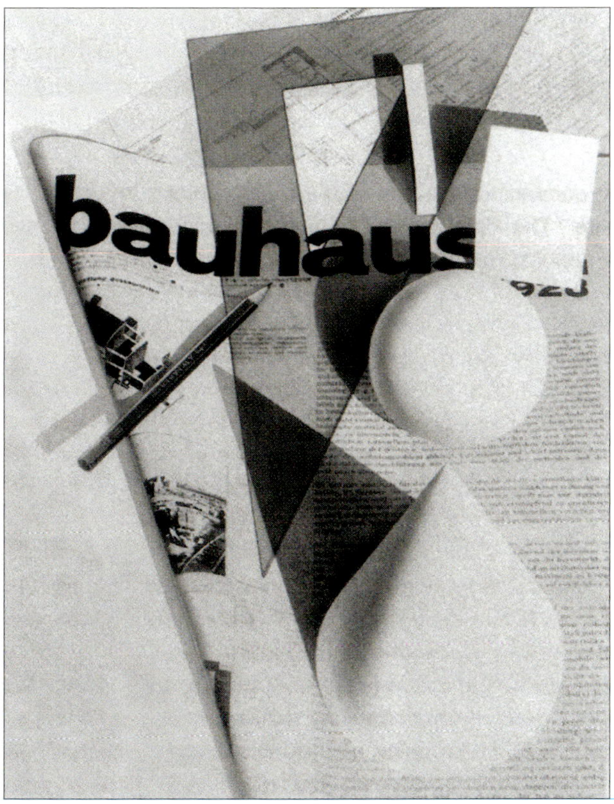

1-6 *Herbert Bayer. Cover for* Bauhaus *Magazine. 1928.*
VG Bild-Kunst, Bonn. © 2005 Artists Rights Society (ARS), NY.

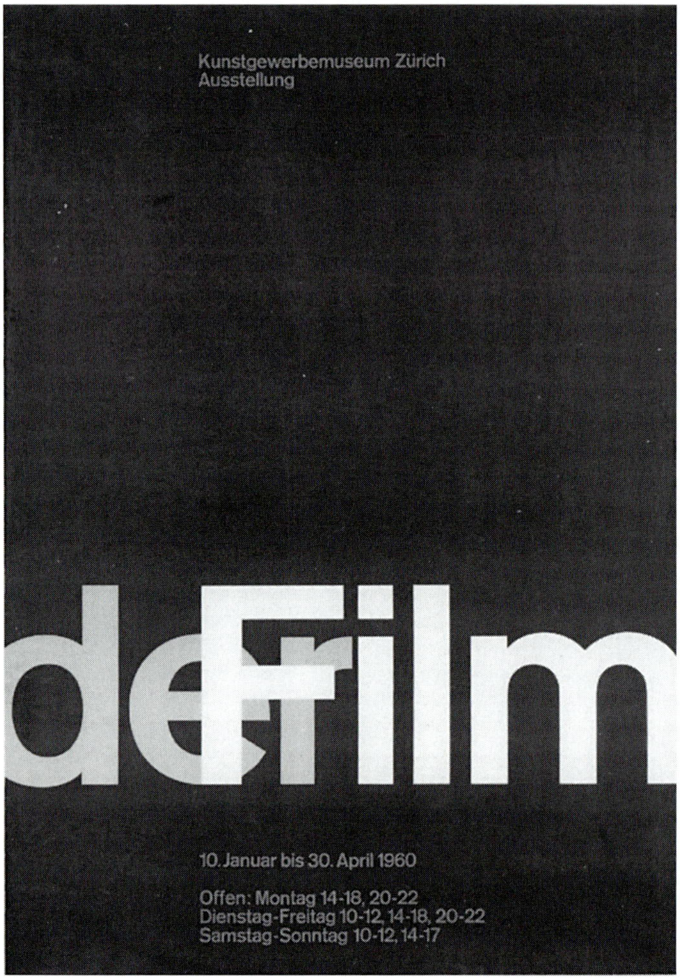

◆ **1-7** *J. Muller-Brockmann.* Poster for Kunstgewerbemuseum, Zurich. *1960.*

the United States. Emerging during the 1950s in Switzerland and Germany, the movement aimed to achieve a perfection of form through the use of the grid. Following the modernist maxim, "form follows function," a grid layout, whether in architecture or graphic design, was intended to standardize and unify a design's content by fitting all the design elements into the grid's geometric parameters. **Figure 1-7** shows how this precise placement produced a balanced clarity and simplicity, as seen in a 1960 layout by J. Muller-Brockmann (1914–1996). The typestyle of choice in the International Style was Helvetica, which itself is an example of unadorned clarity. Muller-Brockmann consistently used Helvetica in his design work, and the effect can be seen in this poster for the Kunstgewerbemuseum. The disciplined, restrained designs of the International Style are visually dynamic, as they engage the viewer and draw the eye across the page.

The graphic designer, as defined by International Style values, was seen as socially responsible for extracting clarity and order out of a chaotic world. Yet the geometric simplicity of this style eventually gave rise to its rejection by artists, designers, and architects who, in the 1970s, launched what became in many ways modernism's antithesis: postmodernism.

A lesser-known movement that also influenced digital imaging, **Fluxus**, was born in the early 1960s. It was a body of ideas that identified itself as a potential for social change and a laboratory, rather than an organized or institutionalized movement. This social intention with an emphasis on experimentation is somewhat like the Bauhaus's mission and echoes a little of Dada's political edge. Its practitioners embraced globalism, multimedia, experimentalism, and playfulness. Like Dada, the artwork created was often ephemeral. Performance pieces and collections, or assemblages, made of "found objects" were not intended to be permanent. The emphasis on creating and interacting within a state of flux also underscored the group's insistence that art could be a system of free, fluid concepts, instead of a salable commodity.

Fluxus formed the philosophical background for Nam June Paik (1932—), one of the most prolific and influential of all electronic artists. Paik is regarded as the originator of video art. His early experiments with feedback, using television sets as ready-made sculpture, echoed the art world's interest in process and ordinary "found object" materials. **Figure 1-8** shows his integration of electronics, sound, sculpture, and found objects. In this creation titled *Piano Piece*, created in 1993, Paik combines thirteen monitors, video cameras on tripods, video players, and a piano as a tribute to the avant-garde composer John Cage. Music by Cage plays on the piano, and the composer's image appears in various monitors. Also shown on the monitors are Paik and the dancer Merce Cunningham as well as images of babies and a live video image of the piano. Today Paik continues to make use of mass-produced products, transforming them into artwork by his alterations and additions. The relationship between the use of commercial, "non-art" materials and unique conceptualizations is of interest to many contemporary artists, and Paik is an inspiration to artists who wish to combine new technology with personal expression.

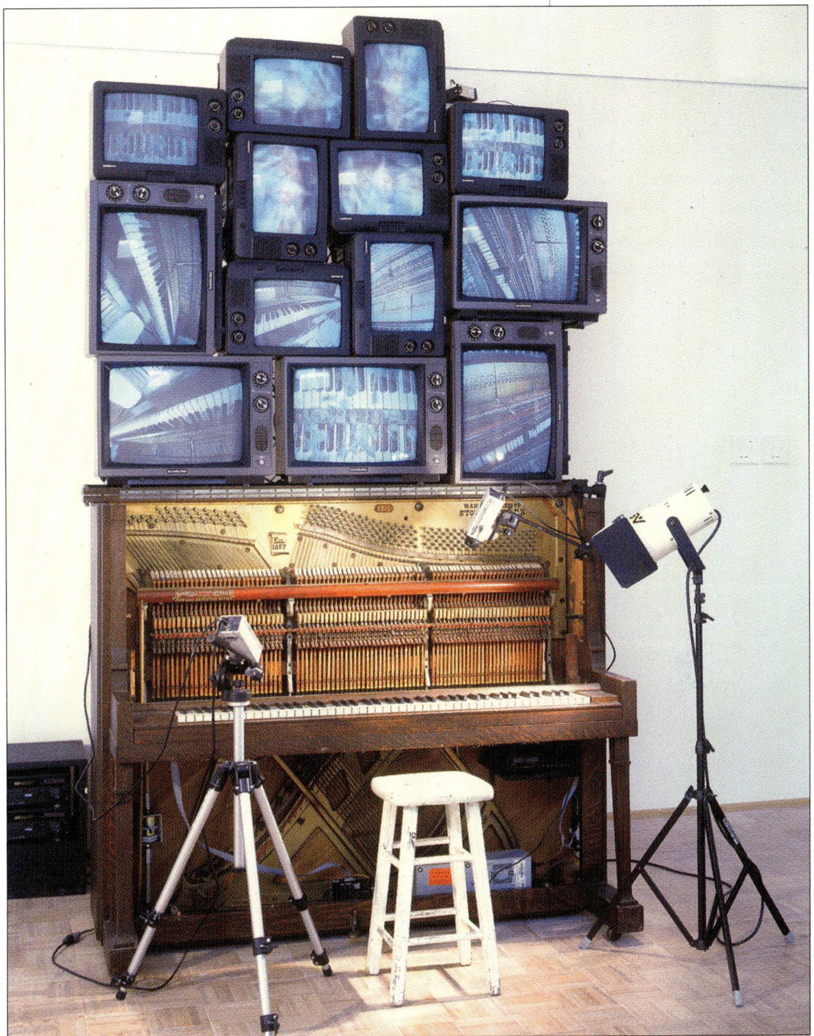

◆ **1-8** *Nam June Paik.* Piano Piece. *1993. Closed-circuit video sculpture, 120" × 84" × 48".* Albright-Knox Art Gallery, Buffalo, N.Y. Sarah Norton Goodyear Fund, 1993.

Early Innovations in Computer Graphics

As stated earlier, an integral member of the creative partnership is the tool itself. The previous section described conceptual innovations in the art world, while the next segment will describe innovations in the technological development of the computer. Contemporary digital images are created through a combination of the creative influences discussed earlier and techniques made possible through our New Media tools.

The Moving Dot

Computers began as number crunchers in the 1940s around World War II. They functioned as powerful adding machines, performing millions of calculations at a speed never before imagined. Important as this invention was, everyone in the field of art and design would eventually be affected by the development of computer graphics at the Massachusetts Institute of Technology (MIT). It came in the form of a moving dot on the visual display terminal.

In 1953 the display of a moving dot had application in the defense industry. It could accurately show the track of an enemy bomber. This visual display's invention was funded by and created for defense, but innovations in computer graphics were quickly adapted in a wide variety of fields such as, but not limited to, medicine, architecture, and communication.

Realism in Computer Graphics

In the 1960s Ivan Sutherland (1938—) invented a device he called "Sketchpad," which could draw lines in response to a marker pointed at the screen. This was the first light pen and interactive display. This display could use **hidden line elimination** to depict a three-dimensional (3-D) object in space. The lines in back of an object were hidden from view, making for a more realistic model. The object's background lines were omitted, remembered, and recalled as the object on the screen rotated. **Figure 1-9** shows Sutherland using his new invention at the Massachusetts Institute of Technology. Later developments at the University of Utah included Jim Blinn's

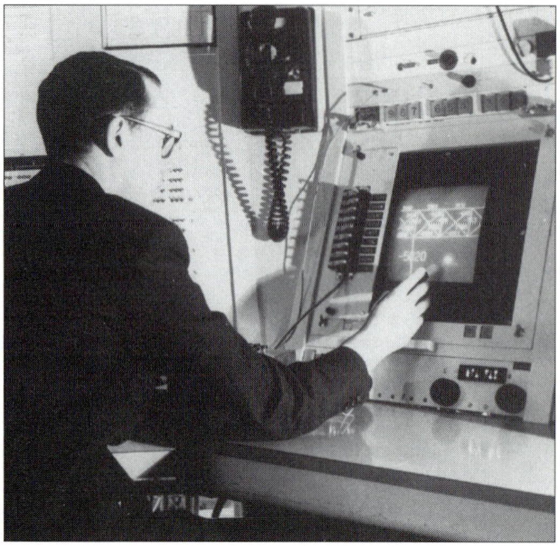

◆ **1-9** *Ivan Sutherland using the Sketchpad, a program for interactive computer graphics. 1963 photo of the artist dates from work at MIT in the 1960s.*
Courtesy, MIT Archives.

wire frame drawing. Highlights and surface textures were mapped onto wire frame drawings as both points and pixels combined to describe these new images. In 1974 Jim Blinn also developed reflectance and environmental mapping to make images even more realistic. Ivan Sutherland, his colleagues, and students also developed the digitizing tablet at the University of Utah during this time. Today, the modern digitizing tablet continues to allow us to draw with a pen instead of a mouse.

An important development in the early days of computer animation was the invention of **tweening**. Tweening allows the animator to omit several stages of the animation and to concentrate on creating key steps. The computer draws the in-between stages. During the 1970s, 3-D animation with **depth cueing** began to display the information in the background lighter than the images in the front to enhance the realism of the animations.

Professor Charles Csuri at the College of the Arts at Ohio State University was a pioneer in early computer graphics and animation. His innovative work began in the early 1960s. When Csuri decided to turn the computer into an artist's tool, the computer confronting him was a huge mainframe that required the entry of its data through punched cards. In 1967 his experimentation led to animated drawings, including one of a hummingbird in flight. Csuri produced over 14,000 frames, which exploded the bird, scattered it about, and reconstructed it. These frames were output to 16mm film. Three still frames from the resulting film *Hummingbird* are shown in **Figure 1-10**. The Museum of Modern Art purchased the film in 1968 for the permanent collection as representative of the first computer-

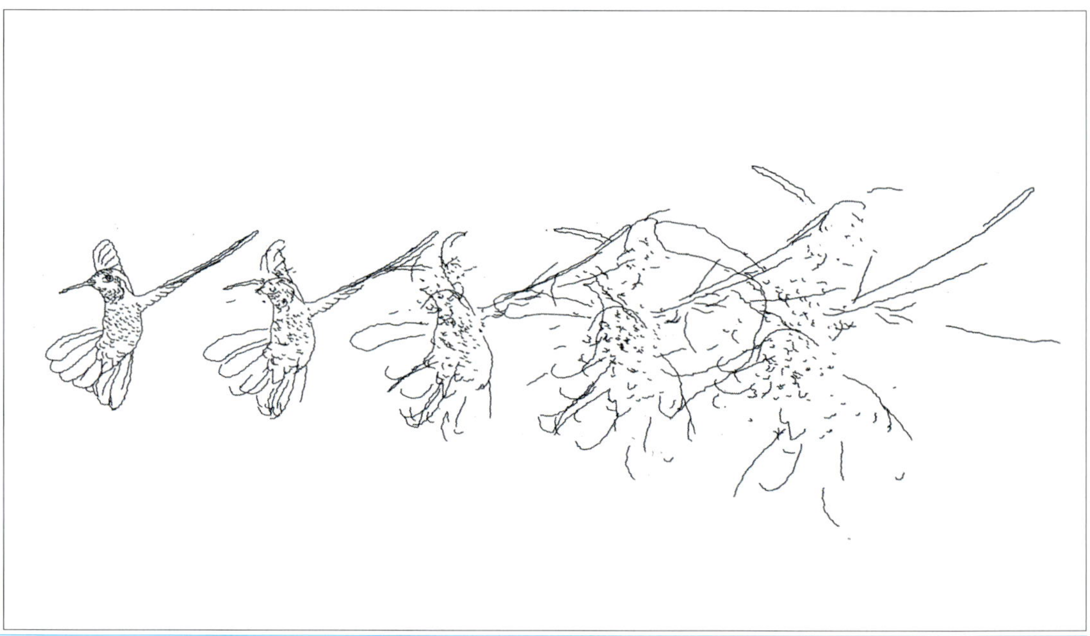

◆ **1-10** *Charles Csuri.* Hummingbird. *1967. Still from computer animation.*
© Charles Csuri.

This still from a ten-minute computer-animated film started as a series of line drawings. Computer-generated motion sequences were recorded by a micro-film plotter directly to film.

animated artworks. Csuri is referred to as an Old Master in a new medium.

Computer graphics also became important in the medical community and was used to map DNA, creating simulations of the double helix. Previous medical models used sticks and balls to represent atoms, but computer graphics made it possible to simulate a moving 3-D image. With this imaging, researchers at California's Lawrence Livermore Laboratory became the first to use computer graphics to design new drugs.

The 1970s saw the development of Pong, the video game based on an interactive moving dot. It was the precursor of a huge leisure time and educational industry. Today's elaborate video gaming can be traced to Pong's interactive, bouncing ball. The last two decades of the 20th century saw an explosion of computer graphics across the art and design field, as well as in science and industry. The development of computer graphics contributed greatly to the 21st-century proliferation of computer technology in everyday life. Between digital phones, digital photography, and the ever-expanding Internet, many non-artists find computer graphics an indispensable part of their day.

Desktop Development

The development of desktop computer graphics was an important part of the computer revolution. Just as the invention of the printing press and moveable type made the printed word accessible to a newly emerging middle class, thus encouraging literacy, desktop computers took computer graphics out of the domain of the scientific and technological elite. This egalitarian development is making clear the importance of *visual* literacy to all of us as we view or create digital images every day. Let's look at the origin of desktop computers.

Apple Computer introduced the first Macintosh in 1984. The screen presented a black-and-white visual display of pixels at a resolution of 72 ppi. Computer graphics became accessible to individual artists and designers, although the integration of type and image on the computer was difficult at this early stage. Interestingly, the first mouse was invented in the 1960s as part of a government research project. It became part of the Macintosh package.

In 1985 Aldus introduced PageMaker software for the Macintosh, and desktop publishing was born. Adobe Systems developed the PostScript programming language that enables printers to output a combination of text and images on a page. This made it possible for Apple to introduce a laser printer that used PostScript fonts. However, it would take some years for image processing and printing in the desktop environment to gain sophistication.

At the start of the desktop revolution, powerful image-processing programs were being used for advanced image generation and manipulation. Systems like the Quantel Paintbox and the Artronics Computer were referred to as "**paint systems**" and were stand-alone systems that contained their own software unique to the hardware packaged with it. These powerful machines were capable of delivering 16,000,000 colors and some color cycle animation in the 1980s, but few artists and designers outside of corporations and educational institutions had access to them. Very quickly, however, these machines were no longer necessary, as the desktop technology grew in sophistication.

Now let us examine some specific artists who were part of the development of computer graphics. Remember the thesis that the tool and the artist are in a creative partnership.

Hallmarks in Electronic Artwork

The innovative artists who created the digital images discussed in this section are as important a part of the history of computer graphics as the people who developed the hardware and software.

Painting and Drawing

Many artists experimented with and contributed to computer graphics during the 1980s. David Em (1953—) began in the mid-1980s to create his illusionary three-dimensional imagery, which he thought of as paintings. He was a pioneer in his conviction that computers and art were natural allies. Em started as a painter but in 1974 began to experiment with electronic manipulations of TV images. His introduction to the Jet Propulsion Laboratory (JPL) and the research work of pioneer Jim Blinn led to Em's mature computer art style. **Figure 1-11** shows his use of the innovations in computer graphics to date, including depth cueing and texture mapping.

Harold Cohen (1928—) developed computer-controlled drawing machines that executed a series of drawings that Cohen edited and enhanced with traditional media. Harold Cohen began his art career as a painter in London. During the 1960s he represented Great Britain in the Venice Biennale and many other important international shows. After moving to San Diego in 1968 and joining the visual arts faculty at the University of California, San Diego, Cohen became interested in computer programming and particularly in the field of artificial intelligence. He is one of the earliest artists to have become deeply involved in artificial intelligence. Much of his work since that time has been concerned with building a machine-based simulation of the cognitive processes underlying the human act of drawing. The resulting ongoing program, AARON, has been seen producing original "freehand" drawings in museums and science centers internationally. AARON paintings have hung in museums around the world. **Figure 1-12** shows one of Cohen's small robot's paintings.

Lillian Schwartz has been an important name in the origins of print-based electronic fine art since the early 1960s. Lillian Schwartz is best known for her pioneering work in the use of computers in graphics, film, video, animation, special effects, virtual reality, and multimedia. Her work was recognized for its aesthetic success and was the first in this medium to be acquired by The Museum of Modern Art. The museum purchased Schwartz's computer-based

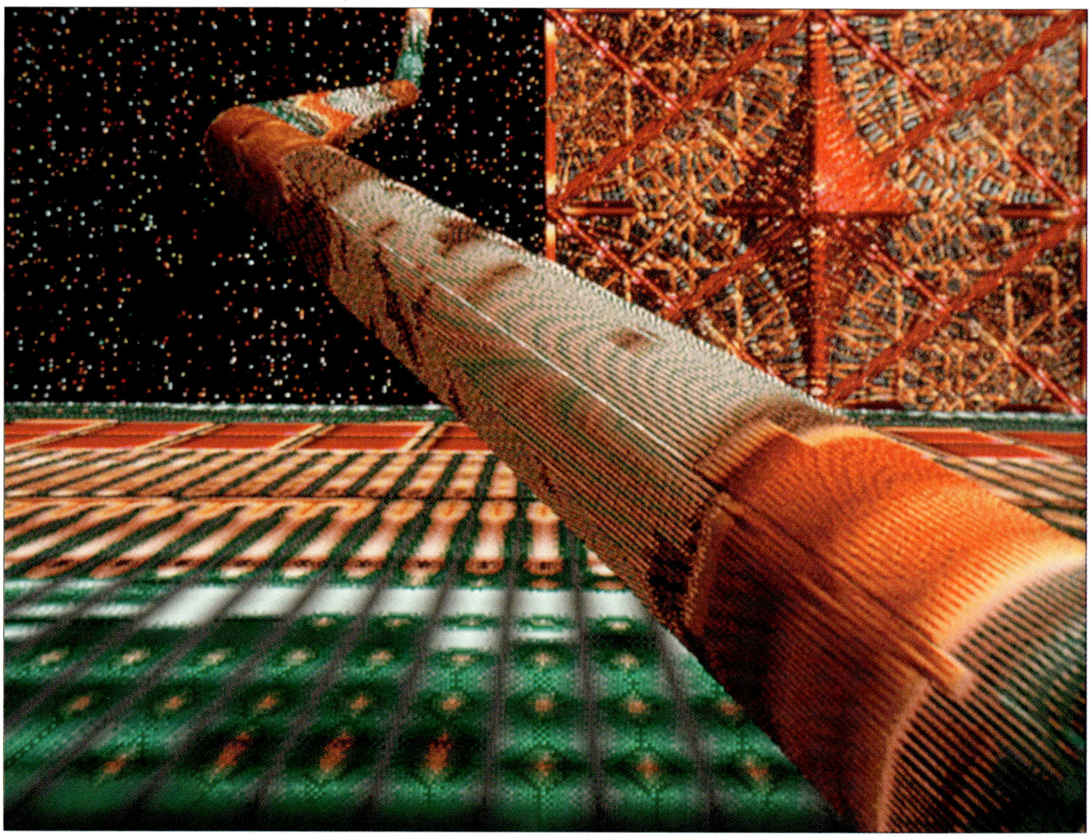

1-11 *David Em.* Transjovian Pipeline. *1979.*
© David Em.

sculpture *Proxima Centauri*. On her own, and with leading scientists, engineers, physicists, and psychologists, Schwartz developed effective techniques for the use of the computer in film and animation.

Joan Truckenbrod (1945—) is a faculty member in the Art and Technology Department at The School of the Art Institute of Chicago. She began her work with computer graphics and paint systems in the early 1980s. Her work included experiments with image transfer to fabrics, and her explorations with available paint system technologies have continued to the present day. Truckenbrod exhibits her computer artwork internationally. **Figure 1-13** shows a recent investigation that is described in detail in a later chapter.

Now we will take a look at pioneers and practitioners in more applied fields.

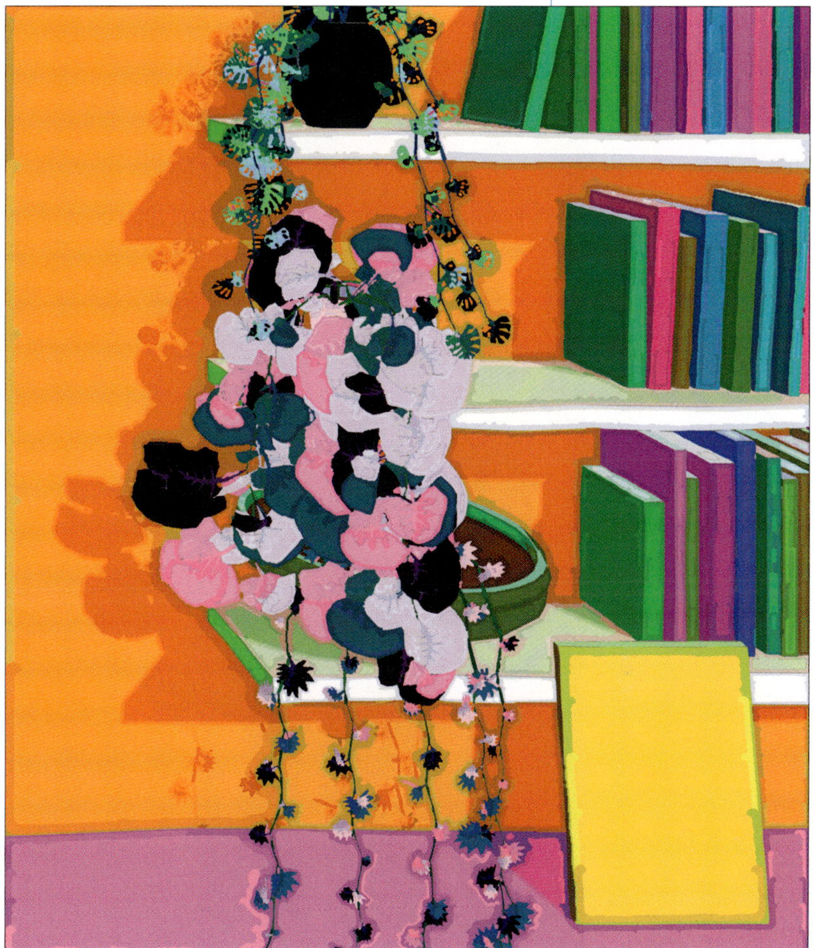

1-12 *Harold Cohen. AARON Painting. 2004.*
© Harold Cohen.

AARON is a cybernetic artist whose paintings have hung in major museums in Europe and the United States.

Illustration and Graphic Design

Pioneers in digital imaging for illustration and design enriched the field with their work during the early period of desktop imaging, and continue to do so. Barbara Nessim (1939—) began using the Macintosh Computer in the mid-1980s to create deliberately pixilated images that suited her preference for simple lines and rich concepts. Nessim is a highly successful New York City–based illustrator, and her career is enhanced by her interest in both hand-drawn and digital art. She lectures widely on the subject of computer art, and her paintings, drawings, and illustrations have been shown in numerous galleries and museum exhibitions. From 1992 to 2004 she was chair of the Illustration Department at Parsons School of Design in New York City, where she continues to teach. Her illustrations often find their conceptual beginnings in sketchbook drawings that she has maintained throughout her career. She is attracted not by the complexity and power of the computer, but by concept and a personal quality of line. **Figure 1-14** is a computer-generated print that is part of a series created in 1993.

April Greiman (1948—) created her first electronic designs on the Macintosh in 1984. Her respect for the modernist Bauhaus and related Swiss graphics, combined with new possibilities opened up by computer graphics, led to Greiman's highly innovative work. She is an excellent artist to study in order to understand the relationship between the 20th-century art movements discussed in the previous section and digital imaging. Her work is characterized by overlapping patterns and shapes, bitmapped fonts, and digital collage, but there is an underlying respect for the grid structure. Her designs are included in several major museum collections and have been the subject of many one-person exhibitions. The pixel is the smallest component that makes up everything in a digital image, and it is something that Greiman delights in pointing out. **Figure 1-15** is a self- portrait that is one of her early computer designs. (See her work featured in a later chapter.)

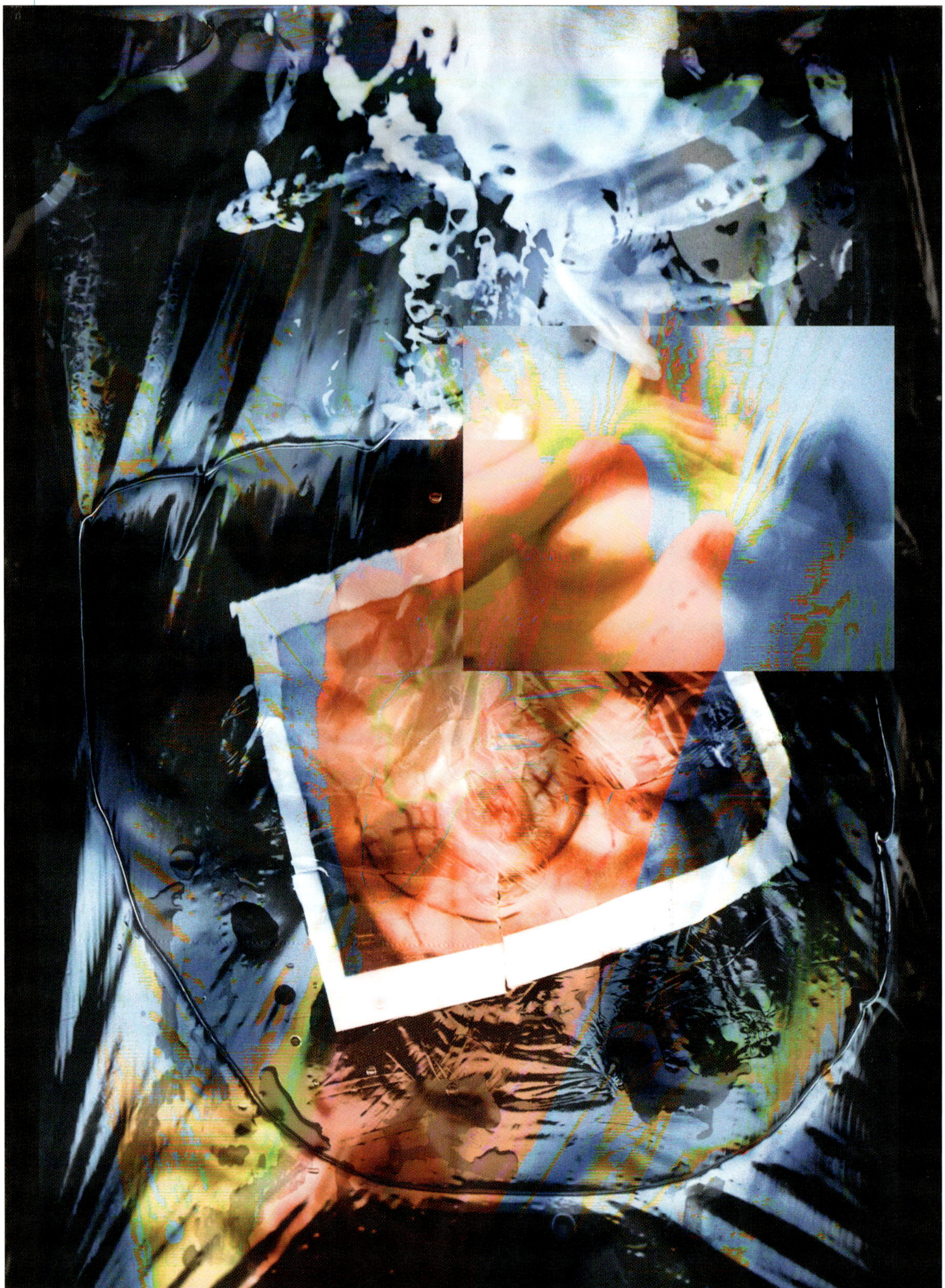

1-13 *Joan Truckenbrod.* Thresholding. *2002. Limited Edition Giclee Print.*
Courtesy of the artist.

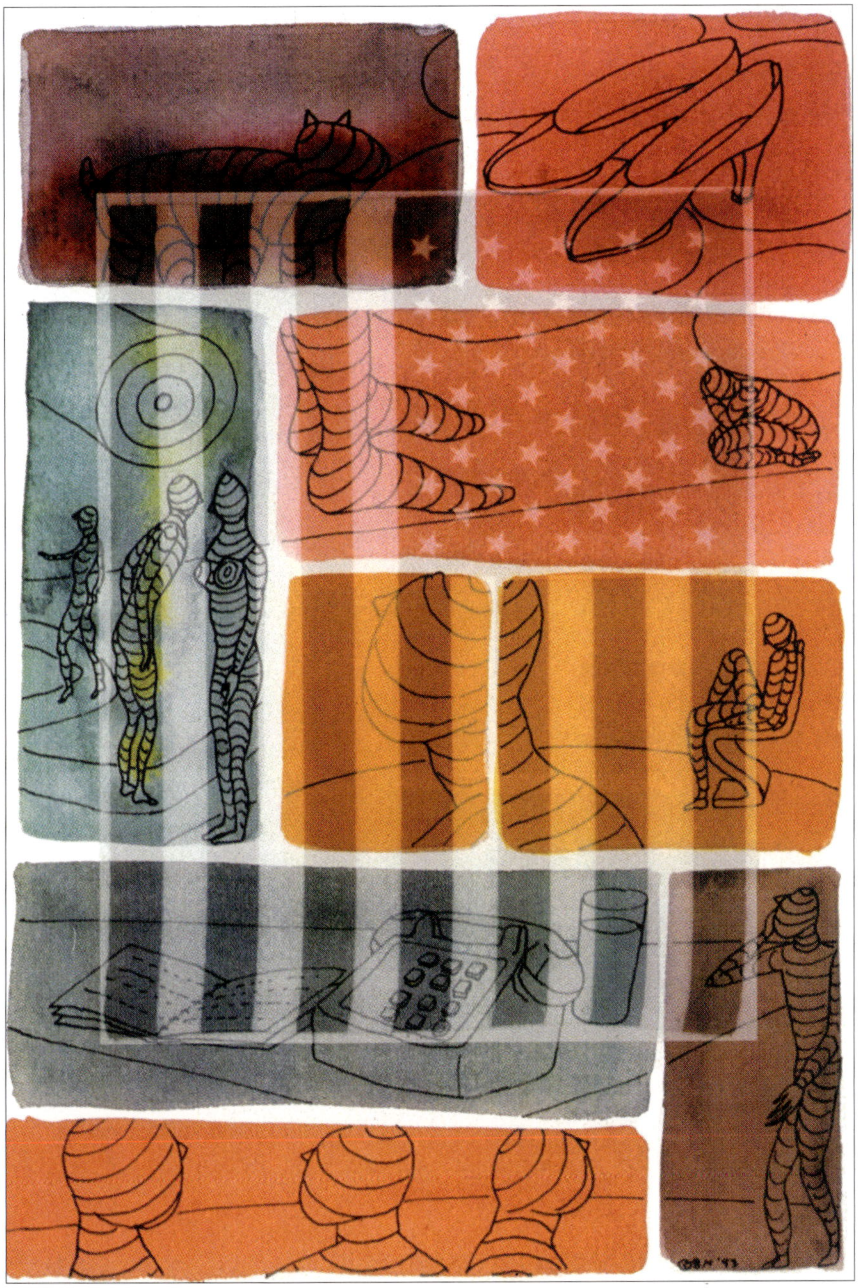

1-14 *Barbara Nessim.* Call Waiting. *1993. Gouache, Book #40. 20½" × 14½". Part of the American Favorites series, output as Iris prints.*

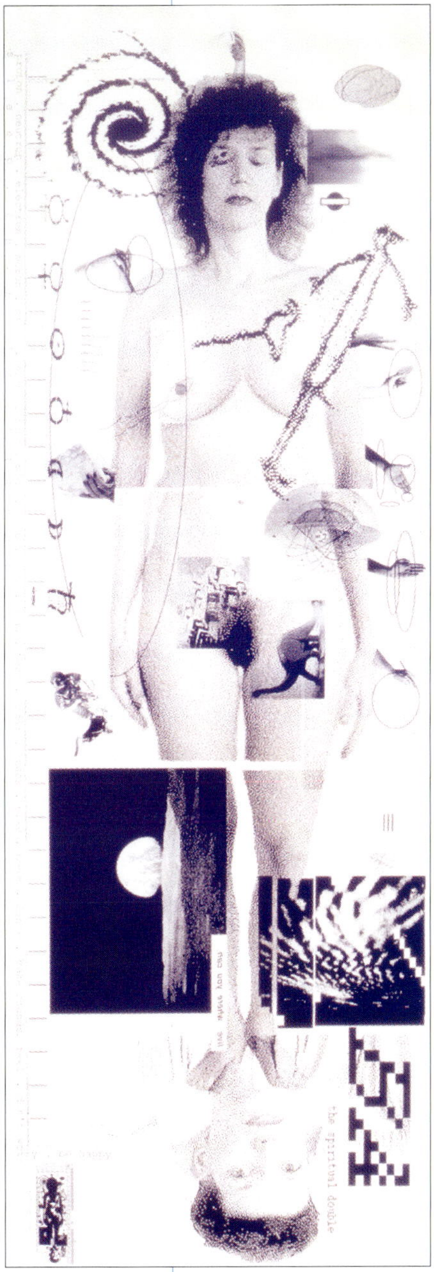

1-15 *April Greiman, art director/designer.* Design Quarterly #133. Does It Make Sense? *1986. Publication insert. Walker Art Center and MIT Press.*

Courtesy of the artist.

Layered Communication

Academic institutions began to incorporate computer graphics into design education programs in the 1980s. Cranbrook Academy of Art in Michigan was an important and influential leader in this movement. Graphic designer Katherine McCoy and her husband, product designer Michael McCoy, co-chaired the design department from 1971 to 1995. During that time, experimentation with computer graphics led McCoy and her colleagues to develop a highly complex layered graphic style based on a concept of hierarchical information. The relationship between the designer and audience was seen as a two-way communication, allowing for various readings of the postmodern design work. This anti-linear exploration of form and visual communication was the antithesis of modernism's strict rules. These designs deliberately revealed the layered structure of the composition, as seen in **Figure 1-16** where type and image overlap and interweave.

Katherine McCoy maintains a website that provides a forum for the discussion of design theory and concept. McCoy now is senior lecturer at the Illinois Institute of Technology in Chicago, but part of the year the McCoys are based in Colorado, where they direct their Higher Ground studio conferences for active professionals. (See the accompanying CD for the Higher Ground web address.)

The computer made possible the visual and conceptual layering that is the hallmark of postmodernism in graphic design. As you can see in Figure 1-16, type can be overlapped to create a rich visual texture that can be intertwined with the photographic image. By the last decade of the 20th century, graphic designers were encouraged to move away from the strict formal and structural approach of modernism and to work more intuitively. By the 1990s this stylistic approach regularly appeared in graphic design across the country. Postmodern typography could be used to explore multiple meanings rather than only to clarify a fixed message.

A combination of the visually rich postmodern stylistic traits with attention to the structures characteristic of modernism can also be successful. Which approach is most appropriate depends upon the intent of the publication.

Computer graphics has strongly influenced typography and layout design in both research-based academic and commercial applications. David Carson is an internationally recognized postmodern designer known for his experimental magazine layouts and typographical treatments. He turned away from the modernist philosophy that "form follows function" and the modernist definition of the designer as an expert problem solver.

Instead, Carson combined his interest in philosophy and various art forms with a career in graphic design that uses layout to explore meaning. His art direction and graphic design for *Beach Culture* magazine have won over 150 awards, an amazing feat considering the publication lasted only three years. Another subculture magazine that provided an excellent venue for his stylistic innovations included *Ray Gun*. The 1993 layout in **Figure 1-17** for *Ray Gun* shows Carson's style, which has its roots in the typographic experiments initiated at Cranbrook. Carson is also an author, and his influential book *The End of Print* is in its fifth printing. *Wired* magazine is one of his many clients. Carson's designs are characterized by the manipulation of type, pushing the notion of a multilayered design that makes several kinds of communication simultaneously. In his treatment of typography, legibility can give way to visually rich variations that make extensive use of computer graphics to manipulate and transform graphic elements.

Computer graphics made a complexly interwoven treatment of type and image accessible. It encouraged the development of lushly layered and visually textured artwork, especially in the graphic design world. The software layers became a metaphor for layers of meaning in the postmodern approach to style.

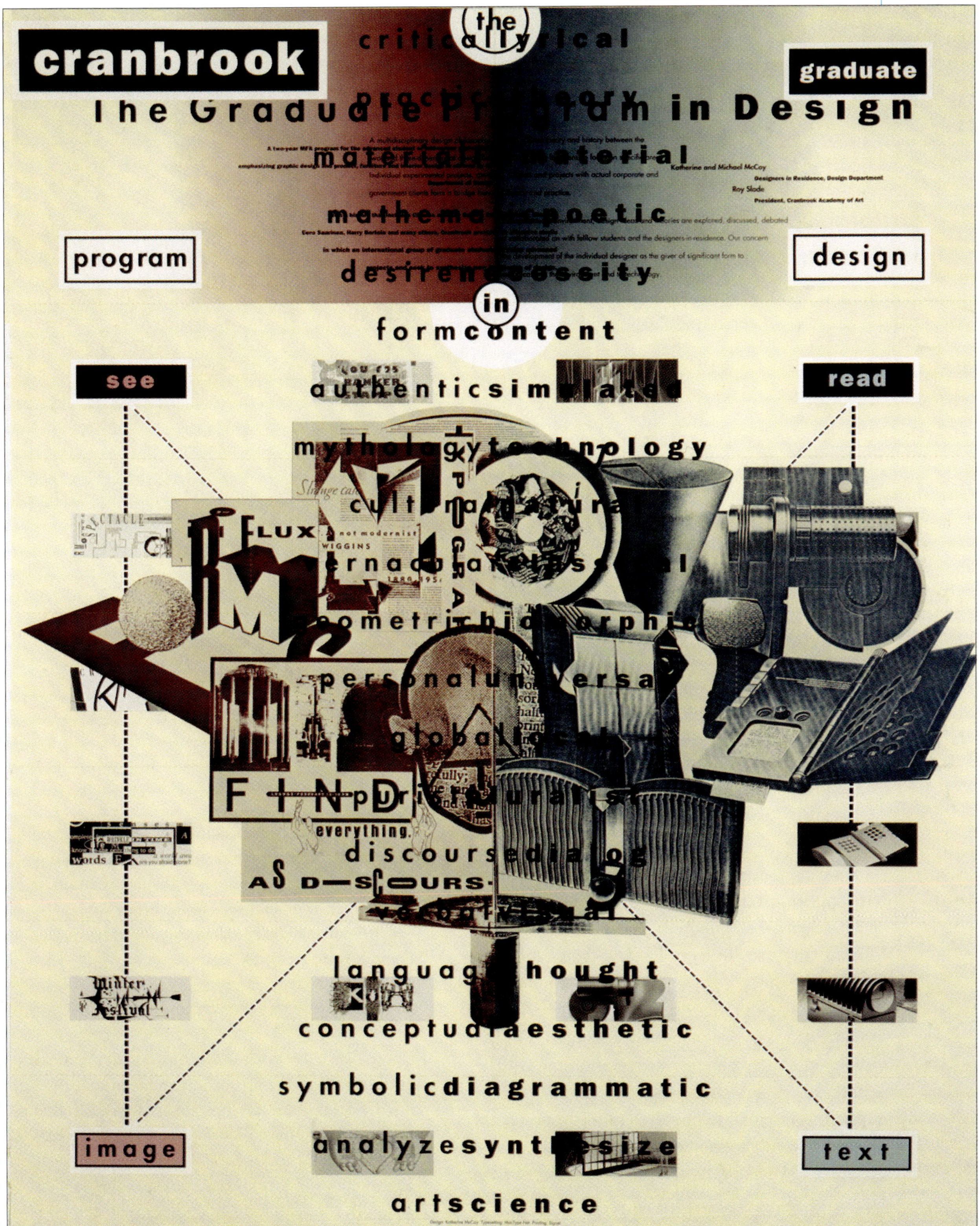

1-16 *Katherine McCoy.* Cranbrook recruiting poster. *1989.*

Courtesy, Katherine McCoy.

Images of student projects are layered with typography and a diagram related to design theory.

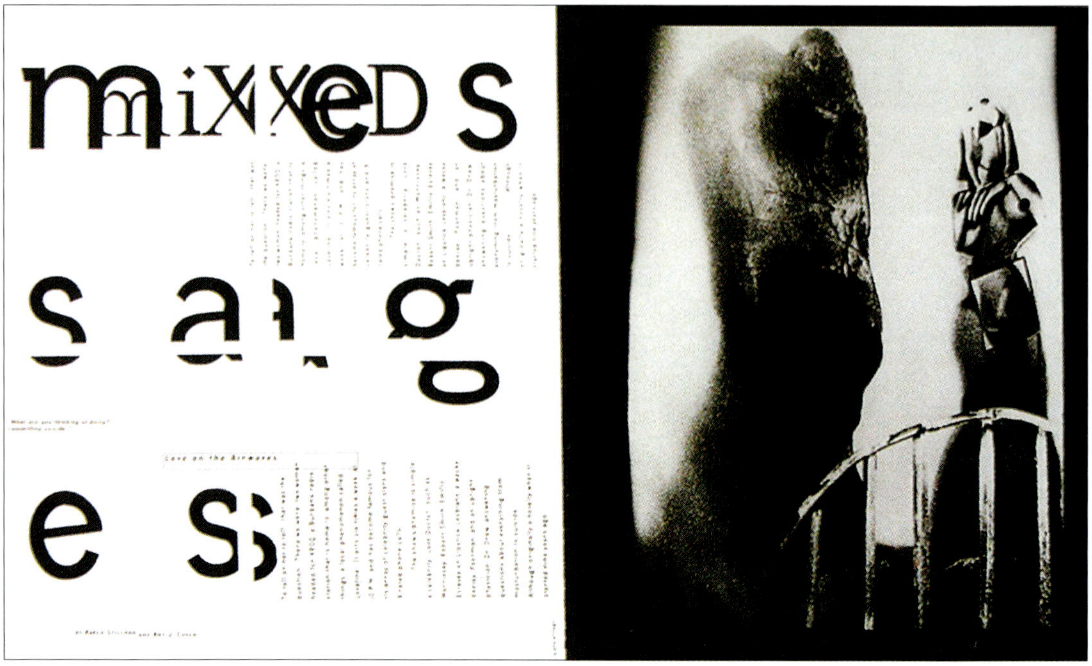

◆ **1-17** *David Carson, art director.* Mixed Messages. *1993.* Ray Gun *magazine, offset lithograph. The spaces within the headline are mixed, reflecting the meaning of the phrase.* Ray Gun Publishing, Santa Monica, CA.

CHAPTER SUMMARY

The mid-20th century saw the development of groundbreaking technology in the field of computer graphics. In the 1970s creative artistic exploration expanded the applications for this technology. The 1980s gave designers and artists access to high-end computer systems as well as early desktop computers. In the 1990s we experienced rapid development of desktop applications and resulting stylistic innovations.

Marshall McLuhan in 1964 wrote: "After more than a century of electric technology, we have extended our central nervous system itself in a global embrace, abolishing both space and time as far as our planet is concerned." In fact we are able to conquer space and time with almost instantaneous communication around the world. An email to another state is scarcely different from an email to another country. The opening years of the 21st century show how relevant McLuhan's vision was. Chapter 7 has a summary of the origins of the Internet, which is an important development in our global embrace.

In The Studio

This is the first of the assignments that accompany each of the chapters in this textbook. The intent of each assignment is to reinforce the information in the chapter. Your solutions in the other Studio assignments will be enriched by your participation in the following art and design research.

Art and Design Research

Choose an artist, designer, or movement mentioned in this chapter, or ask your instructor to suggest additional names. Research this person or art movement. Prepare a three-page report accompanied by supporting visuals, and present it to the rest of the class. Use whatever form of visual presentation you have available, from books to an audio/visual format. Your presentation should take no longer than ten minutes to deliver, but encourage questions afterward. The goals of this report are to enrich everyone's visual data bank and to encourage better studio solutions throughout the class. Your artwork will be inspired and your standards raised by studying the artists introduced in this research. Your instructor may want to spread these presentations throughout the duration of the course.

MOVING ON

Chapter 2 will get you started in using the computer graphics lab and examining the structure of the digital image. As you learn to use this powerful new tool, you will be encouraged to bring your best visual and conceptual skills along with you. Remember, it's a partnership.

TERMINOLOGY

CHAPTER 2

See Glossary for definitions

Renaissance
Illuminated Manuscript
Moveable Type
Camera Obscura
Halftone
Analog
Digital
Pixel
Hardware
Software
Megabyte
Gigabyte
Binary Data
Bit
Bitmap
Byte
ROM
RAM
Resolution
Proof Prints
Visual Perception
Visual Language
Similarity and Variety
File Formats
Raster
Lossy
Mezzotint

2 Old Tools, New Tools

This book's title, *Digital Design Basics*, suggests the partnership between the use of the digital media tools and the use of the designer's eye and mind. This chapter begins by exploring how society gradually evolved new tools of communication, culminating in our current digital media. In particular, the opening focus will be on the development of moveable type and on photography. Those two innovations are central to our current digital media. In the process, we will examine the digital image and how it is structured, discussing the important difference between analog and digital information and learning the basics of scanning and saving an image.

As in every chapter throughout this book, this chapter will present concepts related to visual perception and the elements and principles of design structure. A discussion of the important relationship between similarity and variety will lead to instruction on scanning and the use of Photoshop filters.

Visual Communication Tools

From humanity's origins, we have communicated with a visual language. The earliest artists and designers left their mark on the walls of their surroundings for future generations to find. These European and African marks told stories about hunting and food sources. Perhaps more important to us, these marks were also a record of the presence of life. The bison drawing in **Figure 2-1** was left on an ancient cave wall in Cantabria, Spain. It dates to the Paleolithic period. Our contemporary images continue to use tools both to communicate and to leave a record of our presence, as in the computer-generated image by artist/illustrator Diane Fenster (1947—) that stresses the importance of various senses **(Fig. 2-2).** With its visual and verbal play on sight, sound, thought, and touch, her picture seems a metaphor for communication itself.

As village communities developed through the millennia, their inhabitants began communicating through an oral history, telling stories from generation to generation that preserved their history and identity. The development of written language dates to the Sumerians who communicated with pictographs around 3100 B.C.E. (before the Common Era). Their pictographs were the beginning of written language. Learning from the Sumerians, the Egyptians used a picture- writing system called hieroglyphs for many centuries. The last known hieroglyph was carved in 394 C.E. (Common Era).

The Chinese first invented printing, a technique of great interest to students of digital art and design. It was a form of relief printing that originated with a stamp or an engraved seal. In the 3rd century C.E., seals were made by carving calligraphic characters into a flat surface, pressing that surface into ink, and making an impression onto a second surface. This is much like the hand stamps we can buy in craft stores today. It is the precursor of the commercial printing industry as well as fine art printmaking.

Moveable Type

The development of moveable type is vital to today's information and communication-based world. Again it was the Chinese who developed the concept of moveable type around 1045 C.E. Each hand-cut character, when carved on an

2-1 *Bison. Paleolithic Period. Cave painting. Cantabria, Spain.*

This drawing is one of our earliest records of visual communication.

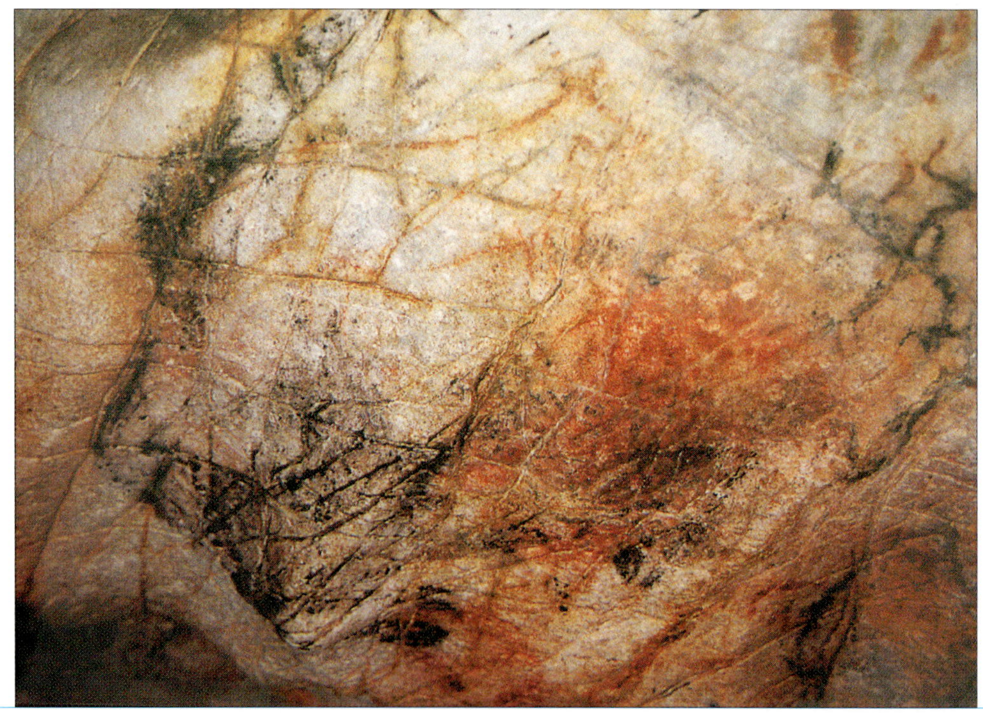

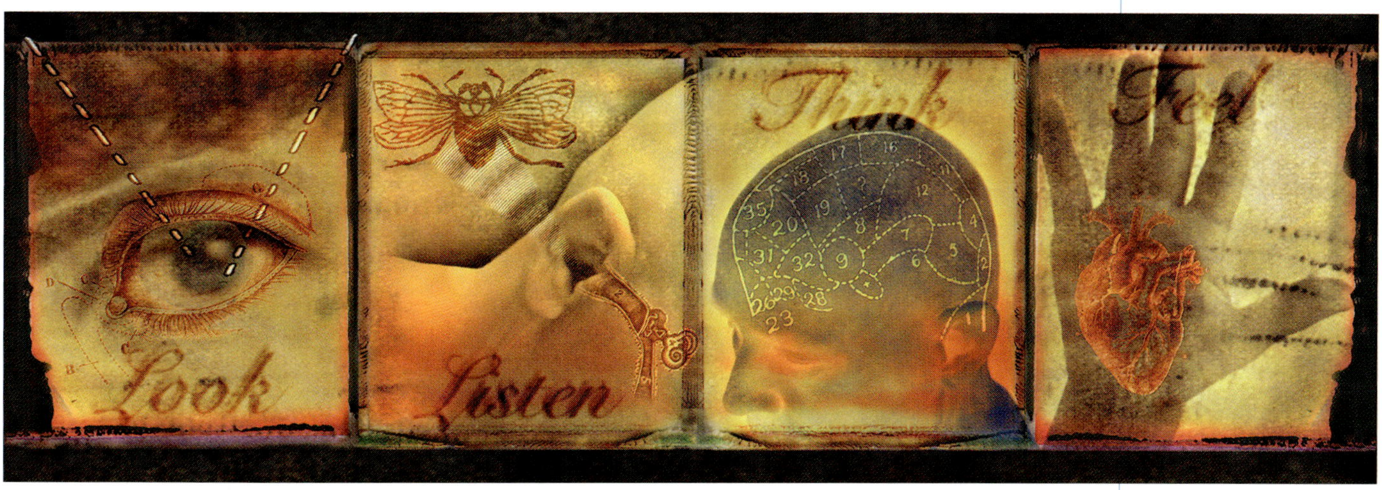

◆ **2-2** *Diane Fenster.* LookListen. *Digital Illustration.*

Courtesy of the artist.

Contemporary California-based artist and illustrator Diane Fenster created this digital illustration that emphasizes the importance of our various senses.

individual block, could be placed in any sequence, inked, and printed on a surface. The Chinese language, however, had thousands of characters, and this prevented the innovation from having much practical application. The hand-cut woodblock continued in the form of intricate illustrations.

In Europe, meanwhile, during the early medieval era, manuscripts were hand lettered in monasteries, and the text was then illustrated with hand inking. These one-of-a-kind manuscripts were usually small enough to be very portable. The written word could be seen or read only by the most elite members of society, who had access to manuscripts and who were able to read. As the **Renaissance** dawned in the 14th century, **illuminated manuscripts** for private use grew in importance. The Book of Hours was the most popular, especially in the following century. The most famous of these is the Book of Hours created for the Duc de Berry by the Limbourg brothers. Shown in **Figure 2-3,** it was filled with elaborate illustrations.

With the growing demand for books, printers began to search for means to increase production and accessibility. Johannes Gutenberg (late 14th century–1468) first developed the method of printing typographic books using **moveable type** around the year 1450. The success of Gutenberg's system hinged on its emphasis on standardization and the fact that the Western alphabet has only twenty-six characters. Another key to his invention was the ability to cast individual letters, thanks to his background in metalworking. The characters were stored in a case, then pulled out letter by letter and set into a trough, called a wand. From the trough, lines of type were then moved into a frame, or galley. After a page was printed, the type was re-filed into the case to be used again. Printers used Gutenberg's press and moveable type system for four hundred years. **Figure 2-4** shows a page from his famous Bible. Although the page *looks* as if it is a hand-printed manuscript, each letter was created by individual metal pieces of type.

The next important innovation was the Linotype machine, perfected in 1886 by Ottmar Mergenthaler (1854–1899). Printers no longer had to arrange type by hand into a frame (or galley). Now a machine composed lines of type. Each time an operator pressed a key, a matrix impression was released and aligned with other characters set in the line. Finally lead was poured into the line of matrixes to cast a line-of-type for printing.

The Implications Gutenberg's moveable type and printing press combination could record and print words that could be shared with many more people than a handcrafted manuscript could. This technology is an indicator of how incredibly important communication tools are in the history of civilization. Moveable type and the printing press are given credit for contributing to the

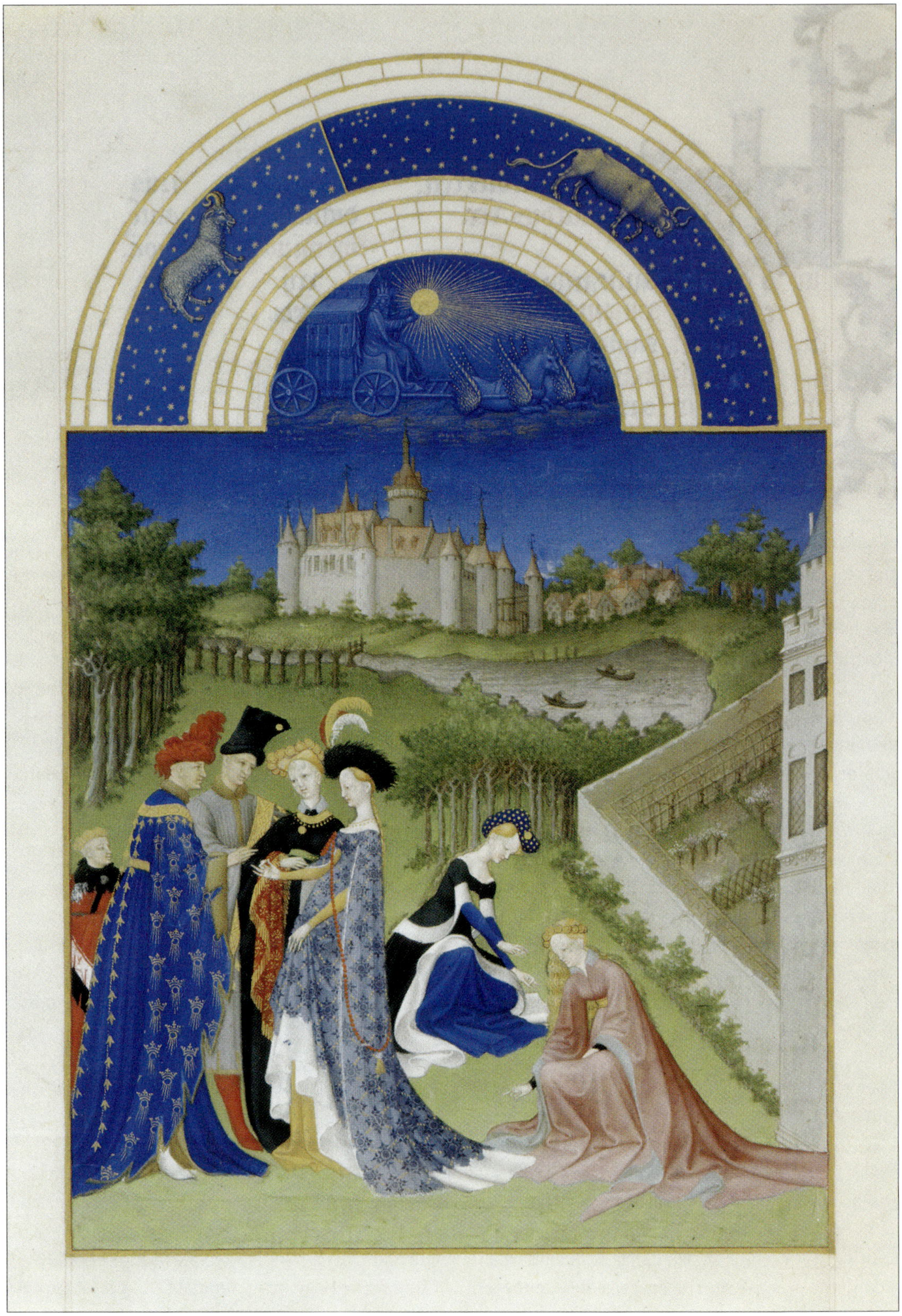

2-3 *Pol, Hennequin, and Herman de Limbourg. Les Très Riches Heures: April. 1416.*
Musée Condé, Chantilly, France/Reunion des Musées Nationaux/Art Resource, NY.

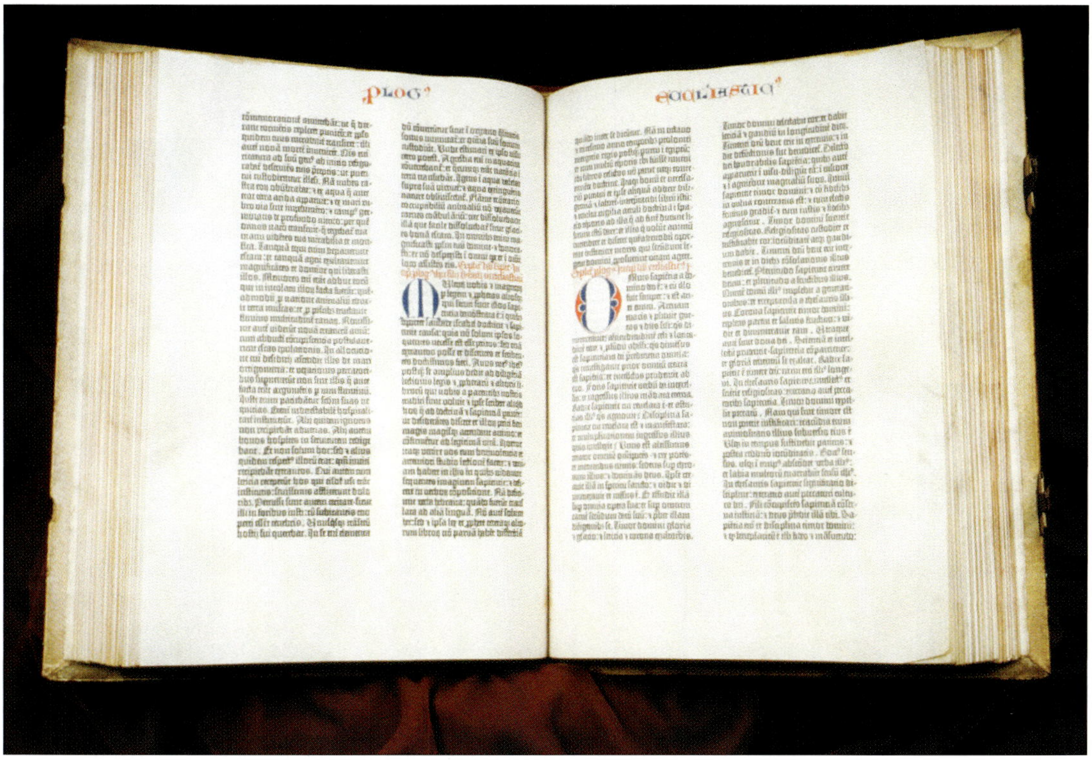

2-4 *Johannes Gutenberg. Pages from the Gutenberg Bible. 1450–1455. 11.75- by 15-inch pages with 1,282 pages contained in two volumes. Color added by hand.*
Corbis.

accelerated growth of a middle class because mass production of the printed word made information accessible to and affordable by many. As is often said today, information is power. The more we know, or can find out about, the more we can control our lives.

Visual art and graphic design can trace their origins from cave painting to the printing press to photography, film, and the computer. As we continue to examine these stages in visual technology, we grow to understand at a deeper level the interrelationship between changes in tools and changes in society.

The Photographic Image

Early forms of photography included the camera obscura. It is a darkened box with a small opening that allows light rays to project onto the back of the box, forming a small, bright re-creation of an object outside the box. The history of the camera obscura is interesting. This process is very old, including projection rooms that were used as entertainment, as shown in **Figure 2-5.** To experience this projection room effect, try going into a very dark room on a very bright day. Make a tiny hole in a window cover and look at the opposite wall. There will be the world outside the window, re-created fully in its color and movement. Why? Light travels in a straight line, and when rays pass through the tiny hole, they do not scatter but cross and reform. It is an optical effect that has been known for many centuries. Some contemporary photographers continue to be interested in this process and create small boxes called pinhole cameras. The outside world is exposed onto photographic paper placed inside the box.

Photographic innovators Niépce, Daguerre, and Talbot are credited with the invention of photography, as we know it. Joseph Niépce (1765–1833) produced a photographic image with a camera obscura onto pewter sheets, cleansed with oil. Louis-Jacques-Mandé Daguerre (late 18th century–1851) shared ideas with Niépce and went on to develop his Daguerreotype prints, which had remarkable clarity and detail. These silver-plated copper sheets went through various steps including exposure to mercury vapors, finally

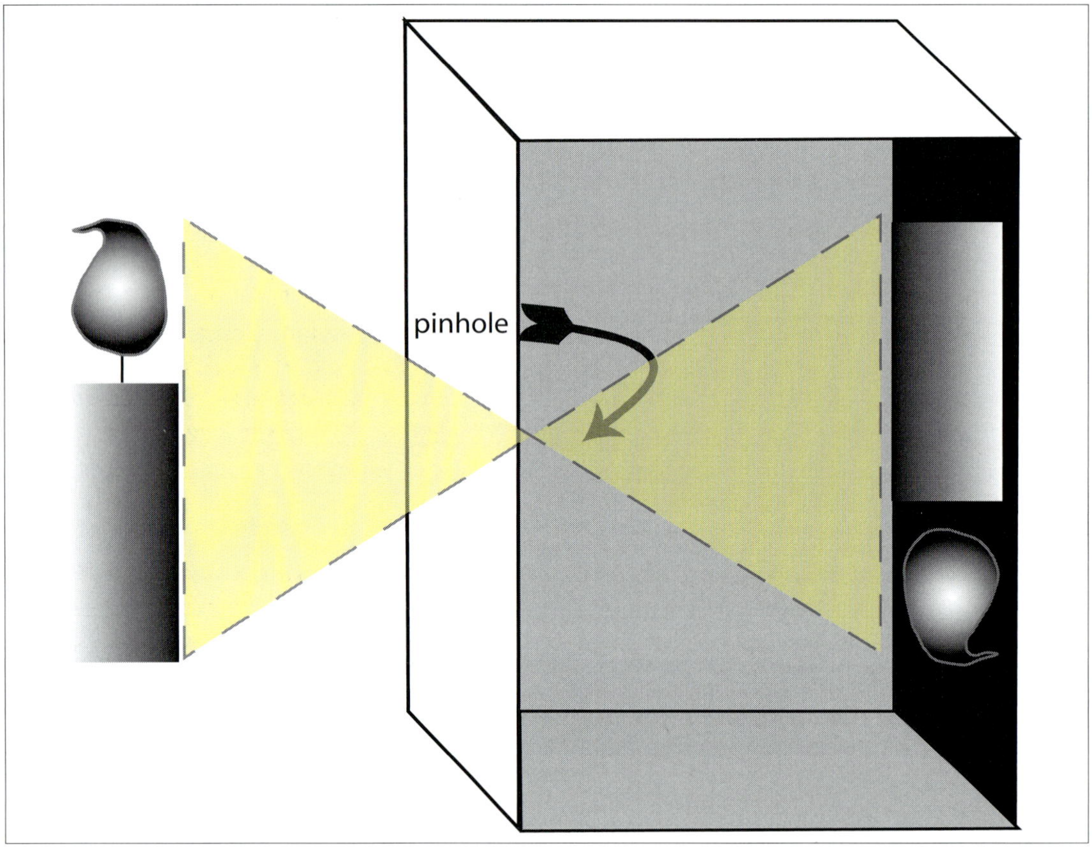

◆ **2-5** *A pinhole of light admitted into a darkened room or a darkened box will re-create an upside-down image of the world outside. A concept used for centuries, this is the premise of the pinhole camera.*

producing an image on the metal plate. Each Daguerreotype plate was a one-of-a-kind image.

William Henry Fox Talbot (1800–1877) developed a process that became the basis for the photograph and photographic printing plates. He developed negatives that could be used to make multiple images and photo-process printing plates. He also invented the photogram, a process in which light passes through an object placed onto a treated surface. When this surface is chemically treated, the image of the object appears. The previous chapter presented the creative work of 20th century photographer Man Ray, who used this technique.

Photographers to this point used a prepared wet plate before making the exposure. The plate had to be developed immediately afterward. George Eastman (1854–1932) introduced the Kodak camera in 1888 and eliminated this problem. Film could be exposed and then processed at a later time. Now ordinary people could readily record images and pose to have their own portraits recorded. By 1881 Frederick Ives (1856–1937) developed a method of etching lines onto glass creating **halftone** printing plates, and it became possible to reproduce photos on printing presses. The halftone was an image made of tiny dots that simulated a continuous tone. Graphic designers need to be familiar with this process, and it will be discussed again later.

The Implications With the advent of photography, potentially anyone could create a "photoreal" image or have his or her portrait recorded. Portraiture was no longer the prerogative of the elite few. Perhaps more important, photography could document events, and it came to be viewed as a visual truth. Mathew Brady (1823–1896), a New York studio photographer, and his assistants recorded the American Civil War. **Figure 2-6,** by one of Brady's assistants, Timothy O'Sullivan (1840–1882), shows troop quarters dubbed Fort Hell. Such images changed the public's romantic vision of war by introducing them to the realities of battlefield suffering. We Americans experienced this again during the Vietnam War in the late 1960s and early 1970s as televised photography brought chilling truths about combat into American homes. Again, in Iraq, the prison abuse photos informed us in a way words never could.

Photography is still considered a form of visual truth. But as digital photography developed, manipulating the photographic "fact" came to be the norm. Next we will look at the fundamental structural difference between film-based photography and the digital photographic image. Film-based photography is **analog** in nature, while computerized images are **digital** in nature. **Figures 2-7a** and **2-7b** show the data that makes up a digital photograph. This data is readily manipulated. Our relationships to analog and to digital data are quite different.

2-6 *Timothy O'Sullivan.* Fort Hell. *1865. Silverprint photograph.* George Eastman House, Rochester, N.Y.

Timothy O'Sullivan shot this documentary Civil War photograph of the quarters of men in Fort Sedgwick, also known as Fort Hell.

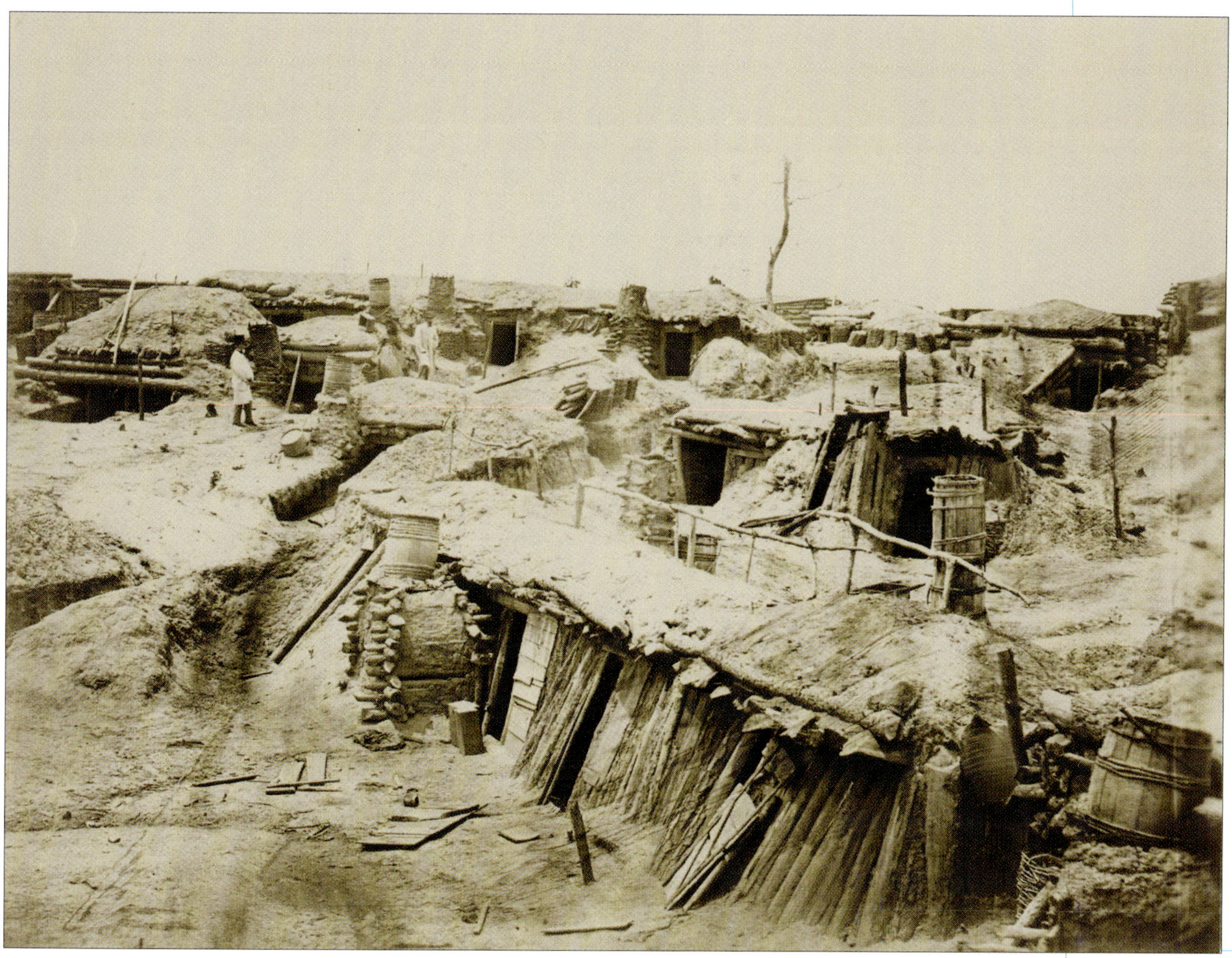

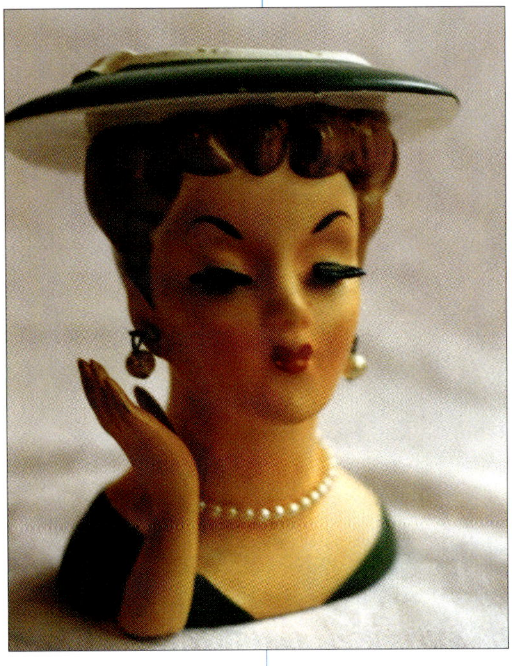

◆ **2-7a** *To our eye, digital photographs can look smooth and full of continuous tones.*

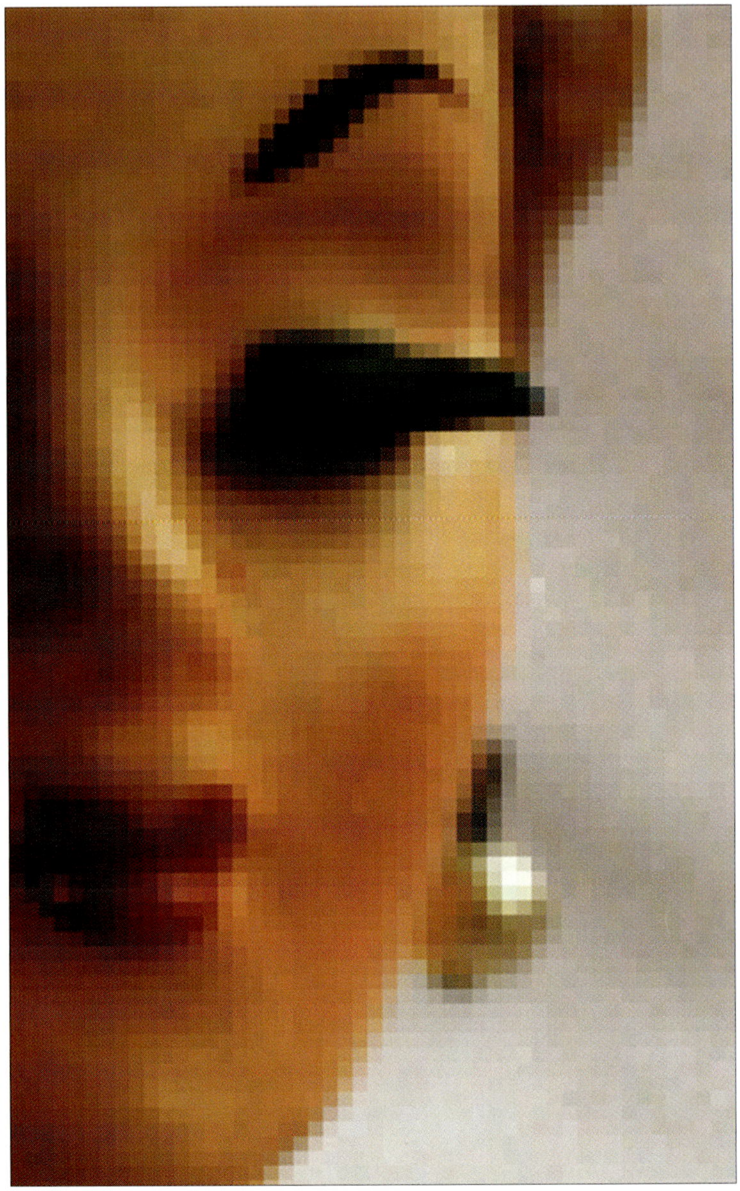

◆ **2-7b** *When a digital photograph is enlarged, we see the individual elements that actually comprise it.*

Analog and Digital Data

The analog world is full of long-playing records and clocks with smoothly moving hands that are reminiscent of the path of the sun and moon through the sky. We ourselves live in an analog world, with time flowing smoothly past, as day fades to night, as we gradually age.

The digital world, however, is full of discrete units of information, like music recorded on CDs and digital clocks. Each piece of music or unit of time is a separate, distinct entity that can be accessed and manipulated. A quarter to seven on sweeping hands feels like a very different kind of time than 6:45 glowing at us in the morning from our digital alarm. **Figure 2-8** is a gracious old analog clock.

What is the difference between an analog and a digital photograph? When black-and-white film is chemically developed and printed into a photograph, it is analog. When we examine such a photograph under a magnifier, all we can see is a close-up of continually changing gray values.

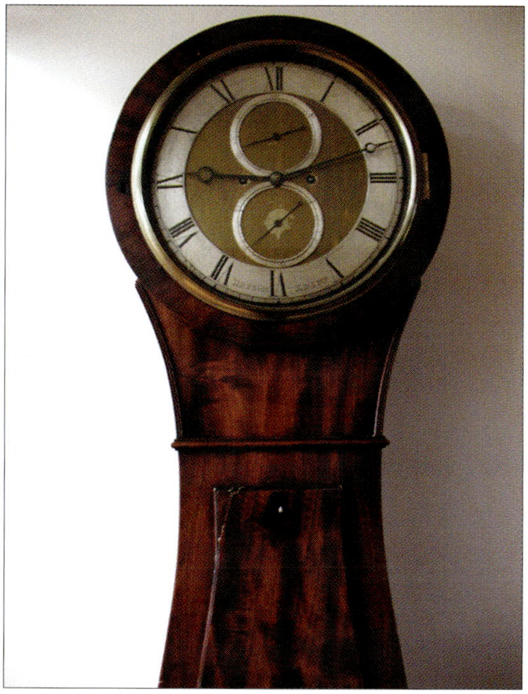

2-8 *Robert Bryson.* Longcase clock. *Edinburgh, 1835. Shown in its traditional case.*

Courtesy George Bryson's daughter.

A digital photograph is captured with a digital camera or scanned. When a digitized photograph is examined close up on a monitor, we see indivisible picture elements or **pixels** that give only the illusion of a continuous gray or color tones. The more pixels, the smoother and more complete the image will be. In **Figure 2-9** the cat's image has been enlarged, showing discrete bits of visual data located in the tiny white square above its head. The top right shape represents a single pixel. The square beneath it represents 3 × 3 pixels in a three-inch square. The bottom represents 24 × 24 pixels in the same size square. The original image shows 300 pixels per inch, which in a three-inch square means you're looking at 900 pixels across. There are many kinds of digital data besides visual data. Consider audio CDs. Digital sound data also exists in accessible units of information that allow for editing.

Each separate pixel or other unit of digital data can be manipulated. Pixels can be accessed and changed by adjusting value, hue, and luminosity. Each unit viewed on the monitor represents a

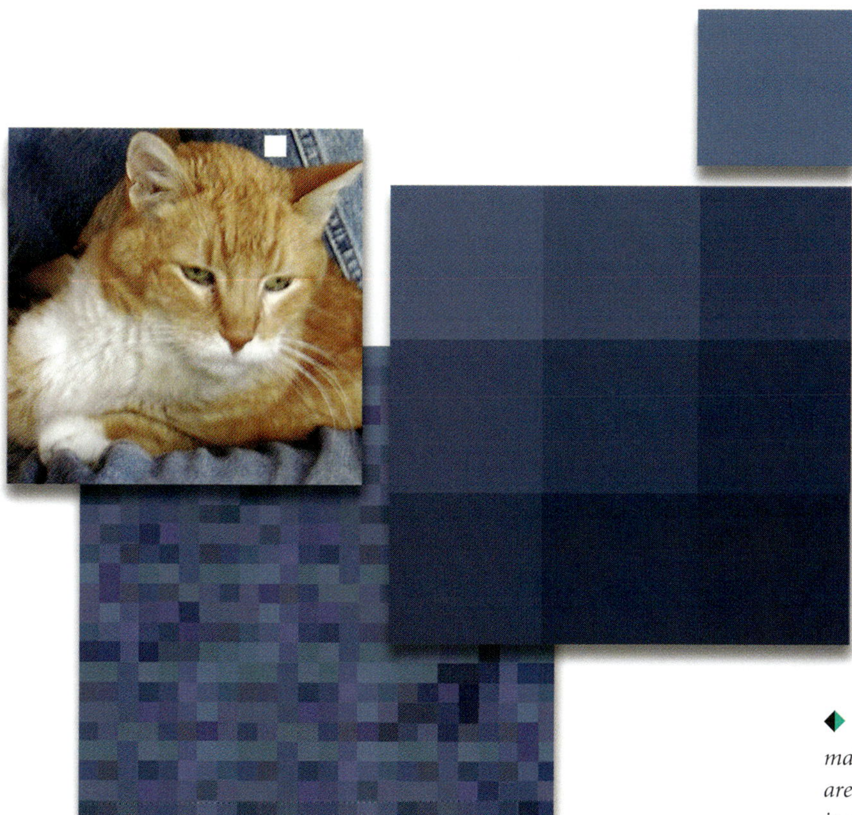

2-9 *The pixels that make up a digital image are represented in three increasing enlargements.*

separate location in memory. This can give the artist/designer, photographer, or filmmaker total control over the image. It can also leave audience members unsure that what they are seeing exists in reality or only in the digital, fabricated world.

Altering Our Senses

Digital data has changed our relationship to the sensory world as it continues to affect our sense of time and space. We can see events around the world as they happen, blurring the notion of distance. Processes happen quickly on a computer, and the fundamental structure of the computer's storage and retrieval has an impact on our perception of time. Its enormous storage capacity has another impact on memory.

A computer graphics student in the early 1980s talked about her grandmother's house and the files that the woman kept in the attic. They were clippings of photos from magazines she had received throughout her life, too beautiful or significant to throw out. This student could keep her significant images on a disk. At this early point in computer graphics, she wondered about the impact of change on our personal memories. Today we can access and share such materials electronically on a global level. Some questions these technologies raise for us are: Is the significance of such images altered? What is the relationship between memories and storage devices? How many images do we store on our computers, and how often do we look at them? Perhaps the answers are different for each of us, but the questions are worth consideration.

Print graphics present material in a linear fashion, paragraph after paragraph and page after sequential page. It is true that we can flip back and re-read. But analog material and our relationship with it are primarily linear, whether it is print, film, or analog video. The computer, however, operates with nonlinear digital, randomly accessible data.

The Digital Image

Why do we see what we see on the monitor? How is the computer graphic display created from a scanned or drawn image? The answers lie in a combination of **hardware** and **software**. Hardware is the physical component that you work with, be it a PC or a Mac or one of the other excellent systems. These systems will have memory in **megabytes** or **gigabytes** (or more) installed. The printers, scanners, and various input devices are also part of the hardware. The software, however, constitutes the programs installed on your computer. Much of this book is devoted to mastering the software on your computer. In order to master it, you will first need to have a background in the structure of digital data.

Analog to Digital Conversions

Now that we know about the difference between analog and digital data, how is digital data created? In a scanner or a digital camera, analog to digital converters (ADCs) transform analog voltage signals to digital red, green, and blue (RGB) values. In a flatbed scanner, for example, a page is placed face down on the scanner and a scan head moves along the page, illuminating it. The light reflected from the page strikes a series of mirrors that redirect it to a lens. This lens focuses the beam of light into a prism that splits the beam into red, green, and blue components. The red, green, and blue light beams strike rows of photosensitive cells where they are converted into an analog voltage level. Finally, the analog to digital converter changes these voltage levels to digital information, storing the RGB levels for all the individual pixels in the image that are seen on the screen. **Figure 2-10** shows how this all works.

Focus On Concept

Oral history and the visual stories told in one-of-a-kind, hand-inked books were ways to bind medieval society together and pass information through generations. What kinds of changes would the invention of moveable type make? Think about its quantity and portability. How might society be linked in a new way?

Each new important invention in our tools of communication, like the printing press and the camera, brings change. Think about a tool that interests you, and discuss the changes it introduced. Consider how oral, written, and web information crosses distances and in what kind of time span. How might this have an effect on our personal sense of time and space?

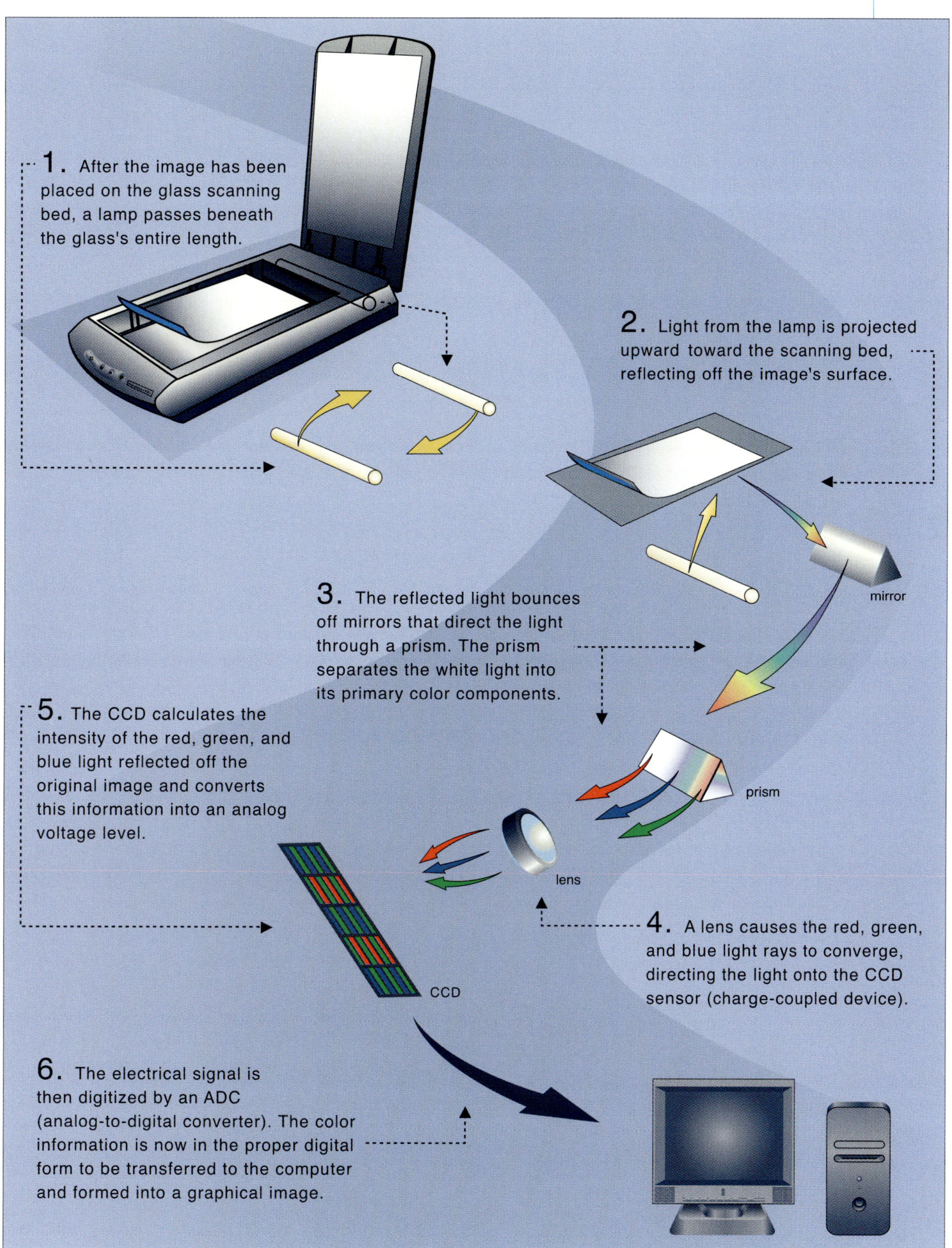

2-10 *The working process of a scanner is shown here.*
Diagram by Tiffany Dorner-Jones.

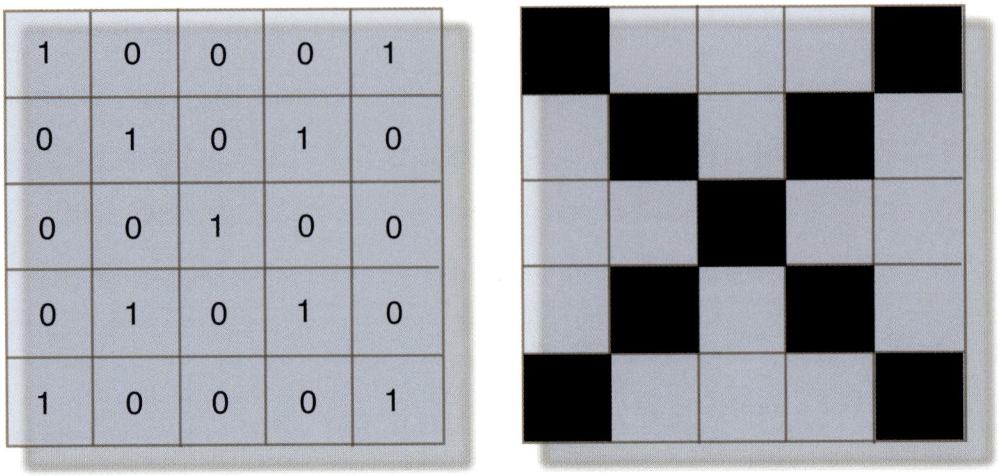

◆ **2-11** *Binary data consists of two commands. This diagram shows how a binary "on or off" command translates to a pixel that is either colored in black or not.*

Bits, Bytes, and Binary It is interesting to understand how digital data is stored, and fascinating to realize that complex, beautiful images of computer graphics are reliant on very basic numbers and mathematics for their creation. All digital design comes down to an "on" or "off" command at the hardware level. This is known as **binary data** because there are only two choices—"0" or "1." **Figure 2-11** shows a simple diagram of "on" and "off" binary code that translates to a pixel colored black or left uncolored. The word *binary* means "compounded or consisting of two things or parts." No matter how elaborate the artwork, this is its structural underpinning.

A single piece of information is called a **bit**, and it is the smallest unit of computer memory. A single bit can represent a black or a white pixel on the monitor. Each pixel on the screen represents a location in computer memory on a **bitmap** that has an "on" or "off" command. This bitmap is usually stored several bit planes (layers) deep to achieve complexity. **Figure 2-12** shows that more complex color can occur when we have a location with multiple bits of information. Three bits exist at each location in this diagram of stacked bit planes.

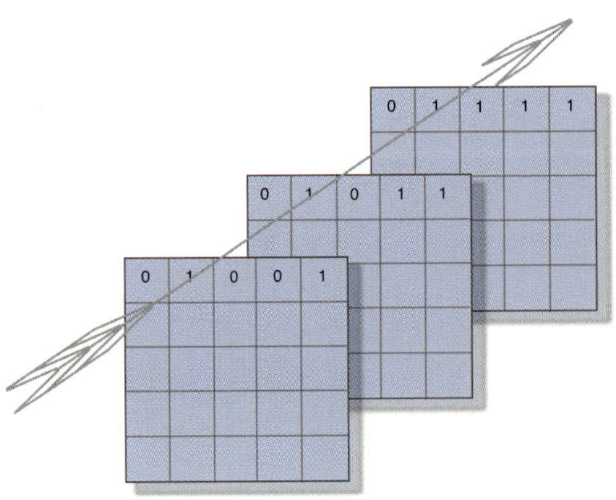

◆ **2-12** *Stacked bits of binary data make more complex color possible. The information at each pixel is no longer "0" or "1," but any of several combinations of those commands.*

When several layers of bits are combined, these bits can display grays and complex colors. A grouping of eight bits is called a **byte** and can represent 256 different grays or colors per pixel. A full-color image will take up much more memory than a grayscale image because it uses more bits of information. Three bytes (twenty-four bits) give the capability of rendering 16.7 million colors. These are the basic units of memory in computer hardware. It is incredible to realize that the visually rich images we create come from such humble origins based on "on" and "off" and multiplication. **Figures 2-13a–c** show the same image created with one bitmap, eight bit planes, and a full twenty-four bits. This is the basic physical structure of computer memory.

Memory There are two kinds of memory in a computer. An integrated circuit chip on the computer's motherboard has a permanent memory called **ROM** (Read-Only Memory). It holds the computer's essential operating instructions. The **RAM** (Random-Access Memory) is the memory used to actively create files. When you launch an application or open a document, it is loaded

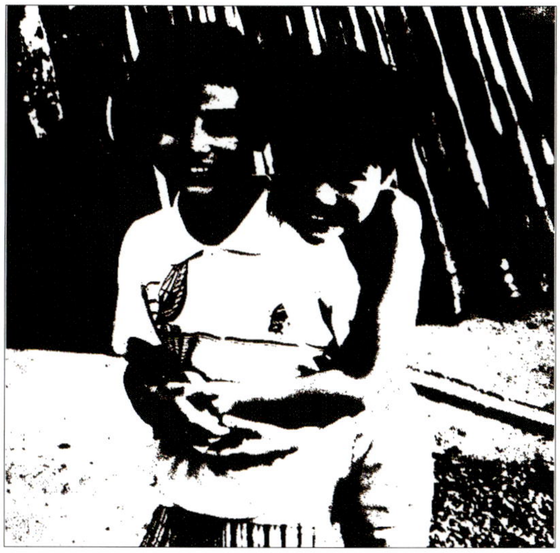

(a)

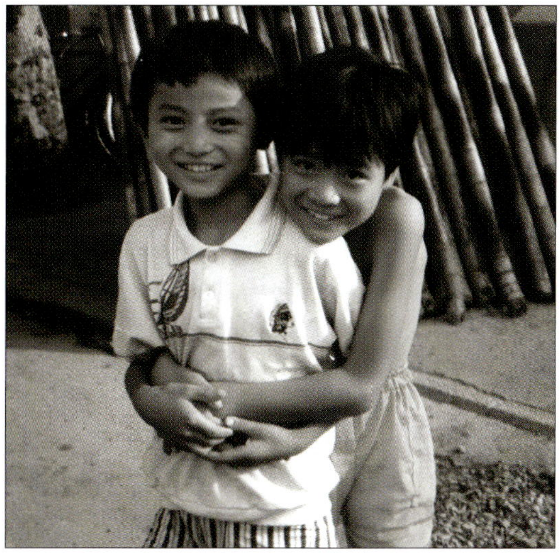

(b)

◆ **2-13 [a–c]** *These three versions of the same image are created with one bitmap, eight bit planes, and a full twenty-four-bit depth.*

into RAM and stored there while you work. Enough RAM is needed to hold both the software and the data you generate. Every year that passes, artists and designers seem to need more RAM to drive their increasingly sophisticated software.

Internal hard drives, small removable mini-drives, DVDs, CDs, and Zip disks have storage space measured in megabytes and gigabytes. There are 1,024 bits in a byte, 1,024 bytes in a kilobyte, 1,024 kilobytes in a megabyte, and 1,024 megabytes in a gigabyte. A deluge of stored data surrounds most people working with computer graphics. When you have been at it more than a few years, a great many of your files are archived on outmoded storage devices. This means you need to continually update the storage of

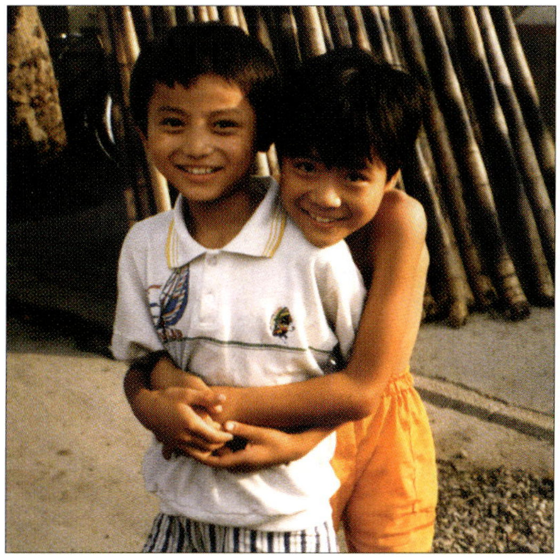

(c)

Focus On Concept

What is the similarity between the prehistoric cave paintings and the marks we make today? Food is a need of all civilizations and is reflected in their communication. Can you think of another need shared across time and across geographic boundaries? How is it expressed and communicated? As you consider these questions, think about both the communications function and the potential for personal expression we find in our writing and imagery.

Our contemporary "New Media" store, retrieve, share, and manipulate data very differently than in the past. What kind of digital data do you encounter every day? What analog data does it replace? Consider the old analog clock in Figure 2-8 or think about various kinds of music storage. How do such technologies make your world different from that of your parents? How might your grandchildren's world differ from your own?

What do you think the next new communication invention will be? Will it bring any significant changes? Can you think of any science fiction inventions that may come true?

important files by transferring them to a new, larger storage device.

Accessing Memory Data storage has a conceptual dimension as well as a physical one. In addition to the physical storage of data, it is interesting to consider the impact such data storage has on us as individuals and as a society. As digital information grows and our access to it increases, how do we sort out the meaningful things? From books to photographs to computer disks to the Web, our personal and cultural storage capacity has increased. How to identify meaningful data is a practical as well as a philosophical question. Remember the student whose grandmother saved decades of images in her attic? Is a different personal value associated with dusty, print pages compared to crisp, digital recordings? What about a painting compared to a digital image? There is a difference between the physical nature of pigment on a surface and a digital file or print.

Next we will look more closely at the physical structure of the data that we are storing.

Pixels and Resolution What is the relationship between image, data storage, and memory? Each of the smallest visual units on the screen (called pixels) represents a location in memory. A digital image is broken down into pixels, each of which can be assigned an individual color. This is similar to the painting technique used in **Figures 2-14a–b** by the Neo-Impressionist and Pointillist Georges Seurat (1859–1891). In this detail from *A Sunday on La Grande Jatte—1884*, you can see that each of his paint strokes is a pigment placed on the canvas without blending. The viewer optically mixes the result.

Resolution refers to the fineness or sharpness of a screen display or computer-generated printed piece. The more memory available and thus the more pixels in the digital image, the higher the resolution is, and the clearer the image will be. The resolution of an individual file depends on what the artist/designer designates when the file is created, as in the Photoshop window **(Fig. 2-15)** where resolution for a new file is set. The number of individual pixels will determine the resolution of the image. **Figure 2-16** shows a high-resolution and low-resolution version of a graphic with straight lines. Note the jagged edges on the image on the right. These "jaggies" are especially noticeable in typography or graphics with straight lines. For print graphics, a final file resolution of 150 to 300 dpi (dots per inch) or more is mandatory.

The resolution of a screen, however, is independent from the image file you view on it. Screen resolution is set by the hardware. It is approximately 72 dpi, varying a little depending upon which computer you're using. Because the screen cannot show the full resolution of an image, it is wise to do **proof prints** of an image, which means printing out the file to paper so it can be seen in a higher resolution than the screen allows. Keep in mind that monitor viewing is in low resolution, and don't plan on evaluating a digital design that is intended for print by viewing the monitor.

Now we have covered some of the hardware, software, and various memory issues in computer graphics. What about the visual and conceptual questions?

Visual Literacy

The basic components of **visual perception** are a fundamental part of all art and design, both on and off the computer. A mark on a page is immediately subject to interpretation by the eye and brain. Our personal experience, cultural background, and physiological makeup help to establish this dynamic exchange between mark and eye and the brain's interpretation. Therefore, all visual perception is interactive by its very nature.

Images and all their visual components are subject to interpretation, as are words. Do you see the same green as your mother does? Do you and your friend see the same painting? There are many factors of visual perception to consider. Features on visual perception throughout this book will remind you to apply the language of design. Now let's look at how to articulate clearly in our visual language. You will be asked to apply this information at the end of the chapter.

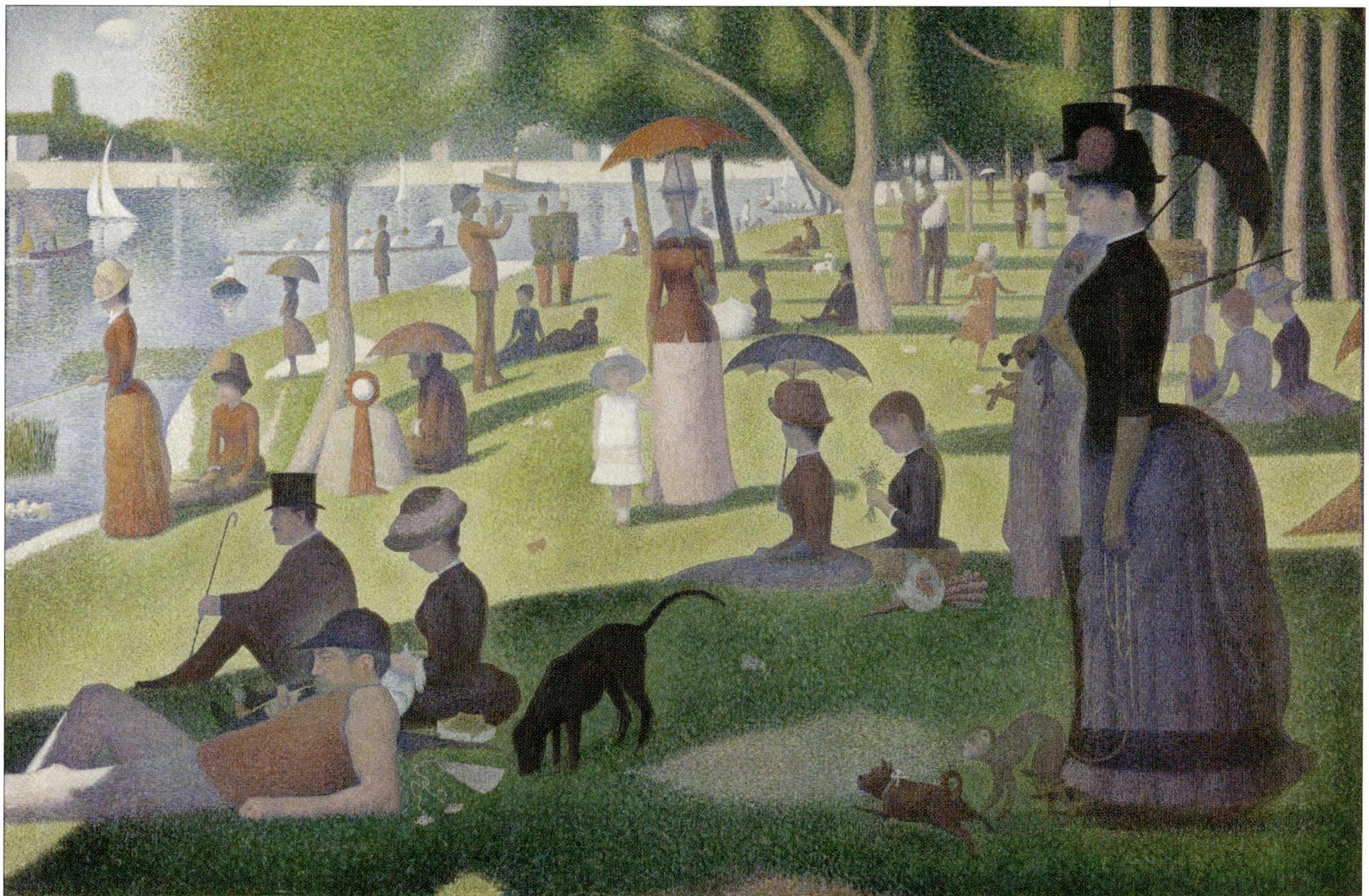

2-14 [a] *Georges Seurat.* A Sunday on La Grande Jatte. *1884. Oil.*
Helen Birch Bartlett Memorial Collection, The Art Institute of Chicago.

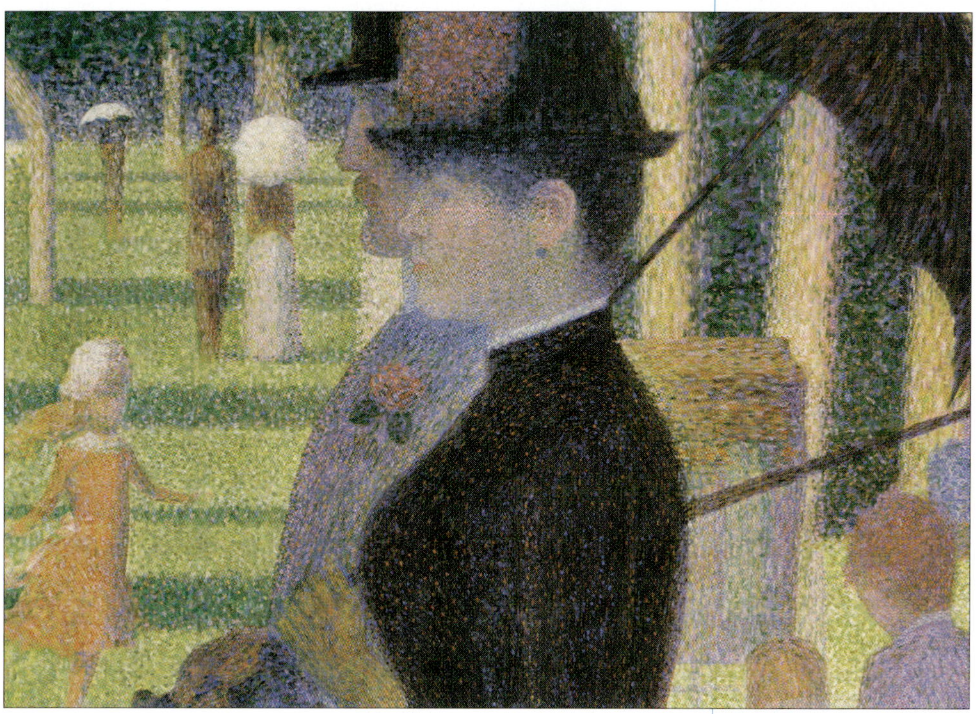

2-14 [b] *Detail.*

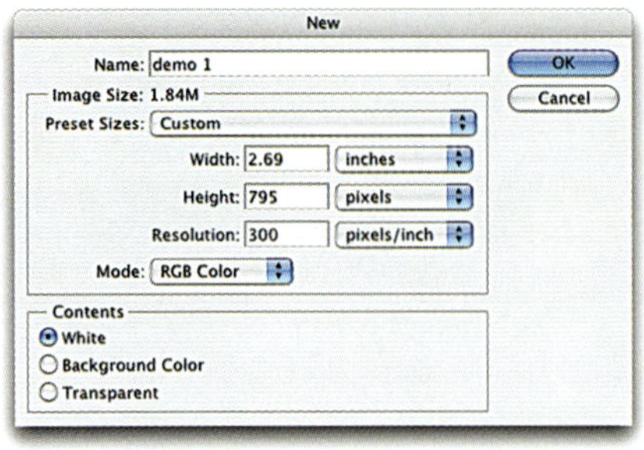

Adobe product screen shot(s) reprinted with permission from Adobe Systems Incorporated

◆ **2-15** *Photoshop window in which resolution and size for a new file are set.*

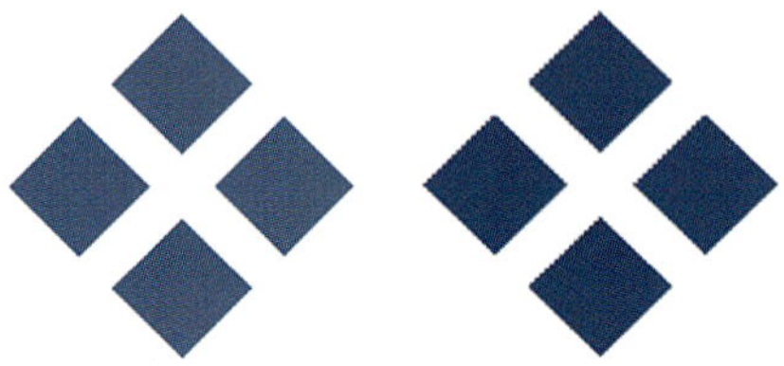

◆ **2-16** *Low resolution results in the jagged quality of the graphic on the right.*

Visual Language

Knowledge of the fundamentals of basic design enriches solutions in all media. We are working with a **visual language**, and it needs to be learned and practiced with control, understanding, and commitment. Although the computer is a tool that brings new design challenges, the fundamentals of design apply to all art and design disciplines both on and off the computer.

Similarity and variety are at the heart of a design analysis. The repetition of unit-forming elements such as shape, angle, color, texture, and size helps to tie a visual creation together. **Figure 2-17** shows a lovely integration of shapes, using repetition and variation. It is a print based on a variety of photographs of lily pads by fine artist Judy Pfaff (1946—).

Variation on a visual theme helps to give this artwork by Pfaff both interest and impact. The computer is ideally suited to this kind of exploration and development of visuals. Because it is possible to compose multiple variations of an initial image without destroying the original, experimentation can flourish. An approach to developing artwork based on theme and variation is a very rewarding one to pursue and can lead to rich solutions. The final challenge is always to edit out the weaker ideas and to recognize and strengthen the most promising.

Throughout this textbook, all assignments at chapter ends will benefit from attention to similarity and variety in shape, angle, texture, value, and color. Now it is time to learn to create a digital image.

How To Basics

Before creating an image, let's read over the various ways to save one. When the image is ready to save, several **file formats** are available to choose from. The way the image is stored on the disk determines which programs can open, read, and edit that image, as well as the amount of storage space they take up. Here is a summary of the most frequently used file formats. These are accessed in the File>Save As> window in your software program as shown in **Figure 2-18.**

File Formats

TIFF (Tagged Image File Format) is a widely used bitmapped file format. It is appropriate for scanned images. Almost every program that works with **raster** images can open this format.

EPS (Encapsulated PostScript) is an object-oriented format that is excellent for storing graphics of any kind. Use it when you want to put type and

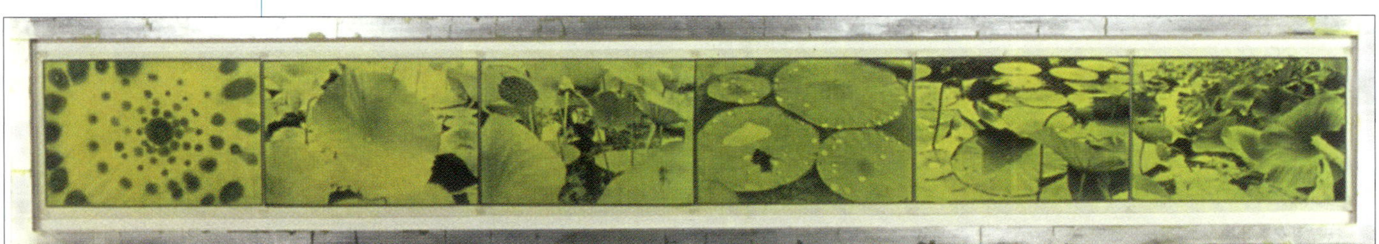

◆ **2-17** *Judy Pfaff.* Sweet Lily. *2002. Photogravure, spit bite, and relief roll in artist's frame, 14 × 71".* Courtesy of Judy Pfaff and Tandem Press.

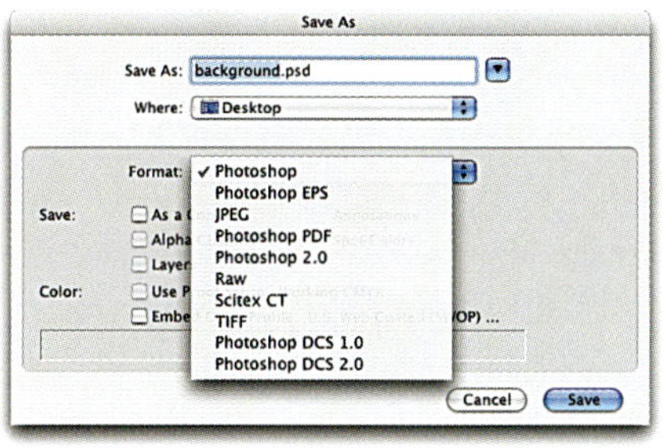

Adobe product screen shot(s) reprinted with permission from Adobe Systems Incorporated

◆ **2-18** *Choose a file format in the File>Save As window.*

images into a layout program for print. It is a refined form of PostScript that will allow a raster or vector program to open the file for editing. If printing for your portfolio, you will need a PostScript printer to handle an EPS graphic.

JPEG is a compressed file format that reduces the pixels in your file to save memory. It is used for web graphics with color gradations or photographic images. Never save a JPEG over itself, because it loses information each time an image is saved in this format. This is known as a **lossy** file format.

GIF is also a file format used in web graphics for images featuring type and flat color. It compresses graphics without eliminating detail. This is known as a lossless file format.

Photoshop lets you save the file in the program's native language. It opens readily in the same program, but may not open in various applications.

PICT is a Mac object-oriented file format. It handles bitmap and vector images well. They should be converted to TIFF or EPS before placing in a page-layout program such as PageMaker, Quark, or InDesign.

PDF files are completely cross-platform and can be opened in Adobe's Acrobat Reader. This program is free and is included on most application disks. You can print from it even if you don't own the fonts in the document or the software used to create the artwork. PDFs are created in Photoshop or with a distiller program, or the full version of Adobe Acrobat will write the files.

Naming Conventions When saving a file, you will need to know what file format to use, but you will also need to give a name to your file that will let you find it again. This seems a simple thing, but imagine how lost you could become looking for one image from fifty you've saved as Computers1, Computers2, or Alice1, Alice2, and so on. Consider what will allow you to successfully search for, locate, and recognize a particular file. Perhaps naming the files Project1a, Project1b, Project2a will work. Even better, creating a new file folder for each assignment could also help to group artwork logically. The folder might be called Project1, and the files inside it called laceA, laceB, Leaf1, Leaf2, LeafFinal. Now that you have an understanding of the basic structure of a digital file, it is finally time to begin work in the studio and create some artwork.

Visual Perception

Whenever we create or view an image, we bring a load of personal experiences and cultural background that help us make sense of that image. We structure the image as we create it on the screen or on paper. We also structure it in our brain and eye in the process of viewing it. The image depends upon the artist *and* the viewer.

Realism in art and design is not an absolute. It is an interaction between the artwork and the mind and eye of the viewer, as we can see in Georges Seurat's *A Sunday on La Grande Jatte—1884* (Fig. 2-14) where abstract color dots appear as people in a park. Seurat painted series of dots, but the result is that we see a summer day. An artist and designer works not simply with the elements of line, shape, and color. Basic principles of design and visual perception are a vital part of this interaction. The principle of similarity grouping occurs when we recognize similarities in shape, size, color, texture, and so on. This similarity helps to visually bind a composition together, as in the texture of Seurat's dots.

In the process of recognizing similarity, the eye and brain also identify those elements that are different. Again, in Seurat's painting, the color makes an important difference that allows us to "read" the painting. A dynamic interplay of similarity and difference makes for an active, successful design.

Hands On Practice

This section will give you step-by-step instruction for scanning an image and opening it in Photoshop. Later in this chapter you will manipulate your scan, creating a variety of filter treatments.

Scanning

The diagrams in **Figure 2-19** illustrate the scanning process. Check to see if the scanner is hooked up to your computer. Then place an image or object face down on the scanning bed.

2-19a *Opening scanner software from Photoshop.*

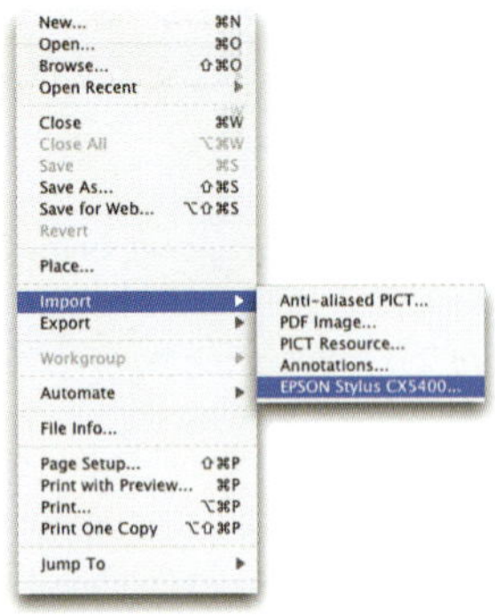

a–b: Adobe product screen shot(s) reprinted with permission from Adobe Systems Incorporated

2-19b *Scanner settings.*

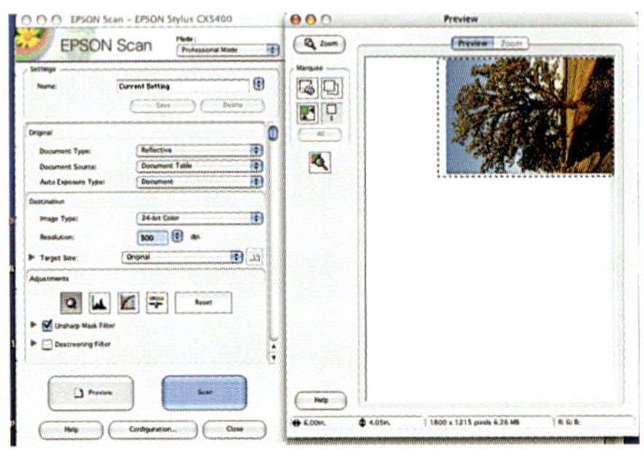

a. Open Photoshop or your scanning software.

If in Photoshop, go to File>Import>*scanning software name*. Figure 2-19a shows an Epson scanning product. Otherwise, simply open the scanning software window. Look for the advanced, not the automatic, scanning option.

b. The advanced window will allow you to enter your own settings as shown in Figure 2-19b. These settings should be:

Reflective. RGB. The resolution can vary from 300 to 72 dpi depending on your need. Generally, as we have discussed, you will use high resolution for print graphics, low resolution for work to be viewed on screen. In a later chapter, you'll use a mid-level resolution for scanning an image to be placed into Illustrator or Freehand as a template to draw over.

c. Scan at approximately the size you will need in the finished piece. Choose a size of 100 percent or more or less, as needed. Keep in mind that 50 percent is half the size of the original, while 200 percent is twice the size of the original.

The brightness, dark, and contrast controls are usually correct at their default settings. (You can move them to see what happens to the preview.)

d. Check the menu for "Descreen" if you are using a printed image from magazines or newspapers because it will be made up of halftone dots. Remember that such images are not your original artwork and involve copyright issues.

e. Select Preview or Prescan.

Use the dashed box tool to draw a rectangle around the area you want to scan. Then select Preview.

f. If everything looks correct, select the Scan button. Otherwise, make adjustments and preview again. Save the file on your disk or computer by selecting File>Save As>*your file name*. Be sure to save it in the correct location on your disk or the hard drive.

Although scanning programs have their own basic image adjustment features, nothing is as good as Photoshop. If you did not scan from within Photoshop, open that program now and select File>Open>*your file name*. Now make a few quality adjustments to the image. The diagrams in **Figure 2-20** illustrate the adjustment process including cropping, levels, brightness/contrast, and Gaussian blur.

a. Select the crop tool from the toolbox, and draw a rectangle around the area of the image you want to save. Press return (Fig. 2-20a).

b. Select Image>Adjustments>Levels as shown in Figure 2-20b. Pull in the dark and light sliders beneath the histogram until they omit any white area on either side of the graph (read more about this later). Or go to Image>Adjustments>Brightness/Contrast and use the sliders to improve your scan (Figs. 2-20c–d).

c. Next apply Filter>Blur>Gaussian Blur. Put the slide roughly (watch the image) to .5. This softens the pixel structure and is especially important if your image is from a magazine or newspaper (Fig. 2-20e).

d. Next select Filter>Sharpen>Unsharp Mask. Set the sliders roughly (watch the image) to 40, 3, 6. This crispens the final scan.

Now resave the image, selecting File>Save As>TIFF.

Setting Up the Canvas There are various ways to open your image in Photoshop. With an existing file, go to File>Open>*your file name*, or simply double click on your Photoshop file. You can specify the desired canvas size and resolution by going to File>Open>New File, as shown in **Figure 2-21a,** and enter your desired data for a new digital file. You can also copy and paste from one Photoshop document to another. Or you can click on an image in one Photoshop file and simply drag it into any open Photoshop window.

If you need to change the resolution or size of your image, select Image>Image Size and in the resulting box specify the resolution and file size as shown in **Figure 2-21b.** Be sure to check the constrain propor-

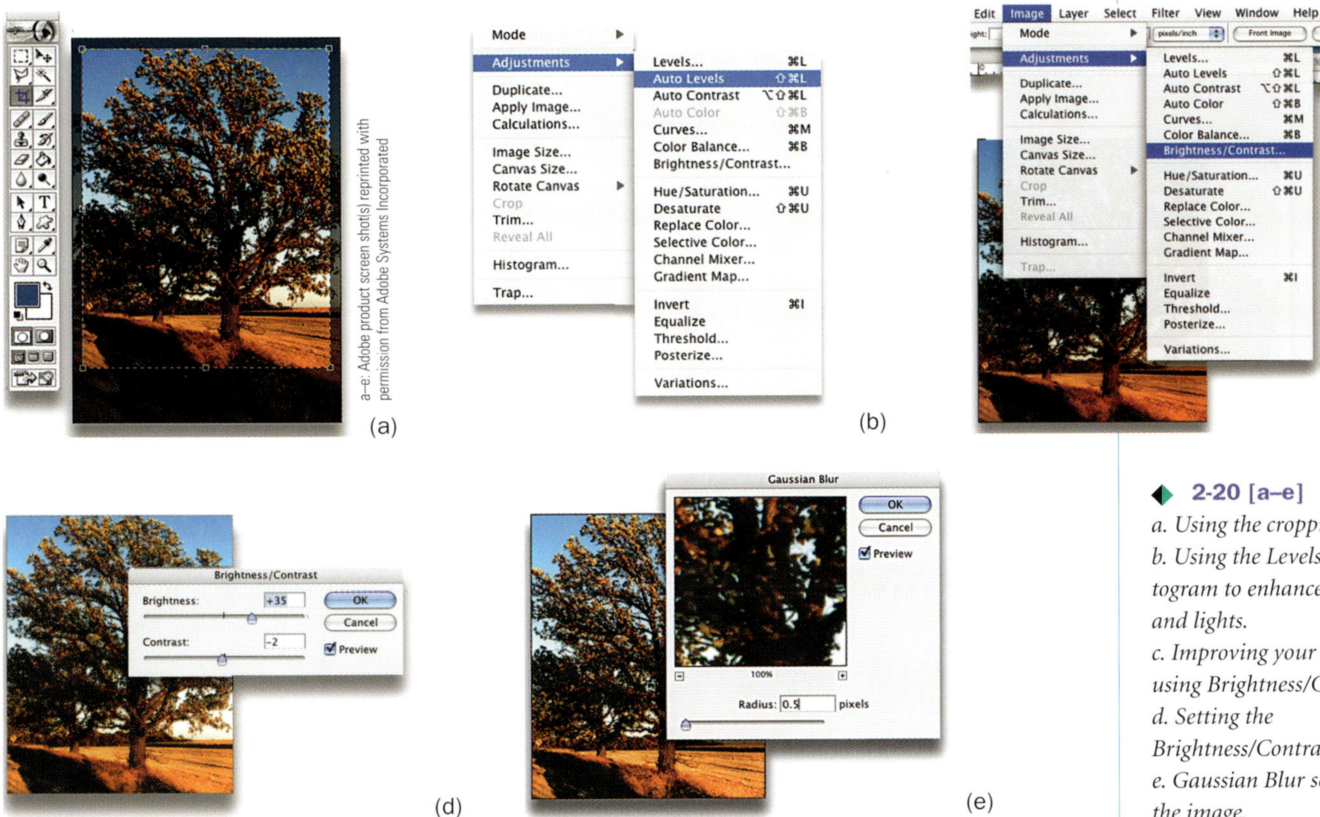

a–e: Adobe product screen shot(s) reprinted with permission from Adobe Systems Incorporated

(a) (b) (c) (d) (e)

◆ **2-20 [a–e]**
a. Using the cropping tool.
b. Using the Levels histogram to enhance darks and lights.
c. Improving your image using Brightness/Contrast.
d. Setting the Brightness/Contrast sliders.
e. Gaussian Blur softens the image.

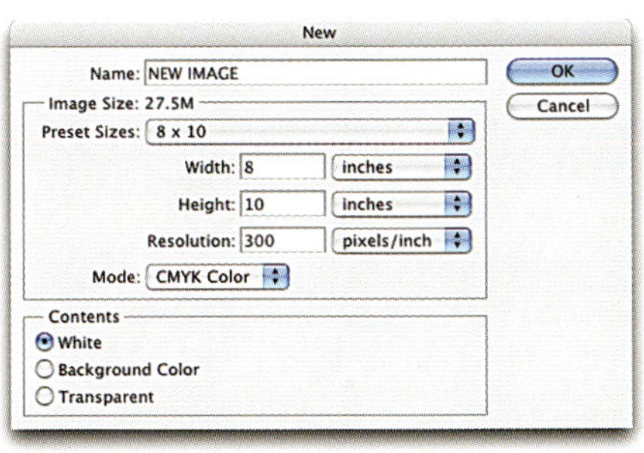

a–c: Adobe product screen shot(s) reprinted with permission from Adobe Systems Incorporated

(a)

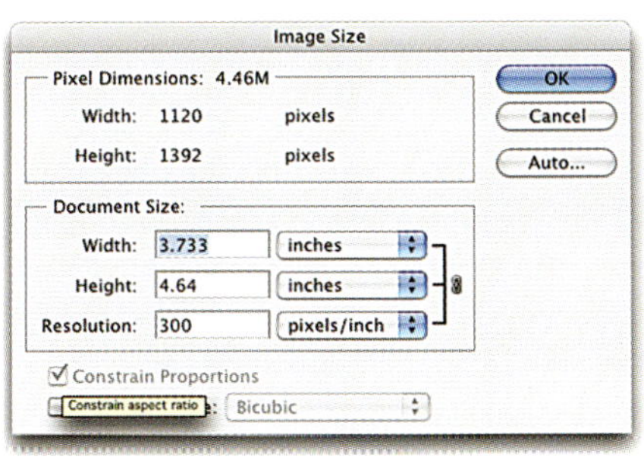

(b)

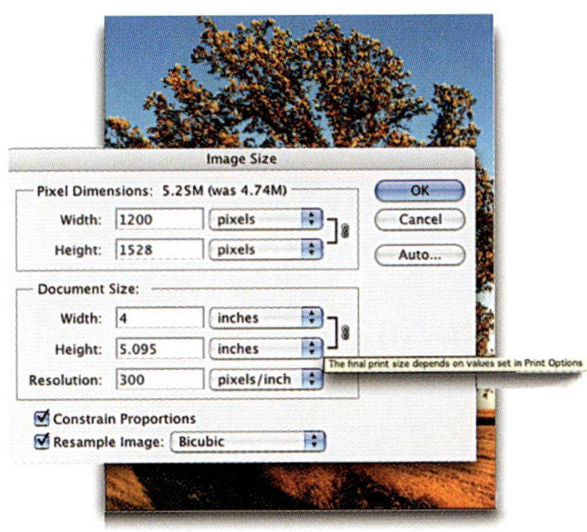

(c)

◆ **2-21 [a–c]**
a. Specifying canvas size and resolution for a new file.
b. Linking image size and resolution of an existing file.
c. Changing unlinked resolution and image size independently of each other.

tions box to keep the horizontal and vertical dimensions true. Unclick the resample image box to make the resolution increase and decrease with changes in the file's physical size. Clicking the box will let you maintain a resolution while changing the physical size, and vice versa as shown in **Figure 2-21c.** If you enlarge the image size significantly, however, it will not stay a clear image.

Warming Up

Begin by practicing scanning. Refer to the How To Basics above. Try scanning a magazine image and a photograph of your own. Save them and open them in Photoshop. Now use basic image adjustment techniques to improve their quality and resave the results.

Scanning a photograph of your own or one that a family member or friend has given you ensures that the image belongs to you. Scanning a professional image from a magazine can produce good-looking results for practice, but it is only suitable for class assignments. Because the copyright belongs to the original photographer, you can never exhibit or sell the work as your own unless you have changed it significantly enough that the image is redefined as primarily your vision. Laws regarding "intellectual property rights" protect the creations of others as well as your own work.

In The Studio

This assignment asks you to create successful initial scans and then experiment with some of the variations available in photo manipulation inside Photoshop to create an interesting final effect. This exploration will enrich your future solutions whether they are in design, fine art, communications, or elsewhere. If there is one computer graphics program that is ubiquitous, that everyone uses to produce files that are imported into a wide variety of other applications, it is Photoshop.

In addition to learning techniques, you are asked to apply some basic principles of visual perception pertaining to similarity and variety. Good visual skills are vital in this dynamic electronic medium.

Exploring Similarity and Variety

Bring a few fairly flat objects with interesting shape or textural qualities. Think about the design potential of the things you choose and share ideas with others in class. Combine these objects into an interesting composition before scanning. Think about texture, figure/ground relationships, how the objects touch the edge of the composition, and the potential for repeated shapes or angles. If the figure/ground relationship of the composition is strong, don't be afraid to stay with one scanned object in a composition. **Figure 2-22** shows a piece of lace with dark, open shapes equally important to the composition as the white areas. The placement within the art frame is also an important consideration. A visual dance can occur among the resulting shapes.

Do your scans at a resolution of 300 ppi (pixels per inch), planning to place them on an 8 × 8" page. Open a new file in Photoshop at 8 × 8" and 300 ppi and place your scanned image inside it.

Once you are satisfied with the composition and quality of the scans, begin to explore the rich potential of filters and image adjustments. (If the program prompt asks about color managing at this point, choose not to.) The accompanying **CD** has a variety of scans inspired by this project that you can use to practice. Interesting objects to scan might be lace, a hanger, sandpaper, leaves, flowers, fabric, hands, or your face.

Choose your best three variations (these may be the least complex) and save as TIFF files to show in class. Plan to discuss technique, concept, and composition in your class critiques on each assignment.

The next How To Basics will give you information on exploring the filter effects you will need to complete your work, and it will also introduce the use of selections.

How To Basics

The various diagrams in **Figure 2-23** illustrate ways to create variety in your scanned images.

Creating Variety

Adjustments In Photoshop select File>new>8×8", specifying 300 ppi. Copy and paste one of your scans into this new file. Be sure to adjust the scan as discussed in the How To Basics above, using cropping and the histogram levels slider.

Select Image>Adjust>Invert>Posterize. If you like the results, save the image under a new name. Now go to File>Revert to get back to the original. Next go to Image>Adjust>Brightness/Contrast and Hue/Saturation. Try anything else in this pop up menu that interests you. Save each satisfying result under a new name. The results don't need to be realistic.

Selections Use the first item in the toolbox menu (rectangular marquee) to select an area of your image. Now whatever effect you apply will only change that area. The lasso tool and magic wand are other ways of making selections. Figure 2-23a shows an active rectangular selection, and a star selection made with the lasso tool. Figure 2-23b shows a scan of used

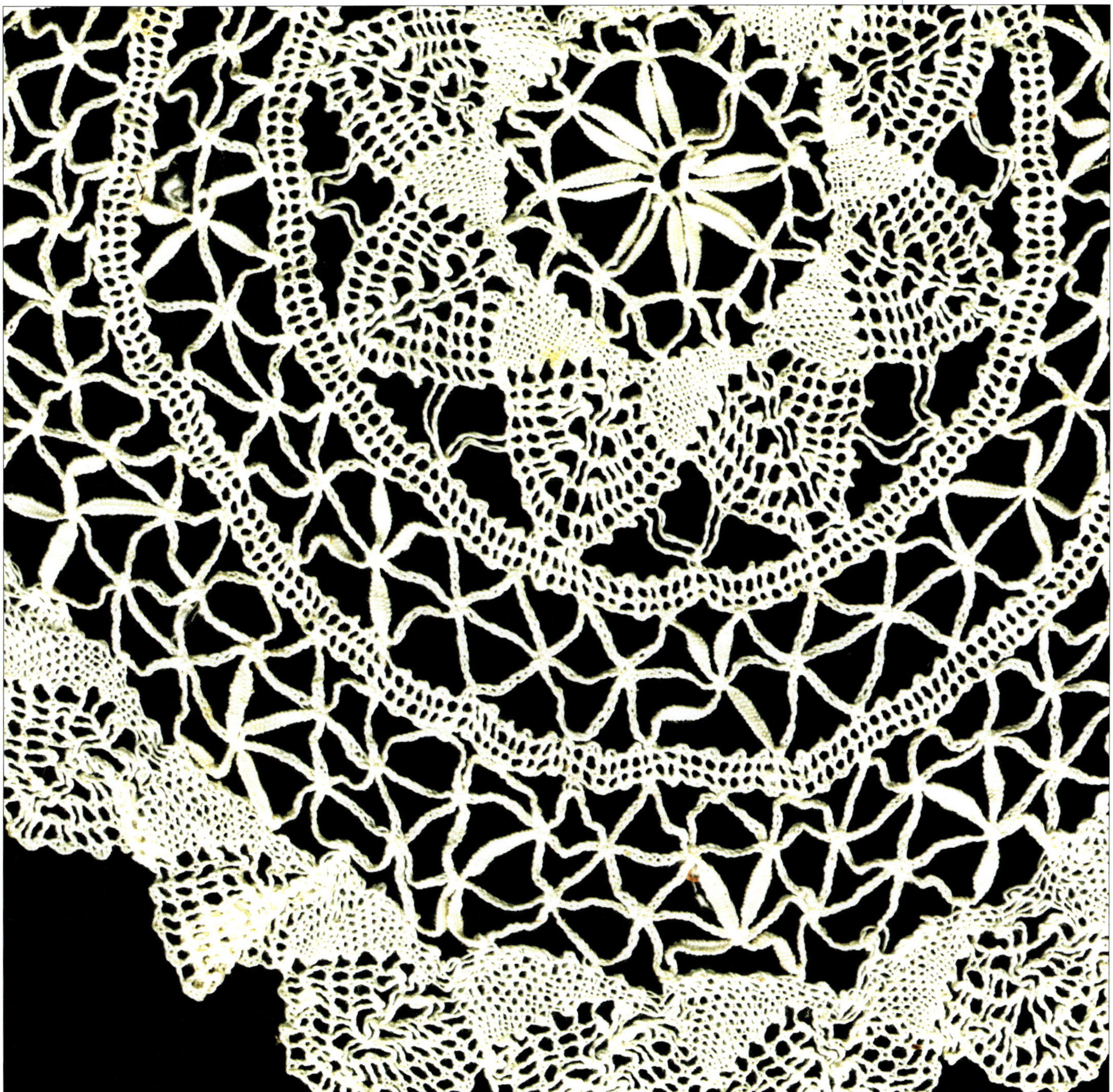

sandpaper on top. Rectangle tool selections were created and manipulated in Image>Adjustments on the bottom part of this figure. As you experiment with these effects, continue to use File>Revert to go back to the last saved version, or Edit>Undo to undo the last command. Window>Show History will let you go backward and forward through all the commands you've selected (Fig. 2-23c). Use the crop tool to select the best part of your final composition. Save it on your disk or folder, giving it a different name than the original scan.

Copy, Paste, and Filters Again, select a visually interesting part of an image. This time we'll use the copy and paste functions to create a collage, then manipulate the various pasted selections. Choose Edit>Copy and Edit>Paste. This will place a copy of the selected image as many times as you select the

2-22 *This scan of a piece of old lace shows off the intricate play of similarity and variety that makes up this handiwork.*

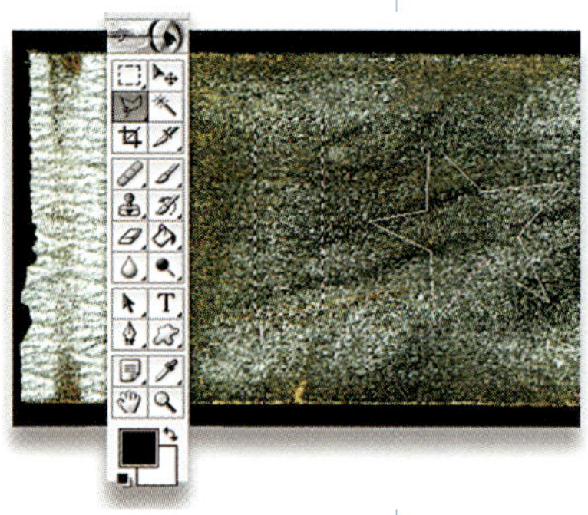

a–e: Adobe product screen shot(s) reprinted with permission from Adobe Systems Incorporated

2-23a *Active selections using the rectangle and lasso tools.*

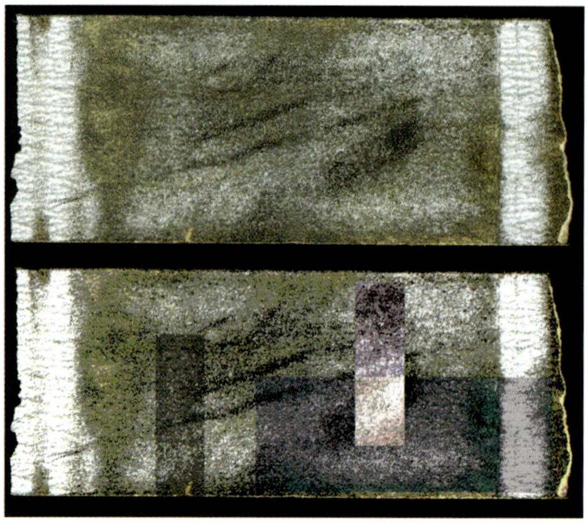

2-23b *Rectangular selections are applied to this scan of old sandpaper and various adjustments made to the selected areas.*

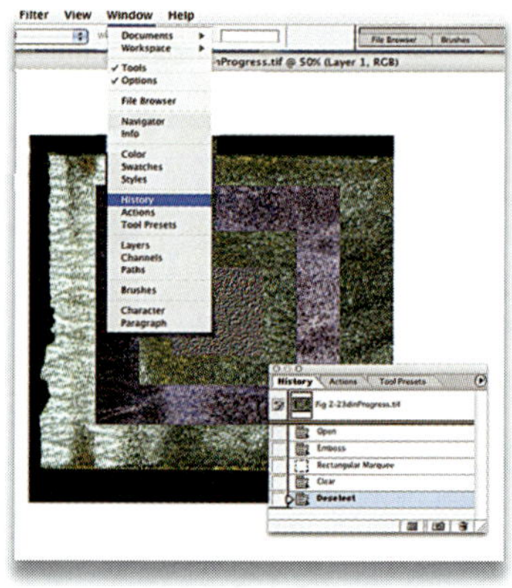

2-23c *Photoshop's History window allows you to move backward and forward throughout your current file.*

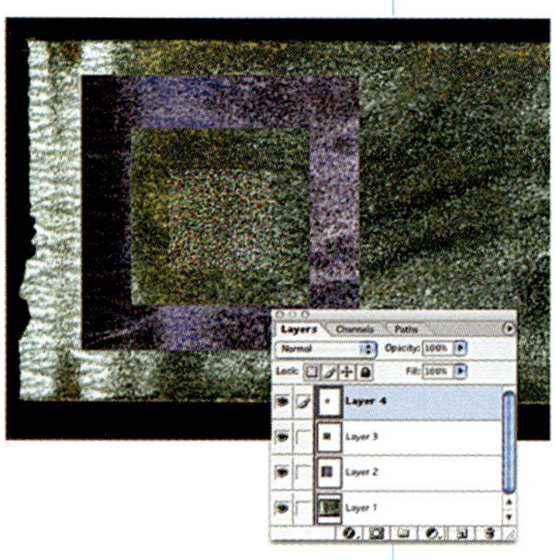

2-23d *The Layers window lets you select individual layers for manipulation.*

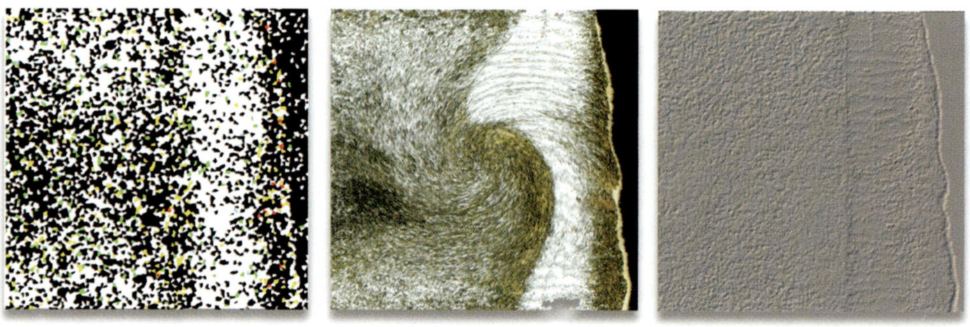

2-23e *Textures created with a mezzotint, a twirl, and an emboss filter are applied to this cropped and repeated section of a sandpaper scan.*

paste function. Now go to the Windows pull down menu and open the Layers window. In Figure 2-23d you'll notice that every pasted selection ends up on its own layer. A series of square selections were copied and pasted in this figure. Layer two was inverted using Image>Adjust>Invert. Layer four was adjusted using Filter>Pixilate>Pointillize.

Compose a collage based on sections or repeats of your original image. Because each pasted element goes onto a separate layer, when you click on that layer, you can manipulate it individually. Now try Filter and its various effects. Figure 2-23e uses a **mezzotint** with crystallize added on the left section. The middle section has a twirl added to a cropped section of the original scan, while the right section has a different couple of filters combined. The same crop of the original sandpaper scan was used in each of these filter treatments, resulting in a study of similarity and variety.

SUMMARY CRITIQUE

We began this chapter by examining the gradual evolution of tools of communication. You read and thought about the differences and similarities between the old and the new technologies. You created and saved a digital image that explored the art and design concept of similarity and variety. Now, as a part of the final class critique of your "warm up" and "studio hands on" workshop, consider and discuss your technique, your composition, and the concepts related to this act of digital creation.

For example, regarding Figure 2-22, you might say the following: "I scanned this as a 300-dpi, grayscale image, and saved it as a TIFF. I opened it in Photoshop and cropped it to

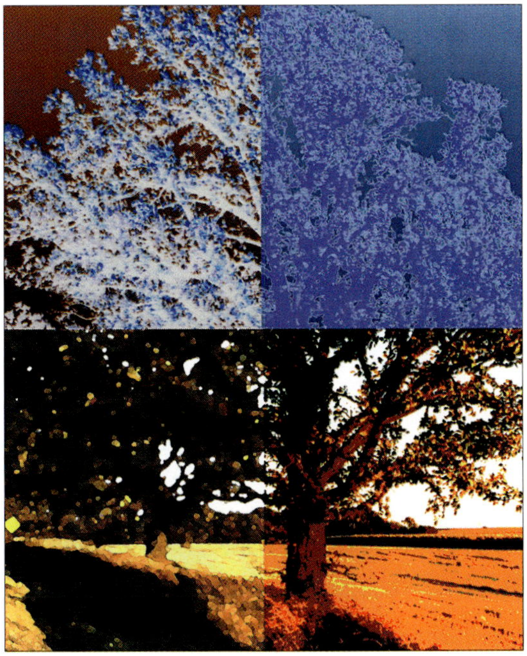

2-24 *An analog photographic print was scanned into Photoshop, and four selections made. Different image adjustments and filter treatments were applied to each selection.*

Adobe product screen shot(s) reprinted with permission from Adobe Systems Incorporated

Gallery Profile

April Greiman (1948—), in 2002, formed a new design consultancy in Los Angeles called April Greiman Made in Space. She created her first electronic designs on the Macintosh in 1984. She experimented with overlapping images and graphical elements, bitmapped fonts, and digital collage in spatial relationship, combining her respect for modernism and Swiss graphics (see Chapter 1) with new possibilities made conceivable by computer technology.

Her current work spans print graphics, web and motion, and architectural applications. Her work demonstrates her philosophy that the pixel is the "DNA," the "architecture" of the computer. She is fascinated with revealing the structure of that architecture, when appropriate, by making reference to it in her design projects.

Born in metropolitan New York, Greiman studied graphic design at the Kansas City Art Institute and also studied in Basel, Switzerland. In 1976 she moved to Los Angeles, and in a few years became the Director of the Visual Communications Program at the California Institute of the Arts. There she began to work with computer graphics and video, combining her interest in Swiss graphics with the multilayering made possible with computers and digital data (see Fig. 1-15). Her work in print, web, and architectural elements has made her one of the most influential figures in contemporary design. **Figure 2-25** shows her combination of enlarged pixels, overlapping layers, and the modernist grid system.

make a more dynamic composition, making the image run off the edges of the page. Because I wanted to emphasize figure/ground relationships, I used the Brightness/Contrast function to enhance the darks and lights. I did not make any additional changes, because the single image seemed visually strong, with a lively play of similarity and variation. I enjoy the presence of this old world item in a new digital venue."

It is always a good idea to put your best foot forward in a critique. But it is vital to be ready to take good suggestions. Make any changes and additions to your work that arise from the class discussion. **Figure 2-24** is a scan of an analog photograph that was manipulated using four different image adjustments and filter treatments.

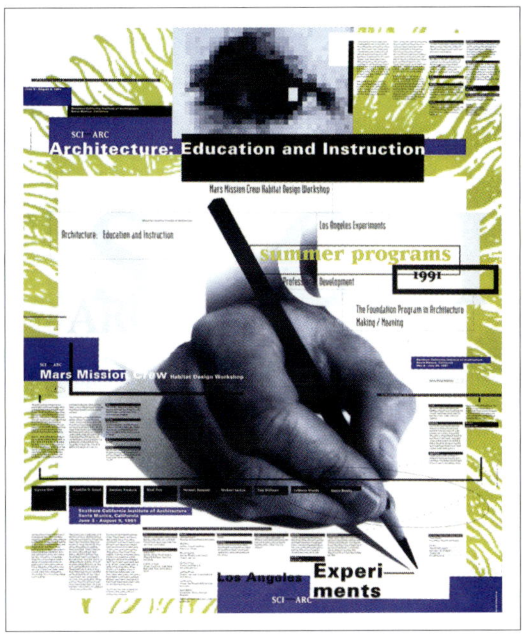

2-25 *April Greiman.* Summer Programs: poster for Southern California Institute of Architecture. *1991.*
Courtesy of April Greiman.

MOVING ON

The next chapter will increase your skills in Photoshop. You will be able to put your scanning ability to good use and learn new ways to create, think about, and manipulate photo-based imagery and hand-drawn computer artwork. You will have an opportunity to learn about another software package, called Illustrator.

TERMINOLOGY

CHAPTER 3

See Glossary for definitions

Vector Graphics
Raster Graphics
Object-oriented
Bitmapped
Cartesian Coordinates
Figure/Ground
Stable
Reversible
Ambiguous
Interpolation
Gestalt

3 Digital Imaging

It is important for artists and designers to understand the differences between object-oriented, vector graphics and bitmapped, raster graphics. Aesthetically, they are capable of very diverse kinds of image creation. Technically, they create very different file structures.

Understanding the key concepts that separate these two kinds of imaging programs is vital to the creation of technically accurate files. This chapter intends to give the reader an overview of and brief introduction to two programs that are prime examples of vector and raster graphics. These two programs are Adobe Illustrator and Adobe Photoshop. The following chapters will discuss each program in greater depth.

Students and instructors may choose to do the How To Basics and Hands On Practice for both programs, learning Illustrator and Photoshop together. Or they may decide to only *read* about both vector and raster file structures, while *practicing* the techniques of a single program at this time.

This chapter presents concepts related to the principle of figure/ground perception. It is perhaps the most important element of design structure. Many excellent examples of figure/ground in art and design are presented. As readers learn to master software techniques, they also learn how to build strong designs.

Drawing and Painting

There are two kinds of image files in computer graphics: **vector graphics** and **raster graphics**. These are also known as **object-oriented** and **bitmapped** graphics for reasons that are discussed shortly. Both are capable of creating dynamic images, depending upon the skill of the artist/designer. Vector graphics are like a cross-stitch embroidery pattern in which the yarn stays as separate interwoven strands. Raster graphics, on the other hand, are like a woven fabric in which the color pattern is dyed into the cloth. The vector color "strands" can be separated and moved independently, but raster "fabric" cannot.

Vector graphics involve creating shapes that are clean edged and are defined as geometric objects. The vector object, whether a shape or a drawn line, can be easily selected and edited, repositioned and transformed. Vector graphics are resolution independent, which means they retain crisp edges when enlarged. This is a powerful concept. However large or small you transform a vector file, it remains perfectly sharp. This is especially important with files that need to be output in varying sizes. A company or product logo design is a good example of such a file. **Figure 3-1** shows the logo for Sandhill Studio at varying sizes.

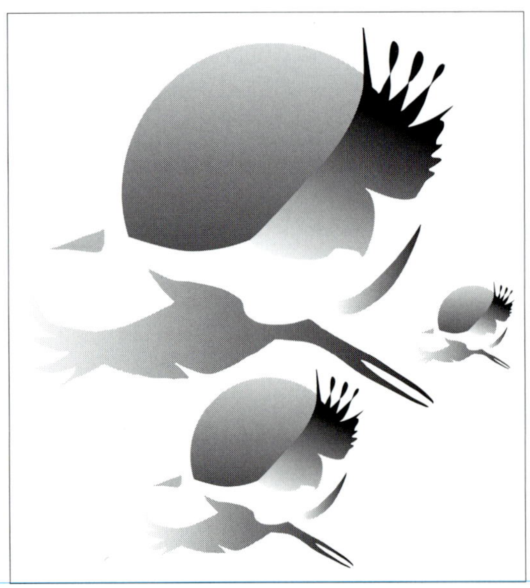

◆ **3-1** *Figures created in vector programs can be enlarged without losing detail.*

Vector graphics are used in typography, which needs to be perfectly crisp and clear. They are also used in illustration, in the creation of GIF files for the web, for animation, and in engineering diagrams. Increasingly, very interesting and varied lines can be achieved with vectors. InDesign, Quark, Illustrator, and Freehand are samples of programs that use vectors. **Figure 3-2** with its soft clouds and crisp train details was created in Illustrator.

Raster graphics are a painterly approach that involves changing the color attributes of pixels. Photoshop and Painter are examples of software programs that create raster files. As you know, pixels are individual picture elements that are the basic structure of raster files. Each individual pixel can be manipulated separately. They form a "map" of your image. The colors in raster graphics can appear to have gradual transitions and softened edges. Each brush stroke appears to blend with the next, and although there is no easy way to separate a stroke from its layer and reposition it, the overall result can be very painterly as you learned in Chapter 2.

Raster graphics are used in anything involving the creation and manipulation of photo-based imagery. They are used in illustration and fine art. They are an important part of web JPEG graphics. **Figures 3-3a–d** compare raster and vector art using the same pair of scanned scissors. The scan in Figure 3-3a is drawn over to create the vector art shown in Figure 3-3b. It has hard line edges and can be scaled up or down without loss of detail. The last two figures show possible variations of a raster file, with its capability for soft edges and image manipulation.

Object-Oriented and Bitmapped Graphics

Let's summarize the differences between these two kinds of graphic data files. Vector graphics programs are object-oriented and create images with clean, sharp lines based on **Cartesian coordinates** (see next section). These images can always be selected and moved independently of other objects in the file. They can be changed in size with no loss in clarity.

Bitmapped graphics are raster graphics comprised of pixels. Each pixel is individually manipulated through color and size to make a bitmapped file based on on-and-off commands. Bitmapped images lose data when changed in size but allow for a very painterly effect. Applications that have tools like paint cans and erasers are usually bitmapped graphics.

Now we will take a closer look at vector graphics and introduce the fundamental skills required to work with them. After this section, we will examine raster graphics. If you choose to follow the raster track and learn Photoshop first, skip to the Visual Language section now and return later to learn vector software.

Vector Graphics

In vector graphics we see the historical integration of philosophy, math, and drawing. The 17th-century philosopher René Descartes contributed to the field of human thought by considering fundamental questions of existence. He asked how we prove that we exist in *fact* and are more than a figment of imagination. When you think about trying to prove that, it's difficult. His most famous words were based upon his conclusion, "I think, therefore I am." He was also a fine mathematician and probably the first person to contribute to the development of computer graphics. His logic has informed us in philosophy, art, math, and science.

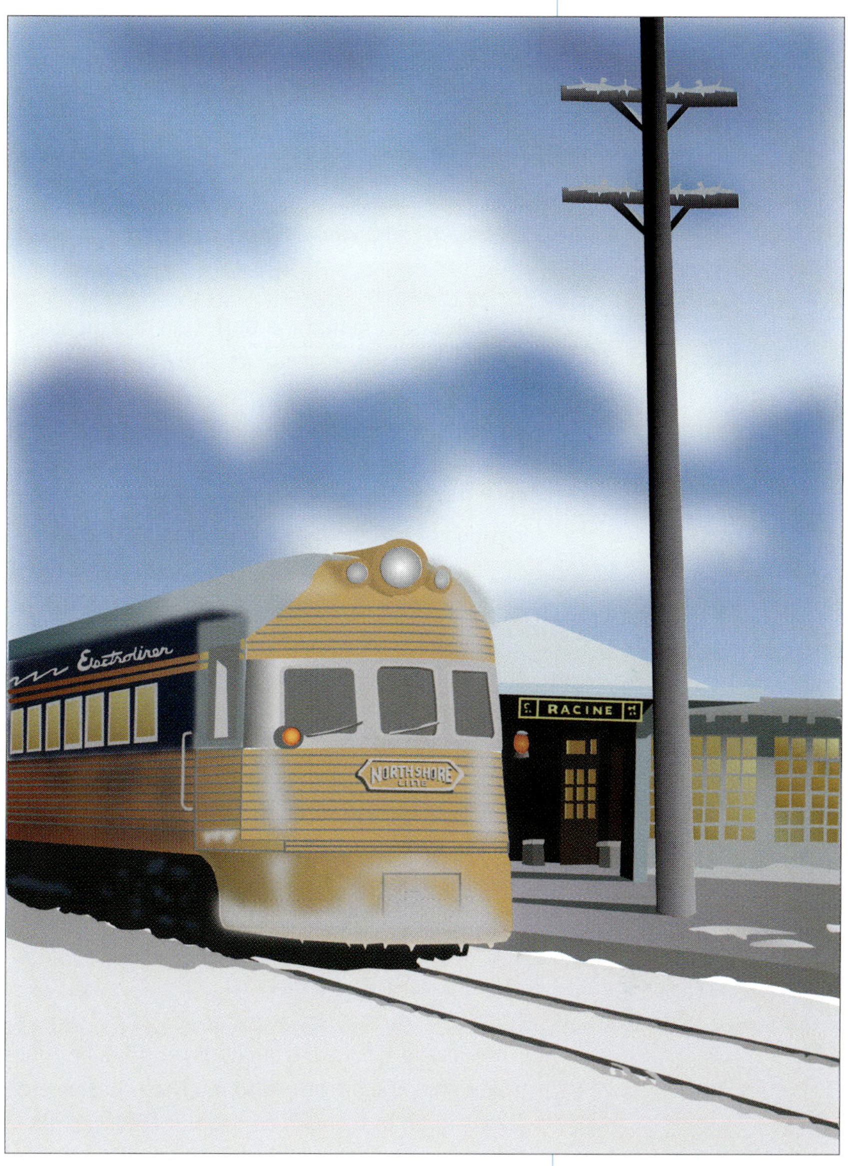

◆ **3-2** *This image was created by Jessica Davis for her student portfolio, using Illustrator software. It references her father's photograph of a local train station.*

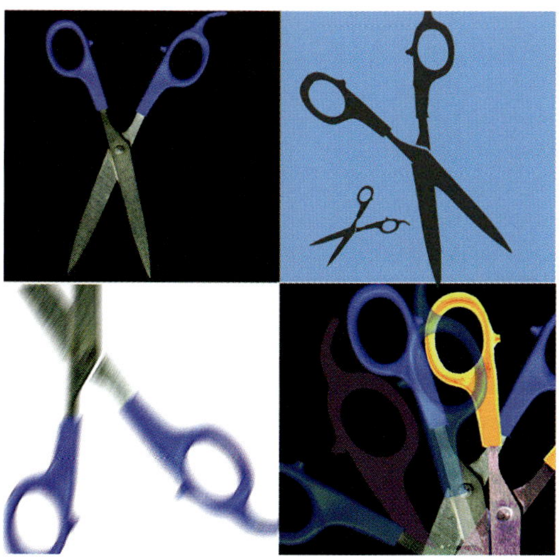

◆ **3-3 [a–d]** *The first scan of a pair of scissors is next shown as a vector drawing. The final two stages are raster image variations.*

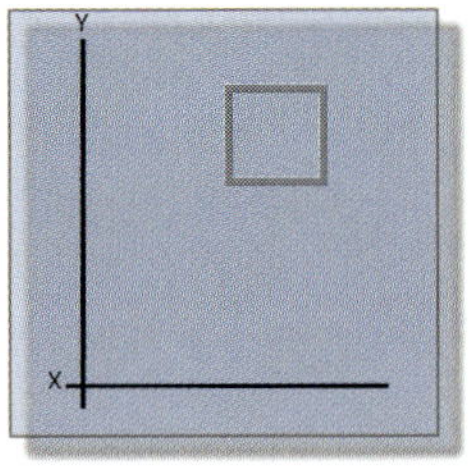

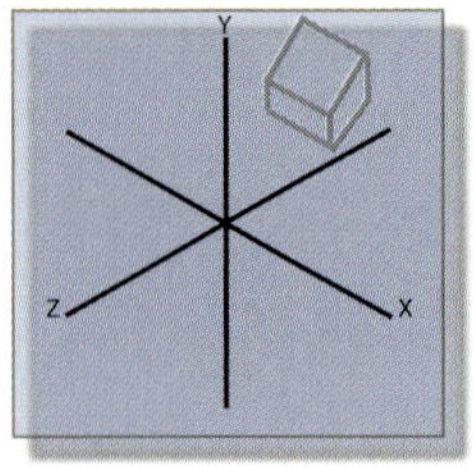

3-4, 3-5 *A two-dimensional Cartesian coordinate system describes the x and y axes, while a three-dimensional system uses x, y, and z axes.*

Descartes created the Cartesian coordinate system upon which vector graphics are based. He was a multifaceted researcher. Familiar to many students of geometry and algebra, the *x* and *y* coordinates represent a two-dimensional shape (**Fig. 3-4**). The *x, y,* and *z* coordinates describe the position of a three-dimensional graphic (**Fig. 3-5**).

Illustrator and Freehand are two-dimensional vector graphics drawing programs. **Figure 3-6** shows the Illustrator desktop. Lines drawn between coordinate points create vector images. These points are referred to in software terms as *anchor points.* Learning to create and control anchor points is at the heart of computer graphics when working with vector programs. We will learn about using anchor points and creating images, using the tools introduced in Figure 3-6 and elaborated upon in the How To Basics section.

Vector Image Creation

The How To Basics are created using Adobe Illustrator on a Macintosh platform. These basics are very similar to techniques used in Macromedia Freehand, which is also a vector-imaging program. The Illustrator tools are similar to its sister program Photoshop, because both are Adobe products. The software interface for all these programs is nearly identical on Windows PC and Macintosh platforms.

The following series of instructions and illustrations demonstrate the basic principles of drawing with vector graphics. You may have a different computer or a different software version, but these principles, along with a touch of imagination, should successfully bridge those differences. For a more comprehensive introduction to your particular software program, look at the various Help menus and Tutorials packaged with it and rely on your instructor. There are also many excellent step-by-step manuals available. The How To Basics below have a great deal of highly condensed information you will want to read, practice, and master. Remember that this book is intended to give you the basics of software operation within a context of art and design principles. It aims to encourage the imagination as well as enable technique development.

The How To Basics section is lecture and study information. The Hands On Practice section asks you to gain step-by-step experience. All of these techniques, however, are only a means to an end. Your eye, brain, and imagination will supply the most important ingredients. As we progress to the In The Studio section, you'll be asked to apply your skills in all three areas of technique, concept, and composition.

Focus On Concept

Math, science, and psychology contribute to today's art and design. Can you think of ways these fields contribute to one another? Perhaps in technical medical illustration? What about architectural design? Math and science contributed to the creation of computer graphics. The psychology of visual perception contributed to images we make on computers.

Figure/ground is a fundamental element of visual perception. How does it affect us in everyday life? Consider the ability to see a bird against the sky. How does it appear in art and design? Perhaps the sky is shown inside a bird. What other examples of everyday figure/ground relationships can you find around you in the classroom? What can you find in historical or contemporary art and design? Examine the examples in this chapter.

How To Basics

The steps described in this section are illustrated in **Figures 3-7a–p**.

Beginning Vectors

Basic Shapes are created with the rectangle tool and the other options located underneath it. Hold down the mouse on the rectangle tool to view and select these options (Fig. 3-7a).

Anchor points and *lines* are created by using the pen tool to establish points. Clicking on another point will connect those points with a straight line.

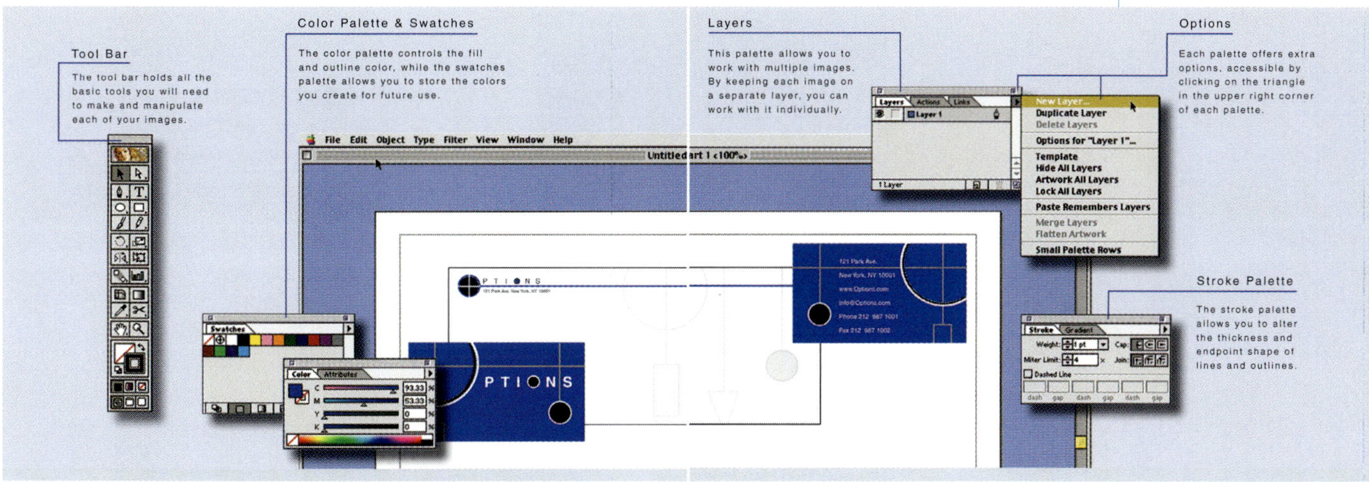

Adobe product screen shots reprinted with permission from Adobe Systems Incorporated

◆ **3-6** *This Illustrator desktop shows various tools and pop up windows.*
Illustration by Tiffany Dorner-Jones.

The width of the line is set in the stroke pop up menu. Figure 3-7b shows this process. Other visual characteristics such as color are set in corresponding pop ups. Most pop up menus are accessed from the Window section of the main menu across the top of your screen (Fig. 3-7c).

Creating a *curved line* is done by pulling before releasing the mouse or pen tool. The next point will be connected by a curve, and both points will have nonprinting "handles" that can be clicked on with the black arrow tool to reposition the curve of the line as shown in Figure 3-7d.

The *white arrow tool* will move the position of the anchor point itself. Be sure the anchor points are selected with that arrow, and that they are "hollow" or white-looking before manipulating. Figure 3-7e shows the white arrow tool.

Connecting the end points from your pen drawing creates closed shapes. Figure 3-7f shows the process of making one end point coincide with the other end

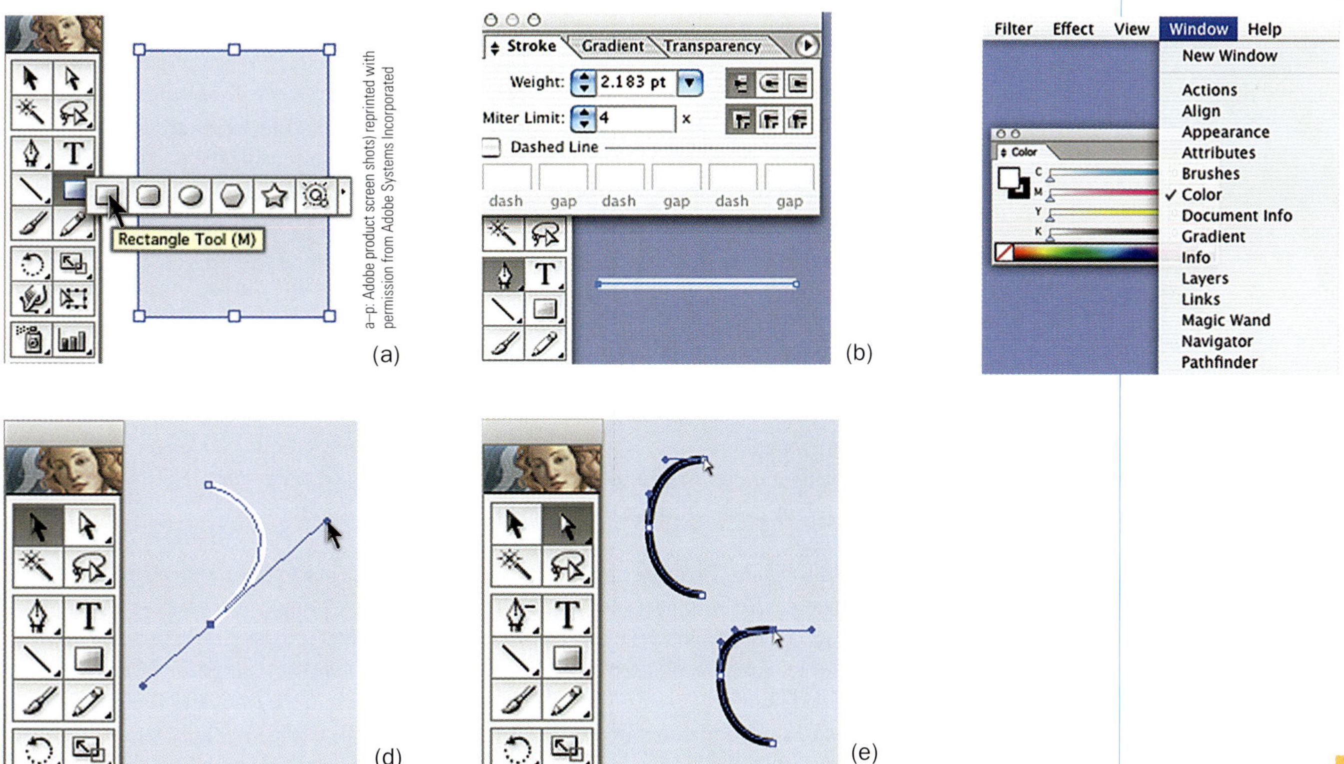

a–p: Adobe product screen shots) reprinted with permission from Adobe Systems Incorporated

◆ **3-7 [a–p]** *The basics of using Illustrator vector graphics are shown in these step-by-step diagrams.*

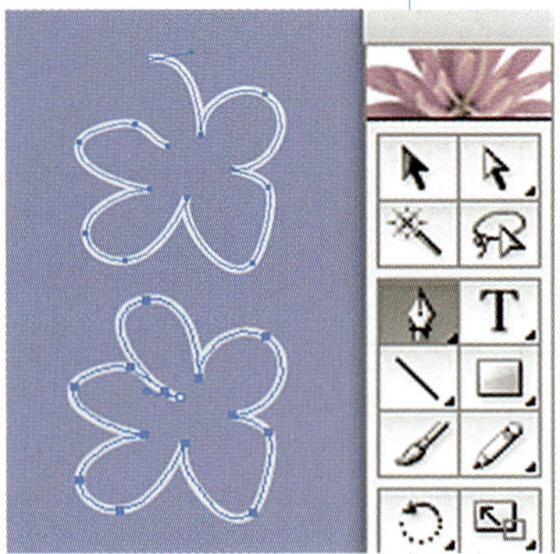

(f)

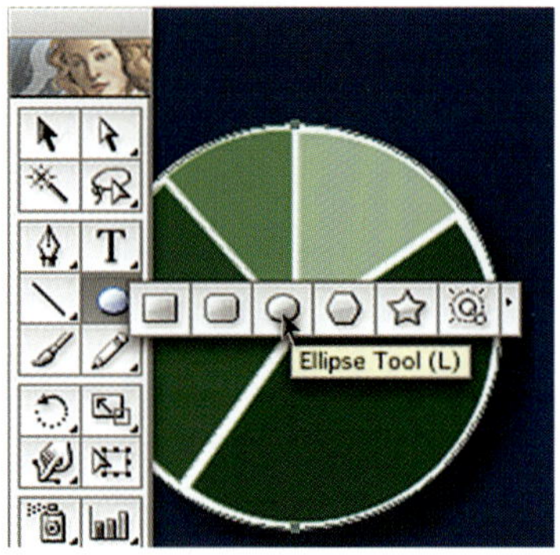

(g)

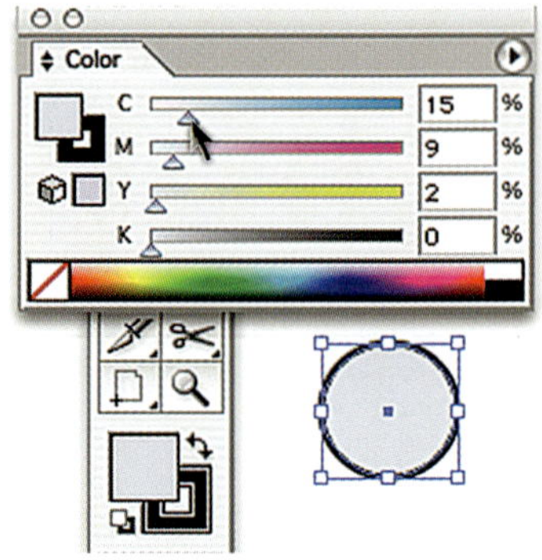

(h)

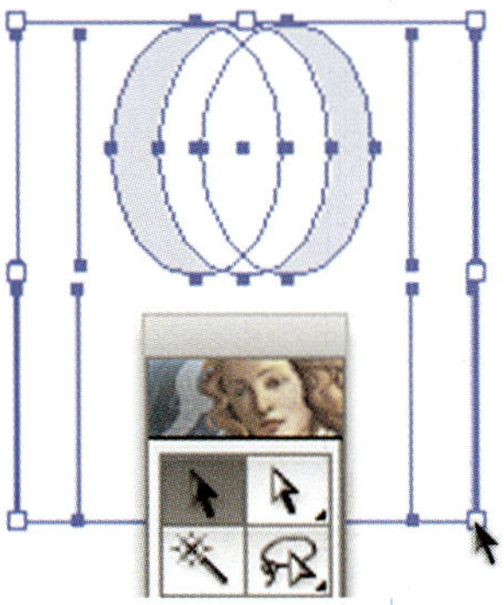

(i)

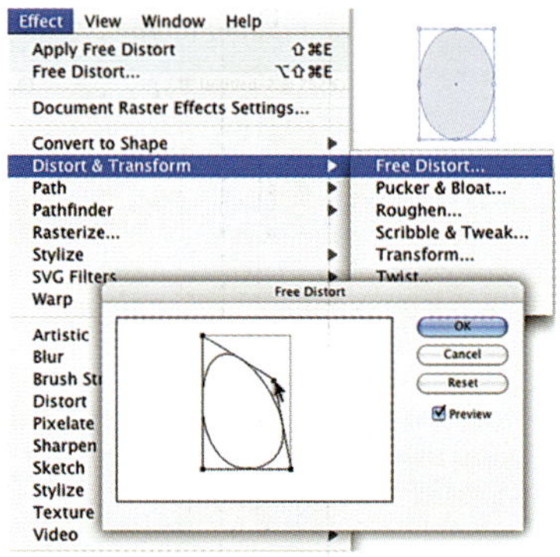

(j)

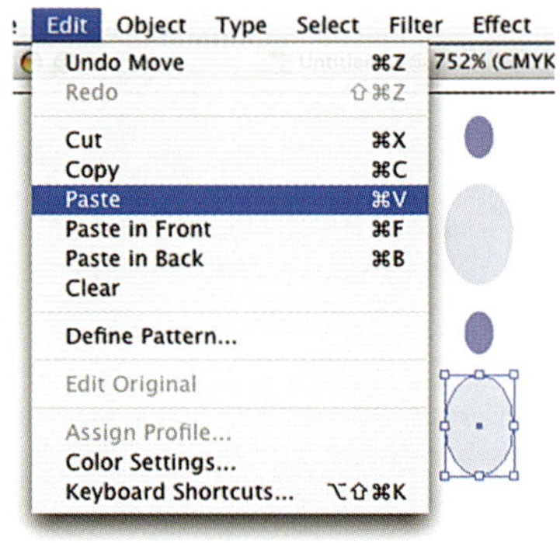

(k)

point to close the shape. Drawing using one of the shape tools from the toolbox also creates a closed shape (Fig. 3-7g).

Fill and stroke commands control the characteristics of the interior of your shape and the line that surrounds it. As shown in Figure 3-7h, you must open the Color pop up Window to *choose a color* for the line or the fill of your shape.

Selecting and *Deselecting* allow you to select one line or multiple lines. The black selection arrow in the toolbox will select a line or a shape. Holding down the shift key will let you select, move, and manipulate multiple lines. Drawing a bounding box around your shape with the arrow key selects everything inside the bounding box. Figure 3-7i shows this selection method. Deselect by clicking off the selected object or choosing Select>Deselect from the menu options.

When selected, objects can be *transformed* and manipulated several ways in Edit>Transform or the Effect menu, as shown in Figure 3-7j.

Undo is available from Edit>Undo. There are quick and simple keyboard commands that you may want to learn. This is one of them. The keystrokes vary between platforms (Mac and PC) but are all listed beside the main menu pull downs.

The *copy* and *paste functions* are fundamental to most programs. Edit>Copy and Edit>Paste let you duplicate any selected object (Fig. 3-7k). You can paste between different open windows and even between some programs, such as Illustrator and Photoshop.

Fonts are created using the text tool and clicking on the screen to activate it. When selected with the black arrow tool (vector) or by backspacing over the type on the screen, type can be controlled by point size and other attributes using the main pull down font menu (Type>Font). Their characteristics can also be set using the pop up character window found under fonts. Figure 3-7l shows various ways to specify font characteristics. Fonts can be converted to anchor points for unique manipulation under Fonts>Create outlines (Fig. 3-7m). This also avoids the problem of various fonts not being available on different computers. After using this function, your font *looks* the same; however, to the computer it is no longer a typestyle but has been changed to an image. Now you have control over every vector point in it.

Layers are fundamental to creating and controlling computer graphics in all vector, raster, and web-based 3-D and interactive programs. There are two ways to layer images. The first is to keep everything on the original layer. Go to Object>Arrange to restack your various selected objects to the front and behind as shown in Figure 3-7n. This works very well. A more detailed technique requires establishing several separate layers.

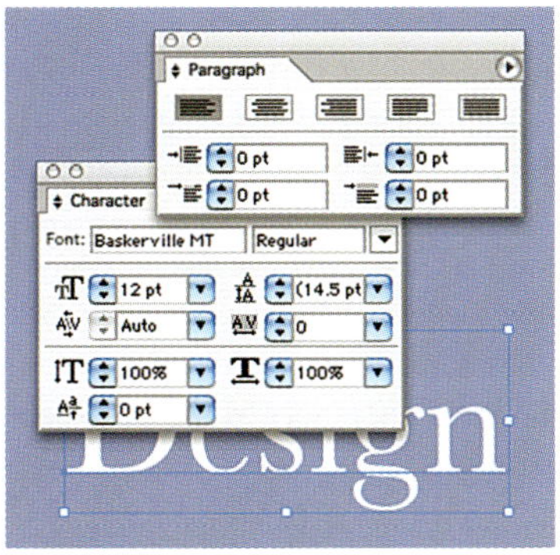

(l)

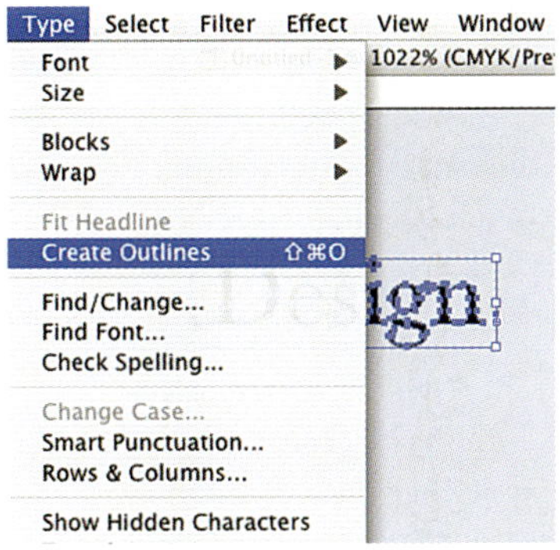

(m)

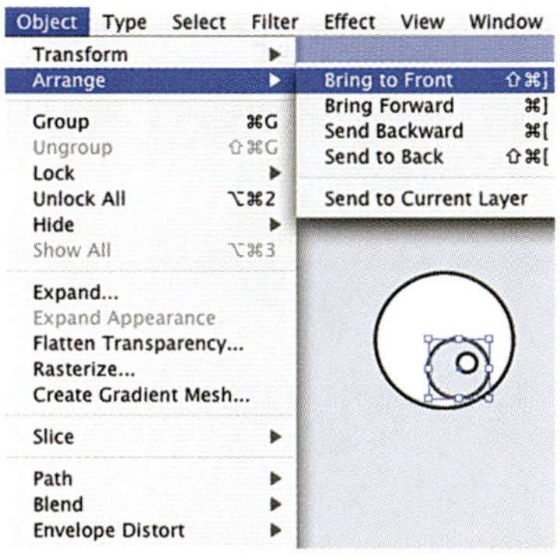

(n)

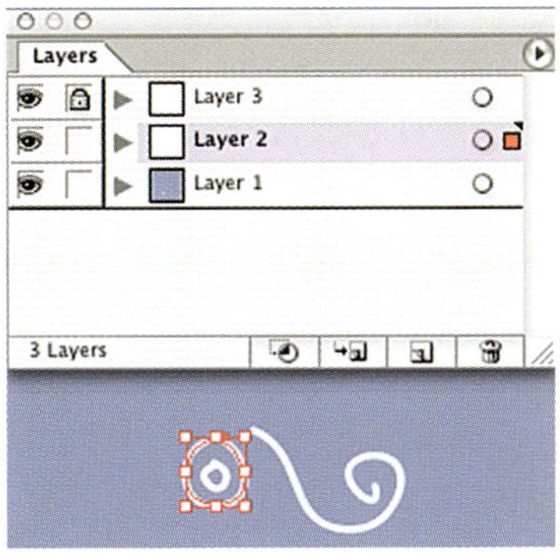

(o)

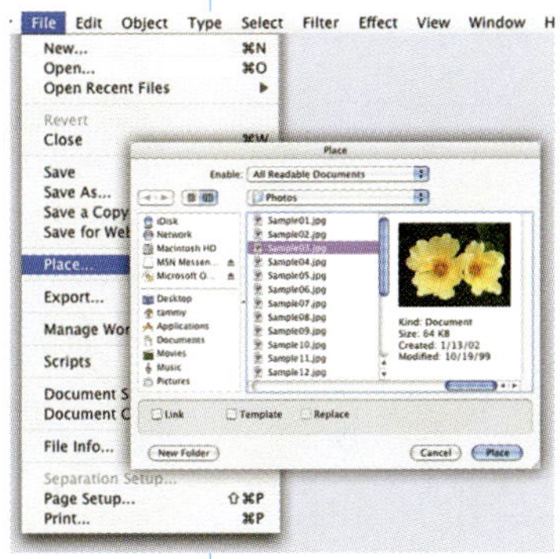

(p)

To access them, select Window>Show Layers. Use the layer pop up to create new layers. Select a layer to make it active and draw on it. Layers can be moved or locked and their visibility turned on and off. Figure 3-7o shows these layers and their attributes. Think of layers as sheets of paper. Each one covers the layer beneath it.

Placing Scans is done with File>Place. Select File>Place and navigate to your file's location (Fig. 3-7p). You will be able to see listed only the files that can be opened in your current application. Once a scan has been placed, it can be traced over using the pen tool to create a drawn illustration. To do this, create a new layer to draw on and lock the scanned reference on the layer beneath.

Hands On Practice

The illustrations in **Figures 3-8a–j** show this process and ask you to work along in the software program.

1. Select the pen tool and move the mouse pointer over the drawing area. Click and move the pointer and click again. Continue doing this until you are satisfied you understand the function and how to draw lines.

2. Now let's draw a curve. Select the pen tool and click the mouse button and drag it up before releasing. Now release the button. This establishes where the curve begins. Attached to the original anchor point are direction lines. Figure 3-8a shows this process, as well as demonstrating what happens when you move the pointer to where you want the curve to end, and click. Try dragging down before releasing the mouse.

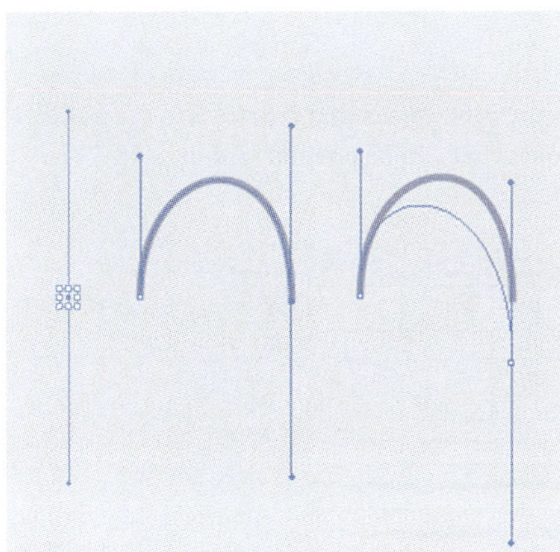
a–j: Adobe product screen shots reprinted with permission from Adobe Systems Incorporated

(a)

3-8 [a–j] *Practice the steps shown in this series of sequential diagrams, as described in the text.*

3. Select the white arrow *direction selection* tool. Click on one of the points you have established and drag it. Notice how the location of the point and the curve is repositioned.

4. Now create some closed shapes. Begin by clicking with the mouse and establishing several points. The end point should cover the beginning point to finish a closed shape. Next, try a different way of creating shapes. Hold down the rectangle tool in the toolbox and select a shape option. Click and drag and release to establish the shape.

5. Now apply color to that shape and its stroke. Select the shape by clicking on it with the black arrow tool. Go to Window>Color. Double click on the solid fill color box and select a color from the array presented. Now click on the outline stroke box and select a color. You should see your shape fill with a color and be surrounded by a colored stroke. Now delete the colored stroke by selecting it, and then selecting the box beneath it with the red slash. Practice this several times. Figure 3-8b shows the fill and stroke controls.

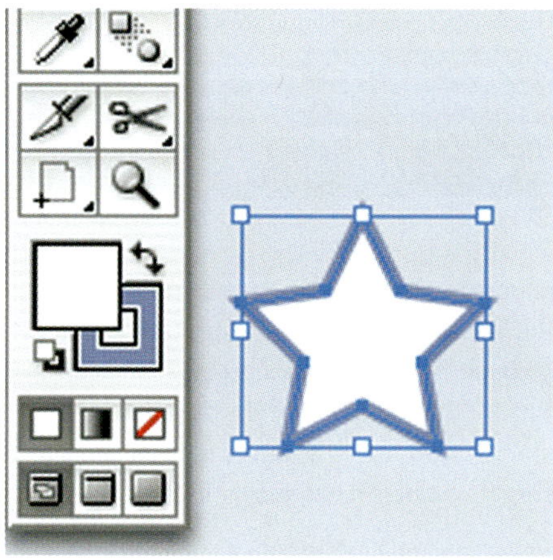

(b)

6. The brush palette allows many variations of the stroke. Figure 3-8c shows that palette and several different strokes that can be created with it.

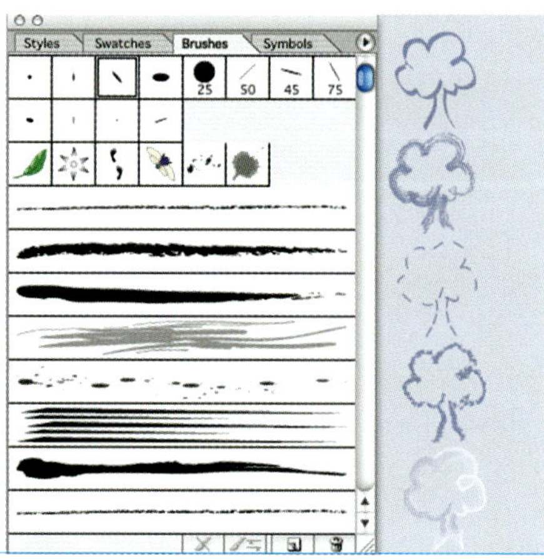

(c)

7. Understanding selections is important. It is different from the raster technique we covered in Chapter 2. Select your object with the black arrow in the toolbox. Drag the object to reposition it. Notice the entire selected shape moves. Now select your object with the white arrow in the toolbox. Be sure the points of the shaped object are hollow or white. Click on a single point to reposition it. Notice only the point moves. Practice this several times. Remember to deselect when desired by clicking off the object.

8. Select your object. Now go to the pull down menu and select Object>Transform. Choose a function from rotate, shear, scale. Observe the results. Figure 3-8d shows a variety of possible transformations.

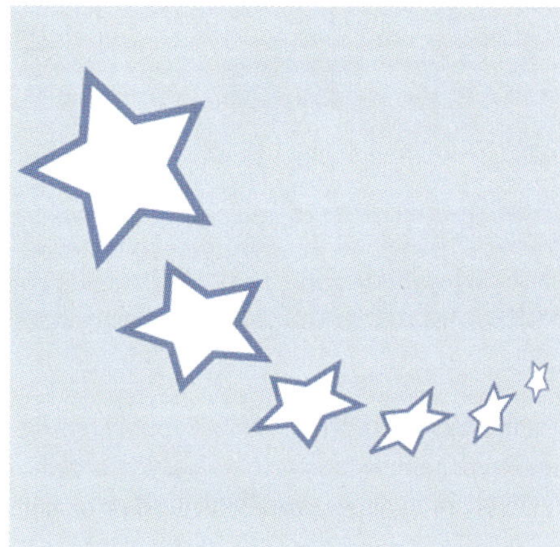

(d)

9. Choose Edit>Undo to back out of your last manipulation. You can set the number of undos by selecting Illustrator>Preference>Units and Undos. While you're there, look at the other options in Preferences.

10. Now we will practice using the copy and paste functions, which are much like Photoshop. The one big difference is that they don't automatically go to a new layer in the layers palette. Select one of your shapes by clicking on it with the black arrow tool. Go to the menu and choose Edit>Copy. Now choose Edit> Paste. This lets you duplicate any selected object. Choose Edit >Paste again. You will notice that the selected object remains in memory until a new object is selected. Any object can also be selected and transformed in Edit>Transform. Try that. Next let's try transforming them in a symmetrical pattern.

11. To make a symmetrical pattern, select a closed shape. Go to Object>Transform>Rotate. Decide how many objects you want to rotate in a circle. Divide that into 360 degrees. Keystroke that number into the rotate function. Do this as many times as necessary to complete a circle, selecting the newest object each time. Figure 3-8e shows this process.

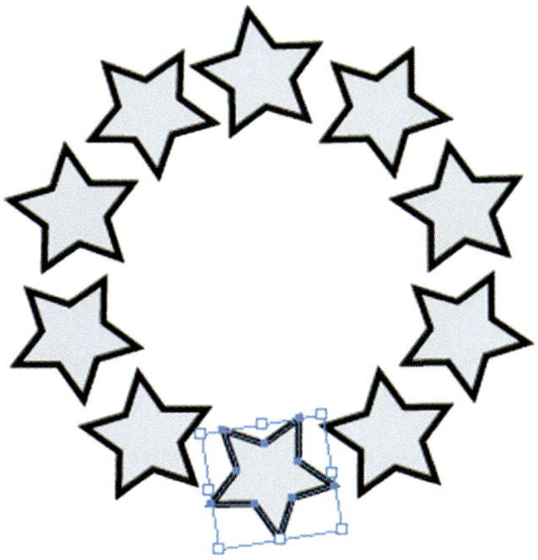

(e)

12. Select the "T" from the toolbox. Click on the screen and type a word. Select that word by clicking with the black arrow tool and go to the Type pull down menu. Experiment with changing the font and size. Then select the word, using the black arrow selection tool, and change its color. Do this by selecting the word and opening the Window>Color menu.

13. Now change your typographic word to an image by selecting it with the black arrow key and selecting Type>Create Outlines from the pull down menu. This file can now be edited using a variety of image editing tools. Figure 3-8f shows an outline word that has been edited. As mentioned before, it can also be sent to press without worrying about sending the entire typestyle with your file.

14. Now we will get further acquainted with creating layers. Select Window>Layers and observe the pop up window that results. Select New Layer from the arrow

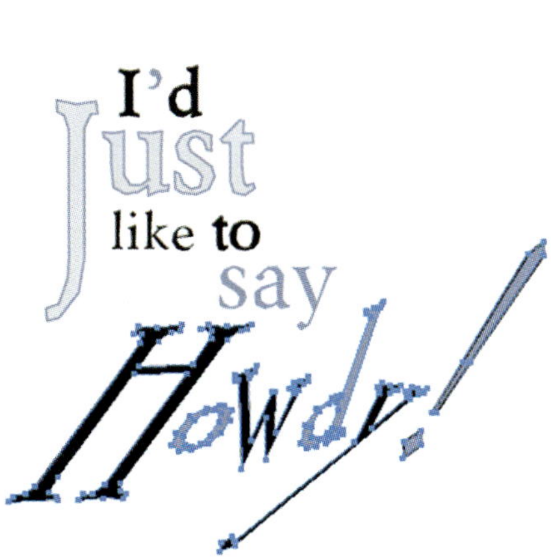

(f)

at the top of the window. Now create an image on the new layer. Observe how it covers the previous layer. You can create many, many layers for a complex piece. Turn the layer visibility on and off by clicking on the eye icon. Lock the layer by clicking on the box beside the eye icon. Practice this several times. The layers can be restacked by clicking and dragging them above and beneath one another in the layers window as shown in Figure 3-8g. For now, keep these layers closed by not selecting the small arrow key in the layers window that opens them and shows the sub layers. Don't open the sub layers to see a list of all the things stacked on each layer. This can be confusing.

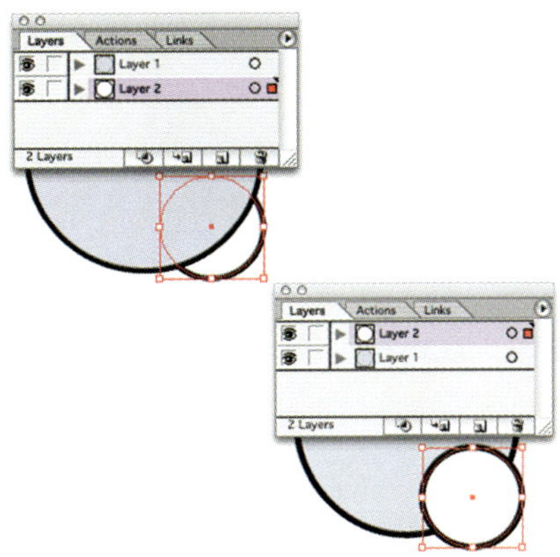

(g)

15. Now you will place a scan. Go to File>Place> *your file name*. Select as your file name one of the scans from the previous chapter. After placing the scan, lock its layer and go to Select>New Layer to create a layer to draw on. Now practice using the pen tool to trace your scanned image, as shown in Figure 3-8h. Be sure you create a closed shape or a series of closed shapes. Lock each shape. You will probably need to create a number of curves, by pulling your points before

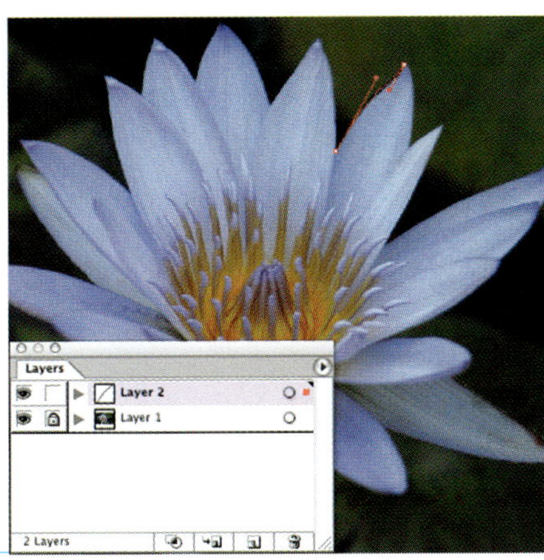

(h)

releasing the mouse. Make as few points as possible to describe the image. Figure 3-8i shows how to do this for the overall flower shape. Open the pull down menu for Window>Layers>Links. When the link box is open, select your scanned image and then select Embed Image (Fig. 3-8j). This way the photo image will stay with your Illustrator file for later reference. If it ever disappears, it will be because you forgot to embed the image.

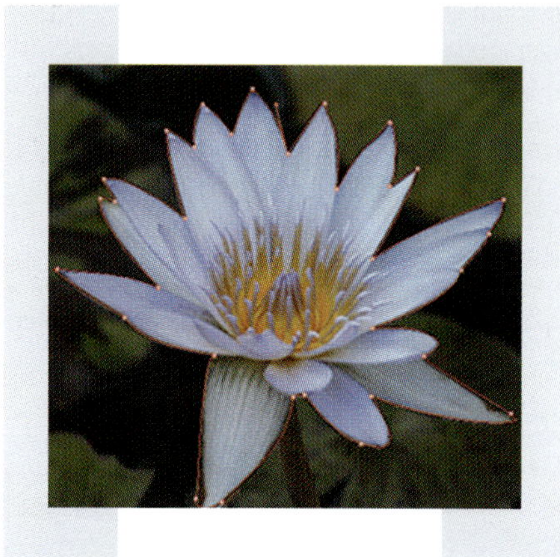

(i)

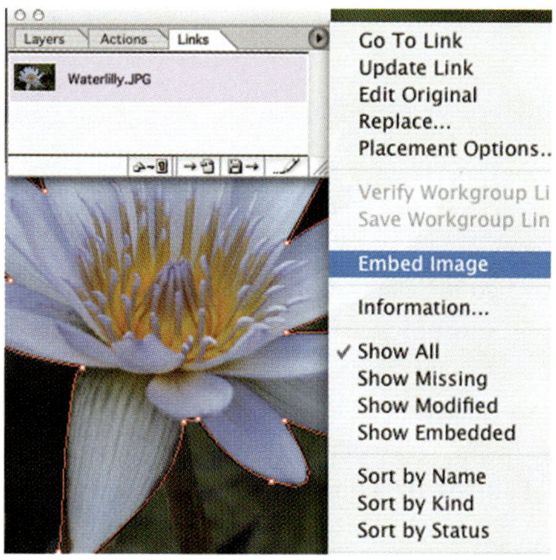

(j)

Visual Language

Now we can move on from learning the basics of vector software technique to thinking about concept and composition. In the preceding chapter we worked with similarity and variety. That principle can help you create good work in any field of art and design throughout your career.

This section introduces an equally vital design concept. The fundamental law of perception that makes it possible for us to identify objects in a visual creation is the **figure/ground** relationship. The eye and mind must always separate an object (figure) from its surroundings (ground). Sometimes referred to as a positive and negative spatial relationship, this principle is crucial to shaping a strong composition.

You should always, in any art and design piece, be aware of creating shapes in the "left-over" ground every time you create a figure. Every area of your composition is a shape, not just the foreground. Many times the relationship between figure and ground is dynamic and ambiguous, offering more than one solution to the eye. There are three kinds of figure/ground relationships. The first is "stable." The next is reversible and the third is ambiguous, as shown in the three diagrams in **Figures 3-9a**, **3-9b**, and **3-9c**. The first diagram shows a definite foreground and background. The second diagram shows shapes that can seem to visually flip from foreground to background. The third diagram shows several shapes that make up an overall whole. These ambiguous shapes can be viewed individually or as a whole. These three relationships are shown using typography but are equally true when creating shapes in art and illustration.

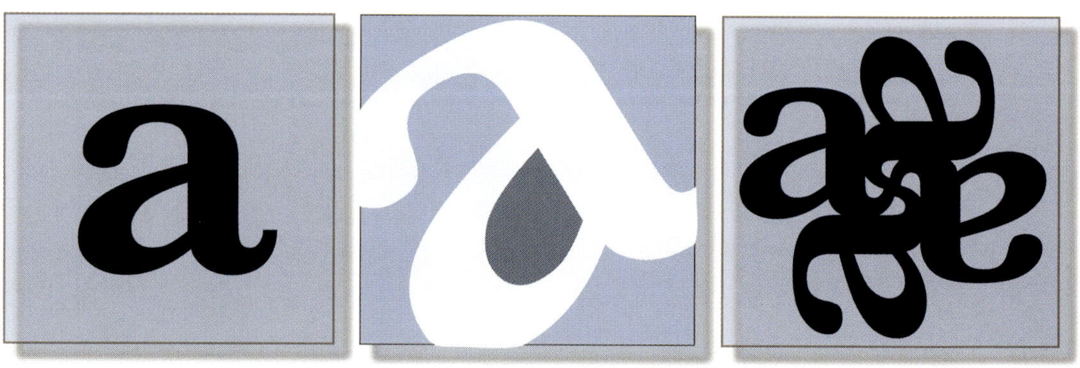

(a) (b) (c)

3-9 [a–c] *Stable, reversible, and ambiguous figure/ground relationships are demonstrated in order in these three type-based figures.*

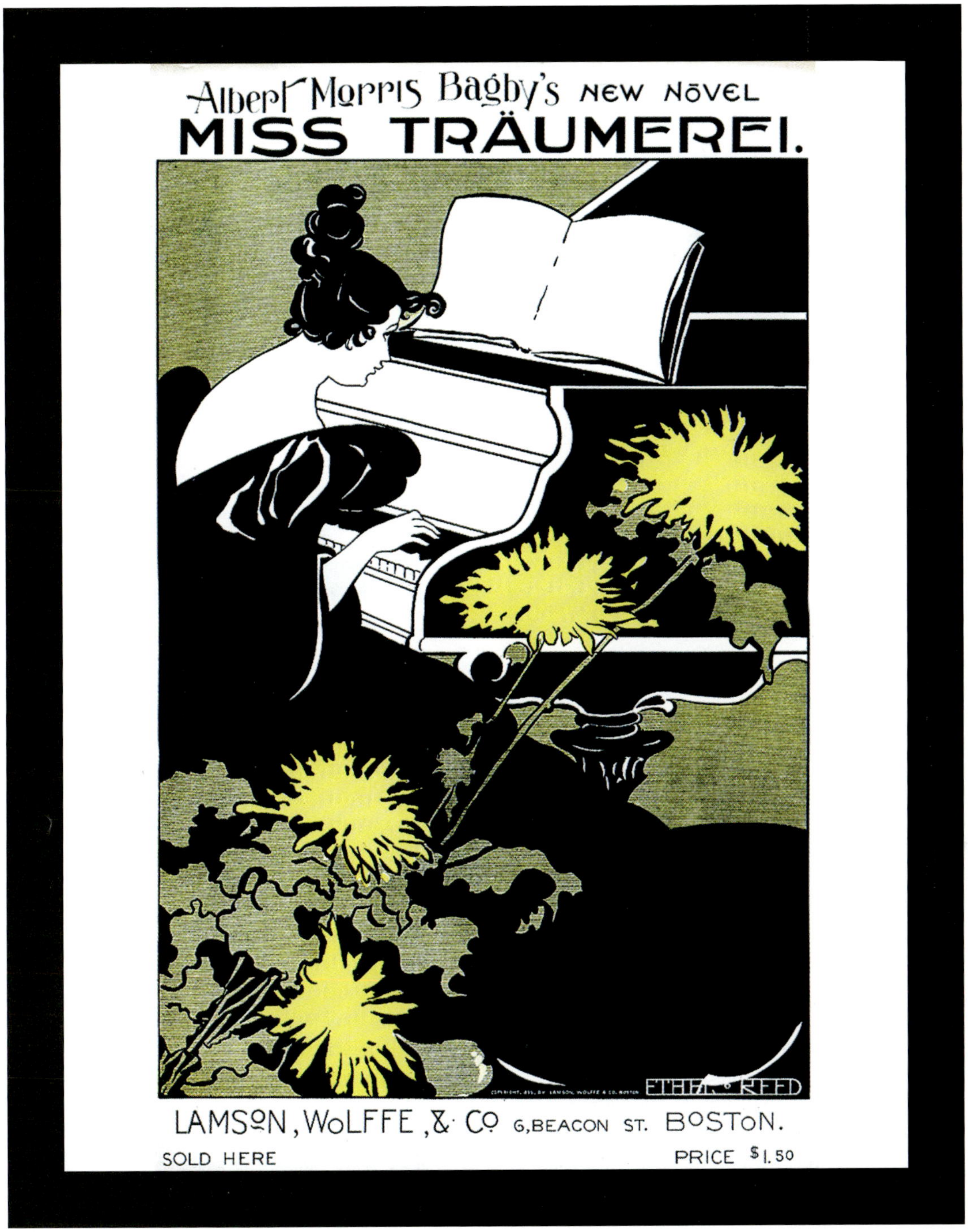

3-10a *Ethel Reed.* Miss Träumerei. *1895. Poster advertising the novel of same name.* Thomas G. Boss Fine Books.

A **stable** figure/ground relationship is seen in an unchanging but dynamic relationship of object against background. How shapes touch the edges of the composition is very important. A dynamically stable figure/ground relationship will often deliberately play with the tension of nearly becoming reversible, as we can see in **Figure 3-10a**, in which the figure of the black dress in this turn-of-the-20th-century poster becomes a background for the flowers.

A **reversible** figure/ground relationship is full of a compelling dynamic tension. Often used in logo design, this type of composition allows us to focus on either the foreground or background

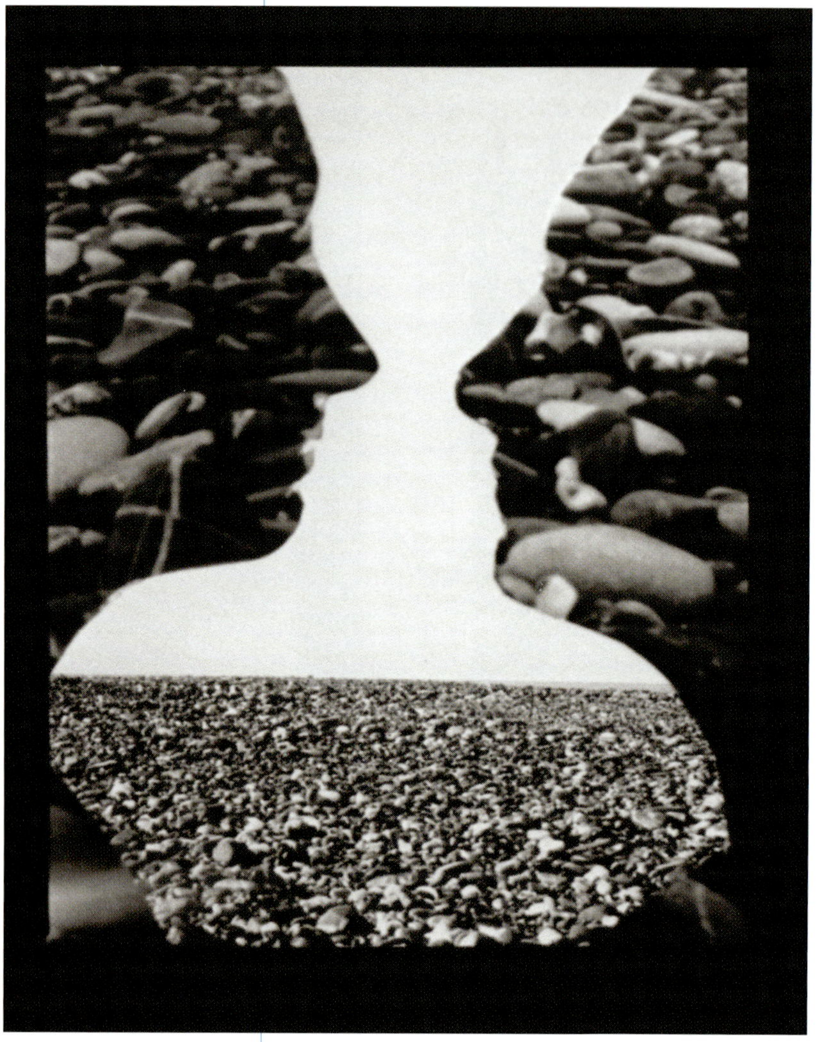

◆ **3-10b** *Ruth Thorne-Thomsen.* Two Faces Are a Vase. *1985. Toned silver gelatin print, 4 × 5″.*
Courtesy of the Artist.

equally. What at first glance is ground becomes figure as our eye and brain keep switching. **Figure 3-10b** shows a photographic composition by contemporary photographer Ruth Thorne-Thomsen (1943—) that pushes our eye into the sky and pulls it back to the face shapes. First one pops forward, and then the other. Research this artist. It will be worth the effort.

An **ambiguous** figure/ground relationship also offers more than one solution to the searching eye. It is often made up of multiple objects that can be read as a whole or as various parts. **Figure 3-11** by Dada artist Hannah Höch (1889–1978) shows a collage that makes a figure out of parts that retain their separate identities. The face and bird are read together but can also be seen as separate. The running figure combines human and beast. These combinations are powerful editorial, allegorical comments by the artist on the political situation of her day.

Now we will move on and begin to integrate both the Illustrator techniques and the fundamental visual perception concepts discussed in this chapter. If you're focused on raster graphics right now, progress to that section.

Warming Up

Spend some time now practicing each of the techniques presented in the preceding vector graphics How To Basics/Hands On Practice sections. Repeat each step until you are comfortable with the pen tool. Study the image and its description shown in **Figures 3-12a–d** to familiarize yourself with the potential in vector techniques. The four layers shown in this figure demonstrate some of the stages involved in the creation of the final effect. See this student's file on the accompanying **CD**.

In The Studio

Now you are asked to create three different vector portfolio pieces. Each should use one of the stable, reversible, and ambiguous figure/ground relationships.

Stable

Select one of your scans from Chapter 2, or one from the accompanying CD. Stay in Photoshop and crop it into a design that goes off the edge of the composition (bleeds) on three sides. Try to create a dynamic but stable relationship between figure and ground. Save it. Now, just for practice, place it into Illustrator and save it in that program. **Figure 3-13** shows the process of placing a scan into Illustrator.

Reversible

Quilt patterns are an excellent example of reversible figure/ground. These overall surface pattern designs are also used in wallpaper, fabric, tiles, and so on. Refer to the diagrams shown in **Figure 3-14a** to get initial ideas for creating your own overall pattern. You may want to use Illustrator's grid, rulers, guides, and copy/paste functions. Remember that only a closed shape can be filled with black or a color. **Figure 3-14b** shows a solution to this problem.

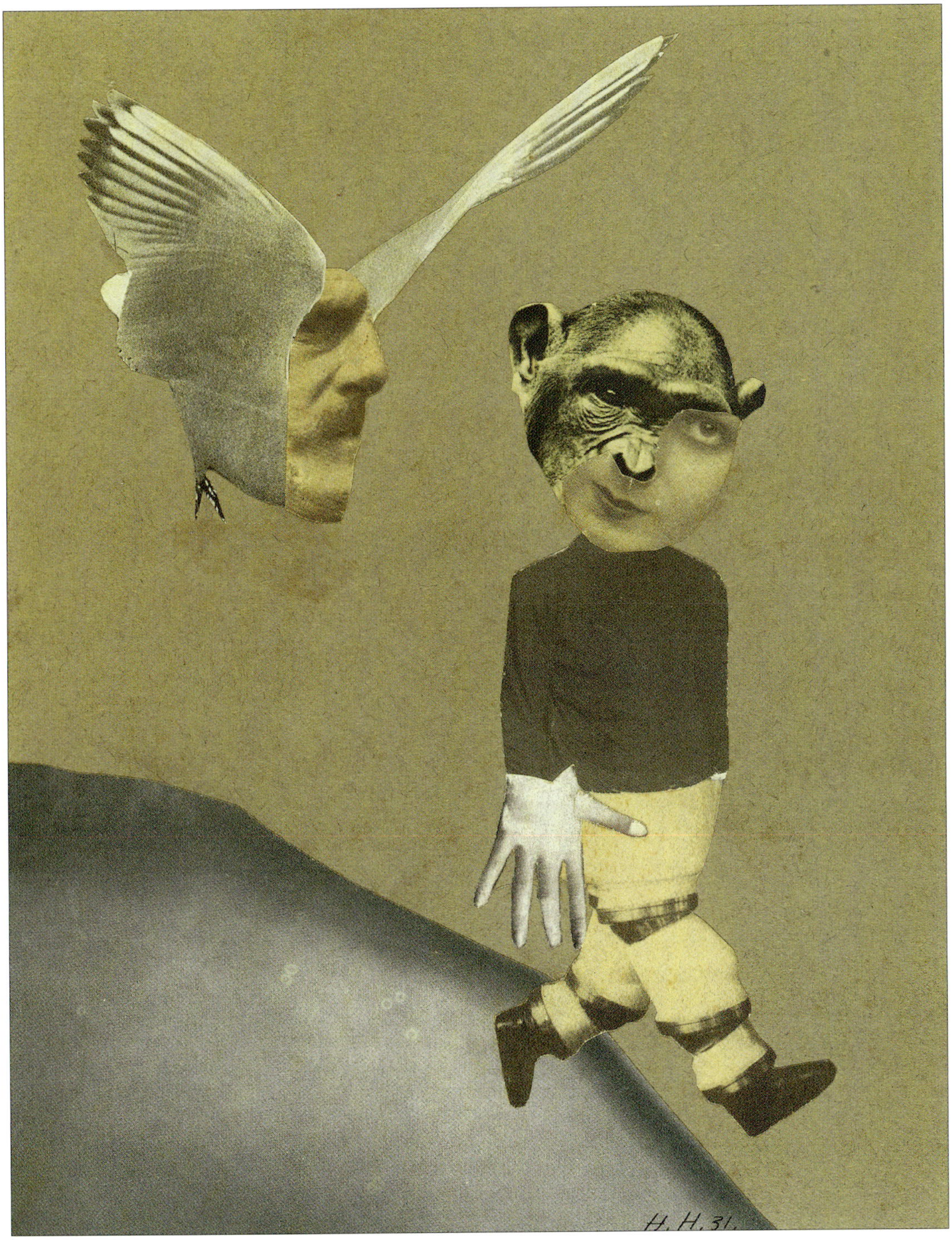

◆ **3-11** *Hannah Höch.* Flucht (Flight). *1931. Photomontage,* $9\,^{1}/_{16}'' \times 7\,^{1}/_{4}''$.
Collection Institut für Auslandsbeziehungen, Stuttgart/©2005 Artist Rights Society (ARS)/VG Bild-Kunst, Bonn.

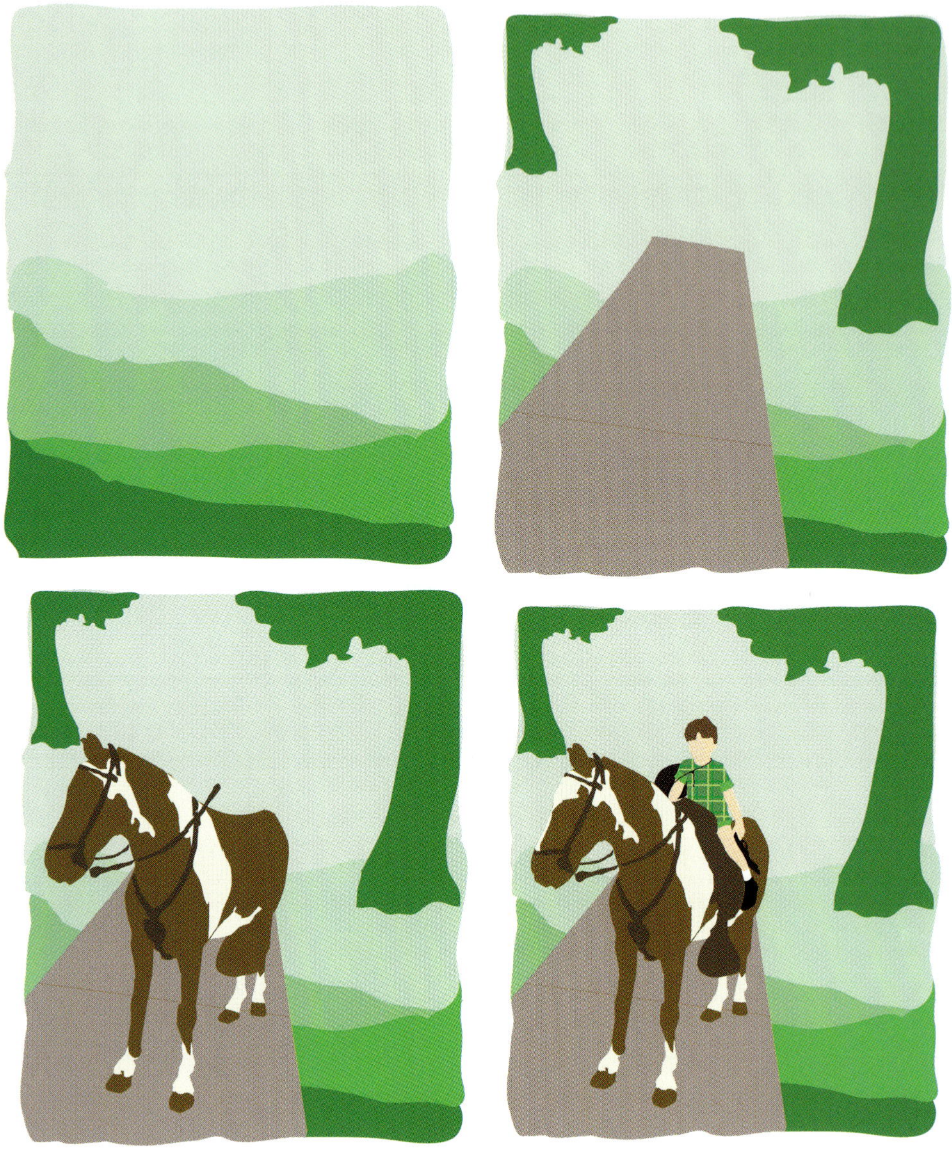

◆ **3-12 [a–d]** *Carla M. Cannistra created this illustration for her student portfolio. Using Illustrator, she worked in many overlapping layers. Four successive stages are shown here.*

◆ **3-13** *Opening a Photoshop scan in Illustrator.*

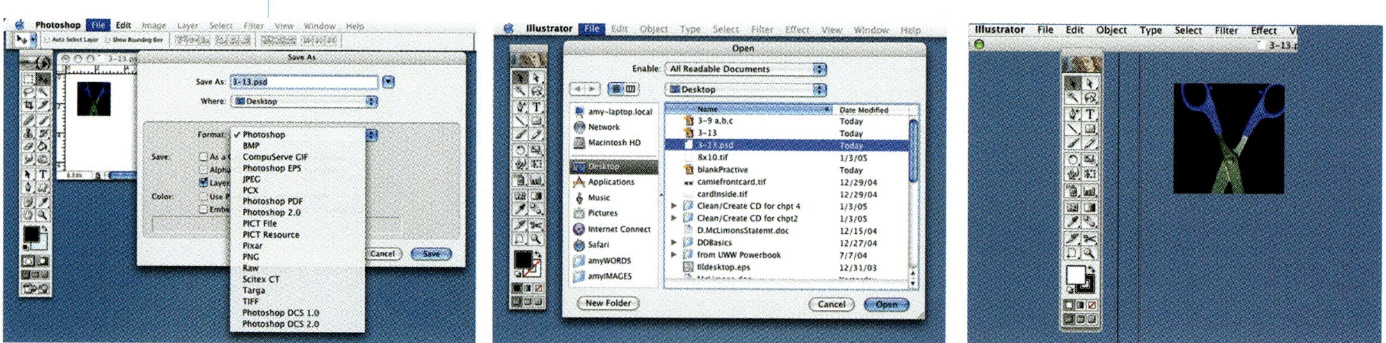

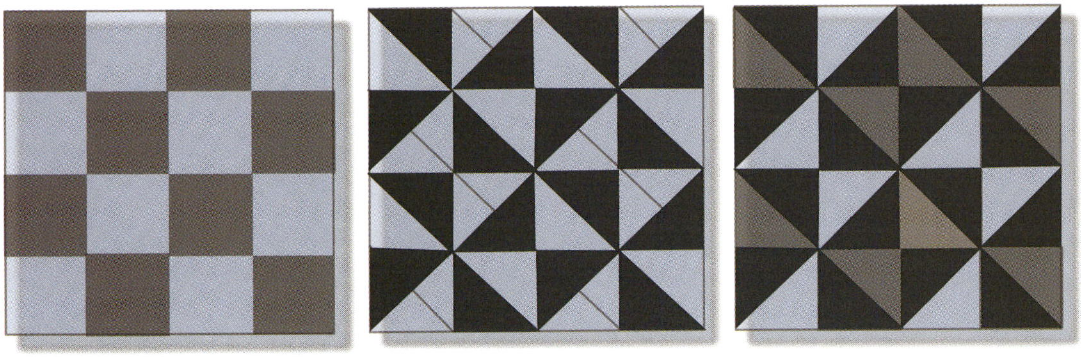

3-14a *Reversible figure/ground as shown in these diagrams is often seen in quilt and tile and other surface design.*

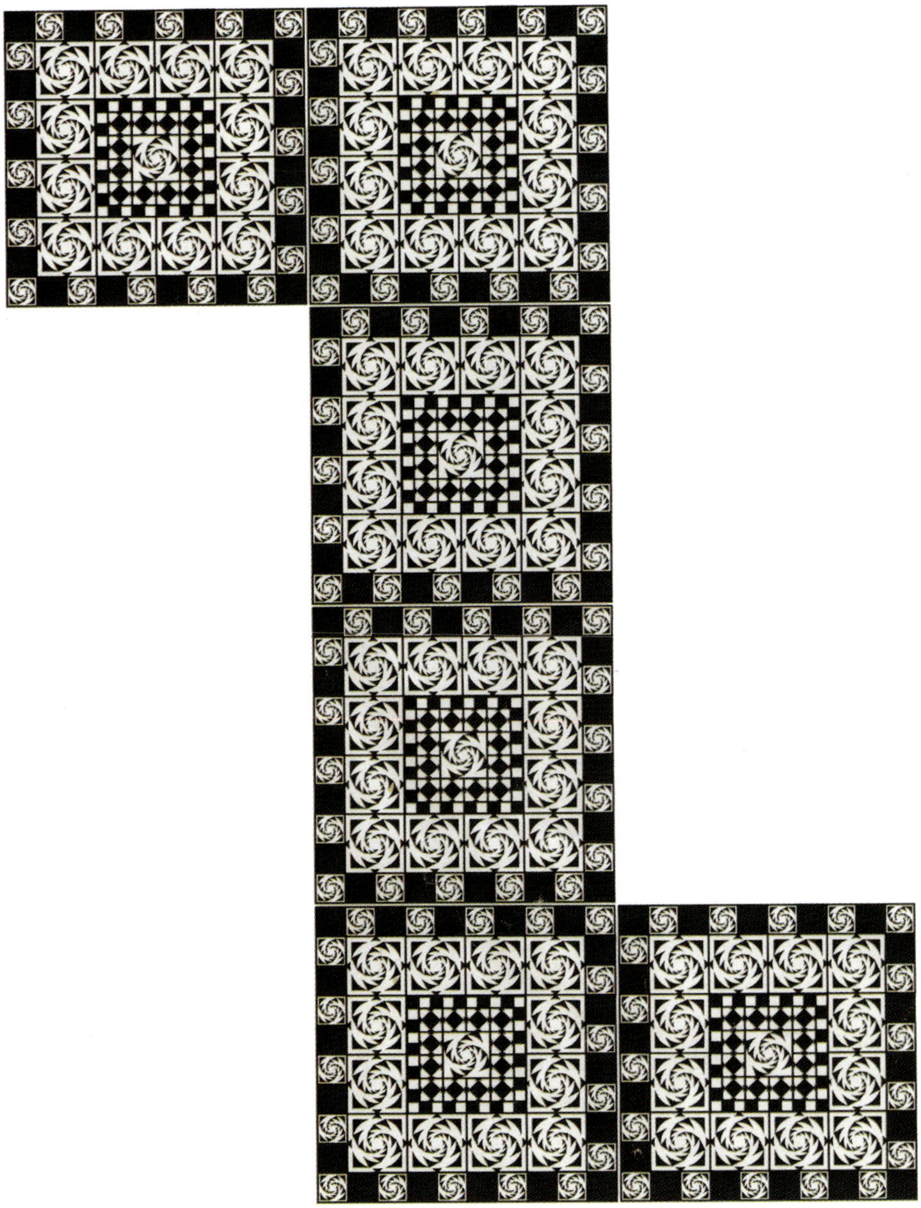

3-14b *Dustin Page created this design for his student portfolio using Illustrator's grid, rulers, guides, and copy/paste functions.*

Figure 3-15 shows a self-portrait paper cutting by contemporary artist and design educator Xiao Zang. An ancient Chinese technique, paper cutting often creates a relationship between figure and ground that is very dynamic. Zang works both with this time-honored technique and with the most current multimedia programs.

Ambiguous

Font animals are an enjoyable way to create an image that incorporates several kinds of typography into a final animal. This task asks you to utilize Illustrator's resizing and image transform functions as well as your imagination. Choose a single typestyle to work with and experiment with its italic, condensed, bold, and other versions to get the result you are looking for. You may want to convert the type to outline to have full control over its visual attributes. **Figures 3-16a–b** show animals created with typography in response to this final vector assignment. In the next section you will learn more about raster graphics and apply those graphics to an In The Studio assignment that also utilizes figure/ground relationships.

Raster Graphics

Now let's learn more about raster graphics. Some of this will review material presented previously. If you are choosing to do only vector software and save the raster for later, skip to the Summary Critique.

Rasters are very different from vectors. Raster graphics are created with individual picture elements called pixels, as discussed in Chapter 2. Think of the entire file as composed of tiny rectangles filled with color. Each pixel can be individually accessed and manipulated for a vast array of effects. Photoshop is a powerful raster graphics program. It has a flexible, intuitive feeling, much like painting with pigments. **Figure 3-17** shows the variety of lines that can be created in Photoshop.

As you know, because each pixel represents a location in memory that is a location on a bitmap, this kind of file is also called bitmapped graphics. When these files are enlarged, they lose resolution. The fewer the pixels, the coarser the image. More pixels create a finer image. Raster images should be created at the size they will be finally viewed or larger than their final size.

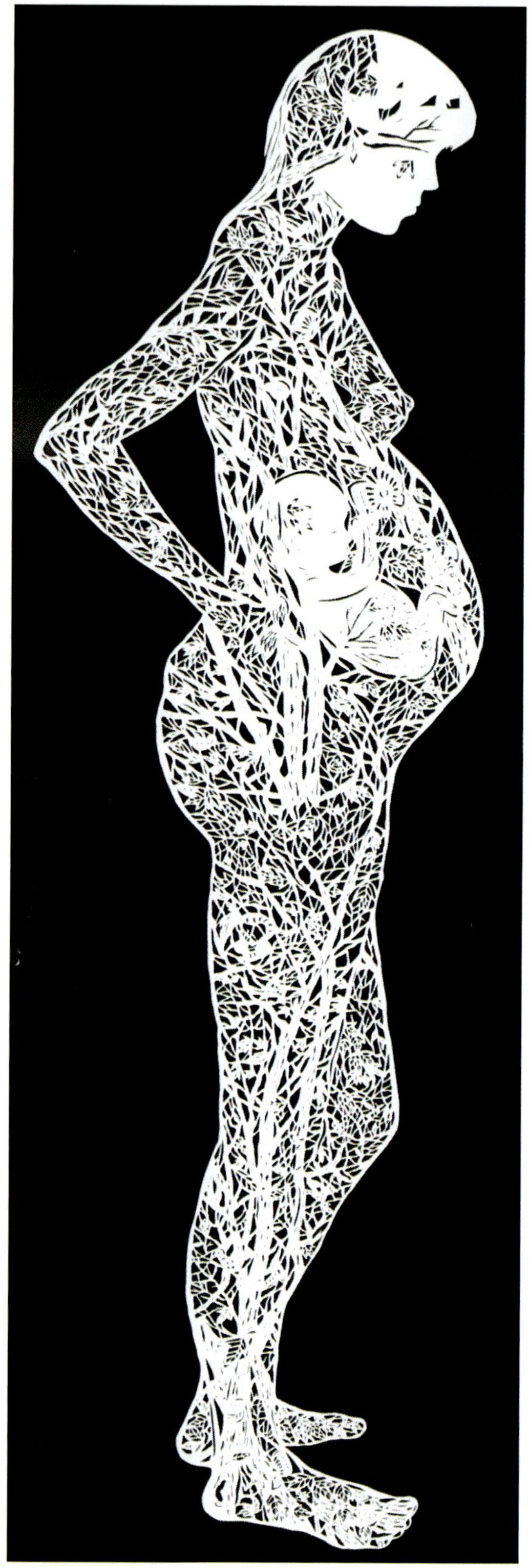

3-15 *Xiao Zang.* Pregnancy. *2002. Cut paper. 40 inches × 100 inches.*

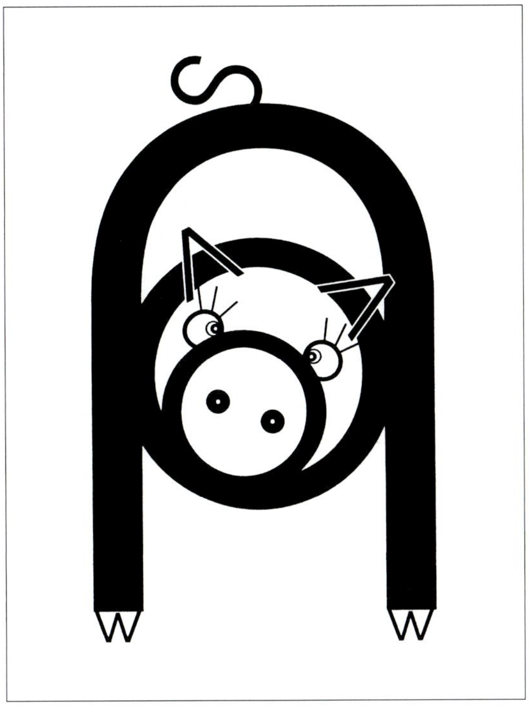

◆ **3-16a** *Stephanie Sura created this typographic animal for her student portfolio. The shapes are all made from ITC Avant Garde Gothic Book.*

Gallery Profile

A world-famous member of the Surrealist movement, René Magritte (1898–1967) was born in Brussels, and in 1916 attended the Academy of Fine Arts there. His classes included Decorative Painting and Ornamental Composition, which prepared him for his early jobs drawing motifs for wallpaper. At the beginning of his career, Magritte did both his mysterious fine art painting and drawings for advertising.

In the 21st century, his work continues to appeal to a wide audience, including those in the art, advertising, and illustration fields. Illustrators often appropriate and adapt his Surrealist vision for sales and editorial images. His highly legible, unusual, and memorable paintings are treasured throughout the world. In his work, skies become solid blocks, flesh becomes wood, rocks become clouds, inside becomes outside, and a leaf becomes a tree.

By the 1950s Magritte's international reputation was well established, and he was exhibiting in America, London, Paris, and Italy. It took longer for him to gain recognition as a leading painter of the time. His paintings deal with the reconciliation of opposites. Thus, a sky is placed almost like wallpaper, inside a room, and objects take on new meaning because of scale confusion (see Fig. 3-24a on page 73). A sky is seen through a window and simultaneously pasted onto the window in Figure 3-24b (see page 74). This becomes a figure/ground confusion, questioning what is space and what is foreground object. Magritte's aesthetic is almost collage-like, reminding us of Dadaist artists like Hannah Höch.

Magritte often stated that his reason for painting was to evoke the mystery of the world. Perhaps that is why his appeal is timeless.

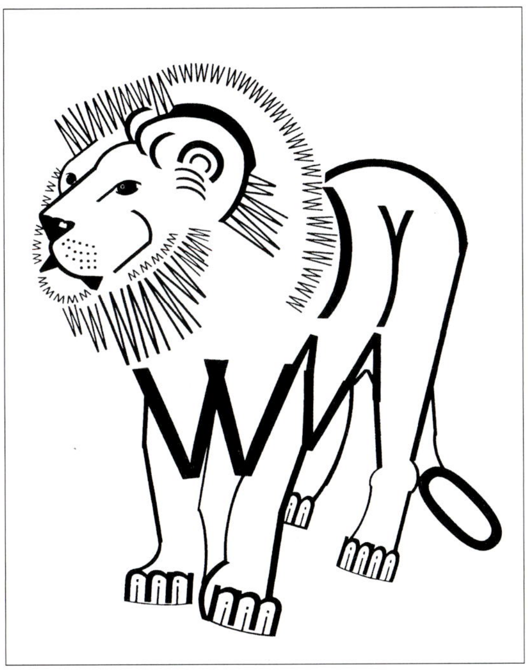

◆ **3-16b** *Andy Hofmann created this typographic animal for his student portfolio. The shapes are made from Helvetica.*

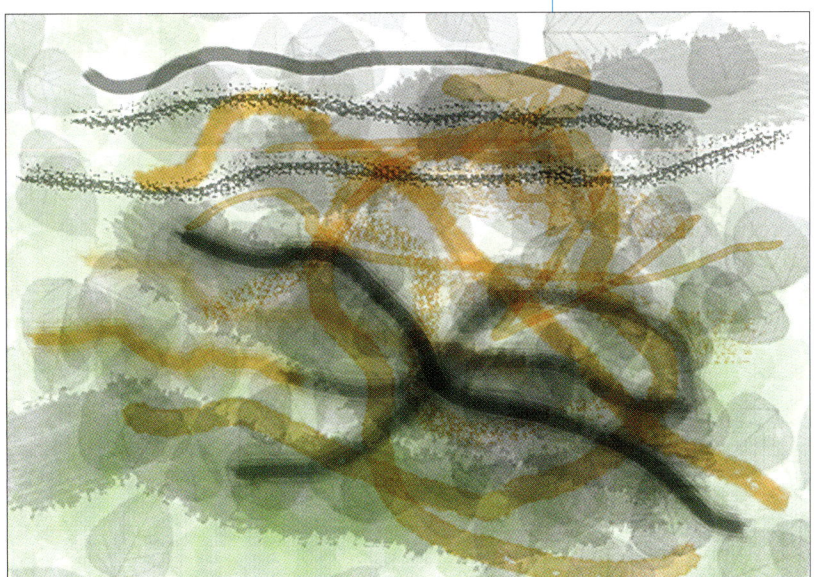

◆ **3-17** *Raster graphics are capable of generating very painterly lines.*

Size and Resolution

Why do raster graphics lose data when enlarged? Because the same number of pixels now cover a greater area. If your file is 8 × 8" and it has 150 pixels per inch (ppi), when that file is 16 × 16" those 150 pixels become larger in order to cover the additional area. You can change the file resolution to 300 after enlarging, but the additional pixels will be interpolated, which means the program has made an intelligent guess at what visual data should be placed with these new pixels. **Interpolation** is an inexact process. It is far better to work with "real" visual data by scanning and opening the original file at the desired resolution. As discussed in Chapter 2, to retain the "real" data while changing size, link image size and resolution by selecting Image>Image Size> *unclick* Resample Image. **Figure 3-18** shows how to enter this information.

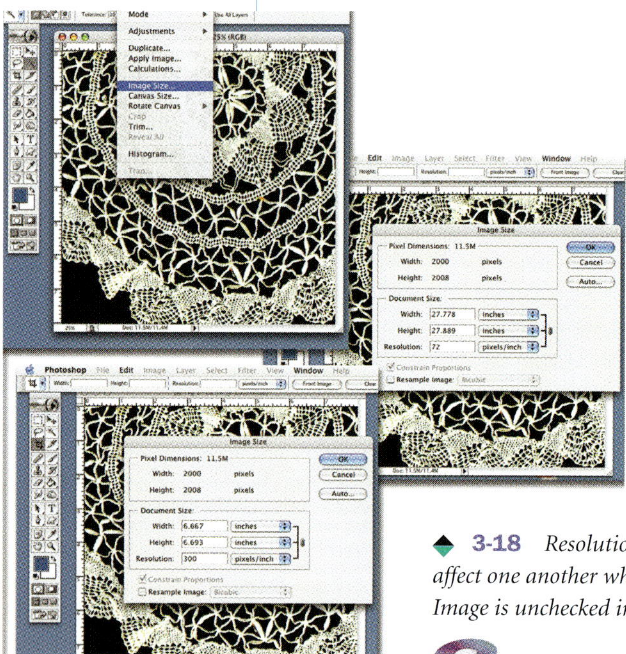

Adobe product screen shots reprinted with permission from Adobe Systems Incorporated

3-18 *Resolution and image size affect one another when Resample Image is unchecked in Photoshop.*

Raster Image Development

Adobe Photoshop is primarily an image-editing program, incorporating digital photography to generate manipulated images. It is a vital program in preparing images for both print and web publication. **Figure 3-19** shows its desktop, with a toolbox different from that of Illustrator. There are other programs that are raster-based. We will

3-19 *This Photoshop desktop shows the tools and pop up windows associated with the program.* Illustration by Chris Eichman.

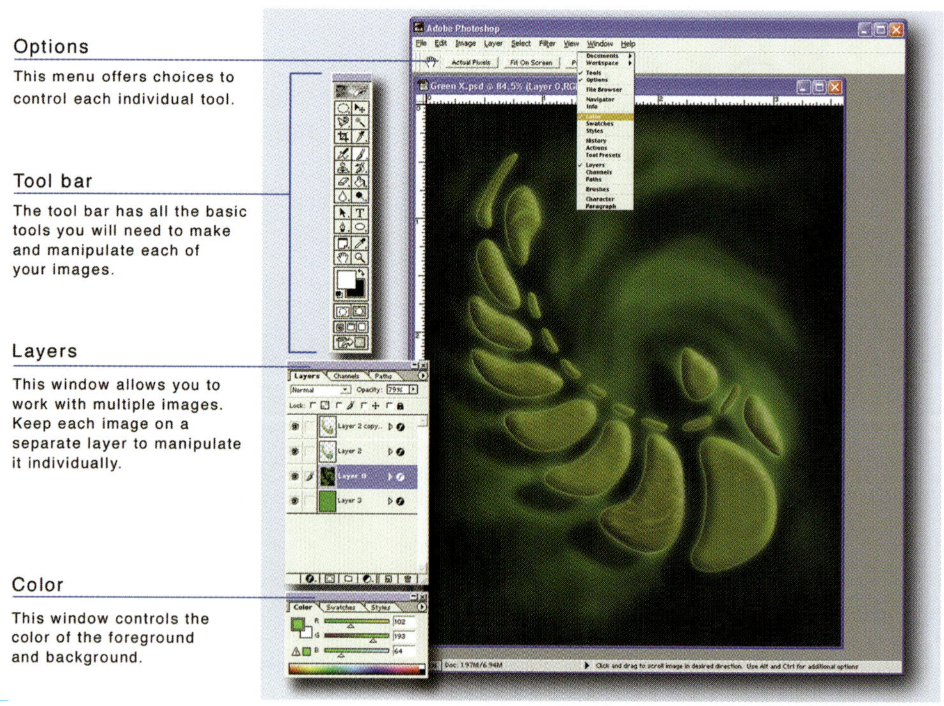

Adobe product screen shot reprinted with permission from Adobe Systems Incorporated

take a look at Corel Painter in a later chapter. Raster programs allow a tremendous freedom of creative effects. The following How To Basics and Hands On Practice will introduce you to more of the concepts of raster imaging using Photoshop.

For a more comprehensive introduction to this particular software program, look at the various Help menus and Tutorials packaged with it, and also rely on your instructor. In addition, many excellent step-by-step manuals on Photoshop are available. Remember that this textbook is intended to present software operation, while encouraging a focus on art and design principles. Technique is a means to an end. Concept and imagination are part of the tool set you bring with you.

How To Basics

Figures 3-20a–m present several learning steps necessary for mastering basic Photoshop techniques. Study these, and you'll have a chance to practice later in the Hands On Practice section.

Resizing Exercise

Practice resizing by selecting an image from Chapter 2 or 3 on the accompanying CD. Reduce it to 50 percent of its size, while retaining the resolution. Now go back to the original, and this time double the resolution, allowing the size to get smaller. Study the linkage relationship between size and resolution. Once you understand it, you're ready to move on.

Image Correction

Once an image has been scanned and imported into Photoshop, it is ready to be corrected. Always try for the best possible original photograph, and the best possible scan, or digital camera image. Each step in digital photographic imaging should be as high quality as possible. However, a major part of the delight of digital imaging is the ease of image correction. We discussed it briefly in Chapter 2; here is additional information.

The *Histogram* controls the distribution of tonal values. Take a look at the histogram function located under the pull down menu Image>Adjust>Levels. It gives a graph of all the pixels contained in an image and their brightness level. The dark tones are to the left, the mid tones are in the center, and the light tones are to the right. The height at any point shows the number of pixels in this particular value in the image. A glance at the histogram tells you the brightness and contrast distribution. The slider will change the distribution in your image. Figures 3-20a–c show how to access the histogram and use it to affect an

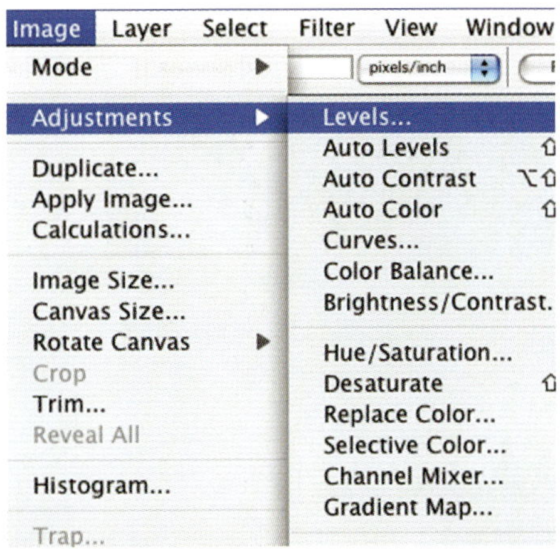

a–m: Adobe product screen shots reprinted with permission from Adobe Systems Incorporated

(a)

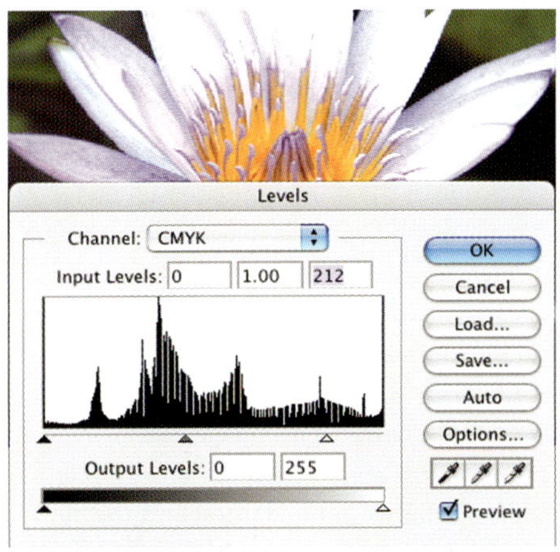

(b)

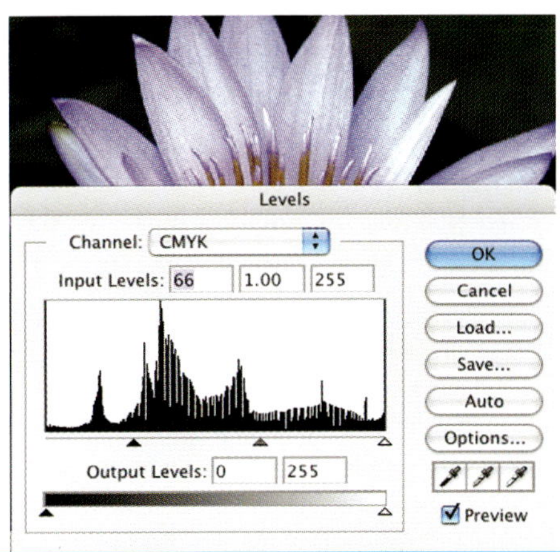

(c)

3-20 [a–m] *Study these step-by-step illustrations of Photoshop basics. They are described in the text.*

image. When images are too flat, you can select Image>Adjust>Levels and pull the arrows beneath the histogram in until they are beneath the distribution of dark and light pixels on the graph. Sampling with the eyedropper will allow you to assign values to the lightest and darkest values as shown in Figure 3-20d. For example, use the left eyedropper and click on your image to establish the darkest area. This controls the tonal distribution throughout the image. A well-exposed image displays a full range between dark and light.

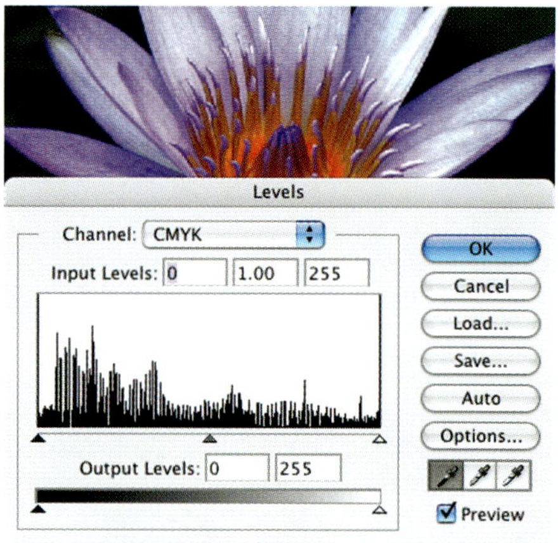

(d)

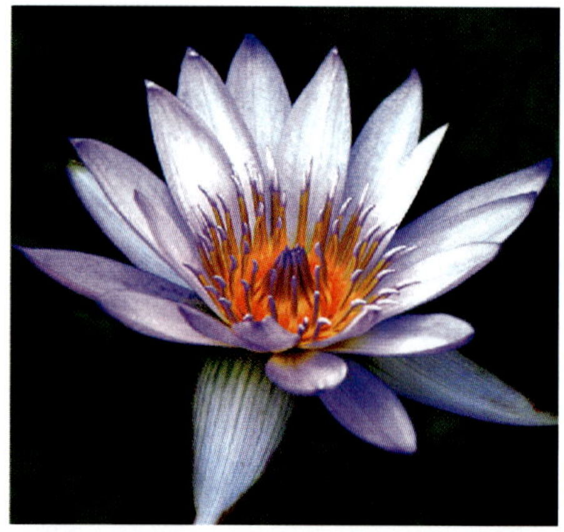
(e)

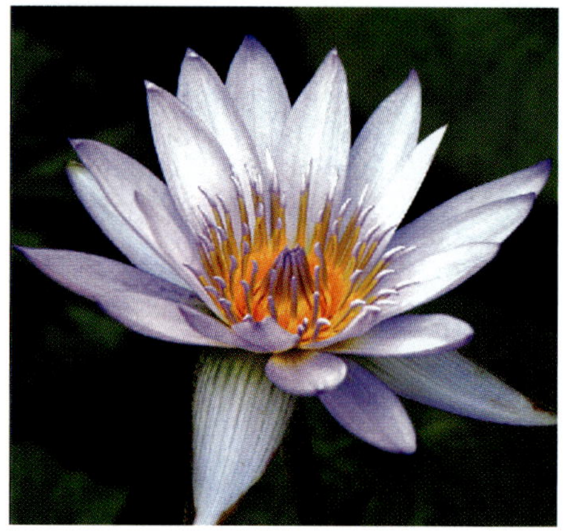
(f)

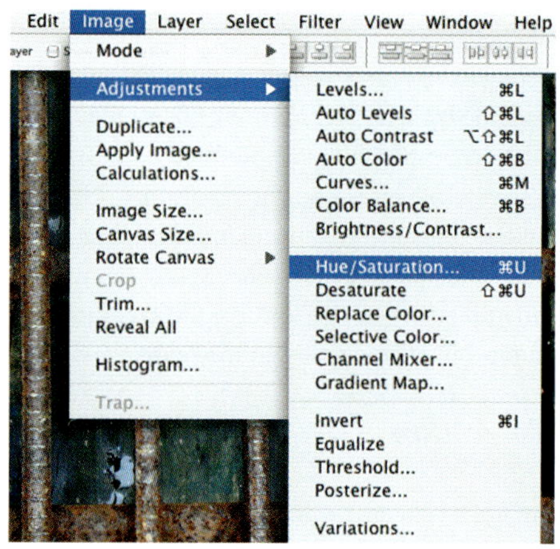

(g)

Brightness and *Contrast Correction* allows you further control of the dark to light emphasis within your image. This is one of the most fundamental image manipulation controls. To use it well, you must understand that *brightness* relates to the exposure of the image and can control photographs that are a little dark or too light overall. Go to the pull down menu for Image>Adjust>Brightness and Contrast. Use the Photoshop sliders to achieve an image that has good detail in both shadow and highlight. *Contrast* refers to the tonal range between the darkest and the lightest points in the image. Try to avoid a "flat" image and adjust the contrast slider so there is a full range of tones between black and white, while retaining highlight and shadow detail. Figures 3-20e–f show various brightness and contrast functions applied to the same image.

Color Correction is also an important part of quality control. There are several options in the Image>Adjust pull down menu that permit control of subtle color details (Fig. 3-20g). A photograph, whether shot with a film-based camera or a digital camera, is dependent upon ambient color conditions. Images are shot under different light sources. The human eye interprets colors "correctly" when viewed under sunlight, candlelight, fluorescent light, or incandescent lighting. A film camera, however, records a color shift in each situation. In a traditional film-based camera, this can be corrected with the use of the proper film for the color temperature and/or filters over the lens. A digital camera is blessed with an automatic white balance function that neutralizes and corrects the colorcast in various lighting conditions. This is considerably easier than using special film or filters.

There will be times when the photographic image you import into Photoshop has an undesirable colorcast. Here are four of the color correction techniques found under the Image>Adjust pull down menu that we explored briefly in Chapter 2.

The *Curves* function can be used for subtle adjustment and control of all the tones in an image. Changes are made to individual pixels by clicking and dragging a section of the line on the curves pop up graph. The shape of the curves determines the appearance of your image. Darken pixels by moving the line to the right, and lighten them by moving the line to the left. Figure 3-20h shows the curves function. Clicking the mouse on the curve will insert an adjustment point to give further control of the line's curve. The line will now have a fixed position at each of these additional points.

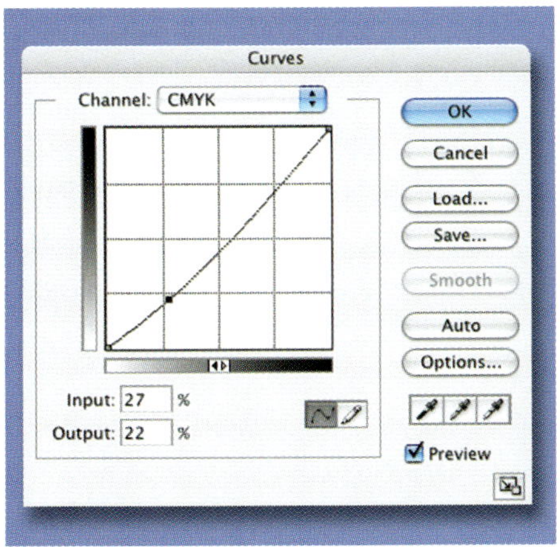

(h)

At the top of the curves pop up dialog box is a menu that lets you choose a channel to edit. This allows control of the overall colorcast of an image (Fig. 3-20i). Channels are accessed in Window> Show Channels. They're usually on the same pop up window as Layers. They show each of the color layers in your color mode. Figure 3-20j shows the channels function in use.

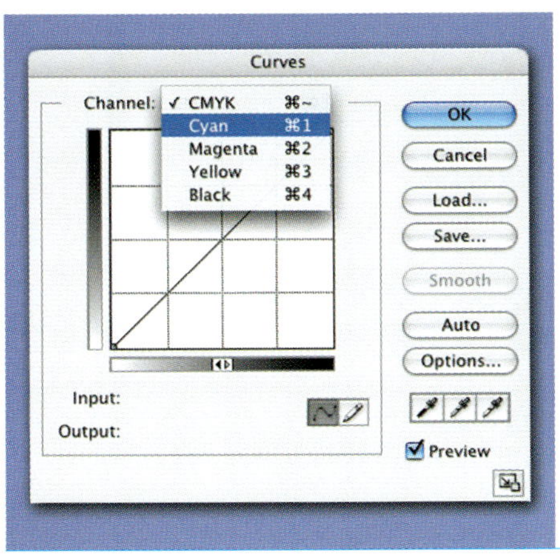

(i)

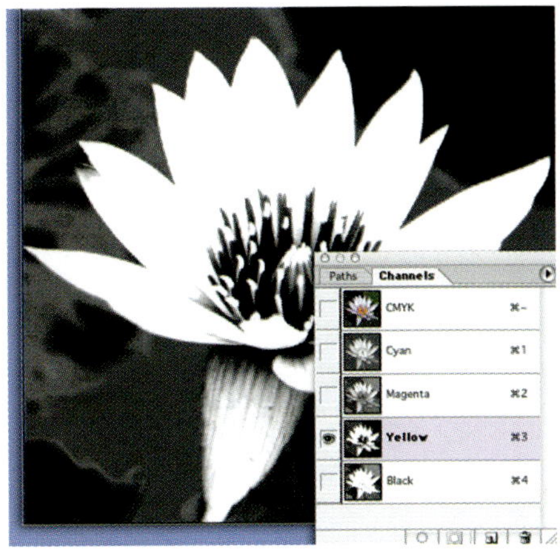

(j)

The *Color Balance* dialog box allows you to adjust color by three groupings of shadows, mid tones, and highlights. The sliders are set up to demonstrate that increasing one color will affect another. This is based on the fact that red, green, and blue (RGB) make up the primary colors of the screen image. The secondaries of these colors are cyan, magenta, and yellow (CMY). Identify the colorcast you want to eliminate on your image, and correct by adding its opposite (Fig. 3-20k).

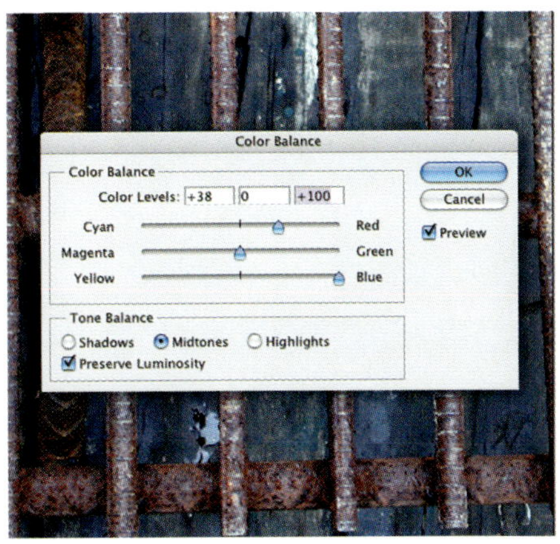

(k)

The *Hue/Saturation* dialog box allows for adjustments of Hue, Saturation, and Lightness, as shown in Figure 3-20l. There are advantages to working in this mode. It simulates conditions familiar to people from a painting and drawing background. Basic 2-D design courses usually discuss these terms, and they are used throughout studio courses. Remember that reducing saturation can keep your electronic colors from looking too harsh. Electronic colors often are harsh in beginning studio explorations.

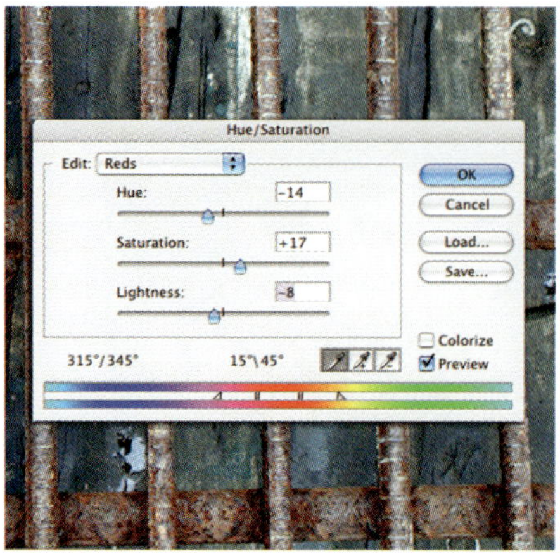

(l)

The *Variations* dialog box provides a quick and easy access to color control. Begin by choosing to adjust color in shadows, mid tones, or highlights, and then choose to make your edits through a visually stimulating menu of choices. The six major colorcasts of RGB and CMY are shown in boxes. Clicking on any of these boxes will add that color to the original. Figure 3-20m shows the Variations dialog box in use.

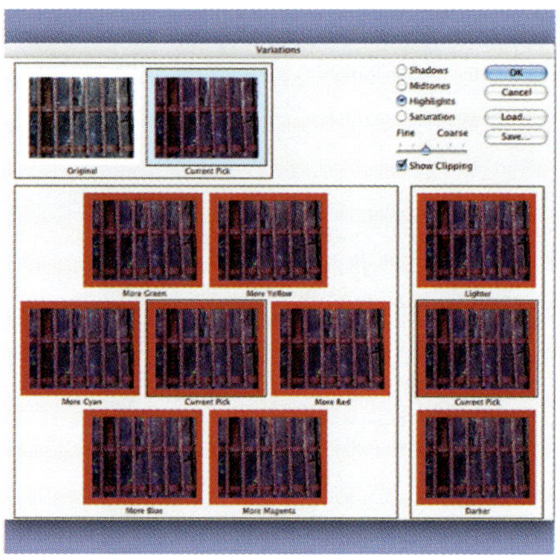

(m)

◆ **3-21 [a–m]**
Practice these step-by-step illustrations of Photoshop techniques. They are described in the text.

Warming Up

Get acquainted with digital retouching of photographic images by doing the following steps. Open an image on the accompanying **CD** from this chapter's warming-up files. Use the Image>Adjustments to repair the image. Adjust the histogram levels. Adjust the contrast and brightness. Finally, correct the color.

Image Creation

The section above discusses working with a scan and correcting it to look its best. The next Hands On Practice section asks you to practice the techniques of creating a collage with your scan(s). These techniques are the foundation for the In The Studio assignment at the chapter's end. Your Hands On Practice may result in an image worth saving for your portfolio.

Hands On Practice

This section asks you to apply the information you have studied in the How To Basics above. Practice the techniques described in **Figures 3-21a–m**.

1. Select the File>New command to establish size and resolution. Remember that 72 dpi is appropriate only for web graphics and trial explorations. Choose 150 dpi resolution.

2. File>Open or File>Place>*your file name* to acquire a scan for you to manipulate. Choose one from the **CD**, or from your previous scans. It will appear on its own layer. Practice turning the layer eye icon on and off, and locking and unlocking the layer.

3. The *crop tool* lets you draw a bounding box around portions of the image to save, while the area outside the bounding box is discarded. As you have done before, select the crop tool and crop your image.

4. Now change the physical size of the canvas that contains your image. Go to Image>Canvas Size. Choose 8 × 10". In the bottom of this window, choose where you want the current image positioned, as shown in Figure 3-21a.

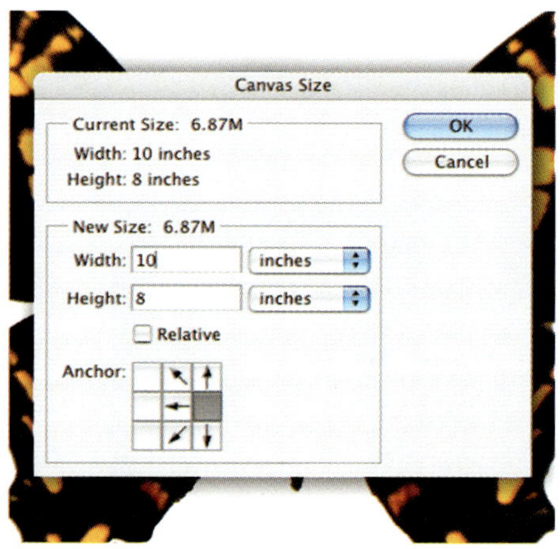

a–m: Adobe product screen shots reprinted with permission from Adobe Systems Incorporated

(a)

Selecting Image>Image Size gives a pop up window that will let you constrain proportions to prevent distortion. As discussed above, deselecting the *resample image* box will tie the resolution with the physical size. Increase the resolution to 300 dpi. As you do, notice the size reduction of the file, as shown in Figure 3-21b. Now Edit>Undo that last command, returning to an 8 × 10" file at 150 dpi.

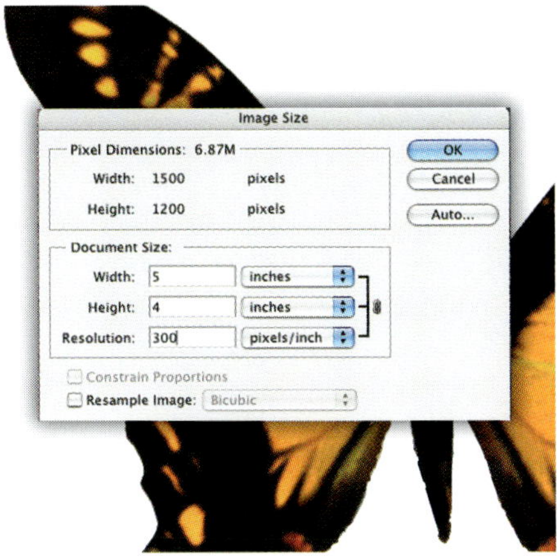

(b)

5. *Selection tools* abound in Photoshop. We discussed them briefly in Chapter 2. As you know, the toolbox, the rectangular marquee, the lasso, and the magic wand will all select portions of your image for editing. The marquee and lasso tools also contain additional hidden tools, accessed by holding down the mouse button on the toolbox icon. The lasso tool lets you make a freehand selection around an area, while the polygon lasso tool lets you make straight-line selections around an area, as shown in Figure 3-21c. The magnetic lasso tool lets you draw freehand borders that snap to the edges of an area. Always check the options bar to set a desirable feather level. Figure 3-21d shows a lasso tool selection with a feather of 10 pixels. The magic wand tool is another useful selection technique. Clicking on a color lets you select all the adjoining pixels of that color, as shown in Figure 3-21e. The tolerance setting helps fine-tune the selection. Practice all of these techniques on your image.

6. Select>Inverse from the pull down menu lets you select the opposite area of the image. Open a new file from the **CD** in the workshop section for this chapter.

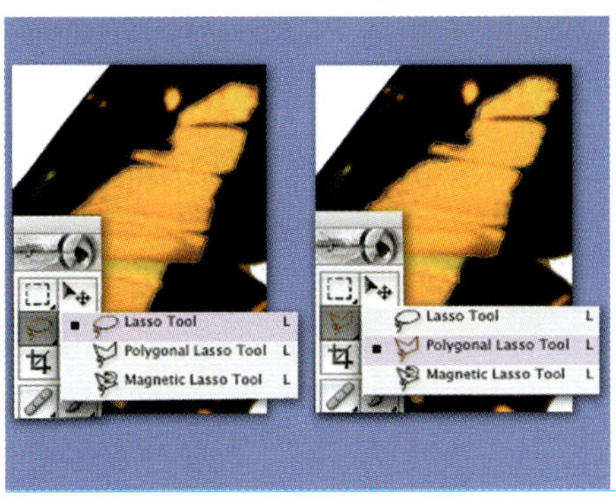

(c)

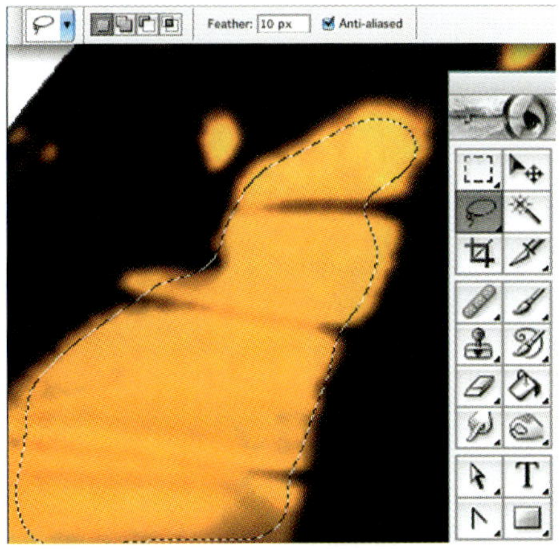

(d)

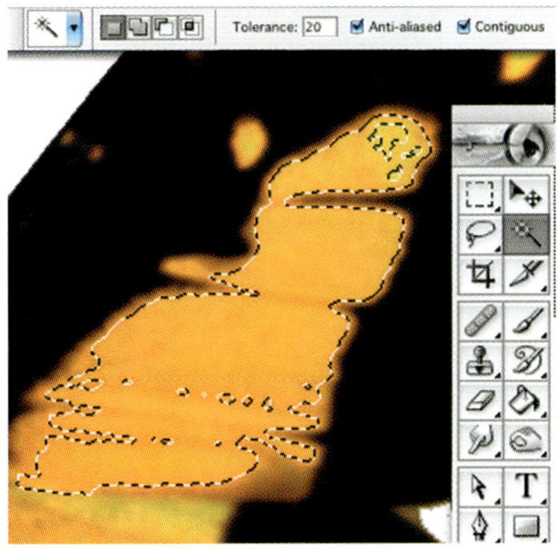

(e)

Use the magic wand in the toolbox to select a solid background area. Begin with the tolerance set to 22. When *only* the background is completely selected, choose Select>Inverse. Choose Select>Save Selection as you may want to load this selection and use it again. Any time you want to reload this selection you can go to Select>Load Selection, as shown in Figure 3-21f. Choose Edit>Copy and Edit>Paste the new selected area.

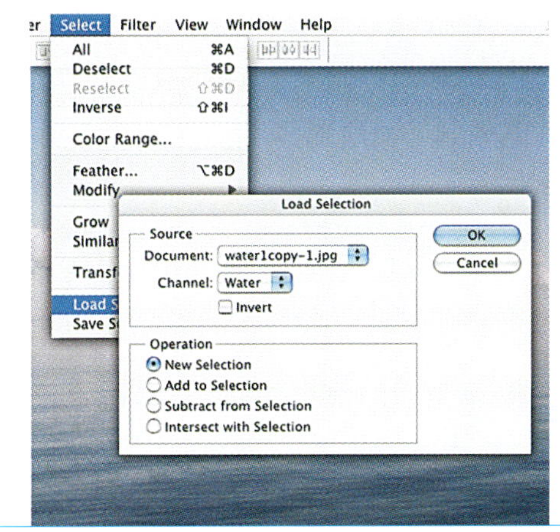

(f)

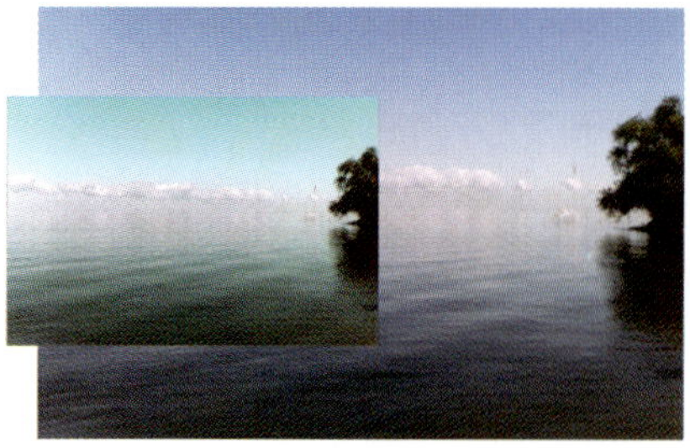

(g)

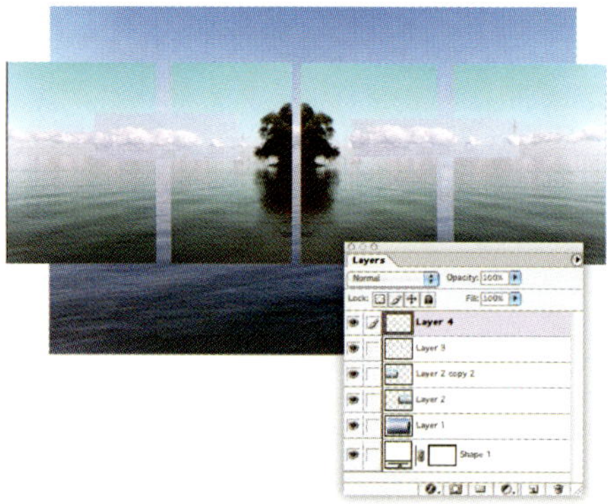

(h)

Select the newly pasted image and use Edit> Transform to manipulate it. Remember any portion that is selected can be edited with various filters and tools or copied and pasted. Change the color and reduce the size to create a new, smaller image (Fig. 3-21g).

7. Edit>Copy and Edit> Paste can be used with selections to create complex collages. Each paste command creates a new layer. Clicking and dragging their stacking order can move these layers, as shown in Figure 3-21h. Changing their stacking order in the layers palette changes their overlapping visual order. Practice with your file.

8. *Filters*, as you know, can be applied to the imported scan for a variety of effects. Select the first layer of your file and then select the Filter pull down menu, and use any of the multitude of effects found there.

9. The *painting tools*, including the brush, airbrush, and pencil, can all be applied to selected areas. Figure 3-21i shows the application of the brush to a selection. Notice that the brush does not affect any area

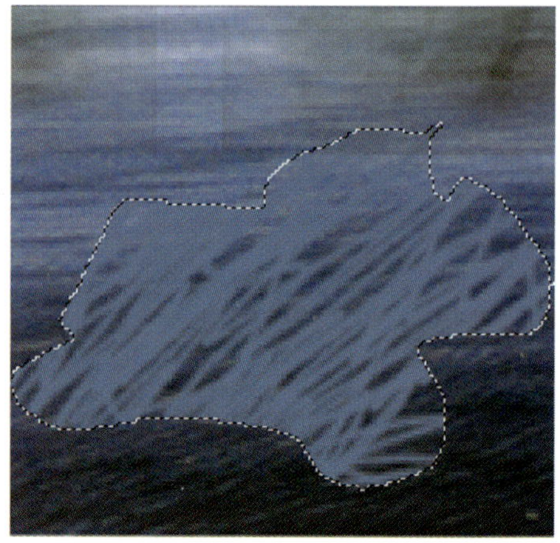

(i)

outside the selection. Wonderfully, raster programs also have an eraser tool. Figure 3-21j shows it in use. Notice the sharp edges of the pasted selections have been erased. Always look at the option bar across the top of the window. It will change with each tool selected from the toolbox and control the visual effect of that tool. Practice with changing tools and their settings in the option bar.

10. *Opacity* options work the same in raster and vector programs. Be sure to have the appropriate layer selected when applying an effect or changing a layer's opacity. The options bar also has an opacity command that allows you to control an individual mark on a layer. Figure 3-21k shows the application of the opacity tool to change layer transparency.

11. *Using vectors in a raster program* is possible. The type tool and the shape tool in Photoshop 7 and beyond can both appear as vectors. Select them to create a vector layer and use vector pen tools and shapes. The information on these vector layers can be resized without losing clarity.

12. Layer properties are reached by double clicking on a layer in the layer pop up window. Experiment with different effects like a drop shadow. Figure 3-21l shows the way to access these effects, and Figure 3-21m shows an application of various effects to the word "Silence." Finally, use the layer pop up window to flatten your image. Flattening reduces the size of your file in memory, but it should not be used until the file is finalized. It is also wise to keep an unflattened version in case you need to return to the file for revisions.

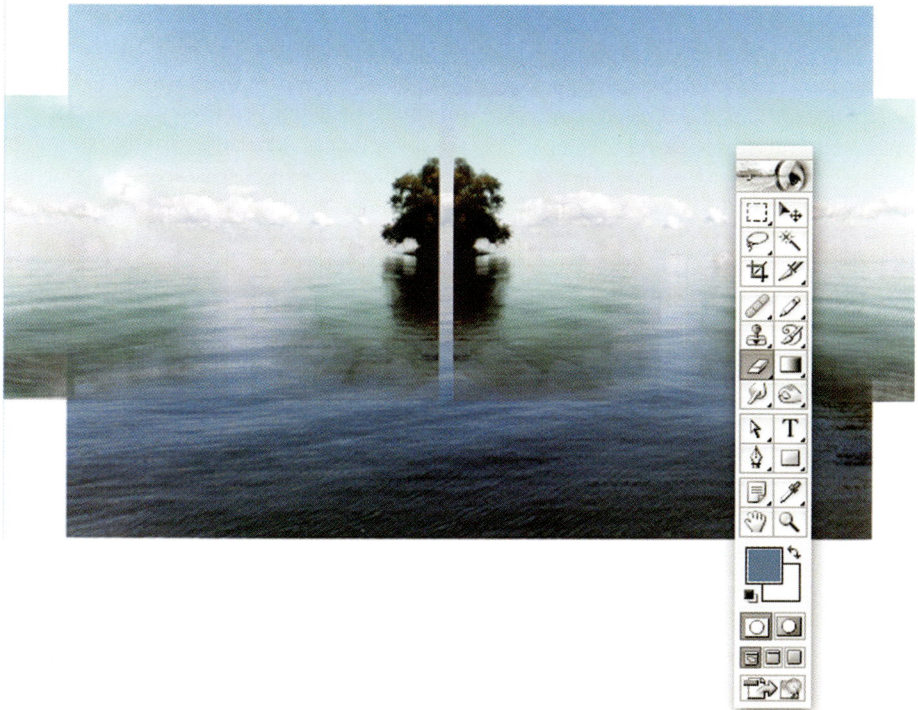
(j)

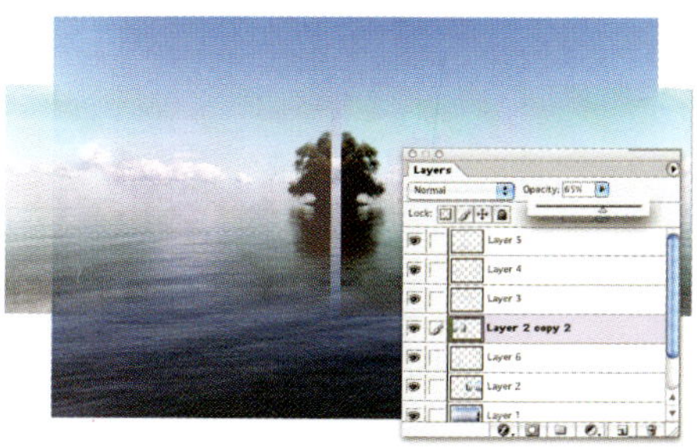
(k)

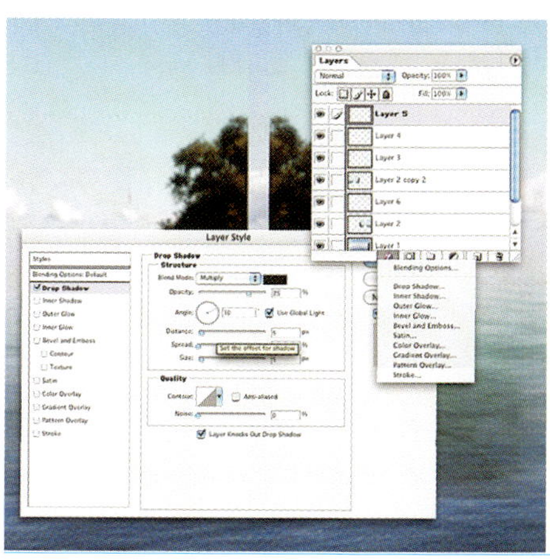
(l)

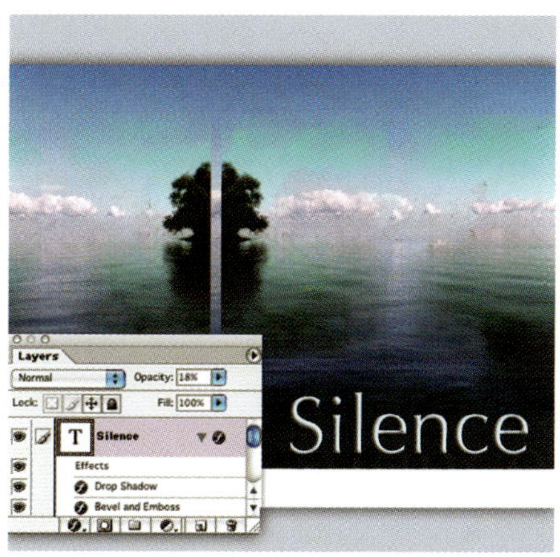
Layers
Normal
Opacity: 18%
Lock:
Fill: 100%
Silence
Effects
Drop Shadow
Bevel and Emboss
Silence
(m)

3-22 *Anna Vo created this image for her student portfolio from a digital photograph of her cat. This Photoshop collage emphasizes a contrast of size between the imaginary landscape (found on clip art disks) and her pet.*

Warming Up

Practice the techniques shown in the How To Basics and Hands On Practice sections above, using your scans from Chapter 2 or the images on the accompanying CD. Now you are ready to begin applying these techniques to create your own artwork.

Select various portions from your different scans to combine into one composition. Begin by opening a new canvas. Make this one at 300 ppi at 8 × 8". Now open one of your 150 ppi scans, or choose one from the **CD** and copy and paste it into the new document. You will notice it comes in at half size. Consider why that is. Remember that the resolution is tied to the size of an image. Mix resolutions, and sizes get mixed as well.

Now open one of the images on the CD (or one of your own) that is an object with a solid color background. Under Image>Image Size, check constrain proportions and uncheck Resample Image. Enter 300 under pixels/inch. Select all and copy and paste into the new document. The size will stay constant. It will come in on a new layer that covers the bottom layer.

Now use the magic wand to select the solid white background. If you do not get it all, change the magic wand tolerance until you do. Change the tolerance by setting the tolerance range in the options menu. Higher numbers are more "tolerant" and see more colors as the same. Holding down the shift key while clicking will let you add to the selection; the option key lets you subtract areas from the selection. Now Select>Reverse Selection. Edit>Copy, Edit>Paste will let you copy this into the current window or any other open Photoshop window.

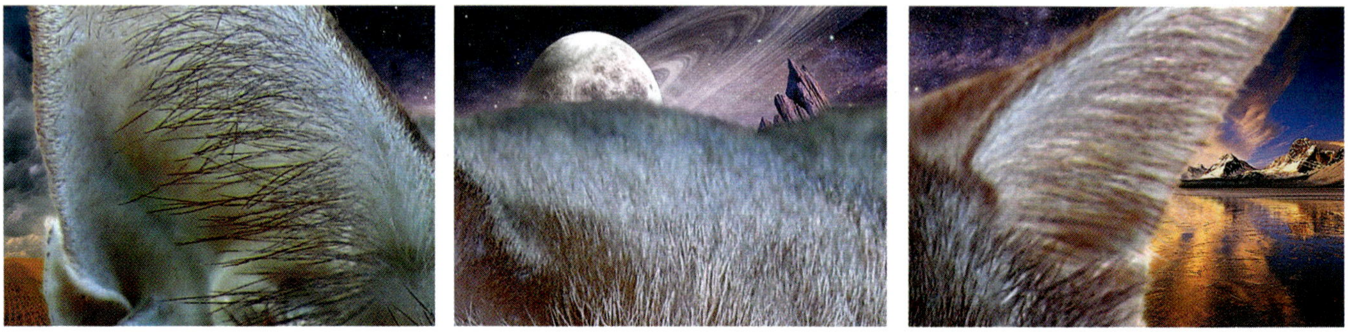

3-23 *Matt Suer created this Photoshop collage for his student portfolio using three images found on clip art disks. He applied the cut and paste function with selected sections.*

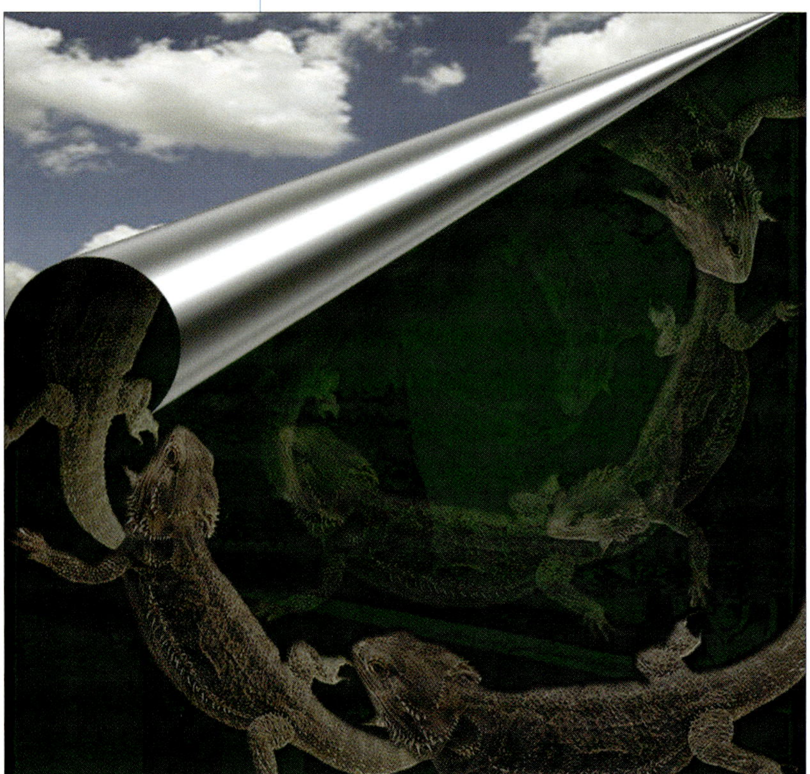

In The Studio

The section on Visual Language introduced the importance of figure/ground relationships in art and design. Review this before beginning to create a collage (the size is your choice) in which the whole is more than the sum of its parts. The student portfolio pieces in **Figures 3-22** and **3-23** are done in response to this assignment. Study the collage aesthetic of Surrealist René Magritte (**Figs. 3-24a–b**) and contemporary electronic artist Diane Fenster (**Figs. 3-25a–b** and **3-26**).

Visual Perception

The **Gestalt** school of psychology began in Germany around 1912 and investigated how we see and organize visual information into a meaningful whole. The conviction developed that the whole is more than the totality of its parts. It becomes a new whole, similar to the way a word is more than the sum of its separate letterforms. In visual language, a unified Gestalt is formed when the parts of the image unite to form a new whole that is more than the total sum of the parts.

Electronic artists work not only with equipment but also with visual elements and with the perceptual structure of the eye and mind. Grouping by similarity is one of the Gestalt principles. When we see things that are similar, we naturally group them. This occurs when we see similar shape, size, color, spatial location, angle, or value. In a group of similar shapes we will notice a dissimilar shape. This is part of the dynamic of visual design that helps to unify a composition.

Another important Gestalt principle is the figure/ground relationship. The fundamental law of perception that makes it possible to separate an object (figure) from its ground (monitor, canvas, or paper) is this principle. Visual artists through the centuries have applied different ways of shaping the figure/ground relationship. Stable, reversible, and ambiguous relationships are discussed in this chapter.

A patchwork figure created by artist and illustrator Diane Fenster using Photoshop is a good example of a new, large soldier/whole made up of small, disparate parts. This is also a good example of ambiguous figure/ground relationship (see Fig. 3-25a). (See the Gallery Profile on Diane Fenster.)

Placing images beside one another suggests a relationship. Creating an unusual spatial relationship or contrast of size begins to establish a new reality in the mind of the viewer. The painting in Figure 3-24a by the Surrealist René Magritte uses an unusual juxtaposition of both space and size to create a new whole. He fills the room with several objects that are larger than life, while the walls are a view of clouds.

What does it mean that the whole is more than the sum of its parts? Can you think of examples in the physical world, as well as the world of art and design? How is visual Gestalt related to a shirt made from a pile of pieces of cloth? Do the parts make a different whole? What about an automobile?

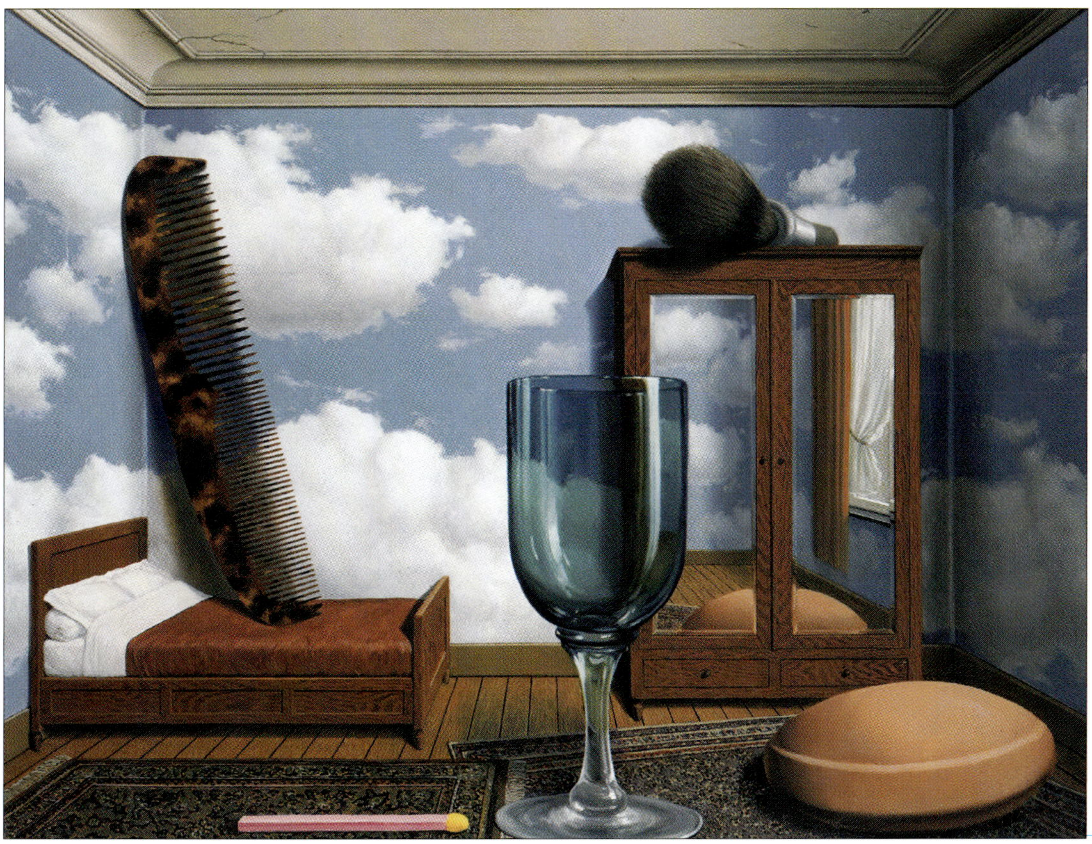

3-24a *René Magritte.* Les Valeurs Personnelles (Personal Values). *1952. Oil on canvas, $31^1/_2 \times 39^1/_2$".* Banque d'Images, ADAGP/Art Resource, NY/ © 2005 C. Herscovici, Brussels/Artists Rights Society (ARS), New York.

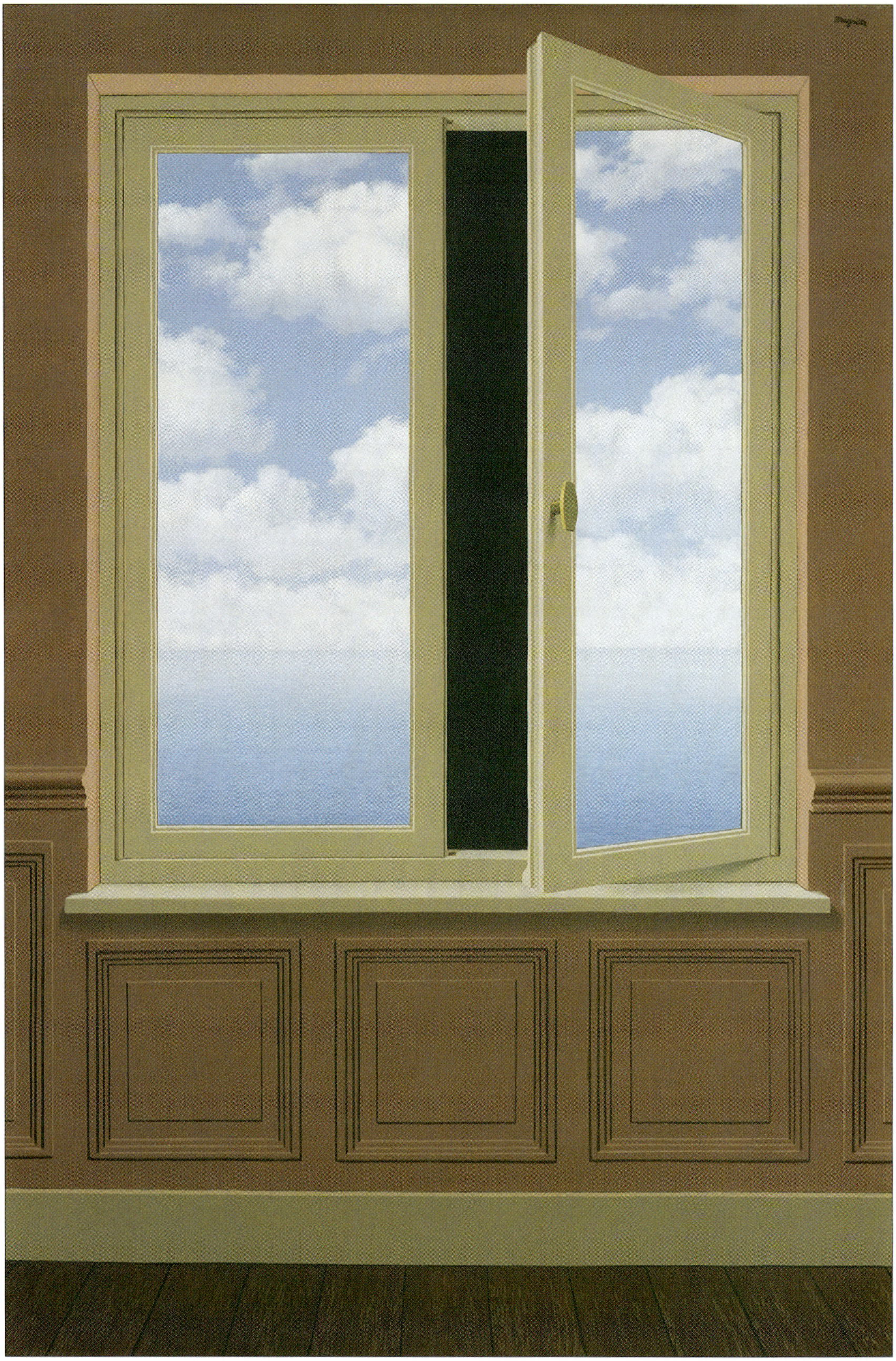

3-24b *René Magritte.* La lunette d'Approche (The Field-Glass). *1963. Oil on canvas, 69 × 45½".* The Menil Collection, Houston, Texas/© 2005 C. Herscovici, Brussels/Artist Rights Society (ARS), New York.

◆ **3-25a** *Diane Fenster.*
Courtesy of the artist.

An excellent digital example of the whole being more than the sum of its parts.

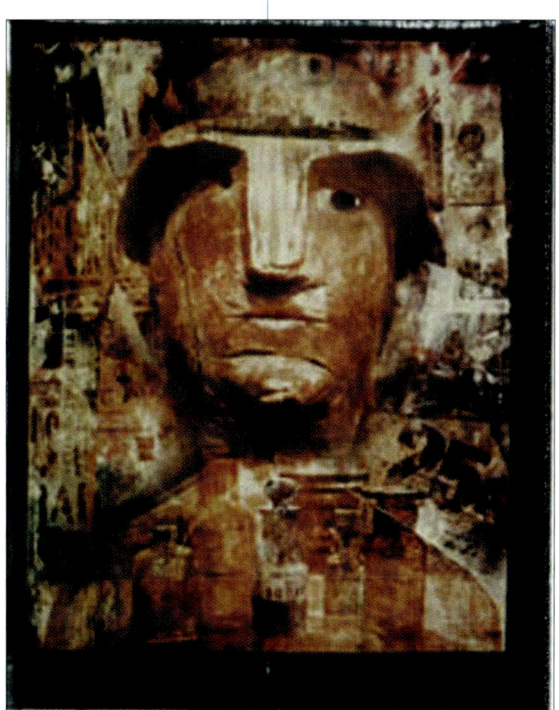

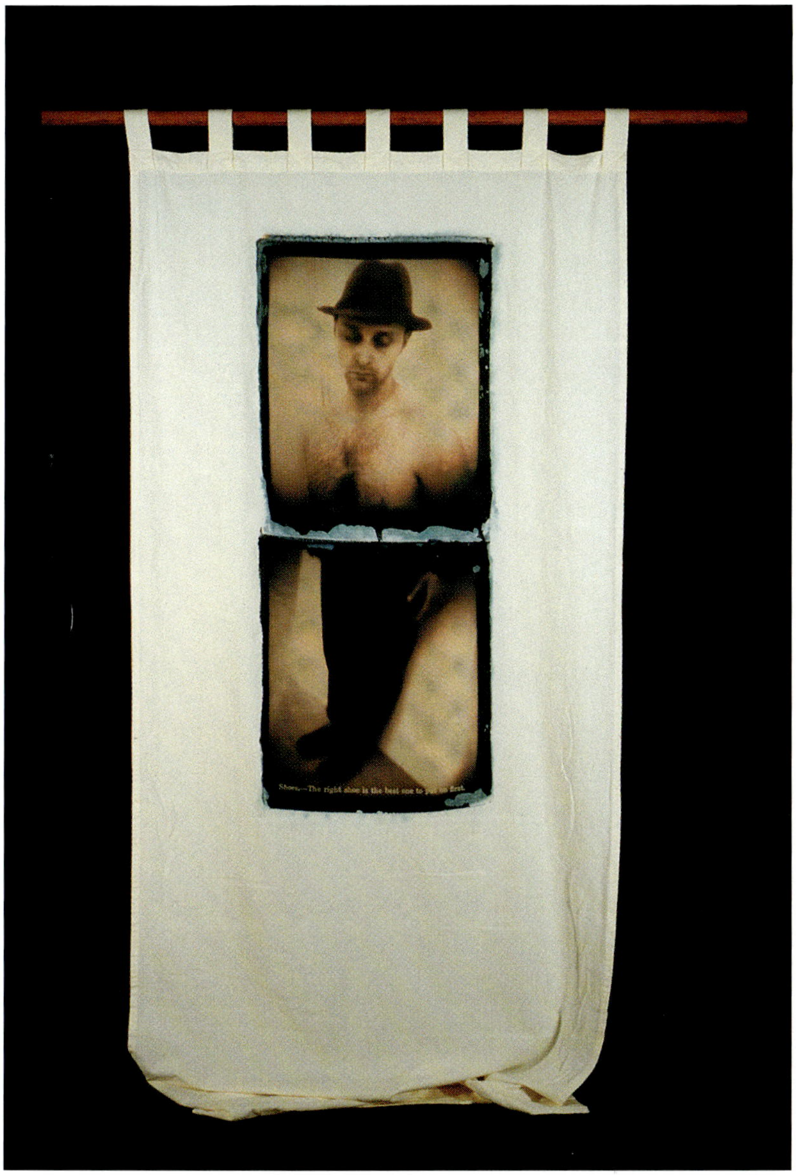

◆ **3-25b** *Diane Fenster.* Untitled (Shoes). Our Dreams and Omens Revealed. *Installation series. 2002. Polaroid image transfers on fabric. 54"w × 108"h.*
Courtesy of the artist.

Gallery Profile

Diane Fenster (1947—) is an internationally exhibited digital photographer and photo illustrator. She began using the computer as an artistic tool in 1989. She has been called an important voice in the development of a true digital aesthetic. She views herself as an alchemist, using digital tools to delve into fundamental human issues. Her work is literary and emotional, full of symbolism and multiple layers of meaning, as shown in Figure 3-26. Her style is an innovative combination of her photography and scanned imagery. Her images appear in numerous publications on digital art and photography, and she is a guest lecturer at many seminars and conferences. Her work ranges from editorial and advertising illustration to installation art and web design.

Fenster's style is an outgrowth of the explorations she takes with her personal artwork. In 2001 Fenster was the first artist to be inducted into the newly formed Photoshop Hall of Fame sponsored by the National Association of Photoshop Professionals and Adobe Systems, Inc.

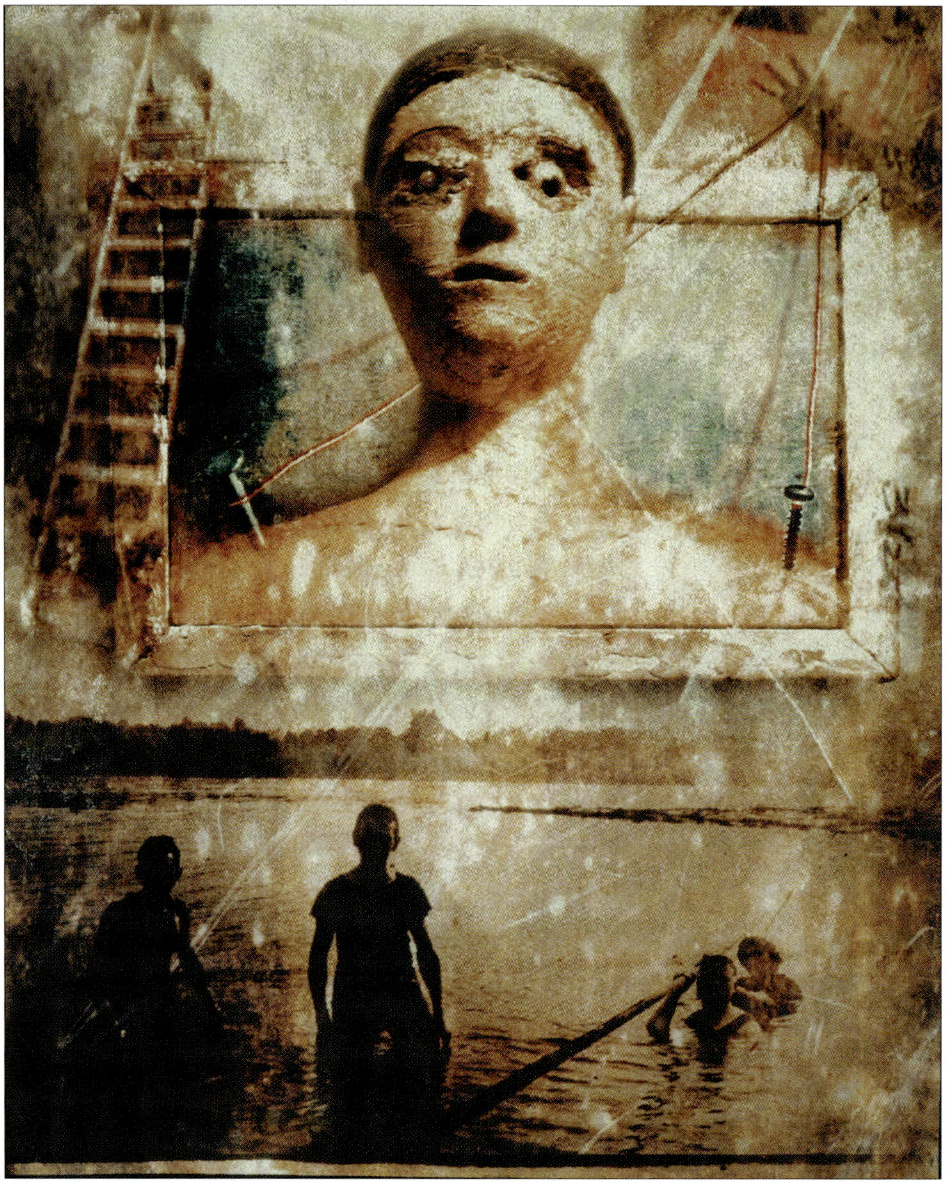

◆ **3-26** *Diane Fenster.* Phlebas the Phoenician a Fortnight Dead. The Waste Land series. *20″ × 24″. Polaroid image transfer.* Courtesy of the artist.

Begin by acquiring images. This can be done by scanning several textures and 2-D images or 3-D objects or by using original photography. Your final collage should transform the original parts into a new whole that emphasizes contrast of size or an unusual contrast of space. You may wish to use a digital camera, as in Figure 3-22, or look to clip art images on the CD, as in Figure 3-23.

SUMMARY CRITIQUE

In this chapter, we examined the difference between vector and raster graphics. As a part of the final class critique of your Warming Up and In The Studio workshops, discuss your technique. Explain your composition, including how it uses similarity and variation. How does it deal with figure/ground? How do the parts recombine to make a new whole? Or choose another student's work that you admire to critique. As always, say what is working well, and mention if there is anything that can be improved upon. It is easy to change and improve an electronic file, so suggesting improvements can be a real help to one another's portfolio development.

MOVING ON

The next chapter will introduce the topic of color theory in art and design, and color practice in electronic imaging. Each chapter builds upon the last, both in terms of software and visual design and concepts. Carry what you have learned about figure/ground and repetition and variation with you into color theory.

TERMINOLOGY

CHAPTER 4

See Glossary for definitions

Color Theory
Color
Wavelength
Hue
Value
Saturation
Color Wheel
Color Scheme
Monochromatic
Complementary
Analogous
Triadic
Split Complementary
Physiological
Simultaneous Contrast
Color Models
Additive
Subtractive
Additive Primaries
Subtractive Primaries
Color Gamut
Bitmap Mode
Grayscale Mode
Duotones
Tritones
Quadtones
Synesthesia
Indexed Color Mode
HSB
Web Color
Iris Print
Calibration
Gradient
Spot Color

4 Mastering Color

A basic knowledge of **color theory** is vital for artists and designers, whether using electronic, photographic, or hand-generated color. Foundation courses in color theory are important to students of computer graphics. Information about how we see and react to color remains true in both pigment-based art and computer graphics. But there is even more to know about using color when you move to electronic media. This chapter begins with an introduction to color fundamentals, regardless of media, and moves on to discuss electronic color, and, finally, various modes of color printing.

Understanding Color

Color is a property of light. This fact has continued to fascinate and inform artists and designers throughout the centuries. *Webster's Dictionary* defines color as "a phenomenon of light or visual perception that enables one to differentiate otherwise identical objects" and "the aspect of object and light sources that may be described in terms of hue, lightness, and saturation." There are more definitions that describe the *psychological* complexity of color.

As you can tell from these definitions, the perception of color is based on an interaction between the way an object absorbs or reflects light and the kind of light that strikes an object. To a visual artist/designer this means looking at how light changes, depending upon the object it falls upon. And the artist/designer must look at the quality of the light itself. Early morning, noon, and early evening present very different views of the same object. In **Figure 4-1** the same spot in a lake is painted at 7:00 AM and 7:00 PM. Because this "object" is full of movement and reflection, it will change even from one moment to the next. Color will also change depending upon whether you are looking at that spot in the lake from a boat, an airplane, or the shore. This holds true for everything, not just water. Is it daylight, lamplight, or fluorescent lighting that is striking your carpet? All of these conditions create a different color perception. Color is not an unchanging, absolute property of an object. It is dynamic.

The Physics of Color

Sir Isaac Newton (1642–1727) contributed to our contemporary understanding of color in the 1600s. He used a glass prism to show that "white light" is actually composed of a range of colors. He let a beam of sunlight shine through a small hole onto a prism in a totally darkened chamber. The light separated into several component colors ranging from violet (or indigo) to red, as shown in **Figure 4-2**. Using a second prism, Newton recombined the colored rays into white light. A hundred years later, scientist Thomas Young (1773–1829) found that light is not a stream of particles, as Newton assumed, but consists of a succession of waves. The size of the waves determines the color. Toward the end of the 19th century another scientific researcher, James Maxwell (1831–1879), found that visible light is only a section of the electromagnetic spectrum. We now know the entire range of wavelengths extends from visible light to gamma rays, ultraviolet rays, X-rays, infrared rays, and radio waves. Colors can now be described with precision in terms of their **wavelength.**

Eye and Brain

The perception of color is a complex interaction between eye, brain, and environmental factors.

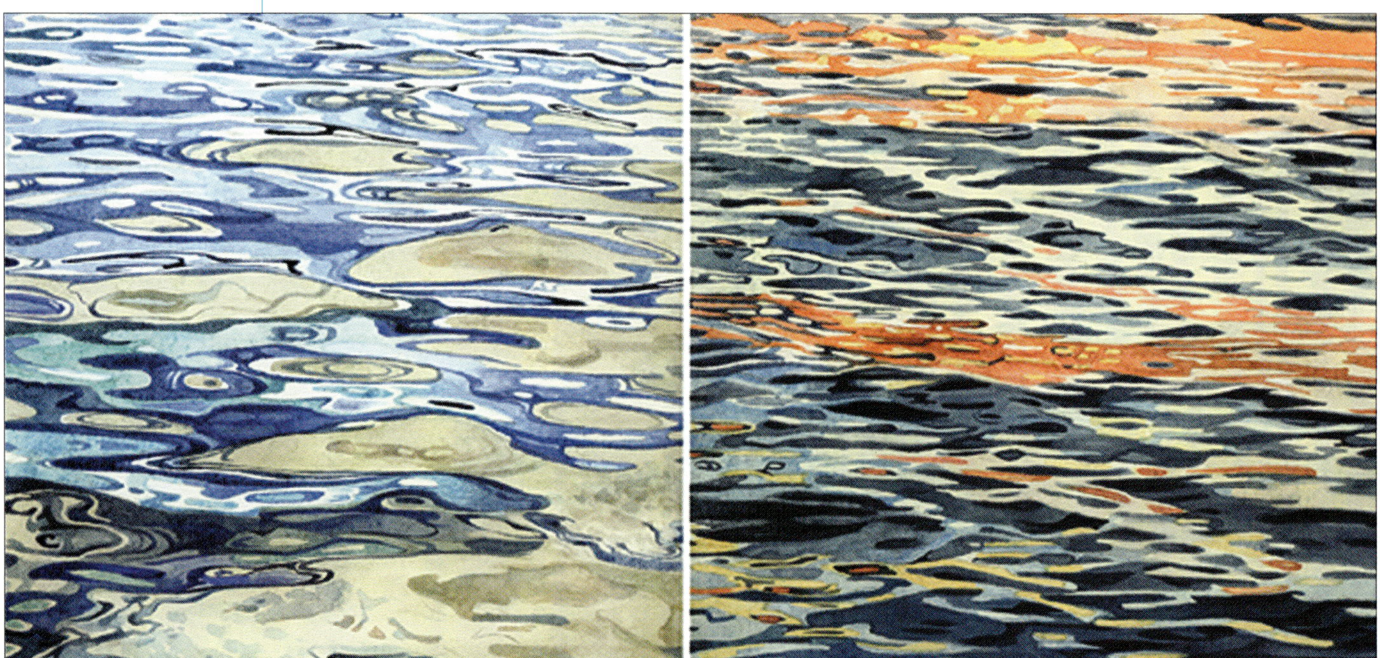

4-1 *Amy Arntson. 7 am to 7 pm. 2000. Watercolor. 12" × 24".* Courtesy of the artist.

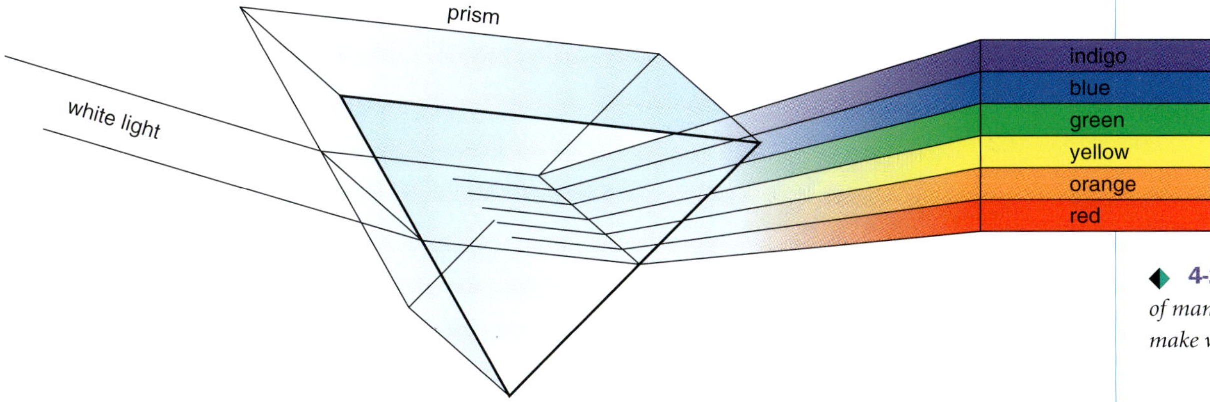

◆ **4-2** *Light waves of many colors join to make white light.*

Signals are sent from the optic nerve to the brain where color perception takes place. When we look at a color, like a red ornament (**Fig. 4-3**), all other colors of the visible spectrum have been absorbed, and only red radiates back to our eye. These rays are waves vibrating at the frequency of red light. The eye focuses these waves onto the retina, activating receptors sensitive to the red wavelength. Other receptors react to other colors caught as reflections in the red ball.

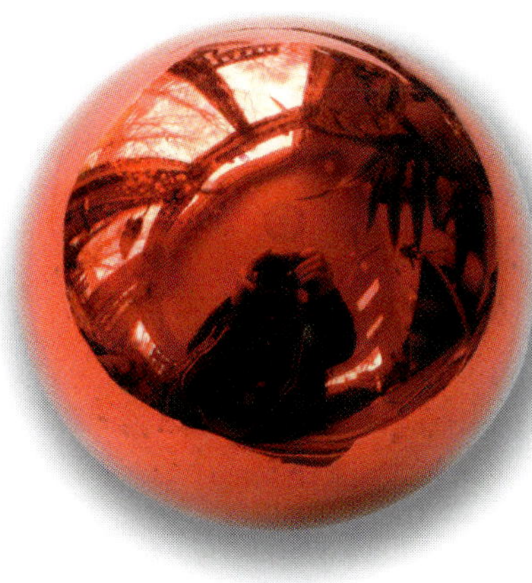

◆ **4-3** *Color is a function of absorption and radiation of light waves.*

Color Theory

Now we will look at the principles of color theory that can be identified, manipulated, and directly used in the creation of an image. These aspects of color hold true whether you are creating an electronic- or a pigment-based piece of art or design.

Properties of Color

Every color has three properties: **hue**, **value**, and **saturation**. The **color wheel** is arranged by *hue*, which is the name by which we identify a color like red or blue. This is determined by its wavelength. *Value* is the degree of lightness or darkness in a color. Value plays an important role in all images. *Saturation* or *intensity* is a measure of a color's purity and brightness. **Figure 4-4** illustrates ways an electronic color wheel shows

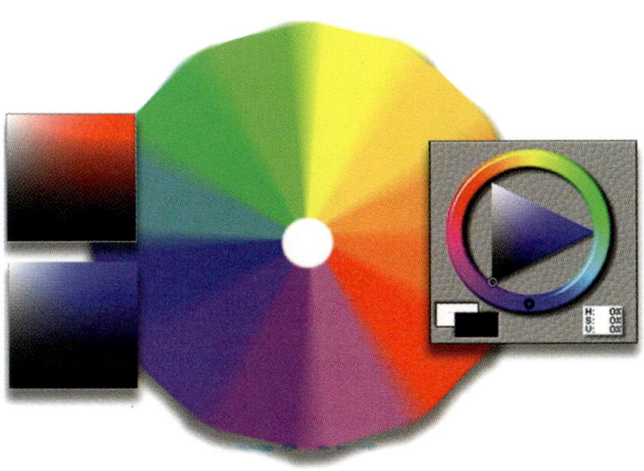

◆ **4-4** *Hue and the properties of value and saturation are shown in various wheels and swatches.*

all three properties, while **Figure 4-5** presents an image that incorporates an excellent, integrated use of all three properties. The red hue is repeated throughout this Illustrator file of a little girl in a landscape, while the hue varies in both value and saturation. The changing saturation and value help give the effect of hills fading into the distance.

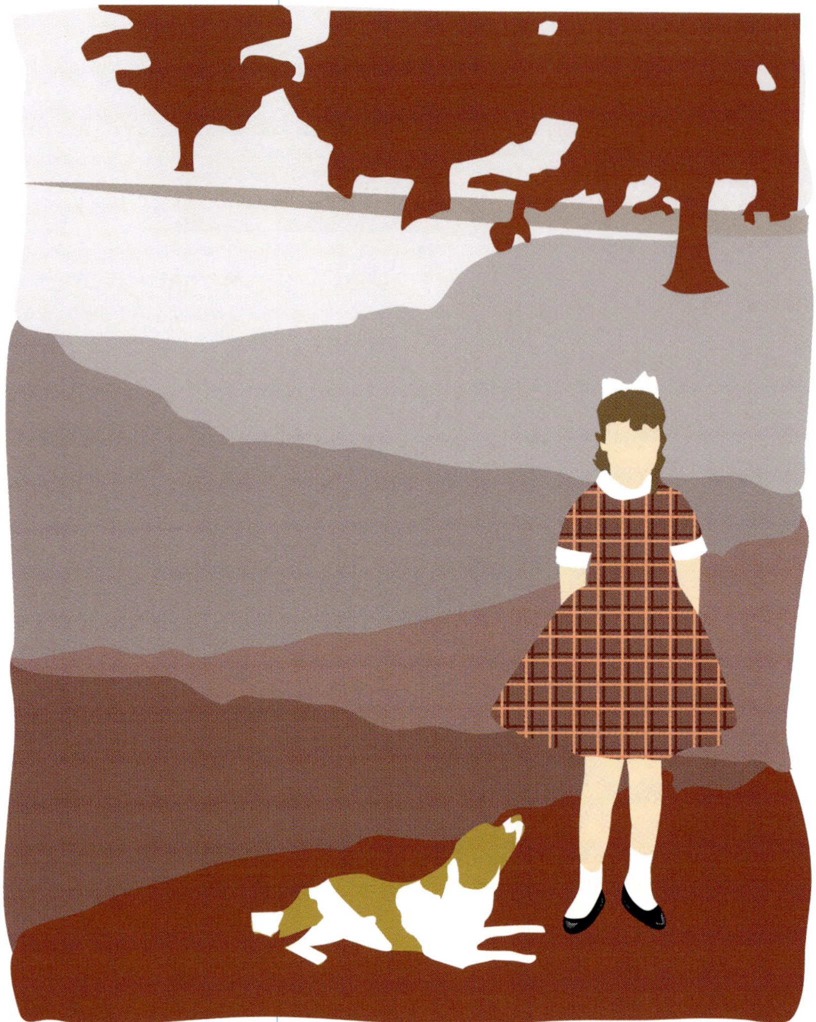

◆ **4-5** *Carla Cannistra. Calendar illustration. 2003. Created in Illustrator.*
Courtesy of the artist.

Color Schemes

Color combinations are grouped into categories called **color schemes**. A **monochromatic** color scheme is composed of one hue with several values. A color scheme comprised of colors that sit opposite one another on the color wheel is called **complementary**. Complements heighten and accent one another. Colors that sit next to one another are called **analogous**. These colors are more likely to be smoothly juxtaposed, in quieter combinations. A **triadic** color scheme is often based on the three primaries of red, yellow, and blue, or any three colors that are equidistant on the color wheel. **Figure 4-6** shows a sample of these different color schemes.

There are other schemes, like **split complementary**, that are rewarding to work with. This scheme includes one hue and the two hues on either side of its direct complement, as shown in **Figure 4-7**. A split complementary scheme can be used to create quiet analogous areas with a

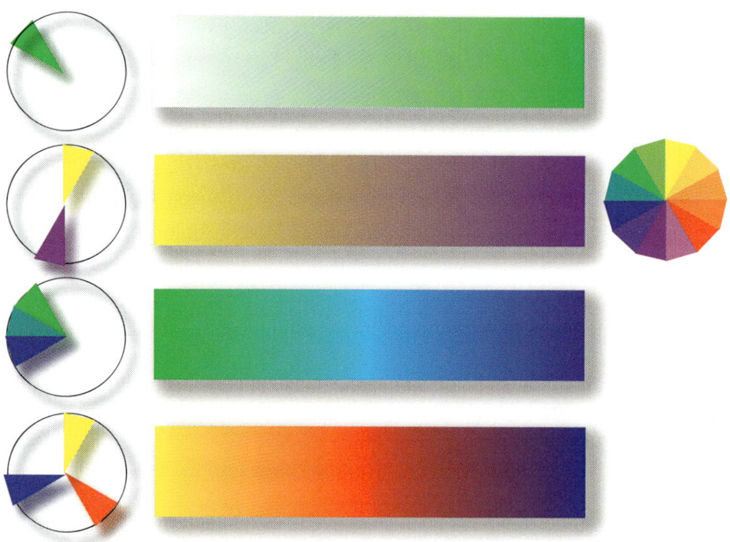

◆ **4-6** *Monochromatic, complementary, analogous, and triadic color schemes.*

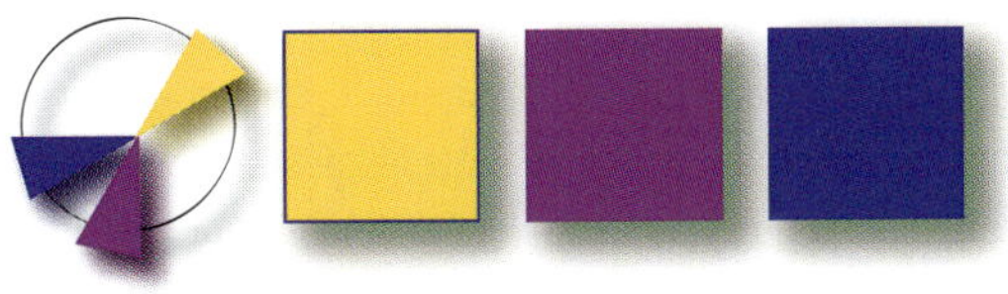

4-7 *Split complementary color scheme.*

Focus On Concept

Consider the notion of relativity and absolutes. To what extent is color an absolute part of our environment? To what extent is it relative, based on individual perception? Consider the relationship between wavelengths and the rods and cones of our retinal vision. Can you identify your individual, psychological color responses?

Because digital tools can enable us to work with over 16 million colors, what is the artistic responsibility of the artist/designer, given this powerful range? How is the digital artist and designer's color palette different from and similar to that of someone working with pigments? Compare your creative solutions in different studio classes.

What color is red? How is it influenced by wavelengths? By lighting conditions? By cultural predisposition?

bright, intense burst of contrasting color for variation. When choosing a color scheme, consider the psychology of color and the emotional effect you wish to create.

The Psychology of Color

Our individual perception of color is also "colored" (whether in life, art, or electronic media) by attitude, cultural background, and personal experience. Colors have the power to evoke strong emotional responses in the viewer. Some of these are based on personal experience, while some are cultural and others seem universal.

Red, yellow, and their variations are referred to as warm colors, while blue and green are considered cool colors. The differences in their wavelengths may account for part of our reactions to color. This would be a **physiological** consideration of how color is received by our eyes, the retinal image, and our rods and cones. The retina contains two types of cells called rods and cones. Rods handle vision in low light, and cones handle color vision and detail. But our associations, memories, and age also play an important part in our response to color. For example, I love soft blue partly because my mother wore blue scarves and suits.

On the other hand, age groups respond to color with different preferences. **Figure 4-8** shows a proposed logo for a children's museum. The logo takes advantage of a child's love of strong color with a heavily saturated, complementary color scheme. Certainly color is an important consideration in the world of advertising and packaging design. The next time you are in a grocery store, look at the cereals targeted for children and compare their colors with those of products aimed at adults. Children's toys, in their highly saturated primary colors, rarely blend well with the adult color scheme in the living room. The next time you shop for anything, see if you can identify a way that color is being used to enhance a product for a particular audience.

The Relativity of Color

The way each color looks is strongly affected by what surrounds it. This principle is known as **simultaneous contrast**. We automatically compare colors that sit side by side. As we know, when

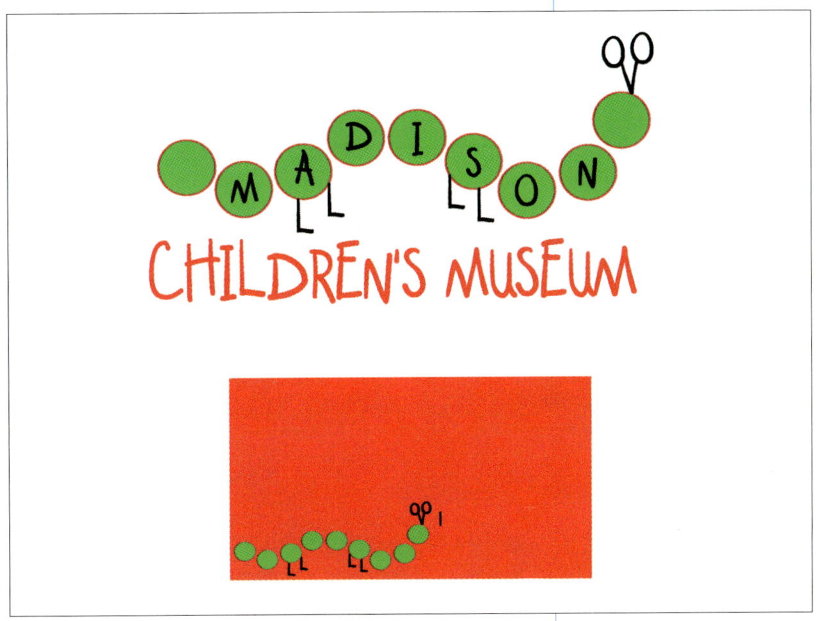

4-8 *Heidi Dailey created this logo and business card for her student portfolio. She used a highly saturated, complementary color scheme.*

Gallery Profile

Josef Albers (1888–1976) was born in Germany and taught at the Bauhaus from1923 to 1933, when he left for America. While at the Bauhaus, Josef Albers ran part of the preliminary course and taught a 3-D workshop "materials class." The autonomy of the student was important in this workshop, which emphasized discovery and invention. In the United States, he taught at Black Mountain College and Yale University.

Albers married Anni Albers (1899–1994), a German-born fiber artist, who was a student at the Bauhaus. In 1933 both were asked to teach at Black Mountain College, an innovative school in North Carolina. Josef Albers taught there for the next sixteen years, and it was at Black Mountain that he began his color studies. Anni taught weaving there and created her own significant body of work. From 1950 to 1958 Albers served as head of the design department at Yale University, New Haven.

Albers began his *Homage to the Square* series in 1949 and worked on it for the next twenty-five years. **Figures 4-9** through **4-11** show three paintings that were the result of this series. He carefully recorded the technical details of each piece, fascinated with the optical effects created through color contrasts. The entire series has only one shape, a square. It is placed in various locations, at varying sizes, with a concentration on what happens as color changes are introduced. As a painter, a theoretician, and a teacher, Albers was an important influence on generations of young artists and designers.

complements (such as orange and blue) are placed side by side, they seem to become more intense. However, the principle of simultaneous contrast describes many different visual effects. Artist Josef Albers is best known for his extensive exploration with simultaneous contrast. Figures 4-9, 4-10, and 4-11 show some of his many explorations with color. Much of what we know about how colors affect one another comes from his work.

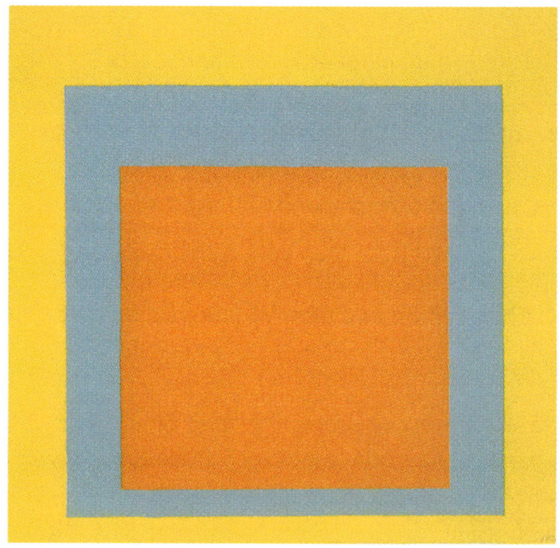

◆ **4-9** *Josef Albers.* Homage to the Square: Confident. *1954. Oil on Masonite, 24" × 24".* San Francisco Museum of Modern Art, Gift of Mrs. Anni Albers and The Josef Albers Foundation.

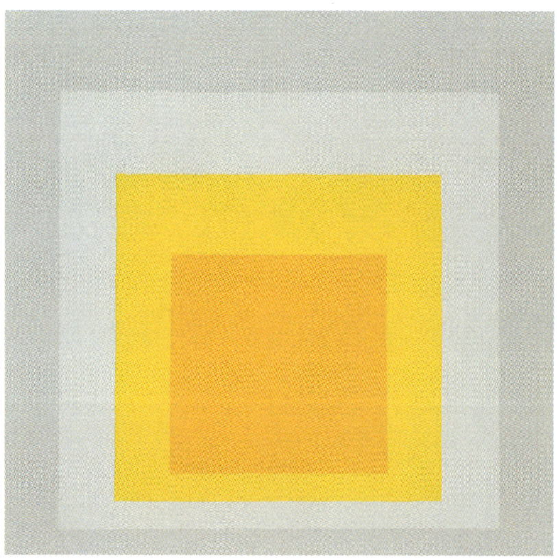

◆ **4-10** *Josef Albers.* Study for Homage to the Square: In May. *1960. Oil on Masonite, 23⅞" × 24".* San Francisco Museum of Modern Art, Gift of Mr. and Mrs. William C. Janss.

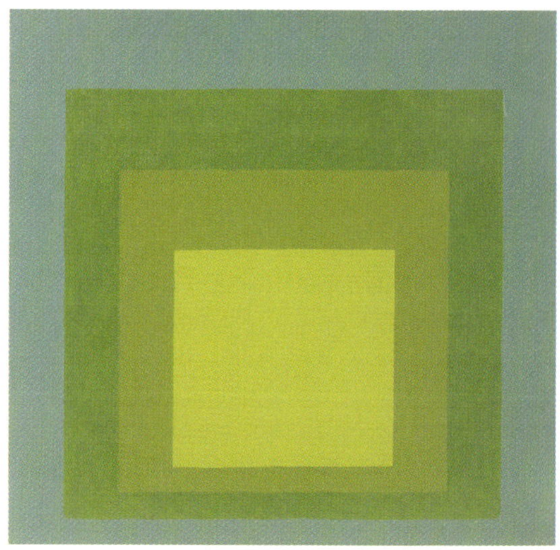

◆ **4-11** *Josef Albers.* Homage to the Square. *1969. Oil on Masonite, 24" × 24".* San Francisco Museum of Modern Art, Gift of Mrs. Anni Albers and The Josef Albers Foundation.

For example, a gray placed beside a color appears to have a tinge of that color's complement in it. This means a neutral gray beside a red hue will appear to be a greenish gray, while the same gray beside a green hue will seem to acquire a red cast.

Value is also affected by simultaneous contrast. A gray or a color placed against a black ground will appear to have a lighter value than the same gray or color placed against a white ground. These relative color behaviors can be interesting for the artist and designer to explore. They can also be a difficult challenge if part of your job is to keep a company logo the same color in every printing environment.

What is the difference between creating color images in traditional media and in electronic media?

Electronic Color

All the information about color described previously remains true in the electronic environment. Understanding the fundamentals of color theory is vital in any medium. But there is more to know about color theory than just pigment-based information. Oil, acrylic, watercolor, and colored pencil create "one-of-a-kind" images. The actual color the artist creates is what people will see unless the lighting is completely wrong! Or the viewer is colorblind.

In print media, color is reflected off a surface, whether that surface is a canvas, a piece of paper, or some other medium. In electronic media, the light emitted from the surface of the monitor creates the color, as discussed below in the section on color models. Even the primary colors are different from those in print media.

The electronic artist and designer work at a distance removed from the final product. Understanding the structure of electronic color is a necessary part of both creating an image and successfully reaching an audience with that creation. The majority of illustrations in this next section will be based on the Photoshop menu options. We will start with some definitions, explaining how color is categorized in electronic media.

Color Models

Color models are a method of identifying, grouping, defining, and sometimes modifying color. The two most basic models in color theory are called additive and subtractive. These names refer to how light is transmitted. **Additive** describes transmitted light, as in computer monitors and photographic enlargers. When this light is added together, you achieve white light, like Isaac Newton's experiments with prisms.

The **subtractive** model, on the other hand, is based on the absorption and reflection of light. Traditional artist pigments and the ink used in printing presses are examples of the subtractive mode. There is a connection between the two color models. If you subtract the values of red, green, or blue from white light, you create cyan, magenta, or yellow. These are the primary colors of reflected light in the subtractive model. They are also the basis for offset reproduction.

The additive color mode in electronic imaging is referred to as RGB (red/green/blue), and the subtractive mode is called CMYK (cyan/magenta/yellow/black). Prints are always sent in reflective CMYK, while the monitor always shows a transmissive RGB color model.

RGB The image on the computer screen is displayed in the **additive primaries** of RGB and is a light-based primary system used in both monitors and photographic reproduction. This additive mode is used in computer monitors and video and for graphics (web or interactive CD, DVD) that will not be reproduced in print.

Red, green, and blue together produce white. Varying the overlapping amounts of these three colors produces all other colors. If a file will be finally viewed on the screen (web or interactive), it stays in the RGB mode. This mode is used for most digital camera and scanner image captures. **Figure 4-12** shows the relationship between RGB and CMYK.

CMYK When an electronic image file is prepared for offset reproduction, it is finalized in the CMY model. The **subtractive primaries** in light-based electronic imaging are cyan, magenta, and

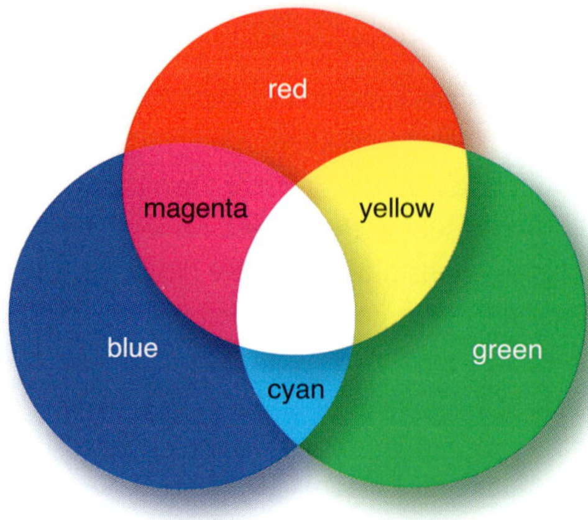

◆ **4-12** *Red, green, and blue are the primary colors in the additive system. Cyan, magenta, and yellow are secondary colors.*

yellow. These are the colors left after subtracting one additive primary from white light. Study Figure 4-12 to see which primary is omitted to form cyan. It is red. CMYK is the basis for the four-color printing process comprised of cyan, magenta, yellow, and black inks. The K stands for the presence of black, although it means Key plate. Black is added to give depth and solidity to the final press print.

What more is there to color models besides RGB and CMYK? There are a variety of models, some created and packaged by manufacturers like PANTONE and TRUMATCH for offset reproduction, while others are based on needs for particular situations. A color mode determines the color model used to display and print images.

More about Modes and Models

The **color gamut** is the visible color range of a color model. The eye can see more colors than can be created in either the RGB or the CMYK color models. The color gamut of RGB, however, is larger than that of CMYK. That means if a design is created with the RGB transmitted light mode, some of those colors probably cannot be reproduced using CMYK colors. **Figure 4-13** shows the varying color range that can be perceived by the eye, shown in RGB, and, finally, reproduced in CMYK. Although the eye can see more than subtractive or additive color modes can show,

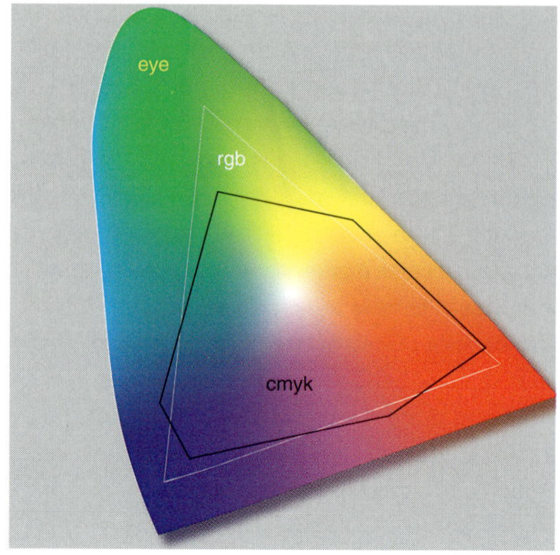

◆ **4-13** *The eye can see more colors than can be shown on the monitor. The colors that can be printed on paper are fewer yet.*

these two color modes are capable of holding over 16 million colors. The color mode that you specify establishes the number of colors that your image can contain. You'll practice doing that inside Photoshop later in this chapter.

The **Bitmap Mode** can have only two colors—black or white—and one channel. **Figure 4-14** shows a bitmap image. It is used for black-and-white (not grayscale) graphics and was also mentioned in Chapter 2. This section gives you a better understanding of this mode.

The **Grayscale Mode** contains up to 256 levels of gray without color. The visual effect can be similar to continuous tone, black-and-white photography. Special Effects within the Photoshop

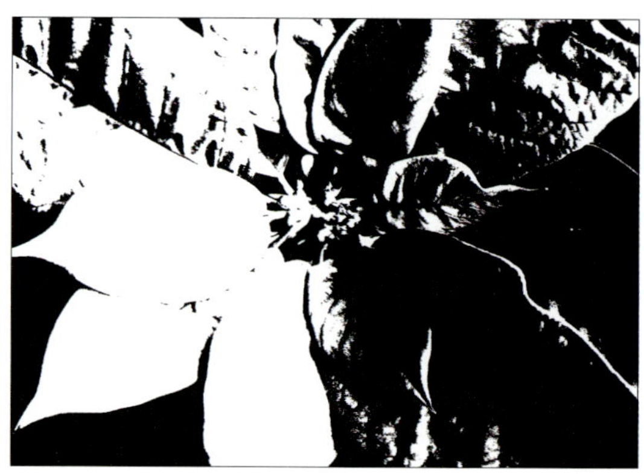

◆ **4-14** *A bitmap image is created in black and white. It cannot show shades of gray.*

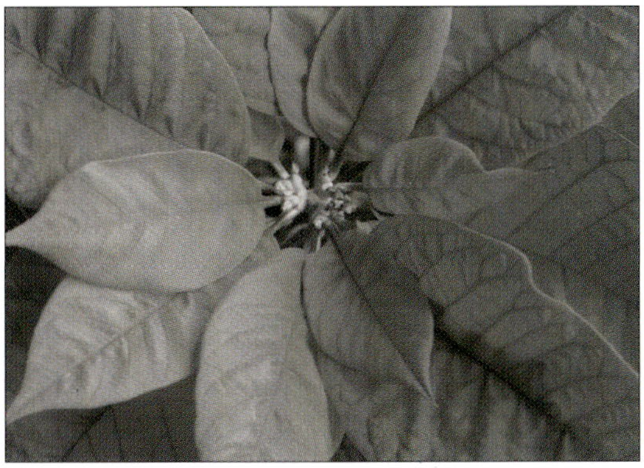

◆ **4-15** *The same image is shown as a grayscale in 256 levels of gray.*

grayscale mode include the Duotone mode, which offers **duotones**, **tritones**, and **quadtones**. These allow for precise control of color assignment and distribution across the grayscale image. They are often the most subtle and interesting effects that are created with a grayscale image. **Figure 4-15** shows a grayscale image, and **Figures 4-16a–d** show an image in varying duotone effects. Duotone effects are often more interesting than full-

Visual Perception

In most computer graphics, artists and designers work with a 24-bit system. In such a system, each pixel is represented by twenty-four bits of color information: eight for red, eight for green, and eight for blue. There are 256 possible values of each of these three colors. These differing values of red, green, and blue can be combined to produce more than 16 million colors. Still, the RGB range of computer graphics is smaller than the range of colors visible to the human eye. Color is powerful!

Color is not simply an inherent property of the objects around us. All the physical and psychological considerations that we bring with us are part of our color perception. The color we see is influenced by our personal experience as well as by the structure of our eye and brain.

Interestingly, color has nonvisual aspects. **Synesthesia** is the word that describes the combining of two forms of perception. Some people see colors when hearing sounds. Painter Wassily Kandinsky (1866–1944) said in his book *Concerning the Spiritual in Art*, "The sound of colors is so definite that it would be hard to find anyone who would try to express bright yellow in the bass notes, or dark (red-purple) in the treble." All our senses contribute to our perception of the world and to our perception of color.

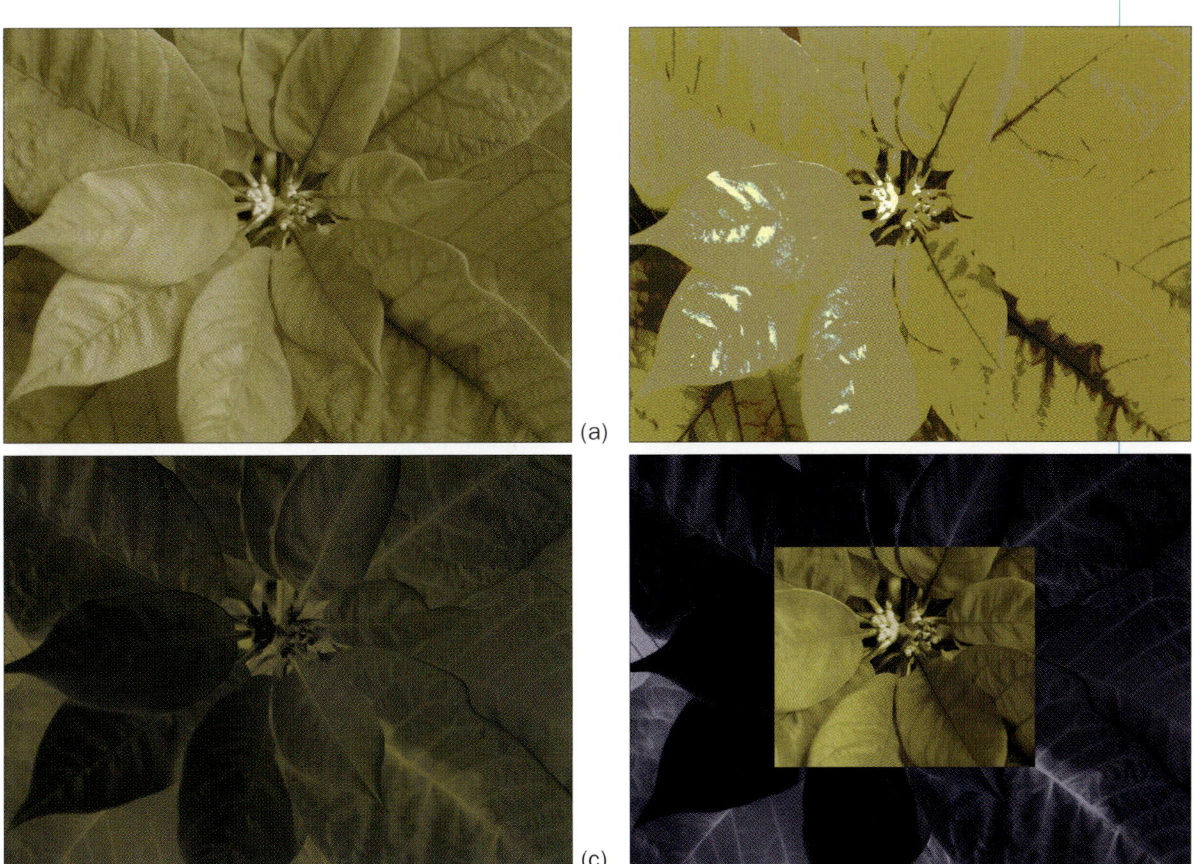

(a) (b) (c) (d)

◆ **4-16 [a–d]** *A single image is shown incorporating different duotone effects.*

color images because their color is full of nuance and close relationships. Now let's discuss the full-color modes.

Accessing Color Options

What are the various full-color modes that can be accessed for use in digital imaging? There are several, and they all have a specific purpose that is related to your file's final output.

The **Indexed Color Mode** contains up to 256 colors and is used in multimedia and web applications to show full-color images while reducing file size. **Figure 4-17** shows a Photoshop pop up window for Indexed color.

HSB stands for hue, saturation, and black (value) and is a highly valuable model for fine-tuning beautifully nuanced color, because it closely mimics the pigment-based intuitive system. Colors can be fine-tuned in HSB, put into RGB for viewing, and, finally, sent to CMYK for printing, if that is the goal. The HSB option is available in the Window>Color pop up of various software programs as shown in **Figure 4-18a**.

Web Color is well managed in Photoshop. It allows you to specify the use of web colors in its picker window and gives sliders for manipulating web colors in its color window. This window is shown in **Figure 4-18b**.

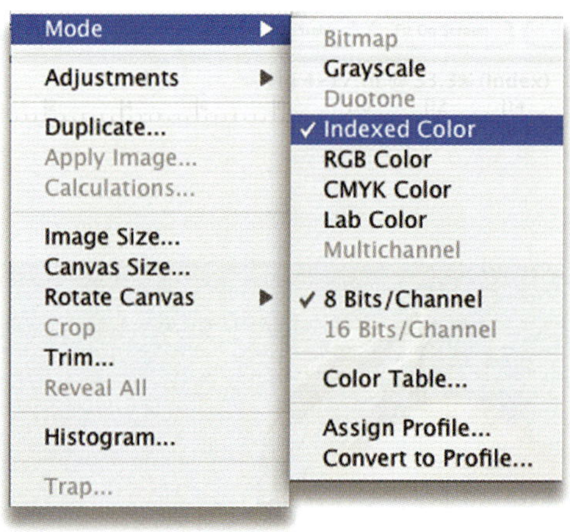

Adobe product screen shots reprinted with permission from Adobe Systems Incorporated

◆ **4-17** *Accessing the Indexed Color mode.*

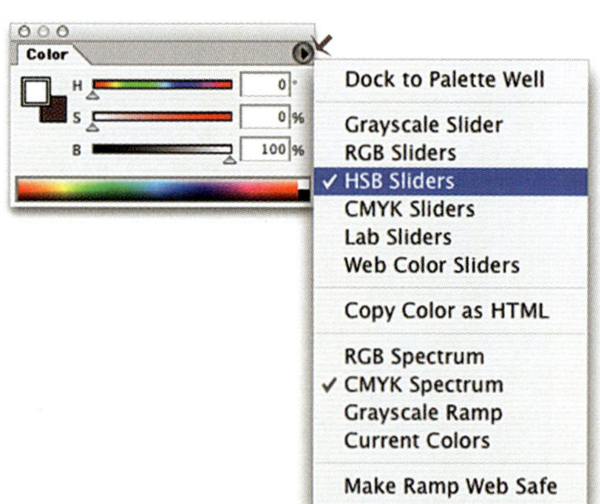

a–b: Adobe product screen shots reprinted with permission from Adobe Systems Incorporated

◆ **4-18a** *Hue, saturation, and black (value) mode is available in the Window> Color menu of various software programs.*

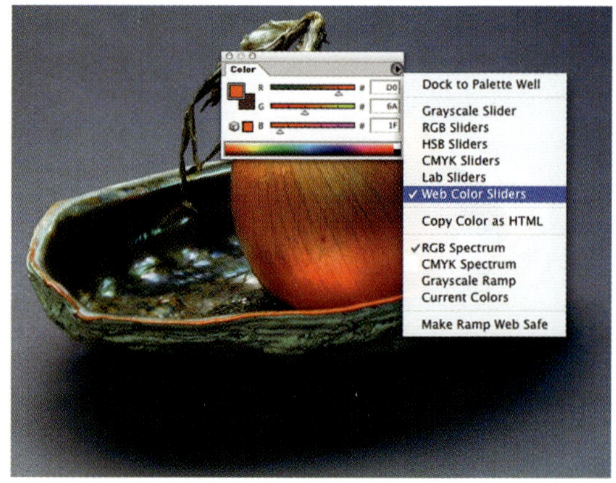

◆ **4-18b** *Photoshop allows you to select Web-safe Color Sliders for manipulating colors for the Internet.*

Output

The way a file will be output makes a difference in how that file is constructed. Will it be sent to a large archival inkjet printer such as an Epson for large, fine art reproduction? You'll need a high-resolution file that can be enlarged without damaging loss of detail. Will it be sent to an Iris printer for limited edition fine art prints? An Iris printer requires a 300 dpi file at the physical size it will be reproduced. Contemporary digital photographer and art professor Leslie Bellavance uses this archival output process. Her work is shown in **Figures 4-19** and **4-20a–b** in the accompanying Gallery Profile.

Will you send your photographic digital files to a printing company for offset reproduction on press? Such files are often inserted into programs like Illustrator or Quark or In Design to combine with type for printing purposes. Always remember that the monitor may not give you a true

Gallery Profile

Leslie Bellavance (1954—) is a contemporary photographer and a professor of art at the University of Wisconsin, Milwaukee, where she has taught photography and art theory since 1981. A recipient of numerous awards, including a National Endowment for the Arts Fellowship, she has exhibited her work throughout the United States and Europe. To create her work, Bellavance electronically manipulates vintage photos and combines them with images of ancient gardens to produce archival **Iris prints**. She varies the size, shape, and color of the original images. Her final image is a composite of selected original portions that have been modified, deleted, or digitally blended. Her photographs make us consider the role of the artist in selecting, altering, and manipulating images to create layers of truth and fiction. Figure 4-19 is a duotone image that is part of her series titled *Threshold*. It is output as a digital inkjet print on an Iris printer. The Threshold series features found portrait photographs from which the people have been digitally removed. The empty space is embellished with her own photographs as well as digital scans. Bellevance states that "both the Threshold and the Wall series are part of an ongoing body of work that pictorially explores the narrative structure of ancient gardens in an effort to examine their pertinence to contemporary life." She also comments that this series "calls to question easy figure/ground relationships."

Figures 4-20a–b are part of her Wall series. The inspiration for the Wall comes from the feminist text *The Yellow Wallpaper* by Charlotte Perkins Gilman. The series also serves as an exploration of the color yellow.

Bellavance constructs her digital montages in Photoshop from scanned 35mm negatives. The final exhibition prints are one-of-a-kind Iris prints with archival ink on archival 46" × 35" Somerset Velvet paper.

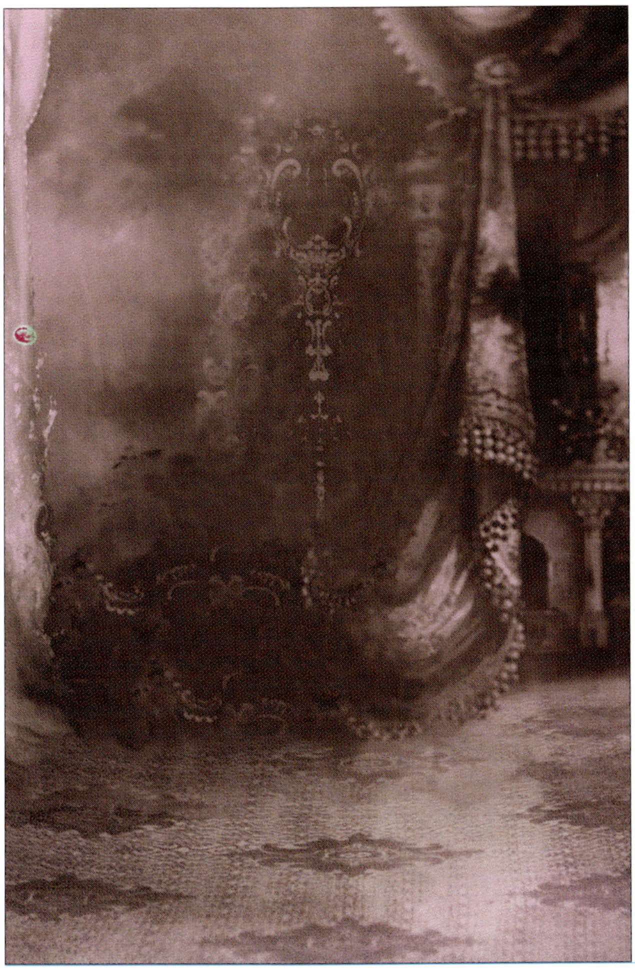

4-19 *Leslie Bellavance.* Threshold. *2001. Inkjet print (Iris) from digital montage. 30" × 20".*
Courtesy of the artist.

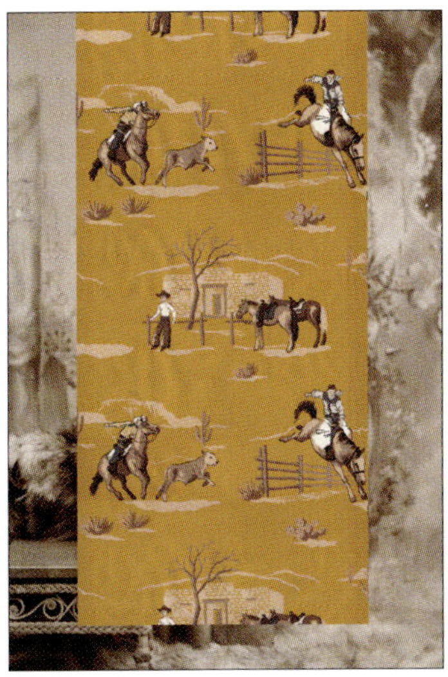

4-20a *Leslie Bellavance.* Wall # 11. *2004. Inkjet print (Iris) from digital montage. 40" × 30".*

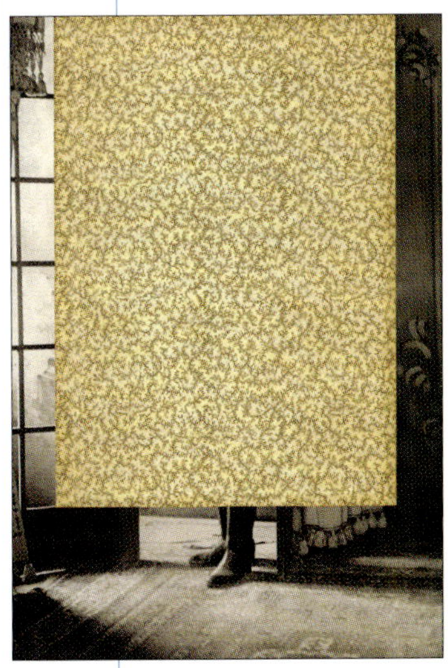

4-20b *Leslie Bellavance.* Wall #7. *2004. Inkjet print (Iris) from digital montage. 40" × 30".*

reading of the file. A close **calibration** between your file, your equipment, and the type of printer you plan to utilize is necessary to reliably predict true color reproduction. In the classroom, you can usually rely on the printer supplied in your lab. Now we'll examine other color options that you will want to explore.

Color Manipulations

Before the computer, graphic designers used duotones in the offset printing process to introduce some color into a black-and-white photograph. Instead of printing it in black ink, the designer specified two ink colors, and the camera at the printing firm created two halftone screens from the original photograph, one for each ink. A lot of visual guesswork was involved.

Now, as mentioned before, Photoshop can generate duotones, easily allowing the designer to view and control both the color and distribution of ink throughout the image. Often these effects are created simply for their beauty in otherwise full-color printing projects. **Figure 4-21** shows a single image split into monotone, duotone, tritone, and quadtone sections. Each of these colored sections was copied from the original duotone mode in Photoshop and pasted into a separate document. It was then changed back to CMYK mode and pasted into a final CMYK composite.

A range of color in a subtle gradation instead of a flat fill is called a **gradient**. It can be specified as a radial or linear fill and can be endlessly modified to create varied effects. Most graphics software offers excellent gradient manipulation through a series of pop up windows. The artwork in **Figure 4-22** created by professional illustrator John Mattos shows the potential beauty of working with gradients in Illustrator. An analogous color scheme filled with gradients helps give this illustration its warm, dynamic sensibility. Mattos has exhibited in the New York Society of Illustra-

◆ **4-21** *Each section of this image is created in a different duotone mode. One by one, the sections are then copied and pasted into an RGB or a CMYK composite.*

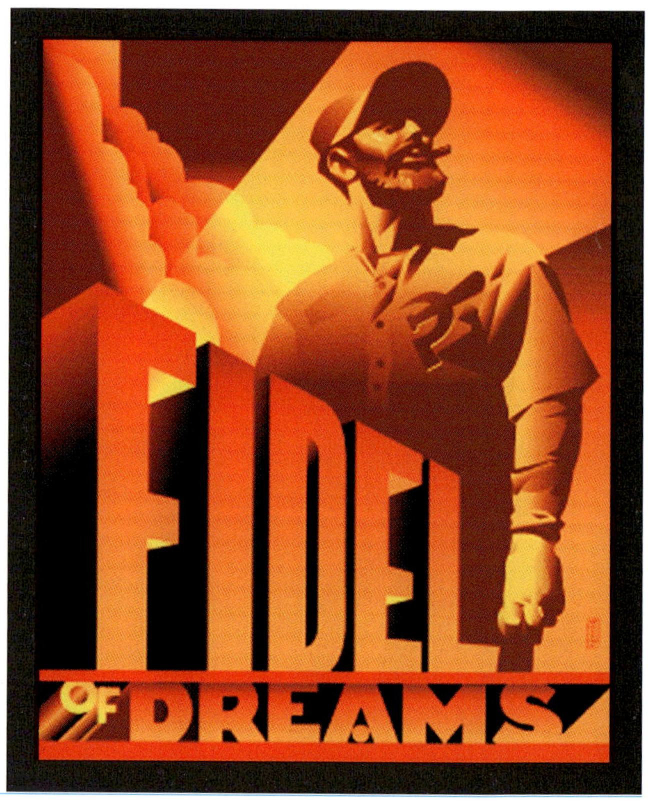

◆ **4-22** *John Mattos.* Fidel of Dreams. *Illustrator document.*
Courtesy of the artist.

This freelance illustrator is based in San Francisco. Visit his website on the accompanying CD.

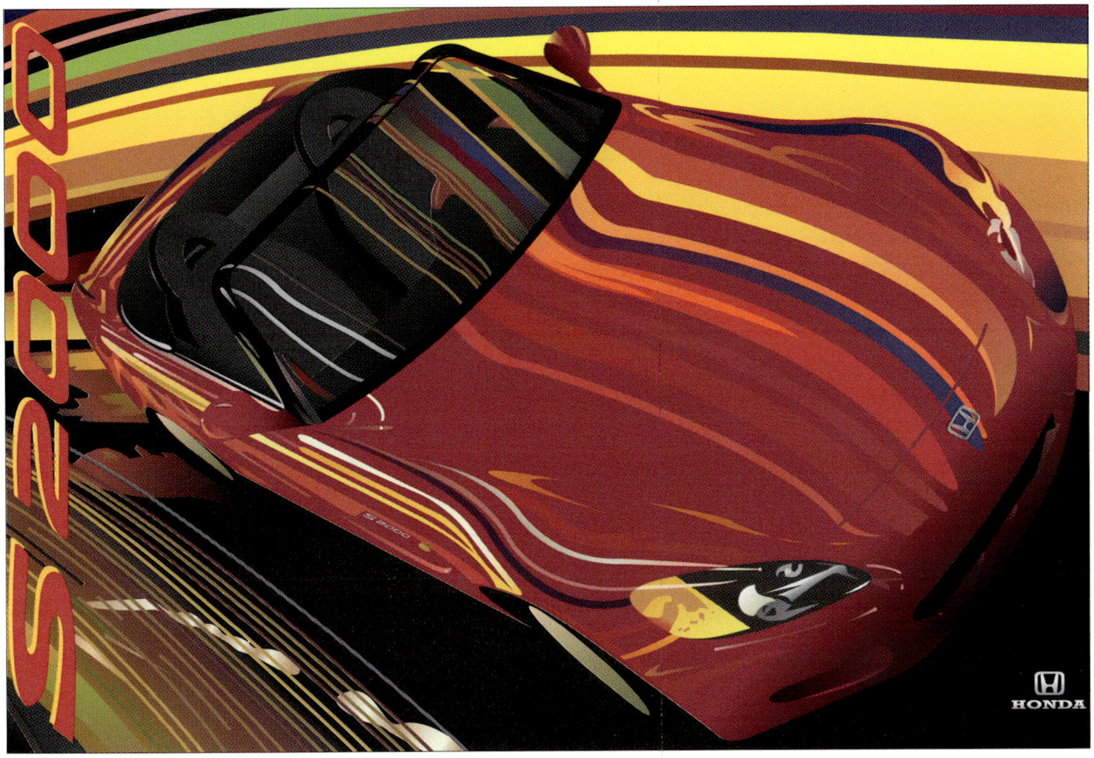

4-23a *Steve Hojinski.* Honda S2000. *This Illustrator document was originally created for a student portfolio.*

a–b: Adobe product screen shots reprinted with permission from Adobe Systems Incorporated

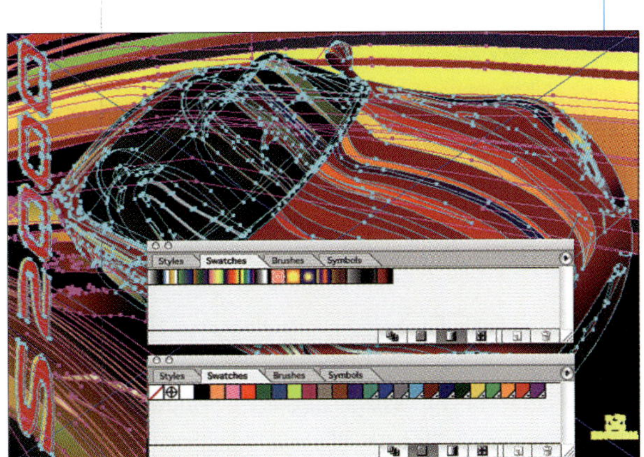

4-23b *Steve Hojinski created these personalized swatches for Figure 4-23a.*

tors show and has works in the collection of the U.S. Library of Congress. His clients include Apple, Adobe, Aerosmith, Disney, Time, Newsweek, and many more. **Figure 4-23a** by Steve Hojinski shows the amazing quality it is possible to achieve with Illustrator gradients, when combined with powerful, repeated shapes and hot colors. This high-intensity color piece was created for Hojinski's student portfolio, and can be viewed in layers in the accompanying **CD**. **Figure 4-23b** shows the personalized color swatches he created for this dynamic color palette. Later sections in this chapter will describe how to create gradients and your own personal color palette.

As we discussed briefly, **spot color** is often used in print graphics for work that will be reproduced by offset press. A selected color ink is inked into an area specified in the electronic file. This ink is specified in a color mode such as PANTONE. FOCOLTONE, TRUMATCH, and TOYO are other choices. These are printing inks that are specified by number. The most widely used is PANTONE, which is available in printed swatch books. If you create a design color #5275, the printing company will put that ink on the press, and it will match the swatch, no matter what your monitor color looks like.

We have covered many of the definitions and categories associated with electronic color theory, and it is time to move on to applying these concepts.

Creating with Color

This section will take a look at creating and using color in Illustrator and Photoshop. You may choose to work with only one software package at a time, returning later in the course to learn a second package. Or your instructor may ask you to learn them side by side as presented here.

How To Basics

Illustrator

Figures 4-24a–f show the steps described in this section that present working in color using Illustrator software. Study these steps (your instructor may lecture on them) and you'll have an opportunity to apply your knowledge in the Hands On Practice section coming up.

The *Color Window* is accessed by selecting Window>Color. In the Color palette, you may mix a color using the Grayscale, RGB, HSB, CMYK, or Web Safe slides. Find those options under the small arrowhead on the right of the color window (Fig. 4-24a). You can also select a color directly from the color bar.

◆ **4-24 [a–f]** *The Illustrator process for creating color swatches and gradients is illustrated in these steps.*

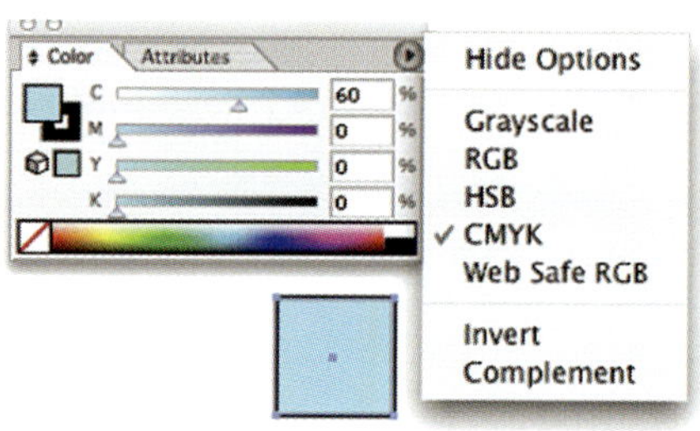

a–f: Adobe product screen shots reprinted with permission from Adobe Systems Incorporated

(a)

The *Swatches* palette allows the creation and selection of a personally defined color library. Select a color on your image. Choosing Window>Swatch then allows the process of saving a new swatch of that color (Fig. 4-24b) that can be the start of a personal palette.

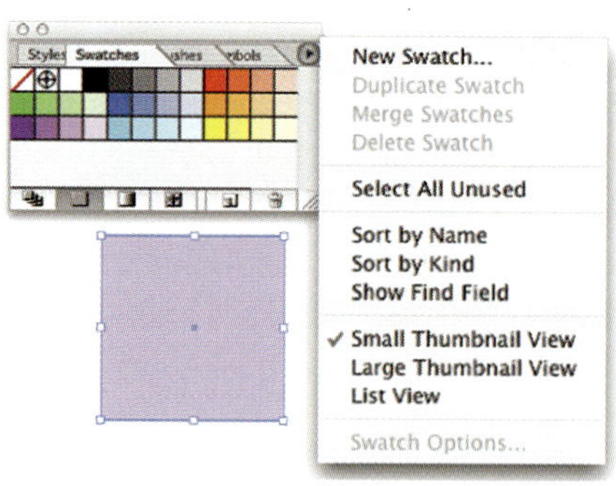

(b)

Spot color modes are reached by choosing Window>Swatch libraries. This lets you select from a variety of predefined color libraries. A swatch can be dragged from the Swatches palette onto an object and dropped to fill the object with color. You can also drag and drop colors from the Swatches palette directly to the Fill or Stroke option in the toolbox. New colors that you create and store are associated with only the current file.

Gradient Swatches can be selected from the Swatches palette (Fig. 4-24c). A gradient is a smooth transition from one color to another. Click one of the buttons at the bottom of the Swatches palette to change your selection to only pattern or only gradient swatches. To delete a selected gradient swatch, drag it to the trashcan. You can save a gradient just like you save a new solid swatch color.

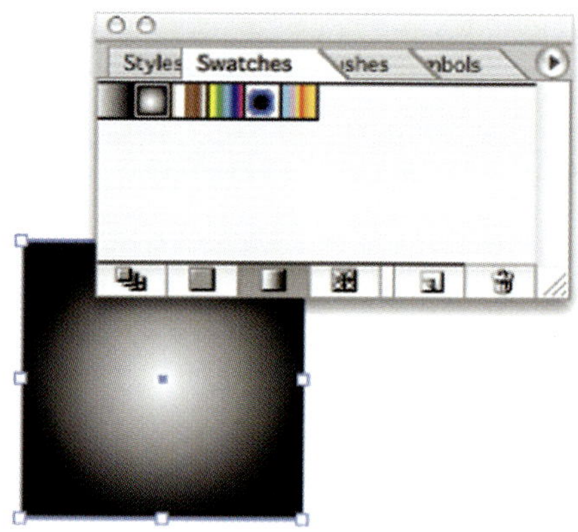

(c)

Applying a gradient is achieved by choosing Window>Show Gradient and clicking the Gradient Fill box at the upper left of the Gradient palette (Fig. 4-24d). Your selected shape will fill with the gradient.

Moving the sliders in the Gradient palette to alter the position of black and white creates new gradients. New colors are introduced by clicking at the bottom edge of the slider to create a color stop tab. Click on the stop and click on a color in the Color palette. Drag the stop to position it in a new location, changing the effect of the gradient blend. Delete colors by pulling down and releasing the color stop tab (Fig. 4-24e).

Adjusting gradients with the gradient tool introduces much more creative variations. Once an object is filled with a gradient, and the gradient tool from the toolbox is selected, this tool lets you reposition the fill along an invisible directional line. Draw this line inside your selected shape (Fig. 4-24f).

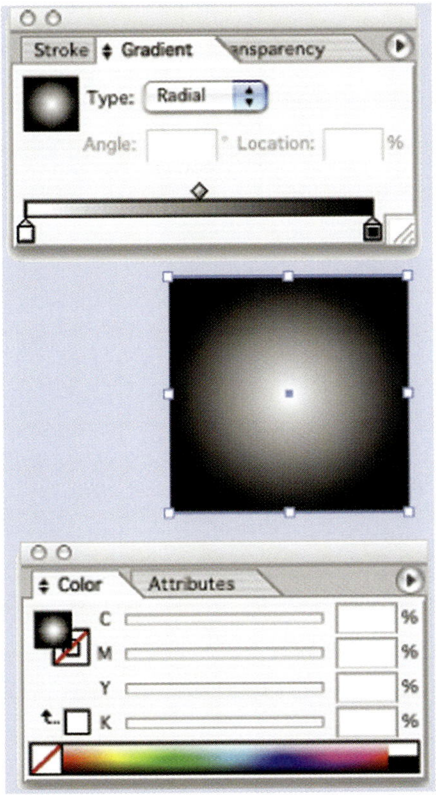

(d)

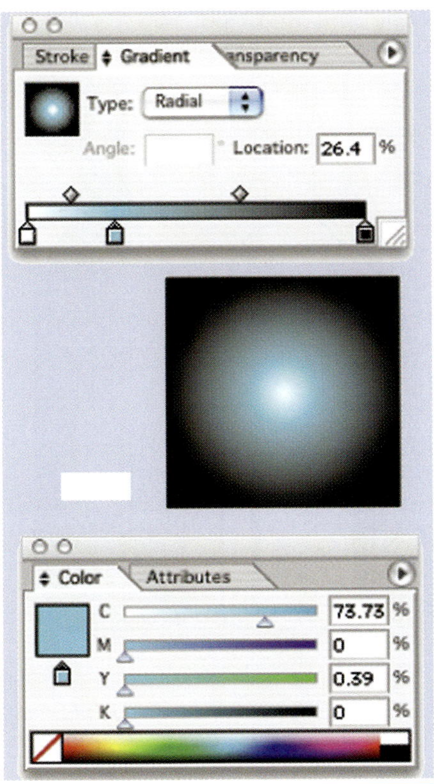

(e)

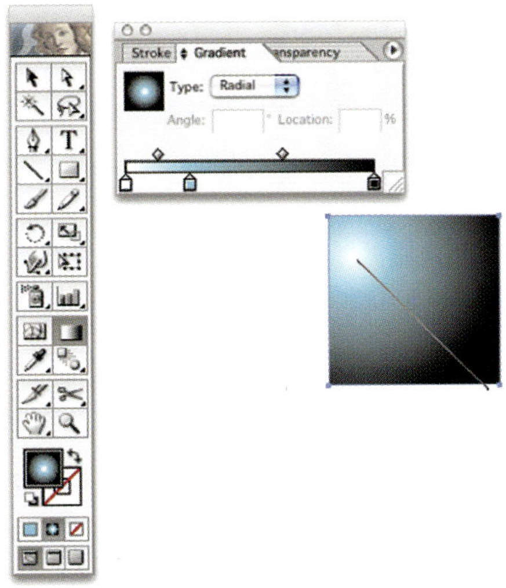

(f)

Figure 4-25 sums up the information about gradients we've covered so far. Study this illustration, and notice the introduction of overlapping layers in varying opacity. We will study gradient mesh in a later chapter. Review and master everything covered in this How To Basics before progressing to the Hands On Practice section. Now we will practice a step-by-step process.

Hands On Practice

Illustrator

You will be creating your own landscape in Illustrator. Think about the mood that you want to establish with your color choices. Think about the color scheme you'll be working with (complementary, analogous, etc.), and incorporate a range of dark to light values. Consider saturation. Take time with this stage.

1. File>New and choose an 8" × 10" page in CMYK.

2. Open Window>Color. Select the rectangle tool in the toolbox and draw a small shape. Click the fill box at the bottom of the toolbox. Now select a color from the Color palette. Use the sliders to make it exactly what you want.

3. Select, copy, and paste the rectangular box several times. Each time, create a new color that will be part of your final composition. Do not include an outline (stroke) color.

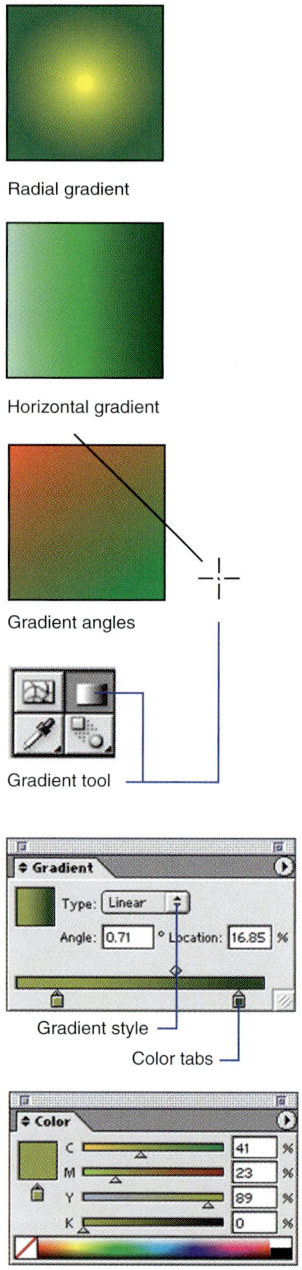

Each gradient tab's color can be controlled in the color gamut sliders.

The gradient tool is able to create multicolor linear and radial blends. You can find existing gradients in the Swatches window or make your own. To make a custom gradient, click on the color tab in the Gradient window. Then pick a color from the Swatches window. If the color isn't exactly what you want, it can be adjusted in the Color window. Your custom gradient can be saved by dragging it to the Swatches window.

The bottles below were created by layering gradients on top of each other. By changing the opacity and layering gradients, you can create a more advanced look.

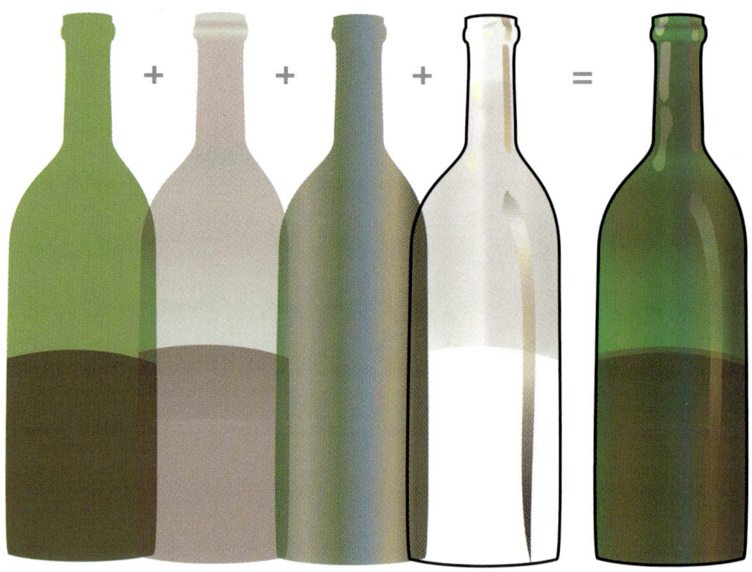

◆ **4-25** *This illustration, created by Chris Eichman, sums up the information covered thus far about Illustrator gradients.*

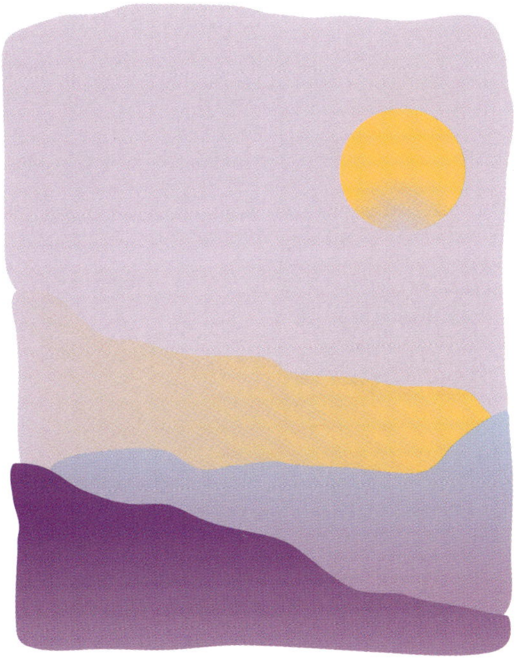

(a)

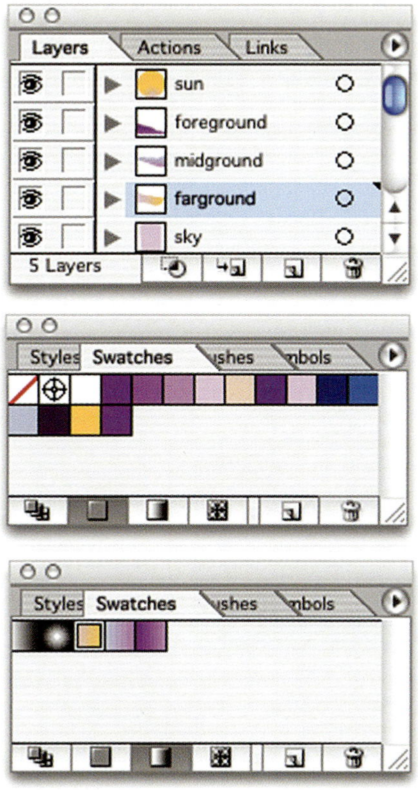

(b)

◆ **4-26 [a–b]** *This image, created in Illustrator, is shown with its personalized color swatches and gradients.*

4. Open Window>Swatches. Make sure you're in the solid color swatch mode. This is the second icon at the bottom of the window. Select New Swatch in the top right of the window. Click on one of your rectangles to create a new swatch color. Name it if you want to. Create and save new colors several times, until you have created color swatches for your entire palette. Delete the rectangles.

5. Use a similar process to create a gradient swatch. Create and select a rectangle on the page, open Window>Gradient and Window>Color. Click on the box at the top left of the gradient window to fill your selected rectangle. Change it to color by clicking along the bottom edge of the gradient slider to insert a new color tab, then clicking on RGB, HSB, or CMYK in the color window. Move the color palette sliders to select a new color for the gradient blend. Delete any unwanted colors in the slider by clicking on the color tab then clicking on the trash icon in the gradient palette.

6. Choose the rectangle tool from the toolbox and draw it over most of the page. Select it and click on an appropriate color from the new swatches. Draw a series of overlapping shapes with the pen tool, simulating land and hills. Putting each on a separate layer is a good way to work. When using gradients, remember to select the gradient tool in the toolbox to indicate fill direction. **Figures 4-26a–b** are simple examples of some of the thousands of images you can create using these techniques. They show the color swatch created for the image and the gradients saved for it. You can examine its structure on the accompanying **CD**.

How To Basics

Photoshop

Figures 4-27a–m show the process of implementing and controlling color in Photoshop. Familiarize yourself with the process before moving on to the Practice section.

Although Photoshop is a premier tool for modifying photographic images, you can also create graphics by painting and drawing. Photoshop's Color Picker gives a good view of color mixing, while allowing access to the various color options. This section will

4-27 [a–g] *These Photoshop steps demonstrate the process of creating raster gradients.*

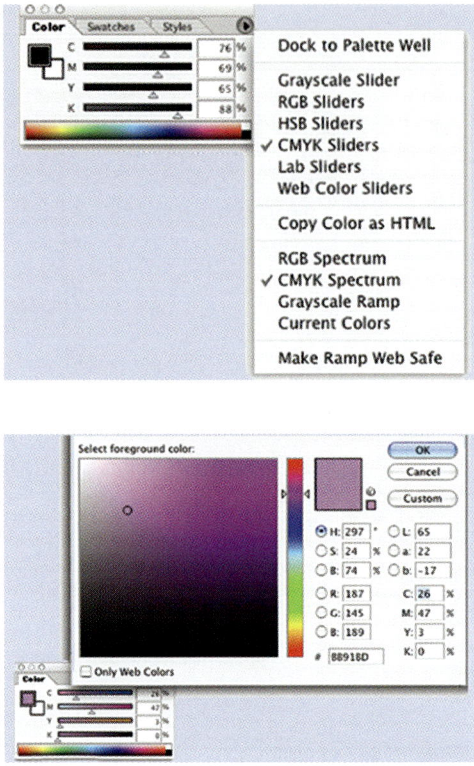

(a)

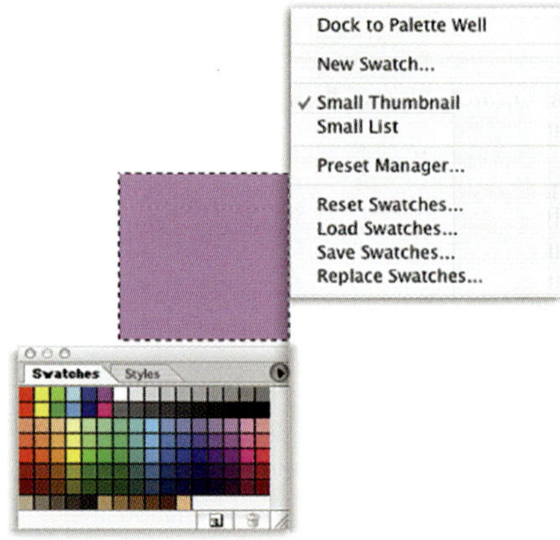

(b)

also introduce using the pen tool in Photoshop to draw shapes.

The *Color Palette* is accessed by selecting Window>Color (Fig. 4-27a). The resulting pop up lets you select a color mode from the arrowhead at the top right of the window. Using the sliders allows for fine-tuning of the color. Use the paint bucket tool to fill a selected area. If you can't find it look under the gradient tool.

The *Color Picker* is accessed by clicking on the color foreground box at the bottom of the toolbox. It is shown at the bottom of Figure 4-27a. Notice that the color mix for each color mode is written in numbers. You can duplicate a color between software programs by keeping track of these numbers and entering them in the new color palette.

The *Swatches palette* allows you to create a personally defined color set from a selected color. A swatch is a color patch. Make a color on your screen and, with it as your fill color, choose Window>Swatches>New Swatch, as shown in Figure 4-27b. Remember you access this command from the arrowhead at the top right of the swatch window. You'll have a chance to name the color before it appears at the end of the Swatch palette.

Spot Color options such as PANTONE are available from the swatches pop up menu. This is also accessed by clicking on the small arrow at the top right of the Swatches window. Choosing PANTONE solid matte option will prompt an opportunity to add or replace these swatches in the current color set, as shown in Figure 4-27c. Solid matte refers to a matte paper surface, while coated refers to a glossy surface.

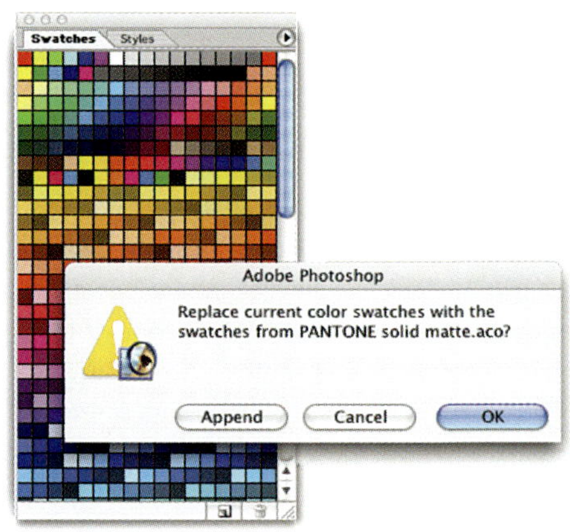

(c)

The *Gradient Tool* creates a graduated blend between multiple colors. You can choose preset fills that the program provides or make your own. The gradient tool is located beneath the paint bucket fill tool. If you can't see the gradient, select the paint bucket and hold it for a moment. To use a preset fill, select the gradient tool and then choose a fill type in the options bar across the top of the screen. Draw across your selection to fill it with a gradient color chosen from the swatches as shown in Figure 4-27d. Practice choosing linear, radial, angle, reflected, and diamond gradients options.

The *Gradient Editor* box lets you modify an existing gradient, to create a totally new effect. Click inside the gradient sample in the options bar shown

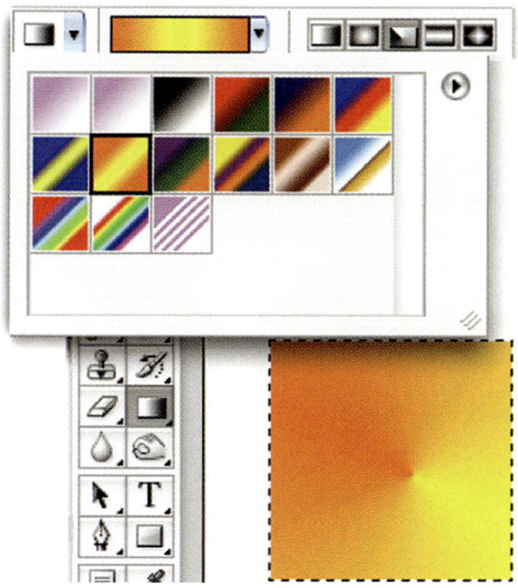

(d)

in Figure 4-27d to display the Gradient Editor dialog box (Fig. 4-27e). To define the first color, double click on the left color stop under the gradient bar. Select from the resulting Color Picker box (Fig. 4-27f). The Photoshop Picker will give an exclamation point alert symbol (as shown) in the Picker palette if a color is not printable in offset. Another color can then be substituted.

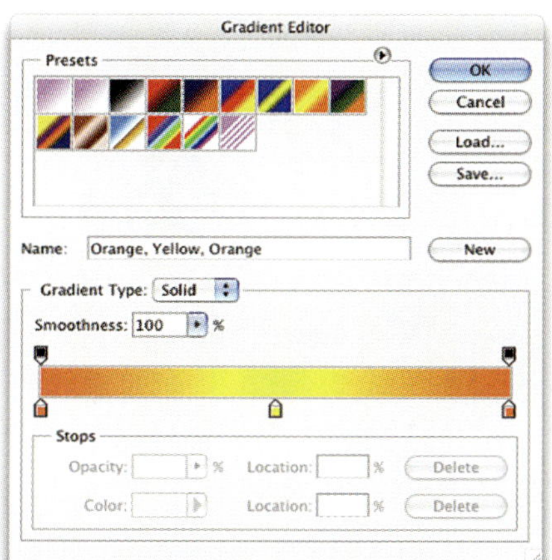

(e)

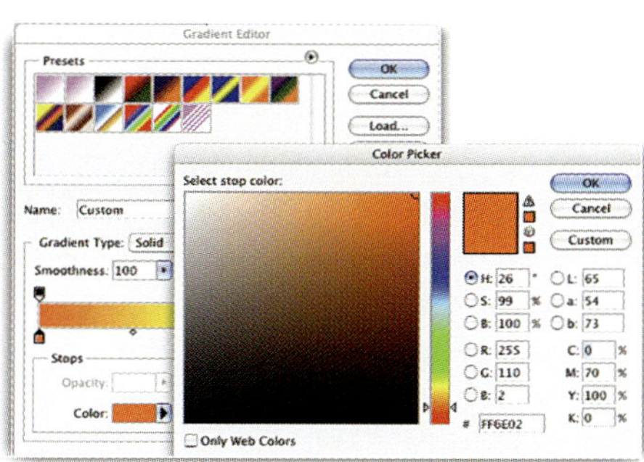

(f)

To add colors to your gradient, click the bottom edge of the slider to create new color tabs. To save your new creation, select Save in the Gradient Editor box. To set smoothness for the entire gradient, enter a value in the Smoothness text box. If desired, transparency values can be set for your new gradient.

To specify the gradient transparency, click an opacity stop *above* the gradient bar. In the stops section of the dialog box, enter a value in the Opacity text box. A different opacity can be set at the other end of the gradient. Figure 4-27g demonstrates specifying gradient transparencies.

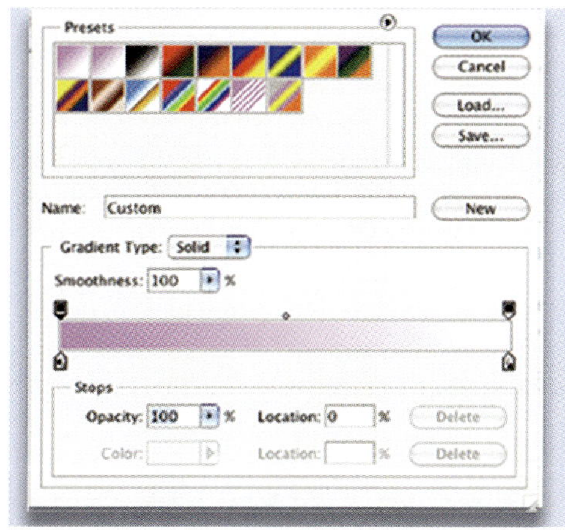

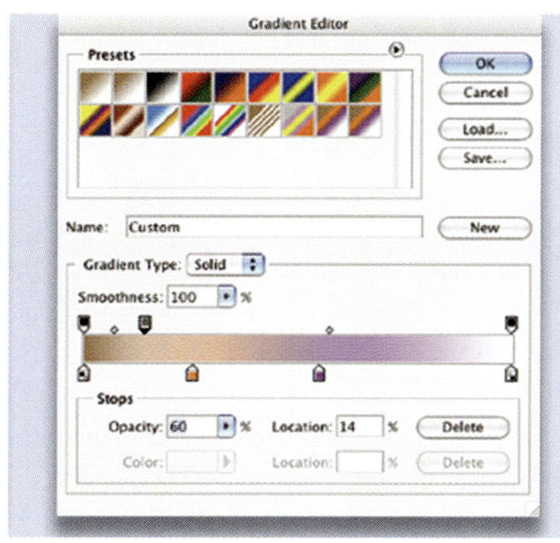

(g)

Vector Paths can be created using the shape tool in the toolbox. The default shape is a rectangle. Select it and hold the mouse down to see the many options beneath. Observe the options bar across the top of the screen. Begin by creating shapes with the pen tool or choosing a custom shape tool from the options bar (Fig. 4-27h). All of the vector anchor points (as described in Chapter 3) can be manipulated using the black and white arrow tools in the toolbox above

4-27 [h–m] *The process for working with vectors inside Photoshop is demonstrated in these steps.*

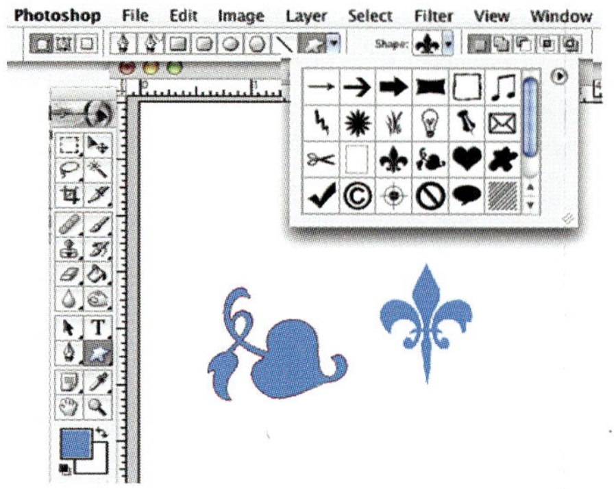

(h)

the pen tool. Figure 4-27i shows a shape selected with the black arrow. The vector points are showing. This shape will show up as a path in the Path pop up window. It can be saved or converted to a selection as we will discuss soon. The pen tools work much the same as in any vector program. If you've studied Illustrator in Chapter 3, they will be very familiar. The vector paths can be converted to raster selections and filled with desirable filter and color techniques. To do this with your new custom shape, select Layer>Rasterize>Shape.

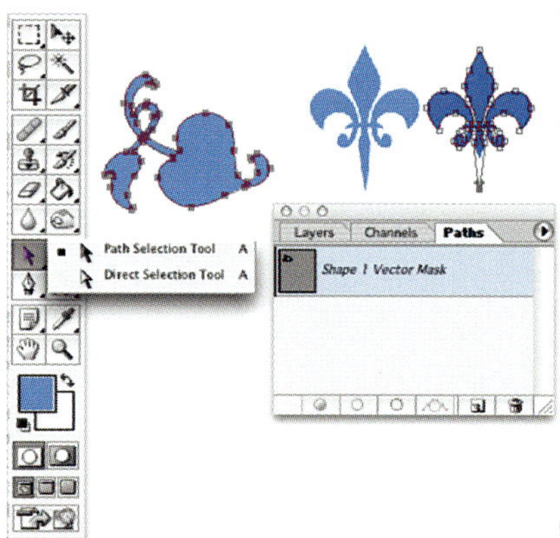

(i)

To save a path you have created, Select>Window>Path and choose the new path or save path option from the top right arrow. Now you can load the path any time. Choose Make Selection in the Path pop up window to convert a path to a selection. Or use the icons as shown in Figure 4-27j at the bottom of the Path Palette to switch a shape back and forth between path and selection mode. Window>Shapes>Load Shapes allows many more shapes to be imported from the library. Once you have converted your path to a selection choose Select>Save Selection in the main menu and now you can Select>Load Selection at any time and fill with color. The fill option will not colorize the path itself, because it only works on raster images. Vector images in Photoshop are not directly editable. You need to use the vector pen tools and path selection arrows unless you have converted the images to raster. Figure 4-27jj shows the selection and the vector path of a shape. It also shows the path window and layers window that are related to this shape.

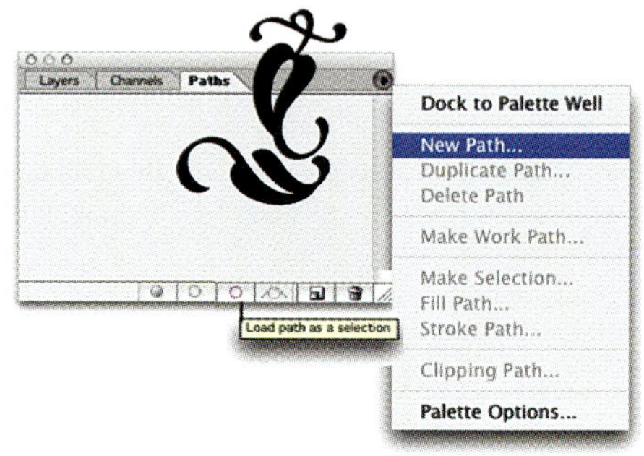

(j)

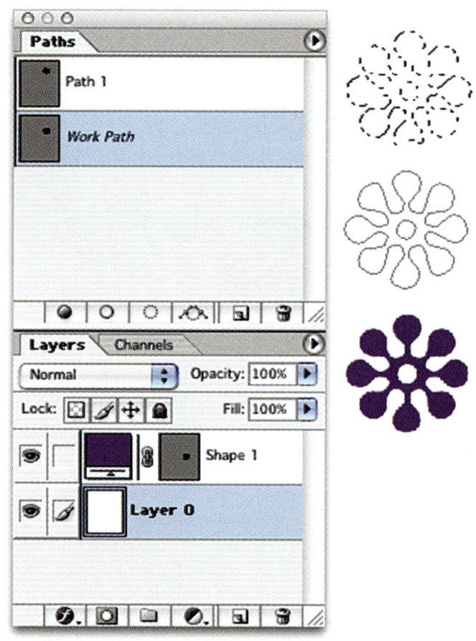

(jj)

Your path can be exported to Illustrator by choosing File>Export Paths to Illustrator. An Adobe Illustrator AI document is created that can be opened directly into Illustrator, where it can be used as a mask. This will be demonstrated in a later chapter. All of this is especially useful if the intent is to create a path of a very complex photographic figure. Beginning with a selection and converting it to a path can be the easiest way to approach the problem.

Type can be treated like vector shapes or raster shapes. Select the T in the toolbox and enter a word. Choose a bold font in the pull down menu (Fig. 4-27k).

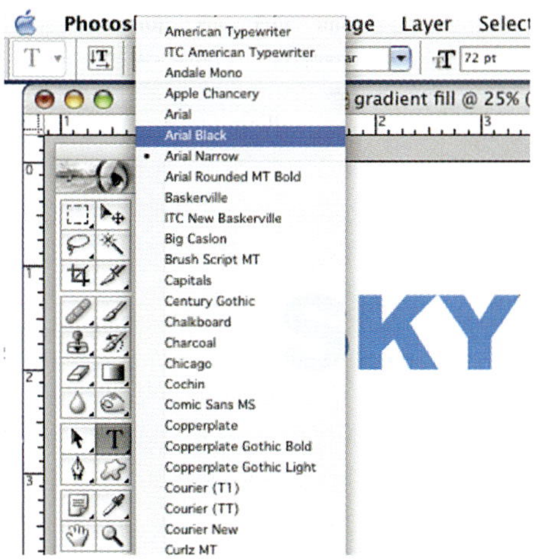

(k)

Choose Layer>Rasterize to change it from vector to raster for editing (Fig. 4-27l). Now select your font with the magic wand tool and drop a gradient across it (Fig 4-27m). Remember to make any size changes before switching to raster. The vector data let you resize the path without losing resolution.

Use all the techniques described in How To Basics and be sure you know where to locate all the commands before moving on.

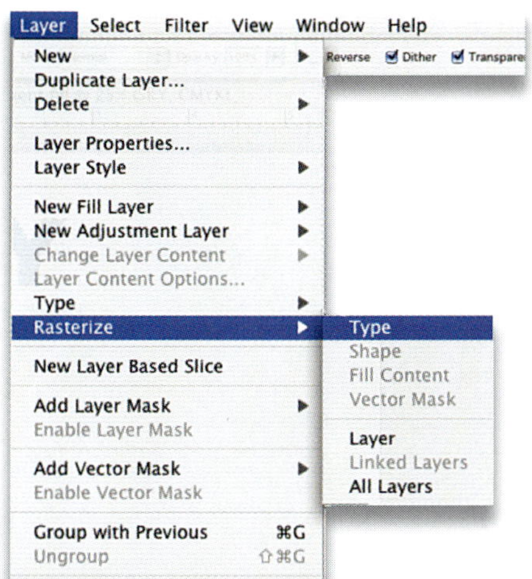

(l)

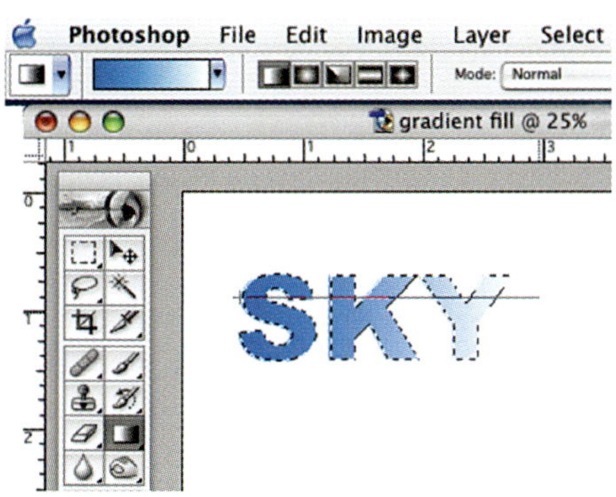

(m)

Hands On Practice

Photoshop

Now we will use a step-by-step process to create a basic landscape in Photoshop. As in the Illustrator version in an earlier section, consider the mood you want to establish with your color choices. When choosing a complementary, split complementary, or analogous color scheme be careful to incorporate a range of dark to light values and some low-intensity colors. This time, you are asked to use the colors from an existing illustration.

1. File>New and choose a 5 × 6" vertical page in 300 dpi in CMYK.

2. Open Window>Color, Window>Swatches. Reset swatches, choosing the top right arrow. Look at **Figure 4-28**, a poster created for the London Transport

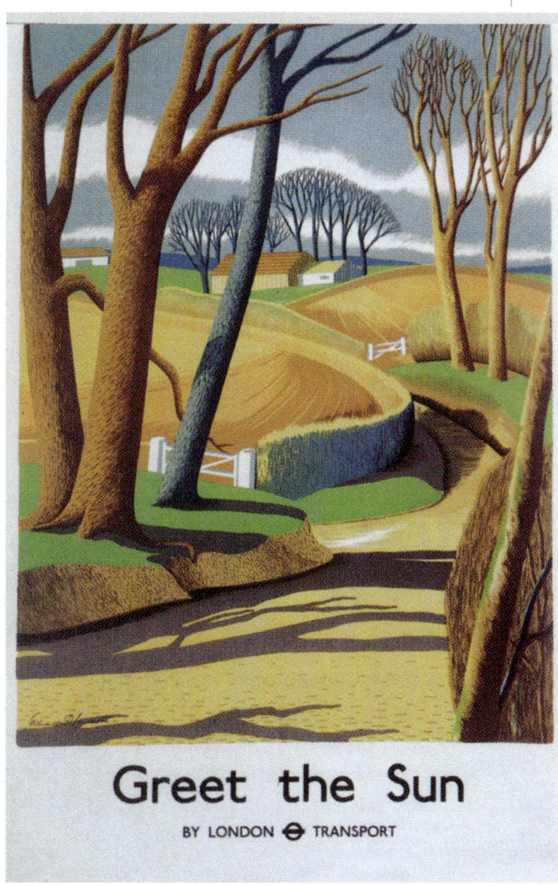

◆ **4-28** *Edward Lancaster.* Greet the Sun. *1930. Poster.* London Transport Museum.

underground rail system in 1939. Create a series of color swatches that match this complementary color scheme. Use the rectangular marquee tool to make a square. Fill with color chosen from the color palette using the paint bucket tool, located underneath the gradient tool in the toolbox. Now use the color sliders to adjust the color. You may prefer to open and use the color picker, by clicking on the color fill box at the bottom of the toolbox. Do this several times, creating your color palette for the landscape and saving the swatches. When you're duplicating colors from an electronic file, you can use the eyedropper tool to re-create them.

3. Mix gradients for your landscape palette by selecting the gradient tool in the toolbox. Notice the options bar that appears across the top of the screen. Click on the color swatch at the top left and begin to mix colors in the Gradient Editor window. Give each gradient color a name, selecting New and Save to keep it in your palette.

4. Now create a simple landscape using your new palette. Plan to draw shapes using the selection tools, shape tools, and pen tool. Remember that you can edit your shapes in either vector (path) or raster (selection) mode. If vectors in Photoshop confuse you, just remember to rasterize them. It would be wise to begin with a pencil or pen drawing for reference. This Practice session may produce a good portfolio piece, if you have enough time to spend on it. Plan to critique it in class and get suggestions for both technique and design treatment. Next, we'll practice applying color theory, and move on to the final Studio assignment for this chapter.

Warming Up

Practice the techniques shown in the How To Basics and Hands On Practice sections before beginning. Study the simultaneous contrast painting studies illustrated earlier in the chapter (see Figs. 4-9, 4-10, and 4-11). Now create several studies that each demonstrate a design principle listed below.

A gray placed beside a color appears to have a tinge of that color's complement in it. This means a neutral gray beside a red hue will appear to be a greenish gray, while the same gray beside a green hue will seem to acquire a red cast.

Value is also affected by simultaneous contrast. A gray or a color placed against a black ground will appear to have a lighter value than the same gray placed against a white ground.

When complements (such as orange and blue) are placed side by side, they seem to become more intense than when placed alone or with an analogous color. Now create a final, more complex surface design that uses one or more of these effects. **Figure 4-29** shows several experiments with these concepts.

An alternate exercise would be to work with synesthesia (see Visual Perception, page 87). This word describes the combining of two forms of perception, both color and sound. Play nonvocal music in the studio, close your eyes, and try to envision colors. Then create those colors. Do this for three different types of music. Samba, jazz, and classical are some musical genres to consider.

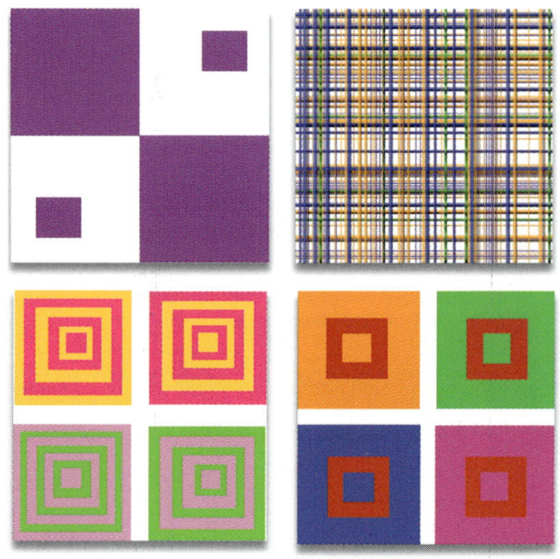

4-29 *Warming up with various experiments in simultaneous contrast.*

In The Studio

The feature on Visual Perception and the first part of this chapter on Understanding Color (see pages 87 and 79) discussed color theory. Review those before beginning.

Using either Photoshop or Illustrator, establish a personal color scheme for your final landscape creation. Make your color swatches and create the artwork shapes by any method we have studied. For example, you might create your images by using software tools to trace over a scan placed in Illustrator, whether it is a photo or a drawing of your own. If you begin with a pen drawing with clear, dark lines, the drawing can be scanned, and individual areas of the scan can be selected in Photoshop and filled with your palette colors. Or, study several successful landscapes in art and illustration history, and then draw your version of a landscape directly with the software tools in either program. **Figure 4-30** is an example created by Casey Swanson in Photoshop for his student portfolio in response to this assignment. He began by scanning a sketch and creating his individual color swatches.

SUMMARY CRITIQUE

In this chapter we examined color theory, while in earlier chapters we examined figure/ground and the relevance of repetition and variation to design. Remember the importance of these design elements as you present your work from this chapter and critique solutions by other students. Also, discuss your technique, successful discoveries, and remaining questions. Feel free to critique and make useful suggestions on other work in the class. Remember that we all learn and grow from these comments. The goal in a critique is not to be "nice" but to be helpful. In a good critique, everyone learns something from each image that is discussed.

For example, critique an image by addressing the following questions:

What is the color scheme? How do the colors incorporate value? What emotional tone is established by the chosen colors? Is that tone appropriate to the image? Are there elements of repetition in the design? Consider repetition of shape, line, angle, and texture. What is the figure/ground relationship? Can any of these elements be improved upon, and, if so, how? What are the particular strengths of this piece?

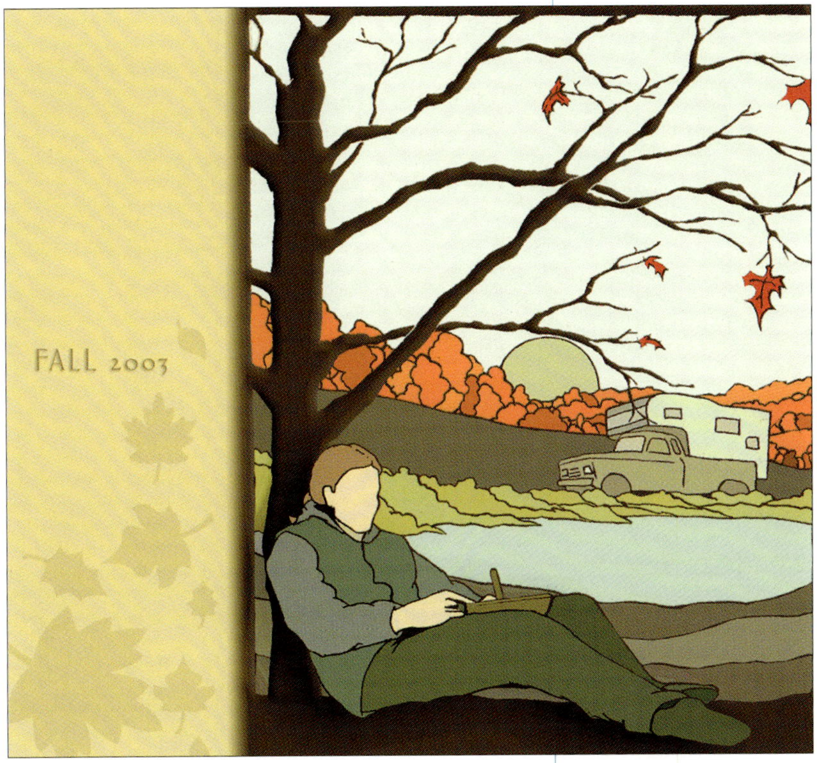

◆ **4-30** *Casey Swanson. Calendar illustration. 2002. Photoshop file.* Courtesy of the artist.

MOVING ON

Chapter 5 will present more advanced techniques in Photoshop as well as introduce another exciting raster program called Painter. The emphasis on understanding color theory and electronic color implementation from Chapter 4 will continue to help you create successful artwork and understand the structure of electronic color as we move on to further exploration of your software program. If you are learning Illustrator vectors before Photoshop, plan to skip to Chapter 6.

TERMINOLOGY

CHAPTER 5

See Glossary for definitions

Silver Print
Surrealism
Diptych
Triptych

Opacity
Masking
Channels
Thumbnail

Rough
Semiotics
Metaphor
Cloning

5 Intermediate Raster Graphics

Photo manipulation in digital design owes a long debt to the history of art. The incorporation of photography into raster graphics gives us the ability to create a wide variety of realistic computer images. These photo-real raster graphics can be re-imaged to mirror a personal vision. Artists have worked with a high degree of realism since the Renaissance. The highly realistic portraits, religious subjects, and environment studies from that period still amaze and inspire us. Artist, author, and professor Roy Behrens (1946—) incorporates an image from the Northern Renaissance painter Rogier van der Weyden (1399?–1464) into the electronic collage shown in **Figure 5-1**. Your other course studies in art history and art theory will enhance your understanding of art movements that had an impact on the development of computer graphics. Even in a class on Renaissance art, look for ideas that can enrich your digital art and design solutions.

Although the ability of an artist to capture the world on canvas and paper continues to fascinate us, our understanding of realism was changed forever by the advent of photography and again by the advent of computer graphics. They make a powerful combination.

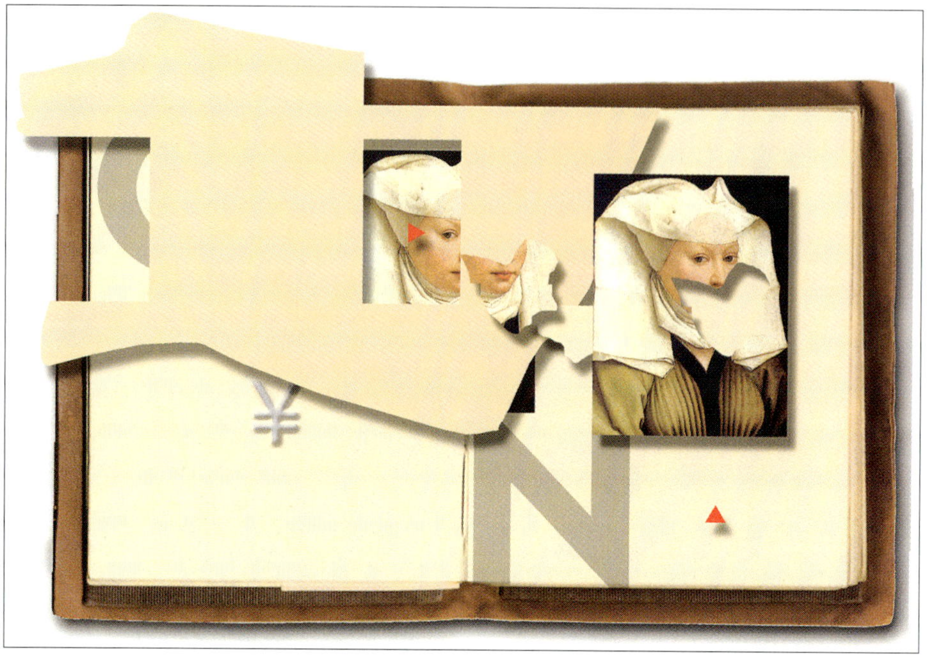

5-1 *Roy Behrens.* At a Loss for Words. *Digital montage print on paper. 2004. 5" × 7.5".* Courtesy of the artist.

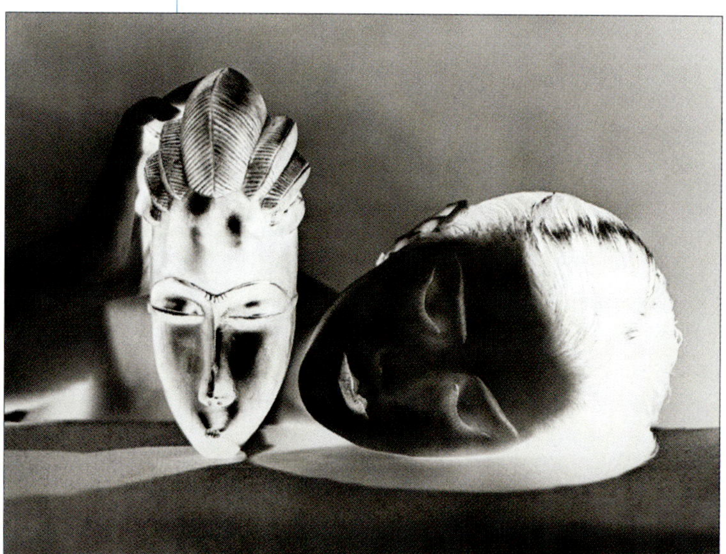

5-2a *Man Ray.* Noir et Blanche. *1926. Reverse negative print.* © Man Ray Trust/ADAGP–ARS/Telimage—2005. © 2005 Man Ray Trust/Artists Rights Society (ARS), NY/ADAGP, Paris.

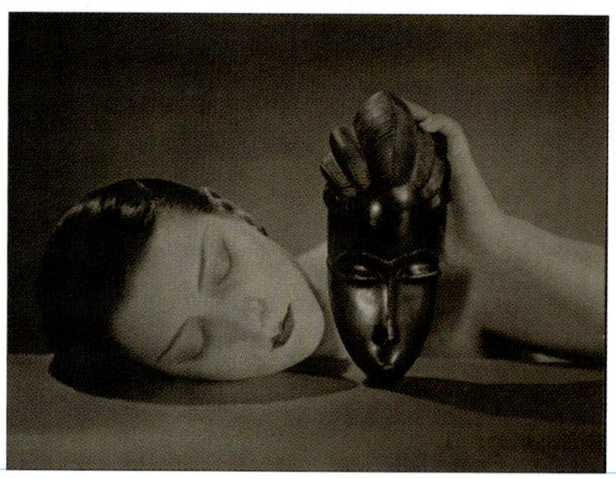

5-2b *Man Ray.* Noir et Blanche. *1926. Positive print.* The Museum of Modern Art. Gift of James Thrall Soby (132.1941)/Digital image © The Museum of Modern Art/Licensed by Scala/Art Resource, NY/© 2005 Man Ray Trust/Artists Rights Society (ARS), NY/ADAGP, Paris.

The Photographic Image

With the advent of photography in the mid-1800s, painters felt freer to investigate images that extended the "realistic" retinal image. The realism of the photographic image drove the 20th-century painters' exploration of other means of expression. "From today painting is dead!" exclaimed the French painter Paul Delaroche (1797–1859), commenting on the invention of photography. Such historical developments in art and design have an impact on concepts in design theory and contemporary computer graphics.

As the 20th century progressed, photography grew to be a vital part of the art world, and some artists began to use it to explore their interest in alternative views. Artists in the Dadaist, Bauhaus, and Surrealist movements developed personalized approaches to the photograph, as shown in the two-part black-and-white image by Man Ray in **Figures 5-2a–b**. (See his accompanying Gallery Profile, page 106.)

Photographers, illustrators, and fine artists continue to be enriched by our long artistic history as they approach the contemporary photograph. **Figure 5-3** is mixed media oil on **silver print** by fine art photographer Holly Roberts (1951—). Her development of multiple planes in the face show a Cubist-inspired approach to the portrait.

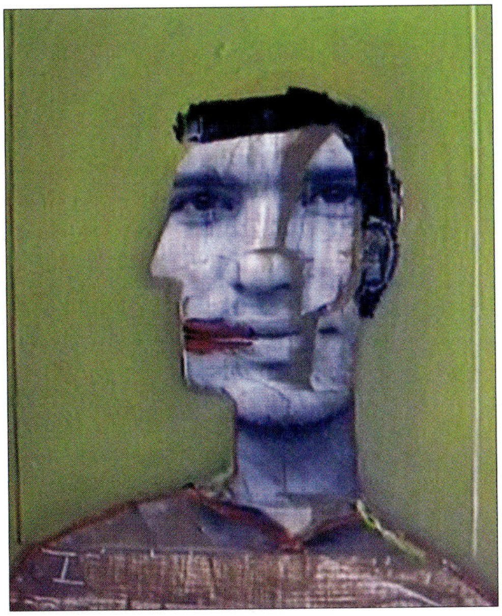

5-3 *Holly Roberts.* Young Man Smiling. *1999. 9" × 6". Oil on silver print.*
Courtesy of anonymous collector.

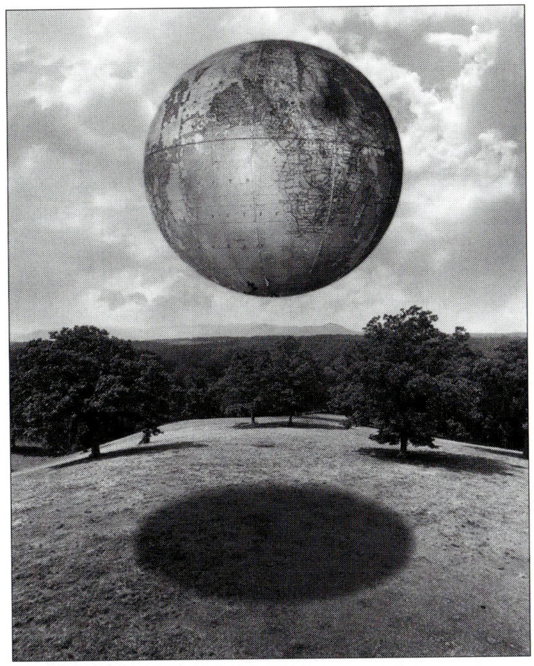

5-4 *Jerry Uelsmann.* Untitled (floating globe). *1981. Silver print.*
© Jerry Uelsmann.

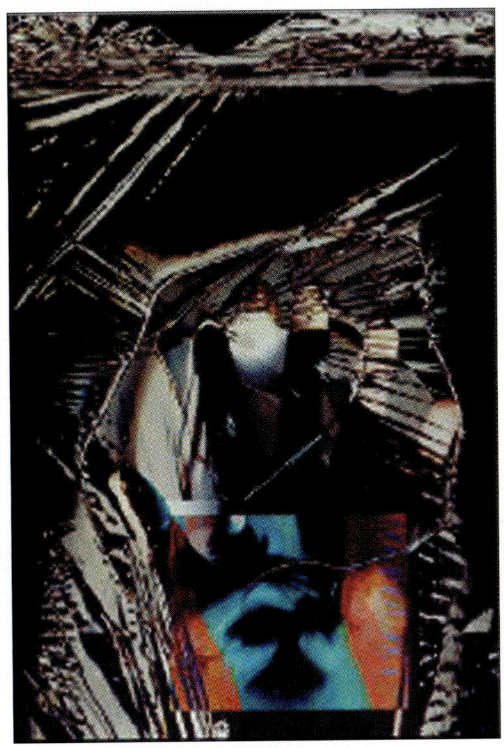

5-5 *Joan Truckenbrod.* Veil of Secrecy. *1999. Limited Edition Giclee print, 56" × 40".*
Courtesy of the artist.

She paints in oil over her photographic original. **Figure 5-4** by photographer Jerry Uelsmann (1934—) is a silver print that uses chemical darkroom manipulation to achieve its collaged look. His work, with its echo of **Surrealism**, continues to inspire artists and designers in both analog and digital photo manipulation. **Figure 5-5** is by New Media artist and educator Joan Truckenbrod. Her computer graphics artwork incorporates photographic imagery into a personal vision. She uses photography and contemporary tools in a variety of compelling ways. (See her Gallery Profile on page 129.)

Computer manipulation of the photographic image is informing artistic choices in many fields. The following sections will continue to cover raster graphics and software manipulation in Photoshop. Throughout these instructions, keep in mind that mastery of the software is a means to an end. The artists mentioned throughout this chapter are excellent references for additional visual research to enrich your concepts and aesthetic sensibilities as you approach your studio solutions. The study, exploration, and application of design principles and concepts are the structural underpinning of your work in digital media.

Applying Design Principles

As you know, there is a variety of ways to visually and conceptually unite images. This chapter will introduce images in a series or presented as sets. These are an excellent way to investigate

Gallery Profile

Man Ray (1890–1976) was born in Philadelphia as Emmanuel Radnitzky. He produced his first significant photographs in 1918 while living in New York, where he helped to form the American branch of the Dada movement. This movement began in Europe as a radical rejection of traditional art and as a protest against the materialism and pretensions of middle-class society. In 1921 Man Ray followed Dadaist leader Marcel Duchamp to live in Paris where, for the next twenty years, Man Ray revolutionized the art of photography.

In Paris, Man Ray was at the center of Surrealism, an art movement established in 1924 that stressed the fantastic and the dream world of the subconscious. Man Ray's often dreamlike, non-photo-real photographs were part of this artistic period. His portrait and fashion photography was also a commercial success. Much of his best-known work from the early 1920s used the cameraless technique of the photogram (or rayograph as he called it) in which objects were placed on photographic paper and exposed to light. He often did several short exposures while changing the position of the objects. These pieces are about time and movement and the relationship between object and image.

Man Ray's photographic creations are often based in some way upon the human form, representing a face or a torso. Others move away from visual resemblance and into the arena of puns and allusion. One of Man Ray's best-known works, *Le Violin d'Ingres*, dates from the early twenties. It shows the back of his model and mistress Kiki, seated wearing only a turban and a loosely draped robe, which has fallen to the bench on which she sits. To the normal photographic print Ray has added two violin "f" holes on Kiki's back, pointing out the resemblance between the shape of her back and the body of a violin. The dress and pose for this picture are modeled on a figure in the Turkish Bath painting by Ingres. **Figure 5-6a** shows a contemporary re-creation of this image on a show announcement for the F5 Photographic Group.

A photogram (rayograph) is a picture made on photographic paper without using a camera. To make the image in **Figure 5-6b**, Man Ray exposed the paper to light at least three times. Each time a different set of objects acted as a stencil: a pair of hands, a pair of heads kissing, and two darkroom trays, the careful placement of which enhanced the faces. With each exposure, the paper darkened where it was not masked. Consider how you might use a scanner and a computer to create a rayograph.

5-6a Quintette et lencore pour Man Ray. *f-5: Dede Bangs, Carol Chae Bjerke, Deone Jahnke, Jan Krieger, Kim Sholly.* f-5 Show Announcement. *2000. Silverprint photography. 5 1/2" × 4". Postcard.*
Courtesy of the f-5 group.

This image is a deliberate re-creation of the original Man Ray photograph by a group of contemporary photographers. Note the name F-5 on the back of their model, instead of the original violin's "f" shapes.

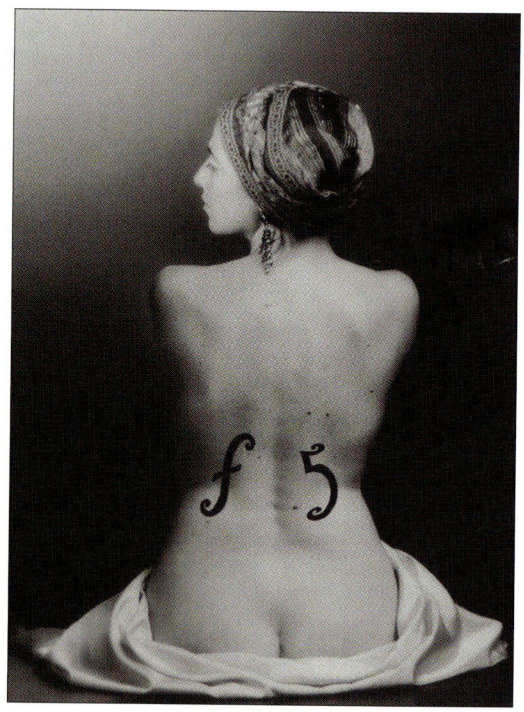

5-6b *Man Ray.* Rayograph. *1922. Gelatin silver print, 9 1/2" × 11 3/4".*
The Museum of Modern Art. Gift of James Thrall Soby (110.1941)/Digital image © The Museum of Modern Art/Licensed by Scala/Art Resource, NY/ © 2005 Man Ray Trust/ Artists Rights Society (ARS), NY/ADAGP, Paris.

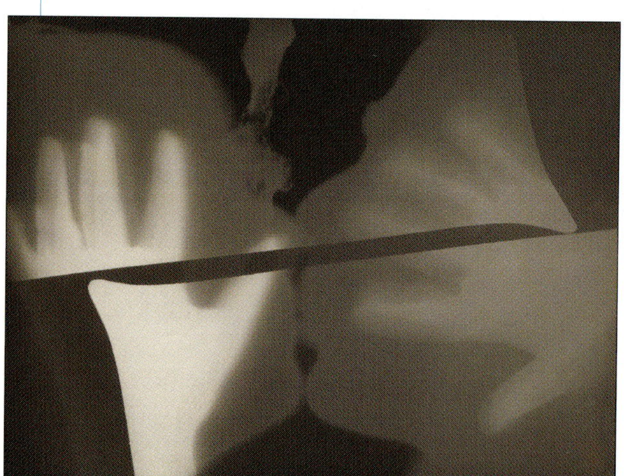

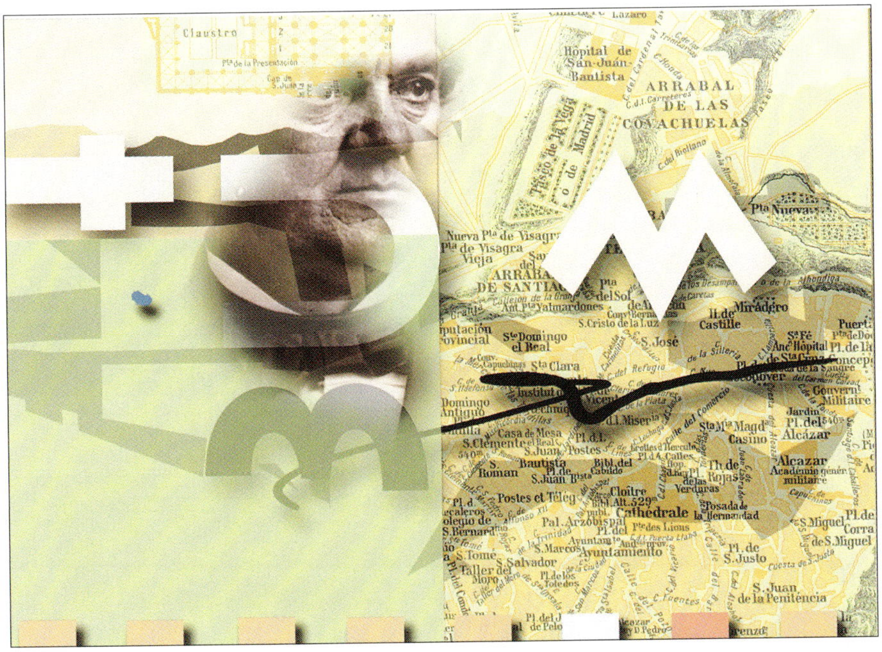

◆ **5-7** *Roy Behrens.* Barbarian Seville. *2004. 5″ × 7.5″. Digital montage print on paper.* Courtesy of the artist.

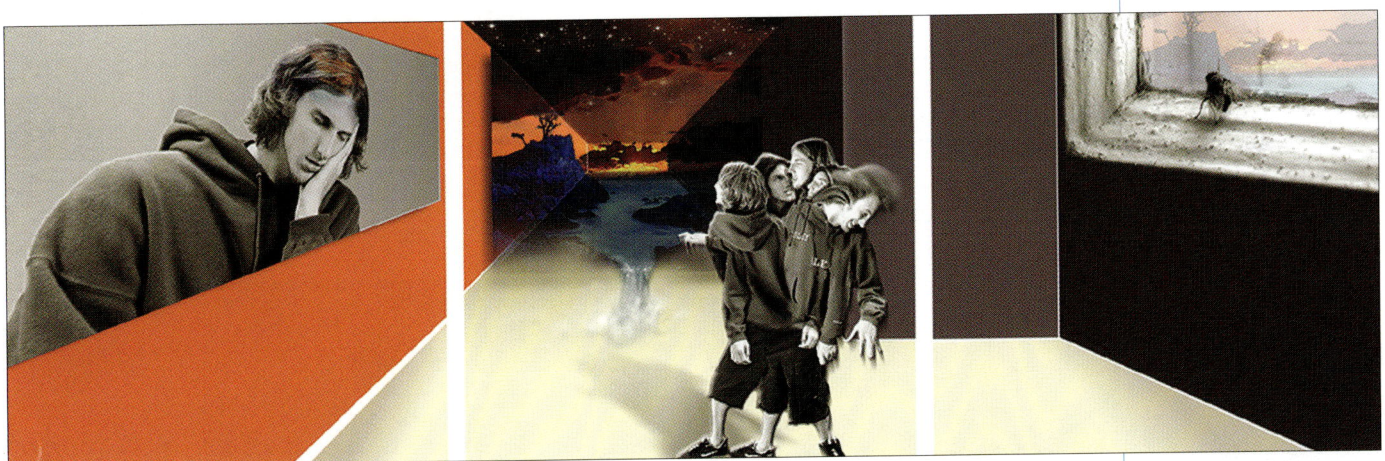

◆ **5-8** *Casey Swanson.* Dream Narrative. *2002. Digital collage in triptych format.* Courtesy of the artist.

the potential inherent in comparisons of similarity and variety. The **diptych** is a work made up of two separate but related images. In the Renaissance, diptychs and **triptychs** (three images) were often hinged together. They were united by content and by visual treatment. Each panel affects how we react to the adjoining panel. Are they a study of opposites? Or are they a comparison of differences? Is the artist making a political or social or religious comment by the pairing of the images?

In more recent artwork, two or three images continue to become a set because of both the visual and conceptual treatment. For example, look at Figures 5-2a-b (see page 104). The photograph by Man Ray uses similarity between the carving and the woman's face in each single image. He also uses similarity by repeating the entire image, varied only by the reversal of values. Interestingly, the white face becomes black, and vice versa. In **Figures 5-7** and 5-1 (see page 104), a series of booklike pages form a contemporary diptych treatment by Roy Behrens. A designer's solutions can also benefit from treating a page layout as a diptych. You might think of your portfolio or "book" in the same way.

In **Figure 5-8**, Casey Swanson uses a triptych to create a personal dream narrative for his student portfolio. Composed of three separate but related images, the triptych has a history similar to that of the diptych. In this contemporary portfolio piece, Swanson combines digital photographic portraits and clip art with Photoshop shapes and gradients. The lines of continuation in the orange swatch on the left and the ground perspective in all three panels help to make a whole of the three parts. The narrative ends with a morning vision of sky and a fly buzzing in the window. Swanson used layers and masking to achieve his final artwork.

Creative Imaging in Photoshop

Layers, gradients, and masking are techniques for enhancing your photographic imagery using Photoshop. The tutorial and help manual packaged with Photoshop gives an excellent in-depth introduction to these software techniques, and it is wise to work your way through it. There are many additional software manuals available for purchase and study. **Figures 5-9a–d** show an extensive use of layers and layer styles created by designer Seth VandeLeest in this illustration for his student portfolio. As you can see in the three progressive stages shown in Figures 5-9a–c, the image was gradually created on a series of layers. Figure 5-9d shows the final artwork. Van-

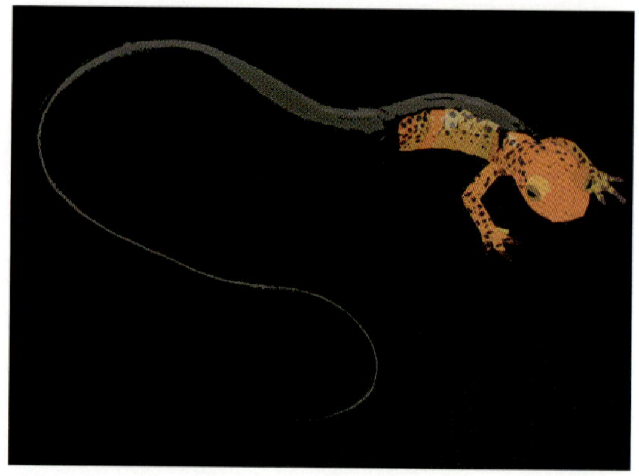

(a)

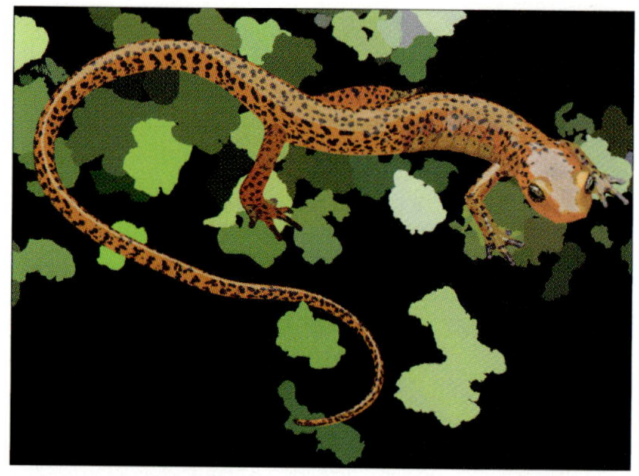

(b)

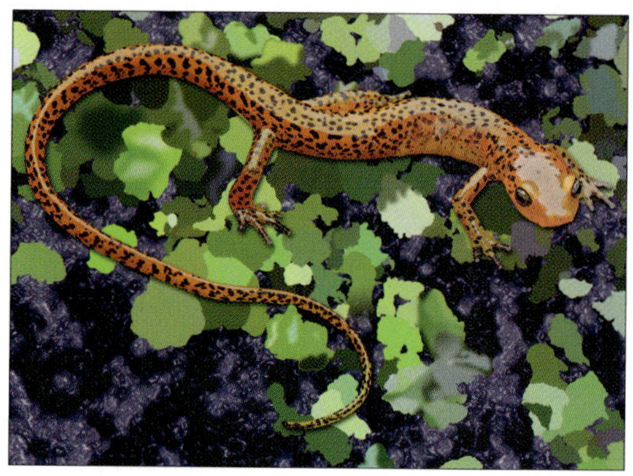

(c)

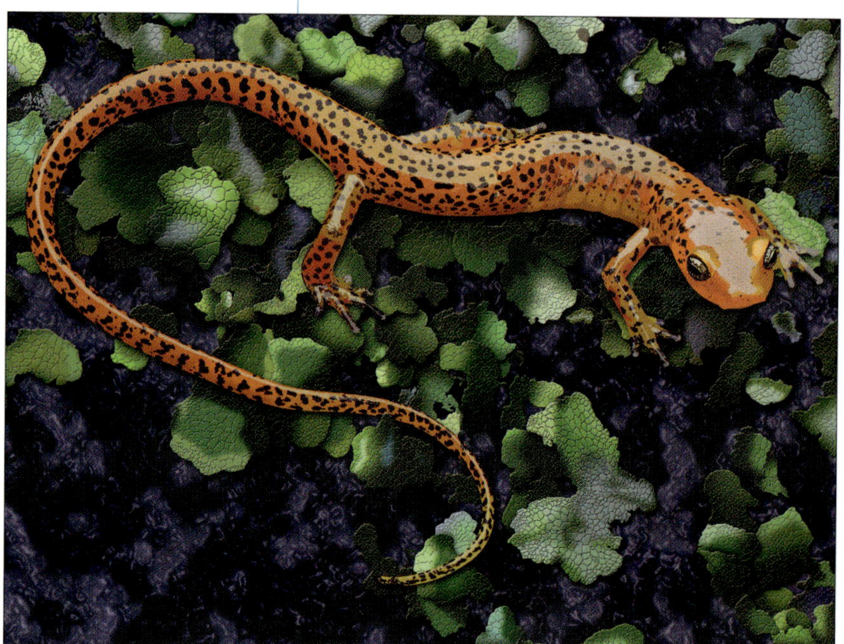

(d)

◆ **5-9 [a–d]** *Seth VandeLeest.* Digital Salamander. *2004. Four steps of a many-layered illustration created in Photoshop.*
Courtesy of the artist.

deLeest created this piece for his final student portfolio using advanced Photoshop techniques in Layer Styles to generate texture. The following How To Basics summarizes some beginning and intermediate techniques used in the preceding illustrations and encourages you to explore their potential applications.

How To Basics

Figures 5-10a–k introduce layering and masking techniques that will help you develop software skills to enhance your concepts and create a successful piece for your portfolio.

Organizing data by layers is a wonderful way to control your image. As discussed in earlier chapters, layers show up in all computer graphics software and behave in a similar fashion in all applications. Every Photoshop file contains one or more layers. Each cut-and-paste function creates a new layer. If the layers palette is not showing, choose Window>Show Layers to display it. You can use the layers palette to view, hide, move, delete, rename, and merge layers. It's always wise to name your layers to easily locate them for later changes. To do this, select a layer and choose the pull down menu for Layer>Layer Properties, entering a name for your layer. Or choose to name the layer when you first go to New>Layer in the layer pop up window, as shown in Figure 5-10a. The layers in Figure 5-10b are named after the parts of a tree frog illustration. Remember that turning the eye icon on and off will let you view and hide a layer. Clicking on the lock icon will lock the selected layer. The bottom of the layer palette has a number of options that are easily reached instead of using pull down windows. Hold the mouse over them to view their titles, as shown in Figure 5-10b.

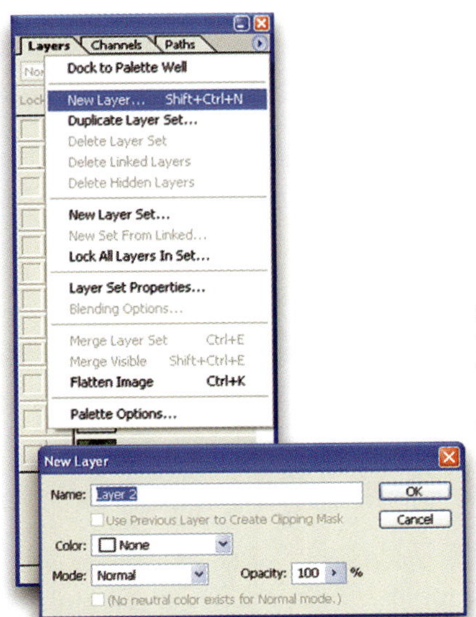

a–k: Adobe product screen shots reprinted with permission from Adobe Systems Incorporated

(a)

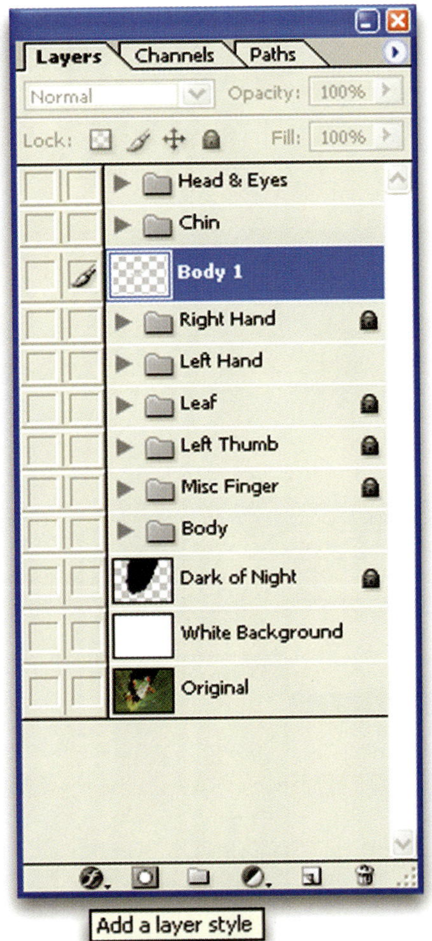

(b)

◆ **5-10 [a–h]** *Various illustrations show the process of working with layers and layer styles.*

Rearranging layers can be easily achieved by dragging and dropping them to a new position (Fig. 5-10c). Select a layer and drag it up or down to reposition it before releasing the mouse button.

The ***Opacity*** of each layer is controlled by the layer slider (Fig. 5-10d). With a layer selected, click the arrow next to the Opacity text box in the layers palette and move the layer slider to select various percentages.

Blending modes offer a variety of effects and are accessed in the Layer pop up in the top left as shown in Figure 5-10e. You can select any layer and experiment with the effects in the mode menu.

Linking layers allows you to move and transform them simultaneously. Figure 5-10f shows that selecting

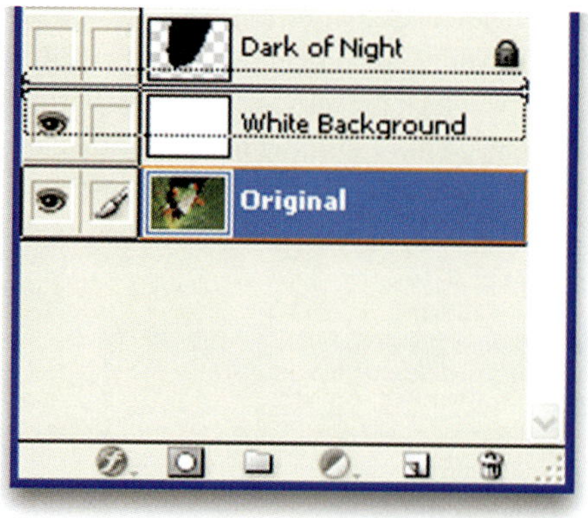

(c)

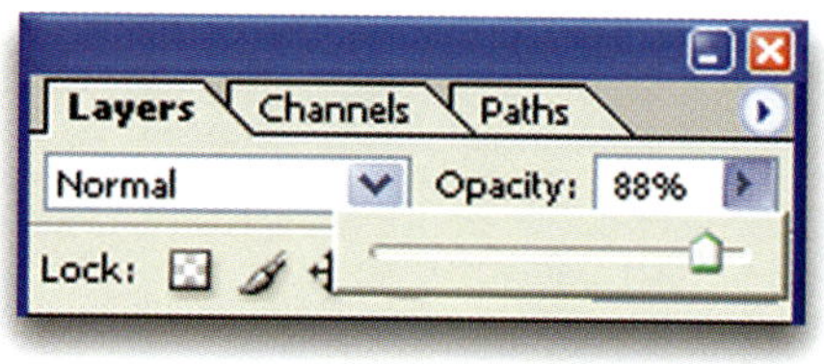

(d)

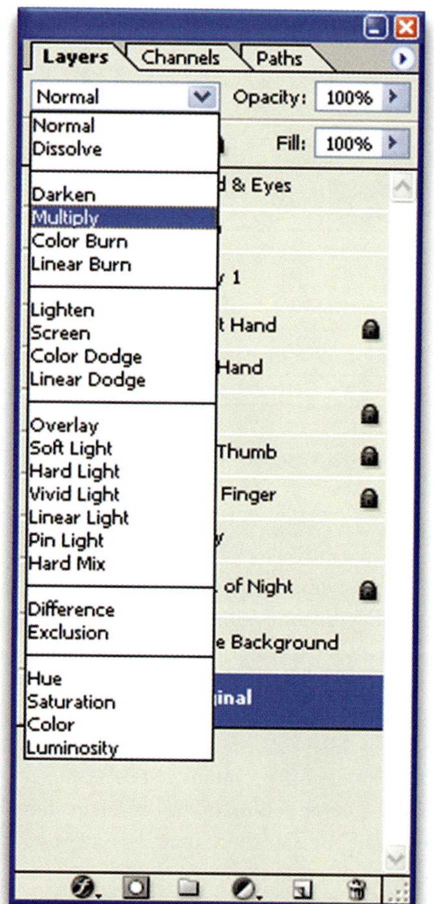

(e)

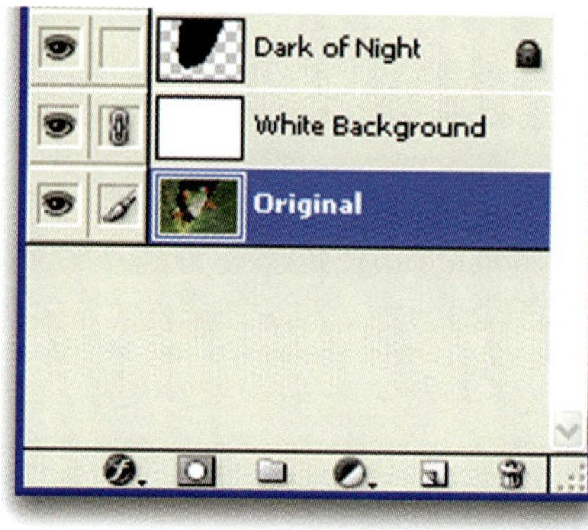

(f)

one layer and clicking the link command on another layer will "link" them. Now a command such as "transform" will affect objects on both the "Original" layer and the white background layer.

Layer Styles are accessed by double clicking on a layer in the Layers window. That produces another pop up window called Layer Style. Layer Style provides a wide array of possible effects from shadow to glow, bevel, emboss, and more (Fig. 5-10g). Clicking on any item in the list on the left on the Layer Style window will show an in-depth array of choices for that style, as shown in Figure 5-10h.

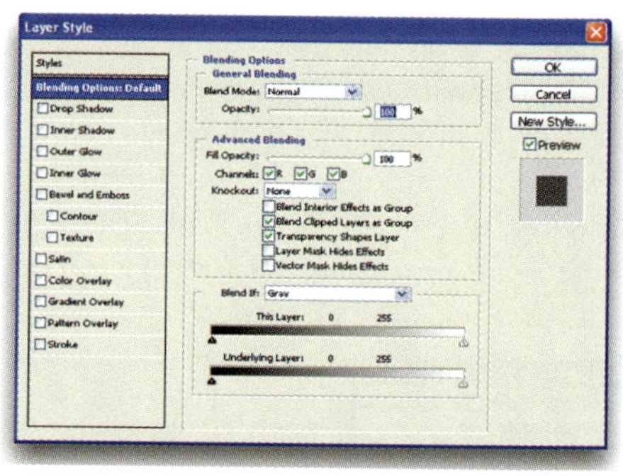

(g)

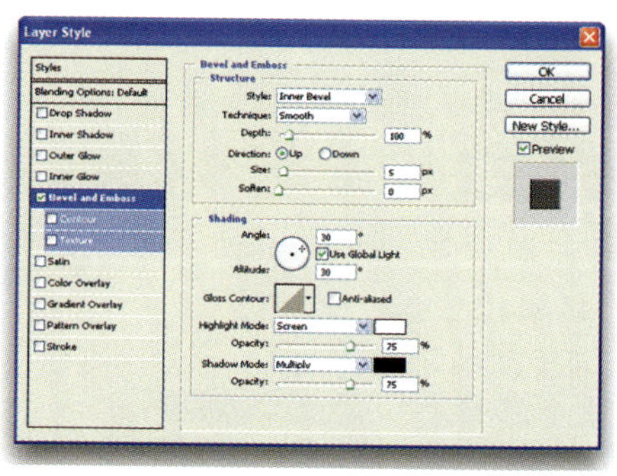

(h)

Gradient effects can be easily added to a layer. To experiment with it, create a new layer and select the gradient tool (beneath the paint bucket tool), choosing a linear gradient in the options bar across the top of the screen. Select or create a gradient color that appeals to you. Now select Foreground to Transparent, which is the second square in the gradient edit options bar, as shown in Figure 5-10i. With your layer active, drag the gradient tool across the image. You can lighten the effect by changing the opacity. The first square in the gradient edit options is foreground to background. Try other gradient effects (Fig 5-10ii).

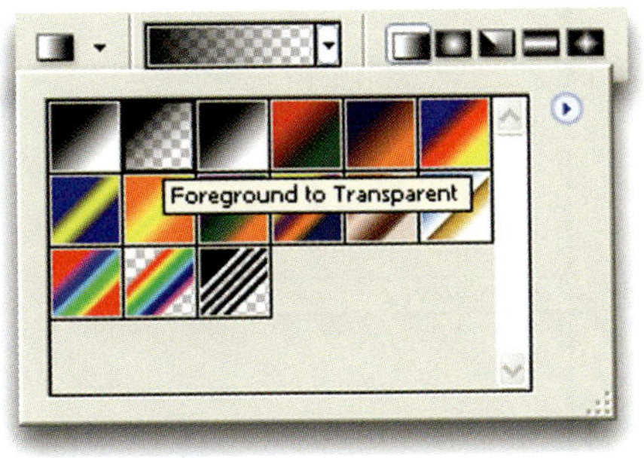

(i)

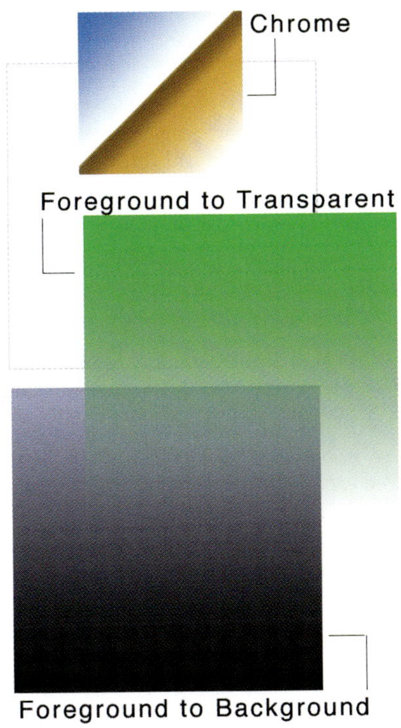

(ii)

◆ **5-10 [i–ii]** *How to access various gradient choices.*

When you have finished your artwork, flattening the layers in your file merges them into a single layer, greatly reducing the file size. This option is found in the Layers window under the top right arrowhead. Don't flatten the image until you are finished, and be sure to save a version with all layers intact, in case you want to return to make changes.

Masking is a powerful technique available in many computer graphics programs. A mask lets you isolate and reserve parts of the image. A selection is a type of mask. When you create a mask from a selection, the area not selected is protected from editing, as discussed in Chapter 3. Photoshop is an excellent place to begin to understand the concepts and techniques of masking, which will carry over to many other applications. In Photoshop you can make a temporary mask in Quick Mask or a permanent mask that is stored in Channels (see the following More How To Basics).

The simplest mask is *Quick Mask,* which is accessed at the bottom of the toolbox. Figure 5-10j shows this process. It allows you to improve your selection of complex objects by adding to or subtracting from them with the painting and drawing tool. Begin by making the best selection possible using the toolbox items such as the magic wand. Keeping that selection active, switch to Quick Mask to begin to fine-tune your selection. Your work area will turn orange-toned. Painting in white and black while in Quick Mask will add to and subtract from the mask. Switch back to standard mode to view the results. Black decreases the selected area by adding to

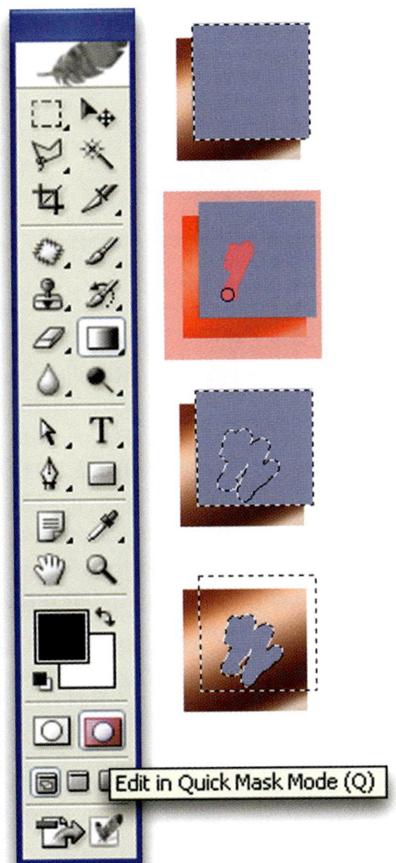

(j)

◆ **5-10 [j]** *Introducing quick mask and layer masking.*

the mask, while painting with white adds to the selected area by subtracting from the mask. Switching in and out of Quick Mask to the standard mode lets you continue to preview and alter the new selection. The final selection can be manipulated however desired. Remember this new, more complex selection can be saved for later use in Select>Save Selection. At any time, you can re-create your selection by choosing Select>Load Selection. The mask (called an alpha channel mask) can be seen by selecting the channels palette in Window>Show Channels. We'll cover channels soon, but it is possible to work successfully by avoiding channels and just thinking in terms of selections.

Layer masks are very powerful and flexible. They are the best way to subtly combine two images. The icons at the bottom of the layer window include one for "add layer mask." This mask will appear on the selected layer. Figure 5-10k shows a masking effect of painting in black on the layer mask that accompanies

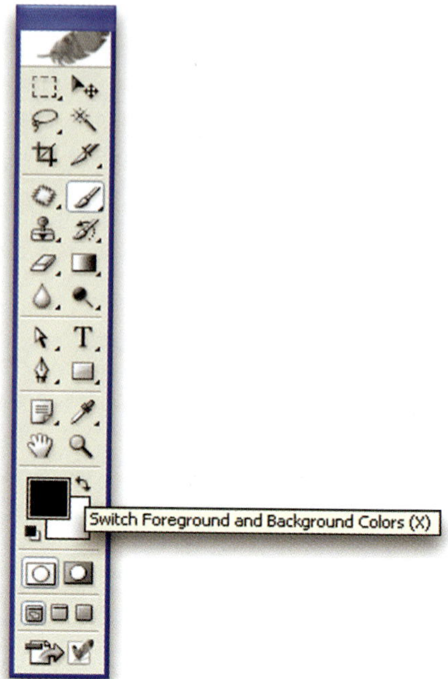

(b)

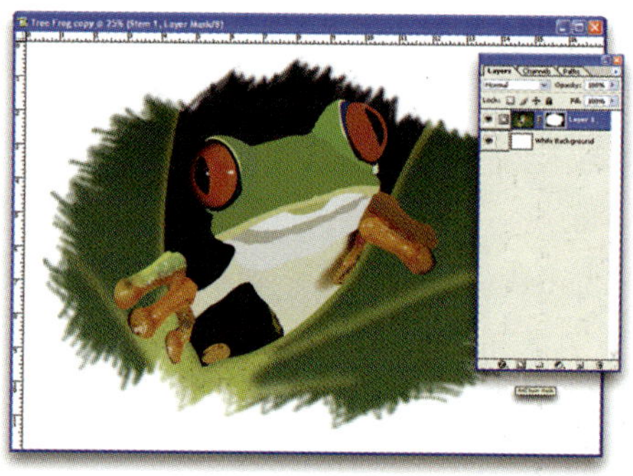

(k)

◆ **5-10k** *Applying a layer mask.*

the tree frog illustration. The white background shows through. Clicking on the layer mask will allow you to draw on the mask in black, white, or gray, while clicking on the original layer icon beside it allows you to continue to draw directly on the layer (**Fig. 5-11a**). Think of drawing on the mask as punching a hole in the mask to see through with any black brush you use. White on your brush will cover over the hole. Switching back and forth between black and white on your pen/mouse allows for adding and subtracting visibility of the image underneath (**Fig. 5-11b**). Black and white *shapes* have the same effect, as long as they are applied to the mask. And using a black and white gradient allows the image under the mask to gradually appear as black gradually changes to white (**Fig. 5-11c**). The image in **Figure 5-12** was created using three same-size faces and layering them over one another on three separate layers. Layer masks were applied to each. Masking with varying opacities of black allowed each face to partially show through, making for a very well crafted final combination of one male and two females from three ethnic groups. If you're overwhelmed when you finish studying masking, skip the advanced How To Basics on channels and integrating raster and vector images.

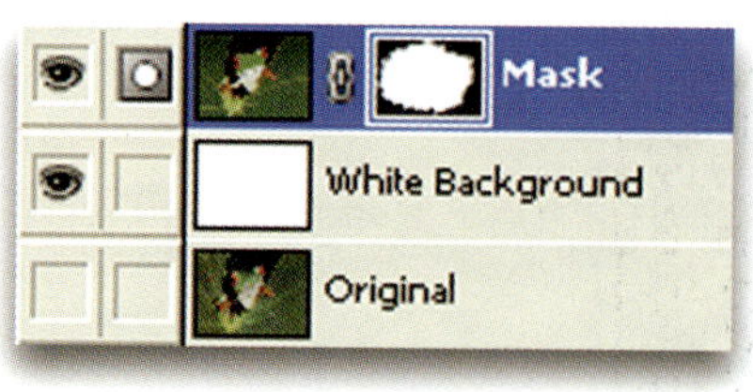

a–c: Adobe product screen shot(s) reprinted with permission from Adobe Systems Incorporated

(a)

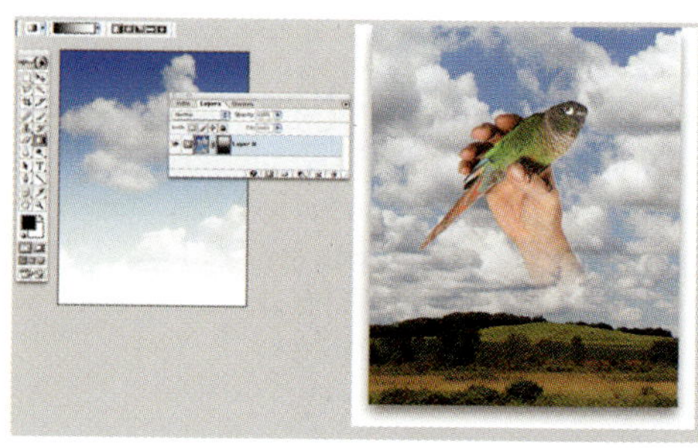

(c)

◆ **5-11 [a–c]** *These three images show the process of working with gradient masking.*

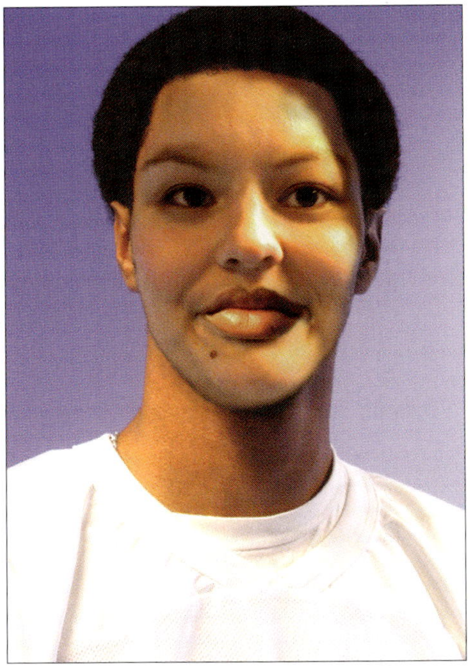

◆ **5-12** *Tiffany Dorner-Jones.* Composite Portrait. *2003. Digital inkjet print. 17" × 11".*
Courtesy of the artist.

Photoshop masking was used to make this individual face from three separate digital portraits.

More How To Basics

We'll take a brief look at *channels* in **Figures 5-13a–b**. **Channels** contain an image's color and selection information. They are located in Window>Show Channels and are usually in the same pop up window as layers. Just click on the tab to bring them to the

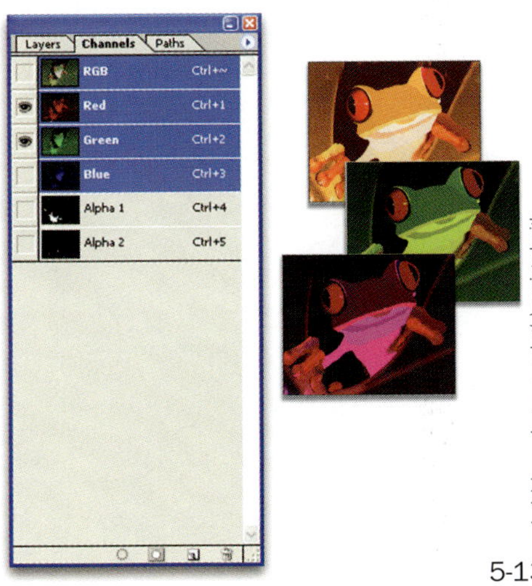

a–b: Adobe product screen shot(s) reprinted with permission from Adobe Systems Incorporated

5-13(a)

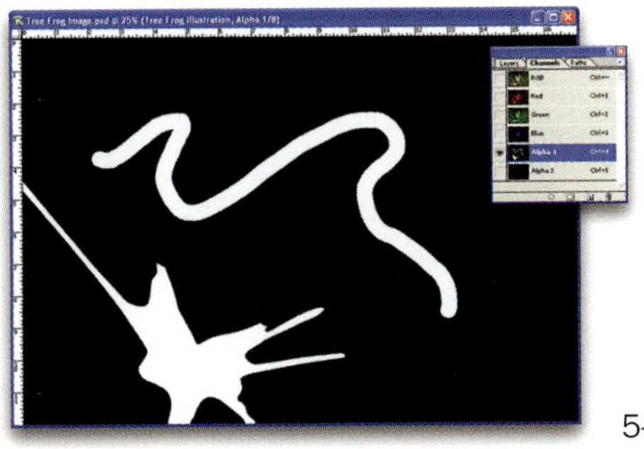

5-13(b)

◆ **5-13 [a–b]** *Channels will show your masks as well as the separate colors that comprise your image.*

foreground. You'll see that the color information channels for your image are there. Open a full-color photograph and look at its channels. Experiment with turning the eye icons on and off to show and hide various channels, as shown in Figure 5-13a.

Alpha channels contain the masks you make and save. These masks can be edited like quick masks. Turn off the eye icon on all channels except the alpha channel you want to edit. Select that channel in the Channel window. Now draw on the image to edit the mask (Fig. 5-13b). Turn all the eye icons back on and return to Layers to view the effect. As you can see, there is a lot of creative imaging potential in masking techniques.

Now let's take a look at *Integrating Raster and Vector*. Integration is possible by moving files back and forth between Photoshop and Illustrator. Combining artwork between applications makes it easy to combine precise vector line art with rasterized paintings and photographs. When you create a precise drawing in Illustrator, you can use the Photoshop Place or Paste command to put it into an existing Photoshop file, as shown in **Figure 5-14a**. Photoshop will rasterize it. If you use the Place command, any resizing you do keeps the graphic as vector until you press Enter (Windows) or Return (Mac OS). If you use a cut-and-paste command to transfer the image, it comes in at the size it was in Illustrator, and rasterized. It is also possible to go the other way and transfer a Photoshop file into

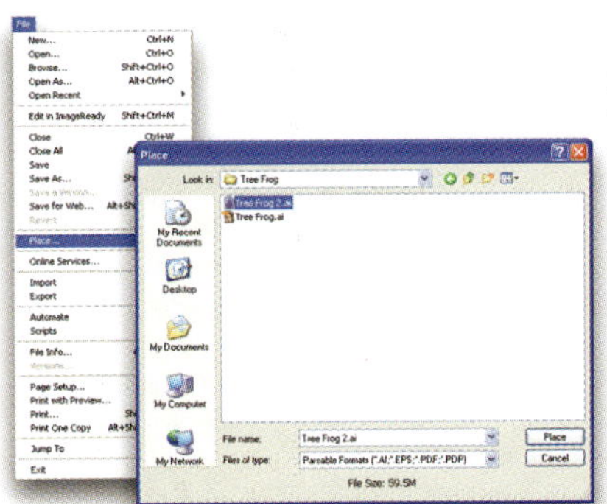

a–b: Adobe product screen shot(s) reprinted with permission from Adobe Systems Incorporated

5-14(a)

◆ **5-14 [a–b]** *Placing documents between Photoshop and Illustrator.*

Illustrator. In Illustrator, simply File>Place and navigate to the Photoshop file and select it (**Fig. 5-14b**). Or use the cut-and-paste function.

The Student Portfolio Profile on the **CD** describes Jorel Tingesdahl's technique for creatively integrating both programs to create his portrait series of American artists in **Figures 5-15a–c**.

Experiment with the many techniques discussed in this section. Several students might each be given a specific process in Photoshop to explain and demonstrate to the class. Working with an assigned partner is also a good idea.

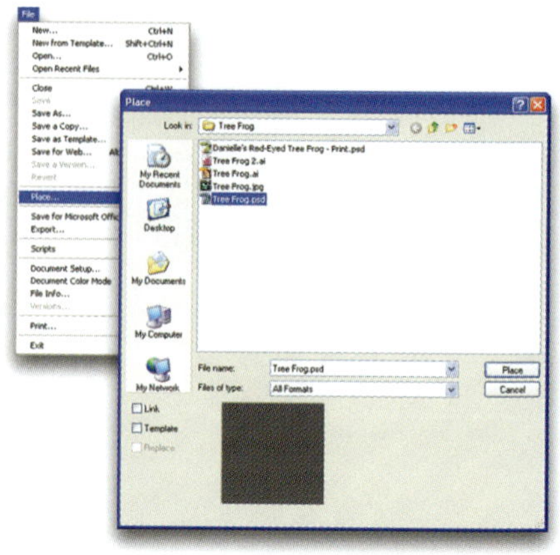

5-14(b)

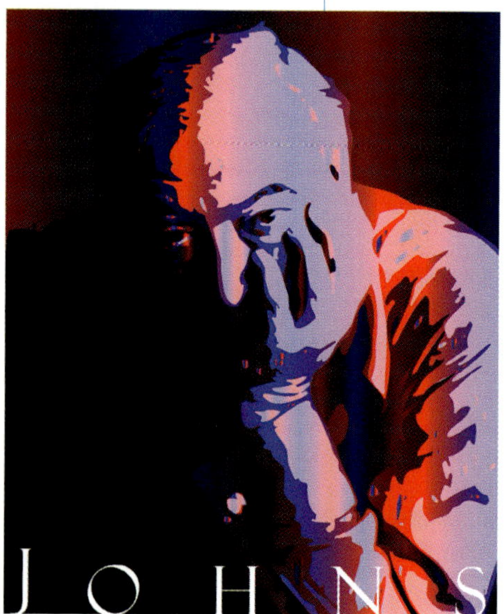

(a)

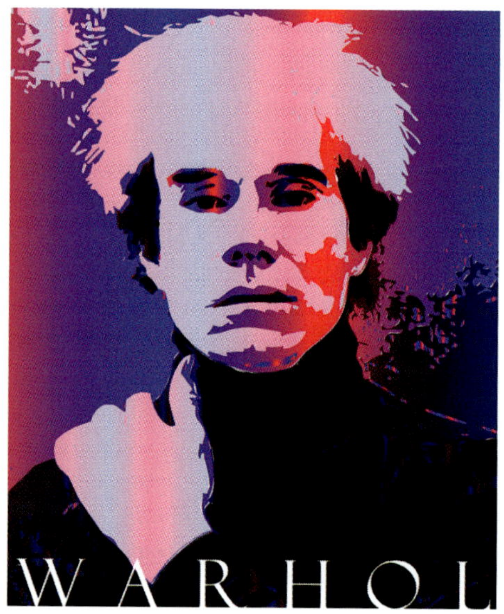

(b)

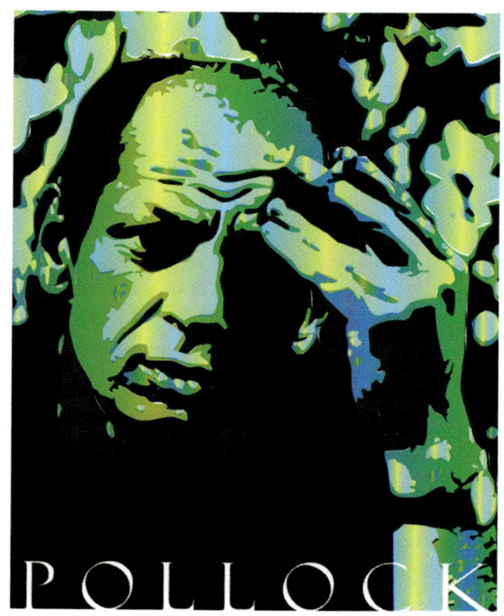

(c)

5-15 [a–c]
Jorel Tingesdahl. Artist Portrait Series. *2004. Digital inkjet on paper. $11'' \times 8\frac{1}{2}''$.*
Courtesy of the artist.

Integrated Photoshop and Illustrator techniques described in the accompanying CD were used to create these digital images.

Hands On Practice

As in the previous chapters, this is your opportunity to practice the techniques introduced in the previous How To Basics sections.

Many wonderful things that are difficult to create with traditional methods are possible with the computer. Combining methods also offers good possibilities. Scanning a small original watercolor created the image in **Figure 5-16**. The file was then run through filters to create a textured background. A Quick Mask creates the "hole" for the face to show through.

1. Create an image (with two or more layers) that uses masking to let one image show through another. Do two or three of these.

2. Now create an image with two or more layers that uses a gradient layer mask. The gradient mask should go from black to white.

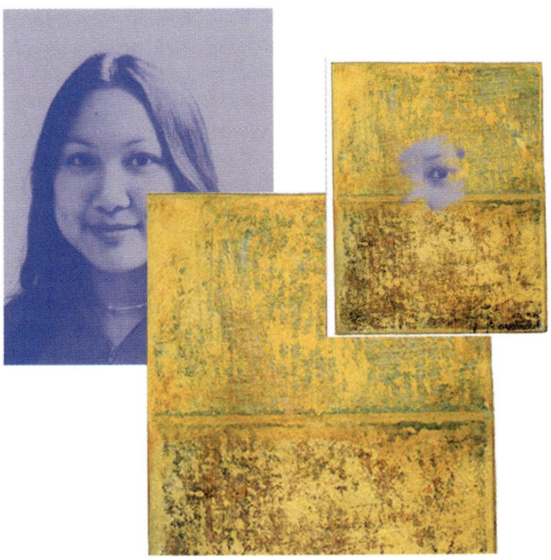

◆ **5-16** *The top layer is painted on in Photoshop's Quick Mask mode to generate the effect of an eye peering through an opening.*

Concept Development

As you begin using your techniques to work on more advanced studio projects, it is a good time to discuss how ideas are developed. The more freedom you have to determine the direction of your art and design work, the more important good skills at concept development become. Consider the message and the audience before beginning a series of **thumbnail** sketches. If this is for a client, you may need to research a product or read a manuscript. Your sketches can be on or off the computer, but are probably more creative if done by hand. They are the brainstorming effort where ideas come alive. The more you push yourself to think of new thumbnails, the stronger your brain muscles become. The word *thumbnail* comes from the fact that these sketches are usually very small and very rough.

The next stage is traditionally called a **rough**. In this step, you refine and upgrade your best thumbnail concepts. Select your best two or three concepts for development after researching available visual references and related materials. This is where you'll need to consider budget, if applicable. In digital design work, the rough stage is completed on the computer.

The finished artwork is completed after a class critique or a client presentation of the roughs. You'll notice that the Studio work in this book usually asks for multiple solutions. As a designer or an illustrator, you'll always need to present multiple solutions for consideration. As a fine artist, it's just good sense to push yourself into thinking in more directions than one. **Figure 5-17a** shows different stages of concept development.

◆ **5-17a** *The four stages of creating a design.*

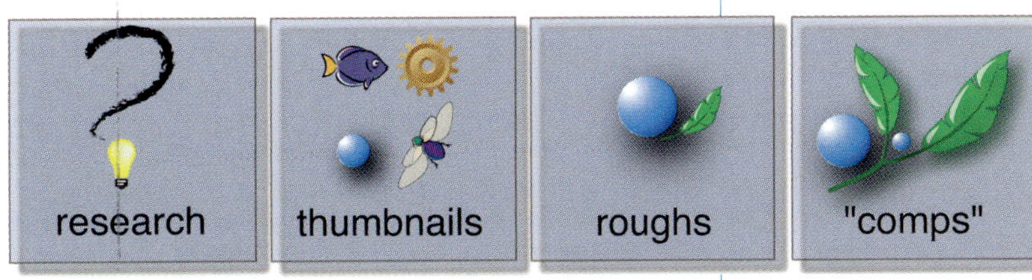

(a)

a–b: Adobe product screen shots reprinted with permission from Adobe Systems Incorporated

One way to approach an idea is to consider **semiotics**. This theory of symbols and signs explores how people derive meaning from words, sounds, and pictures. A basic premise of the study of semiotics is that all things can be classified in one of two ways: the thing itself (signified) or the reference to the thing (signifier). The physical object exists in the real world. Our references to the physical object as artists and designers may be words, photographs, symbols, diagrams, and so on. Four types of signifiers are shown in **Figure 5-17b**. Analyze your subject from the point of view of creating an icon, a symbol, and an index. An icon is the image of the thing. A symbol shows cultural associations

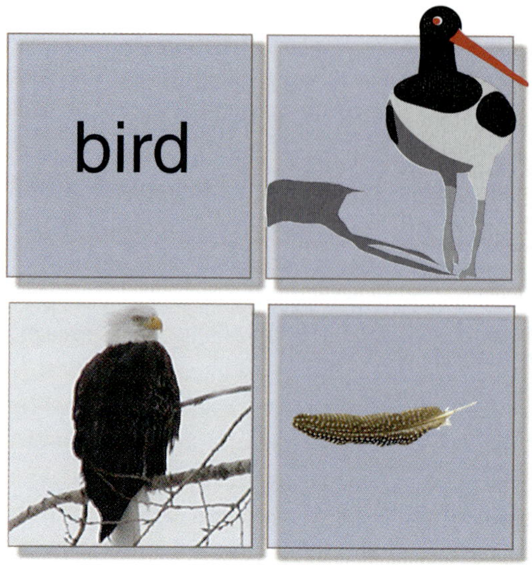

5-17b *Semiotics is a theory of symbols and signs that explores how people derive meaning from words, sounds, and pictures.*

with the thing. An index indicates the presence of the thing. This approach can lead to the creation of visual **metaphors**.

For example, how would you illustrate America? Let's say your choice of an icon or image is a field of wheat in the Midwest. Perhaps your choice of a symbol is an eagle. Your choice of an index indicating the presence of a thing is the shadow of an eagle over the field of wheat. As an illustrator addressing the problem of urban sprawl in America, you might place the shadow of buildings over a field of wheat. These are straightforward examples, but the approach can lead to rich conceptual solutions. The next Warming Up assignment encourages you to use your design skills and to develop your conceptual skills using photography.

Warming Up

Shoot the following series of photographs that are related to the preceding discussion of semiotics and also strongly related to the design principles we have studied thus far (see the instructions in steps a, b, c, and d below). This exercise asks you to be thoughtful about your subject and to pay careful attention to composition. If you do not have a digital camera or a film-based camera available, locate photographs, then scan and crop them electronically to achieve the effects listed below. This exercise will enhance your eye for design details and metaphorical storytelling.

a. Create an abstract photograph that looks primarily at color and shape, as shown in **Figure 5-18**.

b. Create a photograph in which figure and ground can be reversed, as shown in **Figures 5-19a–b**.

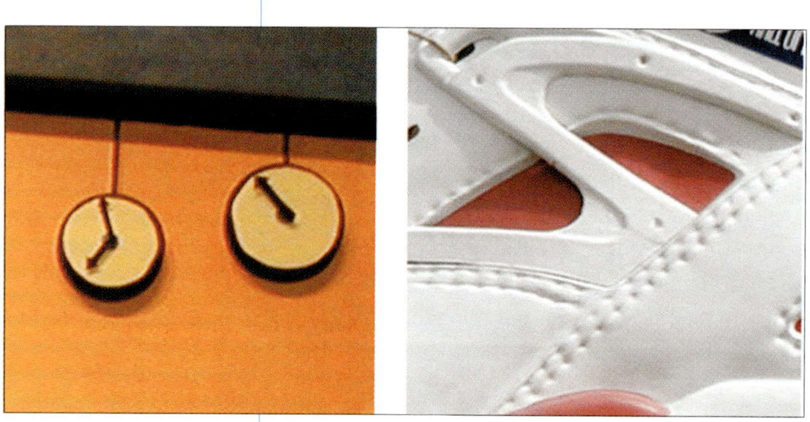

5-18 *Julie LaBelle.* Abstract Photograph. *2003. Digital inkjet print.*
Courtesy of the artist.

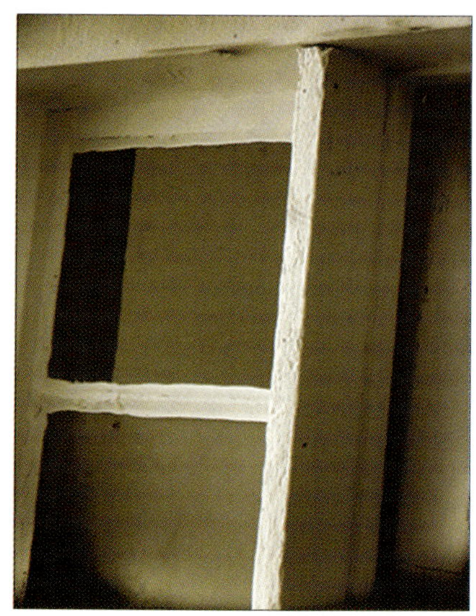

5-19a *Julie LaBelle.* Window. *2003. Digital inkjet print.*
Courtesy of the artist.

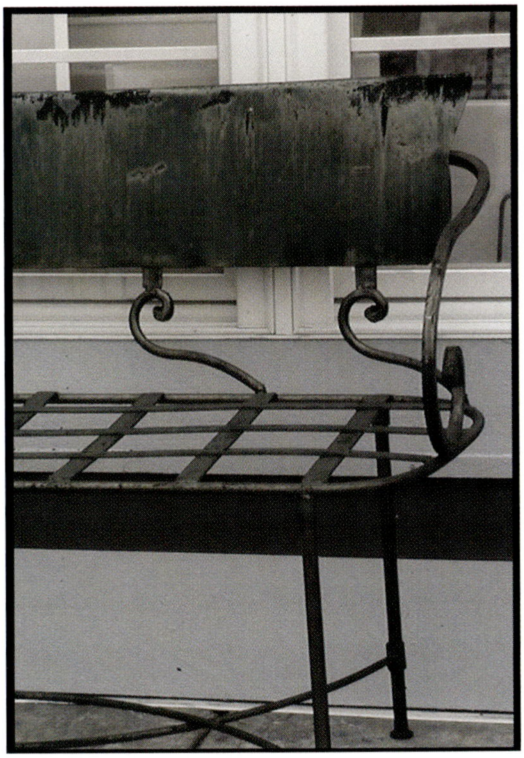

◆ **5-19b** *Julie LaBelle.* Park Bench. *2003. Digital inkjet print.*

Courtesy of the artist.

c. A photograph that is primarily about texture. **Figure 5-20** is an example.

d. A photograph that indicates the presence of something that isn't in the picture plane. **Figure 5-21** hints at but does not divulge such a presence.

Now choose your best two or three photographs and create duotones or tritones of them. Present them together as a diptych or triptych. Reference Chapter 4 for color techniques.

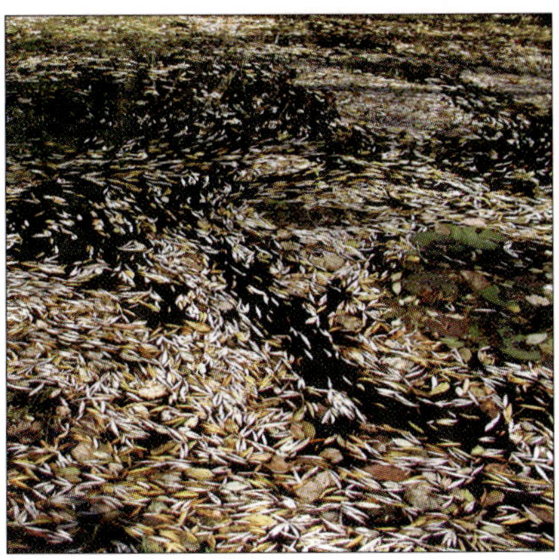

◆ **5-20** *Texture dominates this photograph.*

Visual Perception

Artwork can be unified both visually and intellectually. A visual unity occurs when design elements such as various forms of repetition, continuation, and color theme tie one piece together, or when these elements help to unite several pieces in a series. Visual unity is revealed through *looking* at the design.

Intellectual unity, on the other hand, is based on *thinking* about the subject matter and the underlying concept. The intellectual concept might be displaying the seasons by showing the fruit that grows. The visual concept might be showing that fruit in a close-up, framed by greatly enlarged duotone texture derived from the fruit skin. Figure 5-26 (see page 128) is a series of twelve digital calendar images created by Tiffany Dorner-Jones that is integrated both intellectually and visually. Her chosen subjects of flowers, insects, and snowflakes tell about the passing seasons, while her close-up visual treatment emphasizes the beauty of their design. This artwork was started as a drawing in Illustrator and placed into Painter for color and texture.

The finest artwork is achieved when both intellectual and visual unity support one another to make a final statement. Consider this when working on the Studio projects in this chapter.

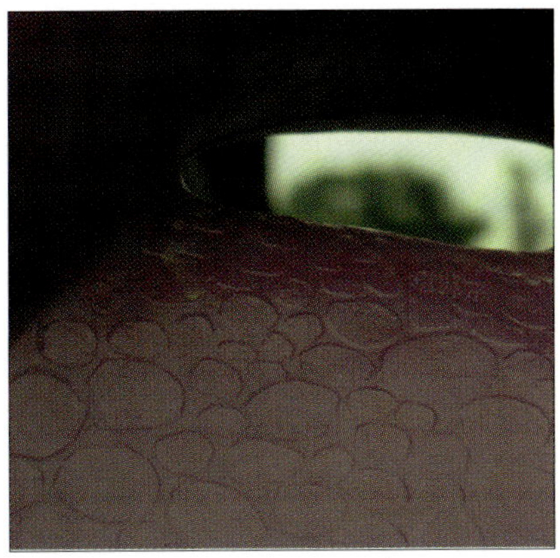

◆ **5-21** *Julie LaBelle.* Presence. *2003. Digital inkjet print.*

Courtesy of the artist.

An unseen presence is suggested in this mysterious photograph.

In The Studio

After forming groups of three, students should shoot portraits of their group's members. If you are using a digital camera, open the photos directly in Photoshop. If you are using a film camera, process the film and scan the prints. Be sure to end up with a file that is at least 150 pixels per inch (ppi) on the monitor. See Chapter 3 for a refresher on how to bring a digital 72-dpi image up to 150dpi. With older digital cameras, you'll need to shoot your digital image at a large physical size at 72 dpi and then on the computer bring the dpi to 150 by reducing the physical size of the file.

Use masking techniques to combine the portraits of the three group members into one image. Try for a smooth, believable effect, or for a collaged look, that makes good use of masking techniques. This project calls for some excellent photo retouching skills and is really fun to create. See Figure 5-12 (page 113) for a student solution to this problem. Compare the three different results in your group.

An alternate assignment asks you to create a diptych or triptych dreamscape that includes one or more photos of yourself, as in Figure 5-8 (see page 107). Remember to use continuation and repetition to tie the separate parts together. Consider the color scheme of each panel, and how to use repetition and variation with color. Be sure to incorporate masking effects.

SUMMARY CRITIQUE

Use this critique on both your Warming Up and the In The Studio creations. Do repetition and variation tie the separate parts of your artwork together? Discuss how you repeat and vary the elements of line, texture, color, and shape. The figure/ground relationship is always important. How have you considered and chosen between stable, reversible, or ambiguous effects? How is continuation used throughout the compositions to tie the elements together? The overall Gestalt of your composition is created by consideration of these principles of repetition and variation, figure/ground usage, and continuation. What was your creative intent? How have you chosen to emphasize the tools and techniques or the personal content? If you selected the dreamscape, describe the narrative elements. Describe how you used masking to achieve your effects and what other techniques you employed. What is the best work you've completed in this chapter? Consider and discuss when sometimes a seemingly simple solution is the best one.

Look at the diptychs and triptychs shown in the chapter. Did they use a unifying technique that would help your work?

Focus On Concept

This chapter presents a variety of excellent images in fine art and computer graphics. It introduces techniques in Photoshop and Painter that can create effects similar to chemical- and pigment-based artwork. What are the similarities and differences between the time-honored traditional studio methods and the newer computer graphics? Think about the kind of time spent creating the image, and where you work, and in what surroundings. In what conditions are they viewed?

Digital design can simulate many techniques in drawing, painting, and photography. What is unique to the new medium? Think about how it is displayed, shared, stored, and structured. Consider its potential for interactivity.

MOVING ON

You may be ready to stop here and take a break until next week (or next month!). If you've been learning both Photoshop and Illustrator, your instructor may elect to skip introducing another raster program at this point. However, the next raster program we'll study is delightful! Next in this chapter we'll look at a program with an emphasis on painterly techniques. The design principles of repetition, variation, figure/ground, and continuation still apply, no matter what the software package. Your eye for color is also vital whatever the application. As you continue to learn new software applications, remember to apply design and color principles.

Creative Imaging in Painter

Corel Painter is an excellent raster graphics program that has an amazingly rich array of painterly techniques to explore. Artists and illustrators prize this program because it successfully mimics a vast array of traditional tools, from pen and ink to scratch board and from chalk to oil paint. While it also incorporates vector files this is a true artist's medium, capable of making a wide array of textured marks (**Fig. 5-22a**). **Figure 5-22b** shows a snapshot of the Painter desktop

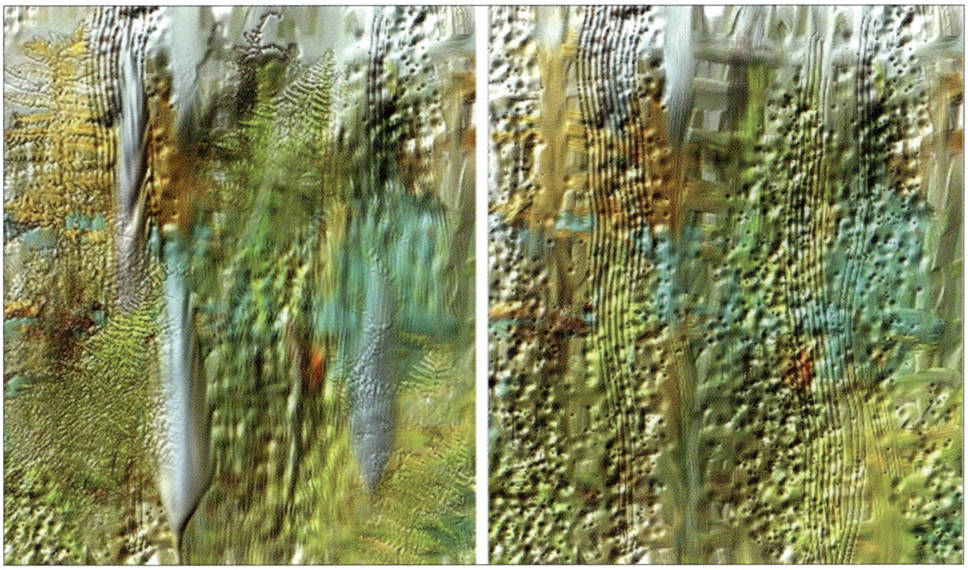

(a)

5-22a *Amy E. Arntson.* Painterly. *2004. Iris print on paper. 7" × 5".*

Painter's brushes are capable of simulating an array of traditional media.

5-22b *The Painter desktop. Illustration by Tammy Roemer and Chris Eichman.*

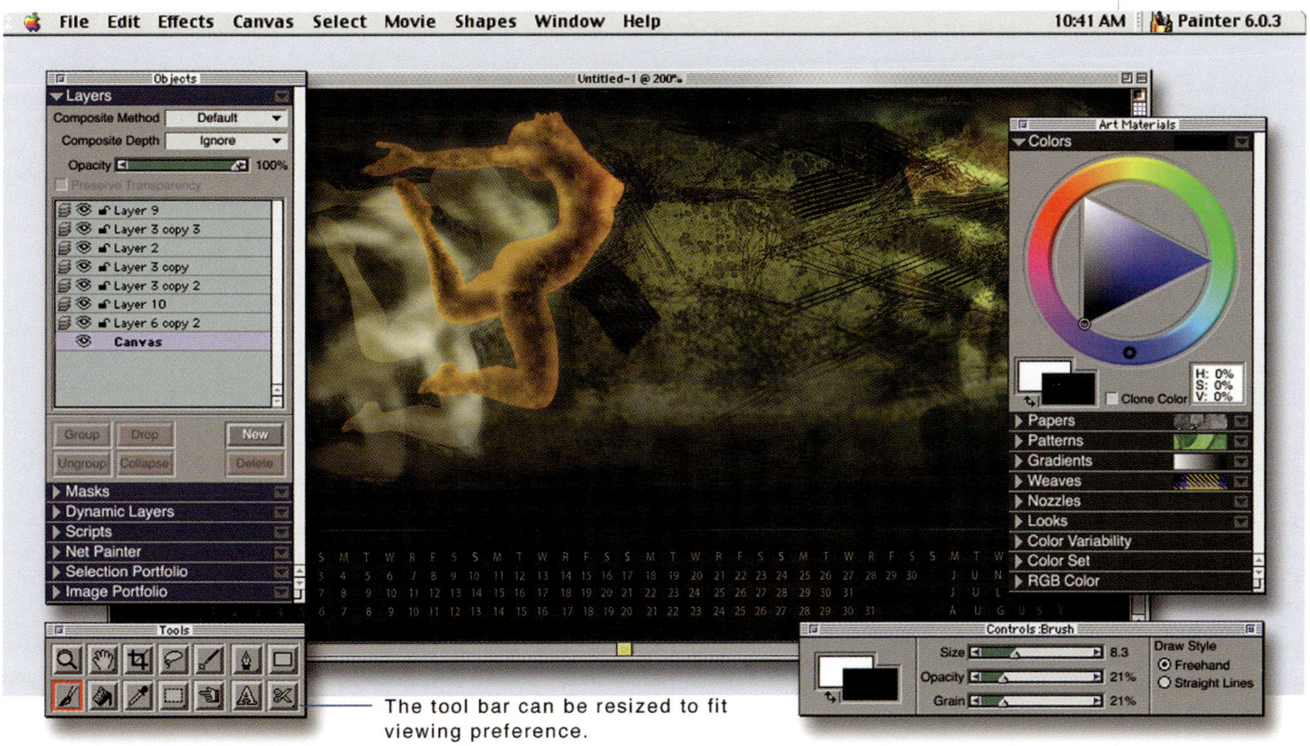

(b)

Corel Painter

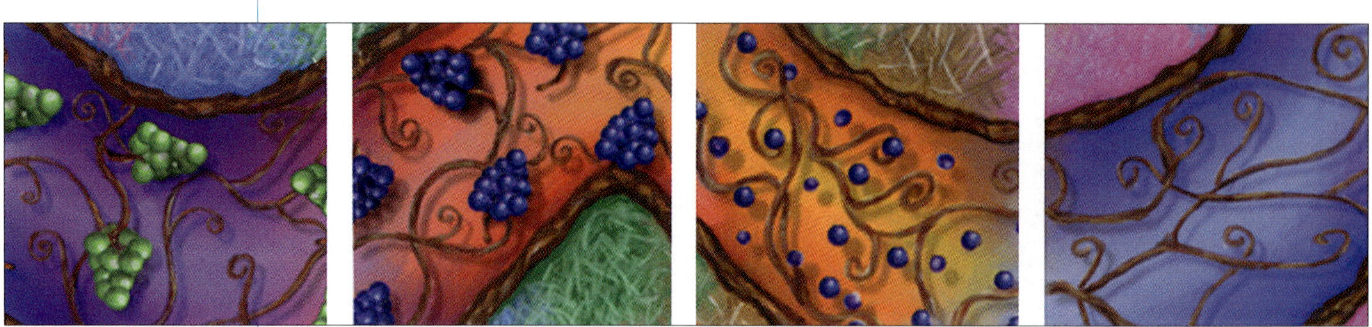

◆ **5-23** *Tammy Roemer.* Wine Calendar. *2003. Created in Painter.* Courtesy of the artist.

This series of four squares is united by intellectual theme as well as by color, stylistic treatment, and the continued lines that flow through all sections.

and a close-up of its toolbox. **Figure 5-23**, created by Tammy Roemer, shows artwork for a wine poster created in Painter, using its many brush and painterly effects. This chapter's instructions and illustrations are based on Corel Painter IV. If you have an older version, things may be in slightly different locations.

The layers, menu pull downs, and many of the toolbox icons work in a fashion similar to those in Photoshop. However, Painter utilizes a graphics tablet and pen to allow you to fully explore its wide array of pressure-sensitive tools. An excellent user guide, help menu, and online training come packaged with the program. This chapter will present an overall introduction to Painter basics, giving you an opportunity to recognize the potential of this complex program. Try it—you'll love it.

How To Basics

Figures 5-24a–w show a step-by-step introduction to Painter software. Study them for later application in the Hands On Practice section.

The *native file* for Painter is RIFF, although the program accepts nearly everything. Open your new file as an image, not a movie (you can do that later). The *File>New command* creates a blank document based on the size and resolution you specify in its dialog box (Fig. 5-24a). You'll also need to specify Picture Type for a single image or multiple frames for a movie. Save your file as a RIFF to retain all the Painter layer information. Do not check the Uncompress box so that your file will be saved in a lossless compression, which saves memory as you work on the document. As your final step, save it uncompressed for print when the file is completed. You can work with it in other programs such as Photoshop by saving a copy

◆ **5-24 [a–b]** *Opening a new Painter file.*

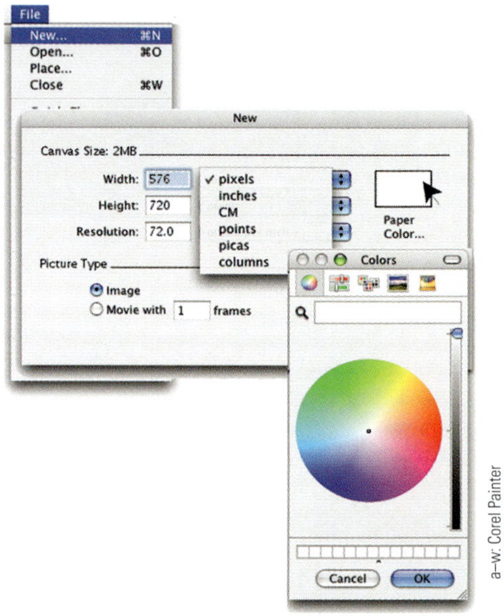

(a)

in an appropriate file format. Painter files can be saved in the Photoshop PSD format as well as in TIFF, PICT, JPEG, GIF, and EPS PC formats and as movie framestacks exported as a QuickTime or AVI/VFW (PC) movie. Painter will open TIFF files, but layered files saved in the Photoshop format must be converted to RGB before being opened in Painter. (Painter prefers to open RGB files.) Painter preserves Photoshop layers, but layer effects must be flattened before they are placed in Painter.

To *open an existing document* choose File>Open (Mac OS) or Select Image (Windows). Navigate to the document you want and click Open. To place a file into an existing Corel Painter document choose File> Place. Then select an image file and click Open. The Place dialog box lets you set options for scaling. To place the image in the center of the document, click OK, or click on a location anywhere in the document.

Much of the *toolbox* is familiar to Photoshop users. Figure 5-24b shows the toolbox with the selection tools revealed. The Zoom tool enlarges or reduces the document. A double click on the Grabber tool will

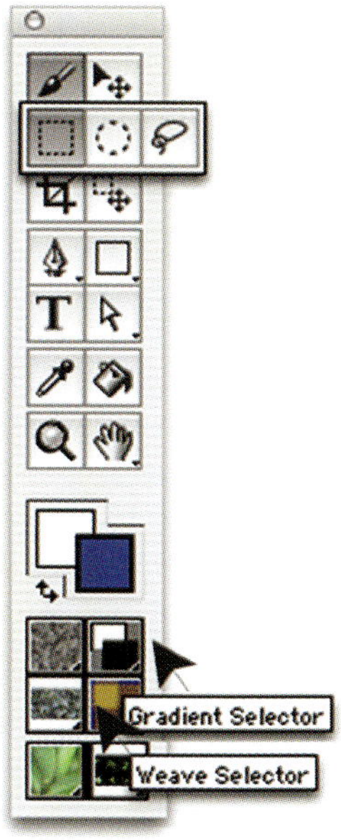

(b)

make your document fit the screen size. The Rotate Page tool lets the user move the cursor to position the image at a new rotation angle. The Crop tool allows you to draw a rectangle around the area you want to keep, while clicking inside the rectangle executes the crop. Holding down the Shift key keeps the rectangle square. The bottom six icons allow access to special effects such as gradients and weaves.

The *Canvas* is the original document window. Choose Window>Canvas>Resize to enter new values for width, height, or resolution. Canvas>Canvas Size lets you specify the number of pixels to add to any side of the canvas.

Preferences allows the user to customize the Painter environment. You might want to read about that in the User Guide if you'll be spending a lot of time in this program. For now we'll assume you'll use the default preferences. However, you may want to set Brush Tracking for the graphics tablet and pen. Choose Preferences>Brush Tracking and drag in the scratch pad in a normal stroke to establish your personal drawing touch.

Layers are accessed in Window>Show Layers. Click the right triangle or arrowhead for a pop up menu of choices (Fig. 5-24c). Most of these are obvious. Drop will flatten the layers, while Group links all selected layers. To apply an effect to a layer, select it by clicking on it in the layers window with the Layer Adjuster tool (the arrow in the top right of the toolbox). As in Photoshop, the bottom of the layers window contains several command icons. Layers can contain either pixel-based or vector-based images. How you work with a layer depends on the type of data it contains.

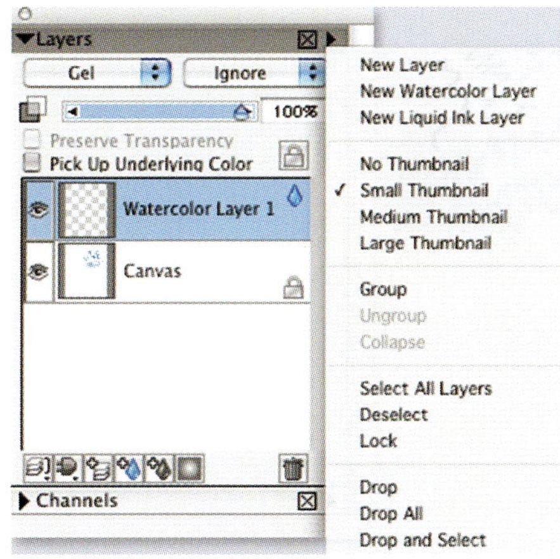

(c)

Pen tool creations and Shapes are vector-based objects. Each shape you create becomes a separate layer. You must convert the shape layer to a pixel-based layer to use raster tools such as a paintbrush or gradation (Fig. 5-24d). As you see, you can also convert to a selection in this window. Shapes can also be selected with the shape selection tool and converted to a selection using the property bar (Fig 5-24e). The property bar contains a great deal of useful information and commands related to the current tool. It's a good window to keep open along with the toolbox. To acquire vector shapes from Adobe Illustrator, in Corel Painter, choose File>Acquire>Adobe Illustrator File. In the

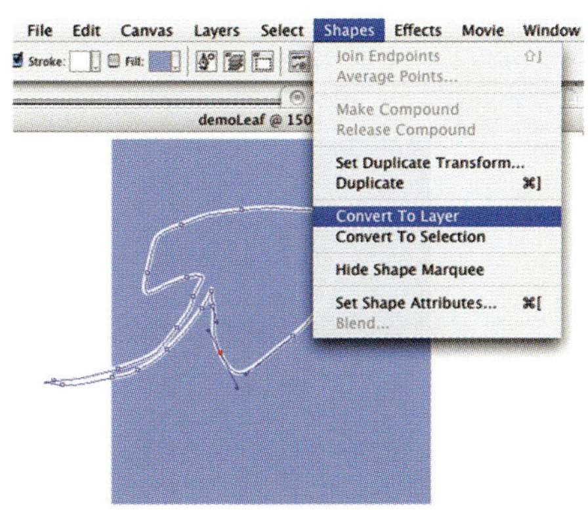

(d)

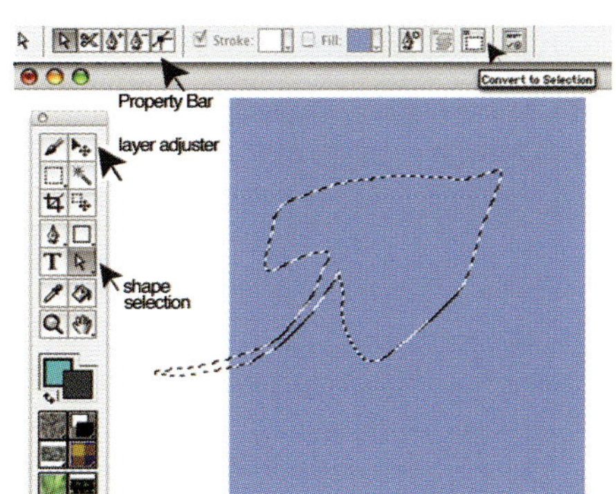

(e)

5-24 [c–f] *Using shape-based and raster layers.*

Adobe Illustrator File dialog box, select the Adobe Illustrator file and click Open Painter.

Specialized types of layers such as Watercolor layers, Liquid Ink layers, and Dynamic layers must be converted to default layers to apply all the Painter features. To do this, select the layer to convert in the layers window and click the upper right arrowhead, then choose Convert to Default Layer. Painter has many types of layers.

With the *Layer Adjuster tool* (black arrow in the top right of the toolbox) you can cut, copy, paste, reposition, and duplicate layers. To create a new layer based on a selection on a pixel-based layer, click the selection with the Layer Adjuster tool. See Figure 5-24e again. To change a layer's position in the hierarchy choose the layer adjuster tool in the toolbox. In the layers window select the layer you want to move and drag it to a new position. To move selected images on a layer, you must "float" the selection by clicking on it before dragging the floating object to a new location with the Layer Adjuster tool. Choose Drop in the layers window to merge the floating object back with the layer.

Unlike in other programs, Painter's layers are only as large as the image on them. Choose Show Layer Indicators on the Layers palette to display markers at the corners of a selected layer. You can choose to preserve Layer Transparency in the Layers palette (Fig. 5-24f). Then only the image can be drawn on, leaving the area outside it uneditable. Think of this as a layer mask. You can use it to fill a shape with patterns, gradients, and so forth. Disable Preserve Transparency restores transparency to the area and allows you to draw on it again. If you can't get a brush to paint, see if Preserve Transparency is selected.

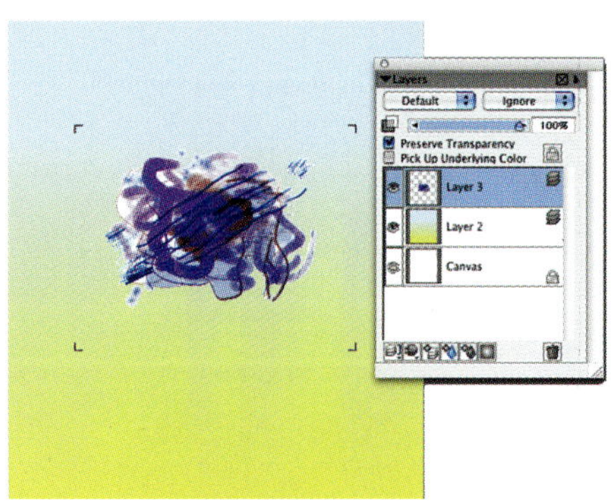

(f)

Painter has many *palette windows*. They are easily docked and grouped together or separated. Click on a window title bar and pull it toward or away from other windows to relocate it. In fact, the many windows and options in this program may confuse you. Plan to close any windows that you don't need.

Colors palette is a window that you will use constantly. It gives excellent control of color choices. To display the Colors palette choose Window>Color Palettes>Show Colors. It is displayed as a Hue Ring and a Saturation/Value Triangle. Choose your color in the hue ring and its value and saturation in the interior triangle. See the top of Figure 5-24g. The selected color appears in one of two overlapping squares displayed on the Colors palette. The front square is the main color, while the back square shows an additional color. In Painter, the "background" color is the paper color, not the second square in the Colors palette. Set the paper color by choosing Canvas>Set Paper Color. Beside the two color squares in the Colors palette is the clone color icon to be used when you want to duplicate color from a clone source.

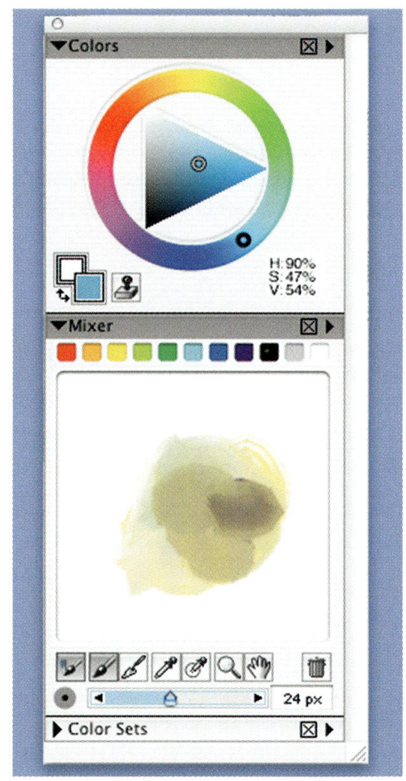

(g)

5-24g *The Colors palette and Mixer palette.*

Color can be selected in several ways. You can use the Colors window palette or the mixer palette shown at the bottom of Figure 5-24g to create your own color. The Dropper tool from the toolbox samples individual colors from an image. Clicking on a current color square in the Colors palette pops open a Colors window, as you are familiar with in other programs.

The Mixer palette works similar to mixing colors on an artist's palette. Colors can be created, saved, loaded, and reset on the Mixer palette. To display the Mixer palette choose Window>Color Palettes>Show

Mixer. The tools on the Mixer palette are used to apply, mix, sample, and clear color on the Mixer pad. The Apply Color Tool acts as a loaded paint source to apply color, while the Mix Color tool mixes colors already on the pad. See Figure 5-24g again. If you wish, use the palette menu arrowhead to choose Save Mixer Colors. Select Load Mixer Colors to retrieve them. To use a mixed color, click the Sample Color tool on the Mixer palette and select the color you want to become the main color in your image. Try creating colors on this palette using an Artists' Oils brush for rich results.

Selections are made using the rectangle selection tool, magic wand, or lasso tool, as shown in Figure 5-24h. Holding down the shift key can combine each selection with others. A selection can be cut and pasted and assigned special effects. Click the icon in the lower left corner of the image window to choose how to work with a selection. Your choices are to draw anywhere, draw only outside the selection, and draw only inside the selection (Fig. 5-24i). As in Photoshop, selections can be saved and reloaded. There are options for whether individual selections should be combined with others or kept separate, as shown in the pop up window in Figure 5-24j.

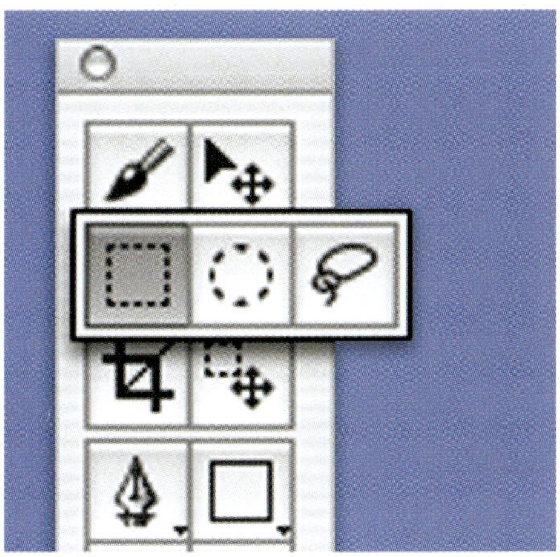

(h)

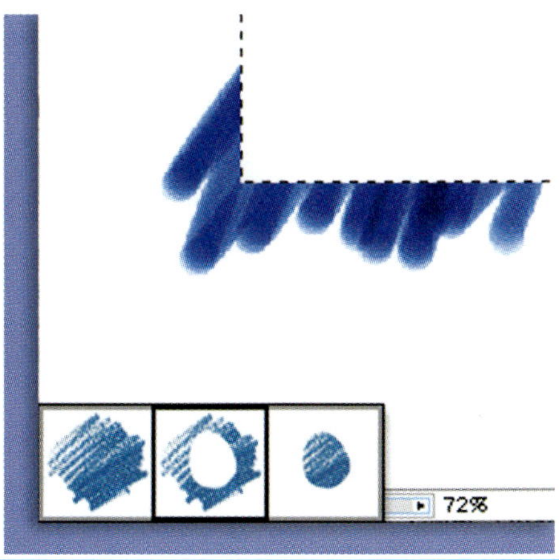

(i)

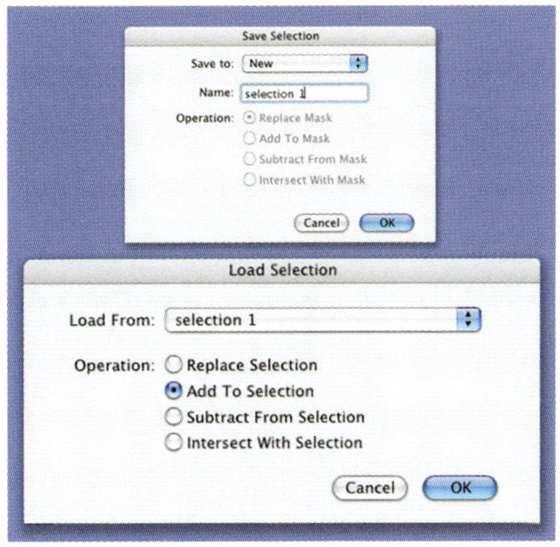

(j)

The *brushes* are wonderfully diverse. The best way to begin to experiment with Painter and understand what it has to offer is to explore the brushes. Click and draw with the various options, exploring the beauty of their sensitive and varied applications. Do not try to make an image, just try to make beautiful marks. Figure 5-24k shows some of the expressive qualities that are possible, especially when using the pressure-sensitive graphics tablet and pen. Window>Brush Control gives options for fine-tuning each brush selected (Fig. 5-24l). The Window>Show Brush Selector Bar is turned on in the upper right. It is the easiest way to choose brushes.

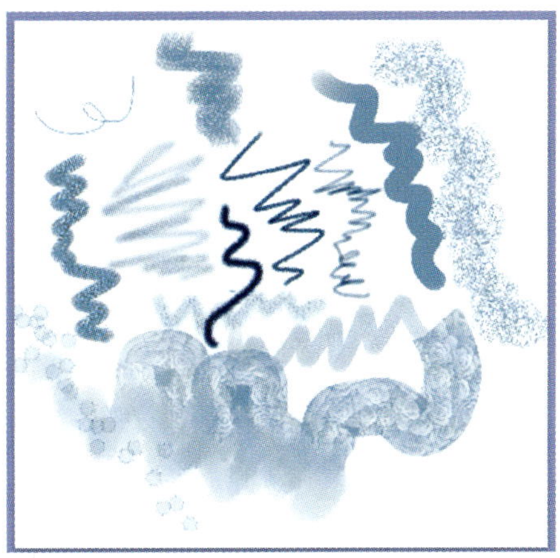

(k)

The Brush tool is organized into many categories such as Artists' Oils, Colored Pencils, Watercolor, and so forth. Figure 5-24m shows the Brush Selector bar with Brush Categories revealed and Watercolor selected. Each brush category has several related variants that are also accessed from this bar. For example, the Watercolor Brush category allows you to select a runny wet camel brush, a simple round wash brush, or a splatter water variant. Figure 5-24n shows watercolor brush variants with splatter water selected.

◆ **5-24 [h–j]** *Using and saving selections.*

◆ **5-24 [k–w]** *Utilizing the brush categories and variants.*

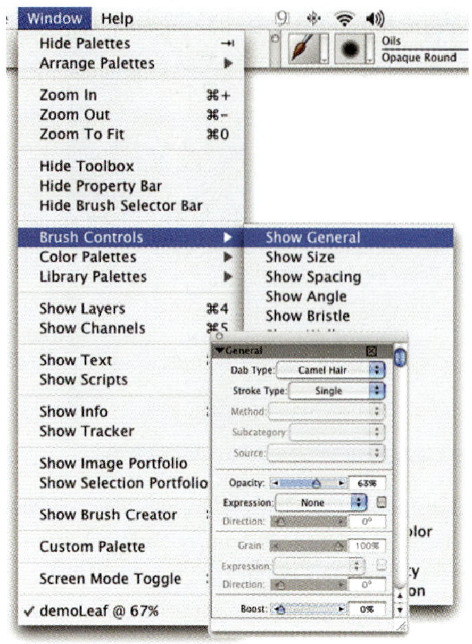

(l)

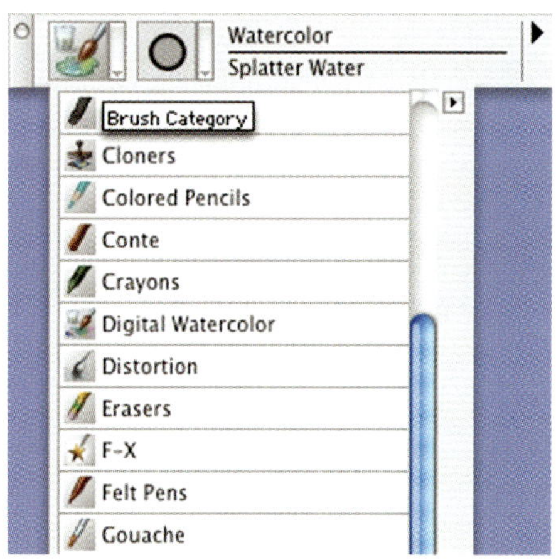

(m)

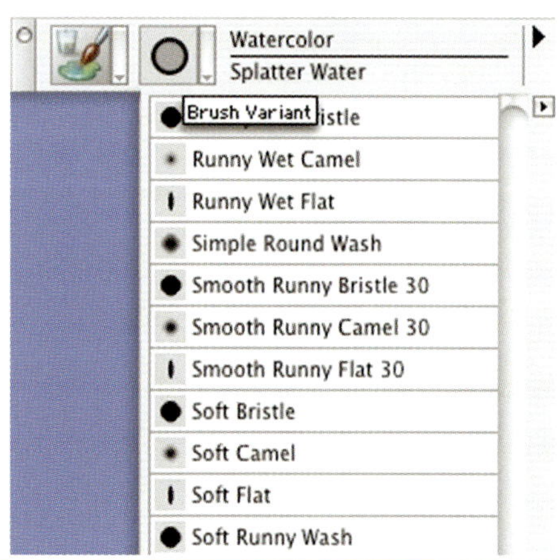

(n)

Double clicking the toolbox Brush tool also turns on the Brush Selector bar. Turn on the Properties bar at the top of the screen to easily set your brush characteristics. Type a value for the size in the Properties bar, or adjust the pop up slider. The Properties bar also provides opacity and grain sliders to fine-tune the brush effects. Many Painter brushes respond to stylus pressure when you are using a graphics tablet. The brushes also allow media to build up or "pool" when you move a brush slowly. The Properties bar gives an option for Freehand Strokes or Straight Line Strokes with vector anchor points.

Open the *Paper Selector* to select from various papers by clicking on the top left icon at the bottom of the toolbox. Choose a paper or launch the Papers palette by selecting the launch option under the arrowhead in the Paper Selector window. Papers create a surface texture that simulates paper grain. Your brushes are affected by this texture. Make a selection and choose Effects>Surface Control>Apply Surface Texture. Don't make a selection if you prefer to apply the effect to the entire image. The Papers palette lets you adjust appearance with sliders for softness, light, and depth. See the top of Figure 5-24o.

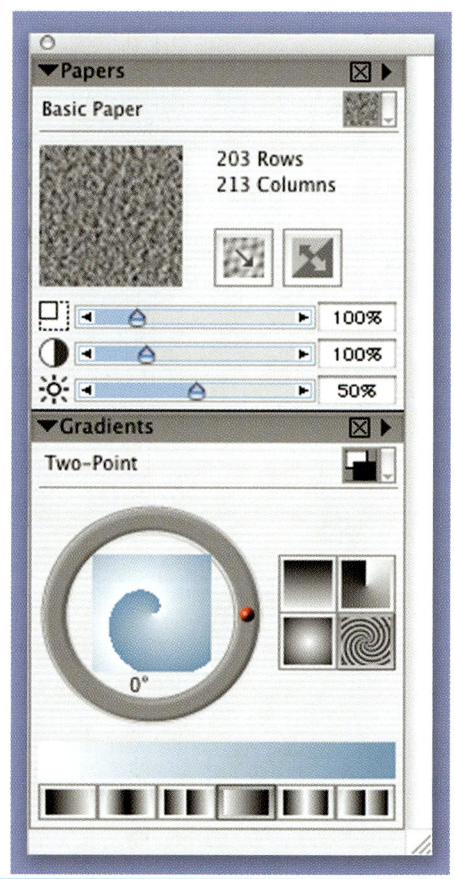

(o)

Many brushes allow you to apply a *gradient* or a *pattern* to your stroke. The pattern can be scaled up or down. To paint with a gradient select a brush and open the gradients palette by choosing Window> Library Palettes>Show Gradients. Choose a gradient from the Gradient Selector. You can now choose the orientation of the gradient using the Gradient Order buttons. The *gradient editor* is used to create gradients. See the bottom of Figure 5-24o. In the gradient window click the left triangle in the Gradient section bar, then click the right triangle to choose Edit> Gradient. Again this works much like the gradients in Photoshop and Illustrator. Selecting a color control point lets you choose a color from the Color Picker. Add new color control points by clicking in the color bar, and delete points by selecting them and pressing the delete key. Moving the control points will change the gradient effect .

You can fill an area of an image with a gradient, pattern, weave, or color (Fig. 5-24p). If you want to fill part of any image, select that area. If you want to fill a layer, select the layer on the Layers palette. Choose Effects>Fill. In the Fill pop up window select Current Color, Pattern, Gradient, or Weave and adjust

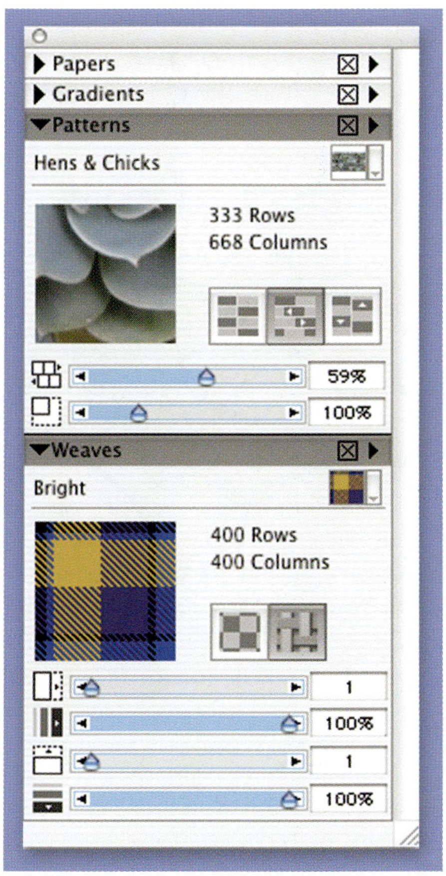

(p)

the Opacity slider. Before filling be sure to select the media you want to use from the toolbox. If the fill leaks beyond the boundaries, select Edit>Undo .

Cloning is the process of taking an image from one source and re-creating it in another document. The re-creation can incorporate a wide variety of special effects. Begin the process by choosing and opening a clone source. You can use a cloning brush to develop your image in the new file, simulating an artistic style. The final new file can be a combination of several clone sources. Figure 5-24q shows a landscape photo and its cloned re-creation.

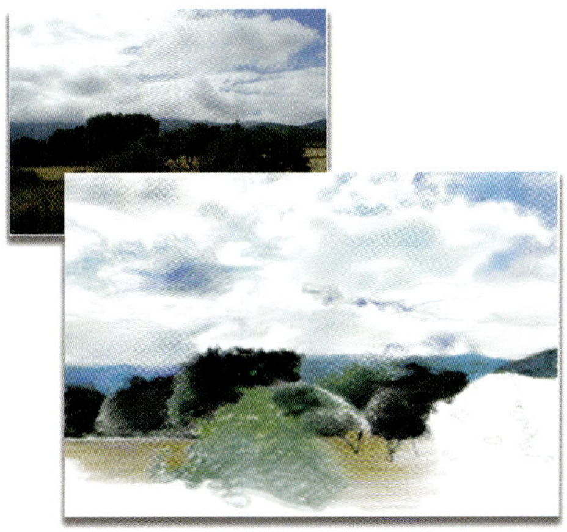
(q)

Begin to clone an image by opening your source document. Then choose File>Clone (Fig. 5-24r). With the clone window selected, choose Select>All. Next press delete (Mac OS) or backspace (Windows) to clear the canvas. Click the Tracing Paper icon in the vertical scroll bar (Fig. 5-24s) or choose Canvas> Tracing Paper. A 50% ghost image of the source will show through the tracing paper. Trace over the image using any Corel Painter brush variant. Click the Tracing Paper icon again to turn it off and see your

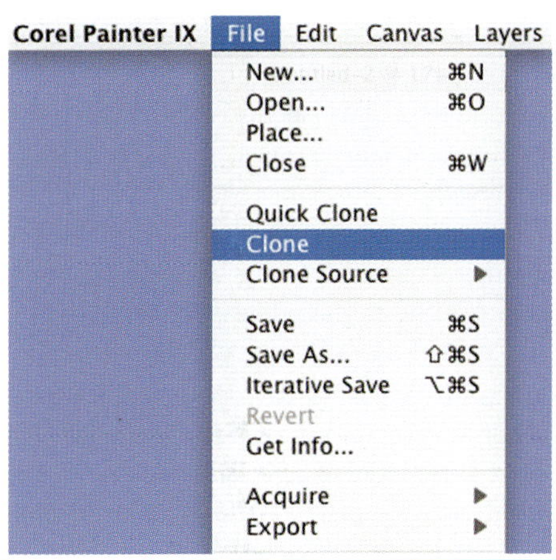

(r)

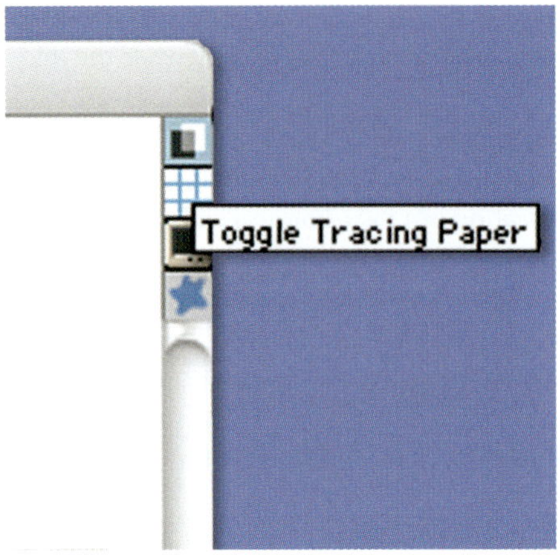

(s)

document's progress. You can turn clone color on to ensure that any brush will use the color of the original document. There are several ways to do this (Fig. 5-24t). Choose File>Clone Source to select any open document as your new source.

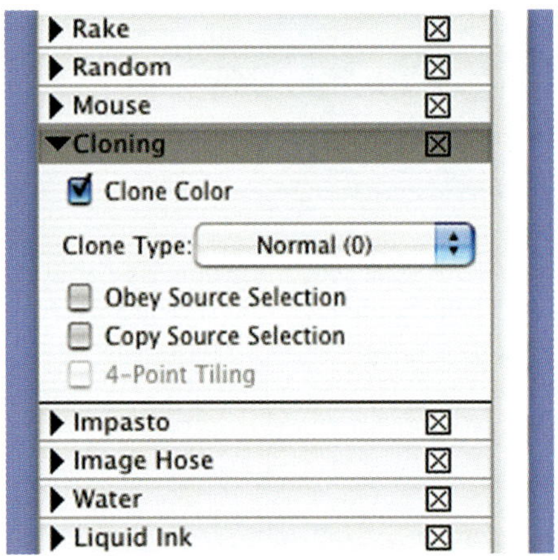

(t)

Select a cloner brush variant from the Brush Selector bar. Set the desired size, opacity, and grain penetration before painting in the image. The cloner brush will take its color information from a clone source instead of from the Colors palette. Figure 5-24u shows a 50% tracing paper source image of a horse that is being traced with a furry cloner brush.

Masking is achieved by making a selection on a layer in Painter. Then click on the layer mask icon at the bottom of the toolbox. The mask can also be viewed in Channels (Fig. 5-24v). A mask is basically a selection, controlled using Save and Load Selection. Once the selection is saved, it shows up as a mask. This can be altered and saved to an existing or a new selection. You can also select a clone source to insert into the masked area using a clone brush (Fig. 5-24w).

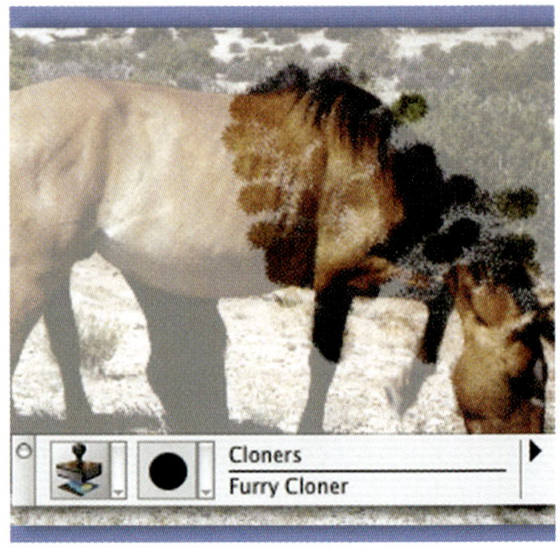

(u)

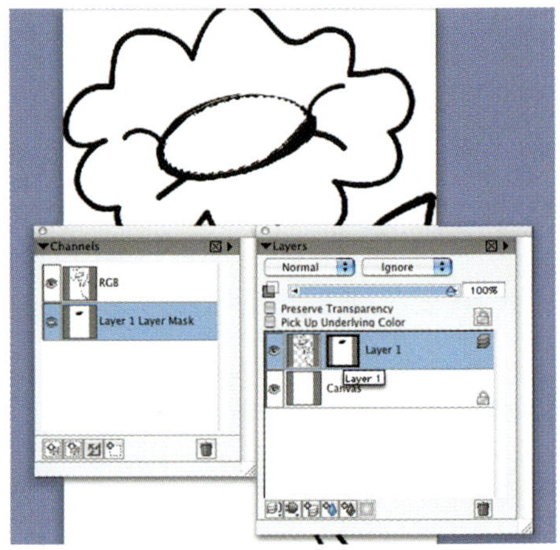

(v)

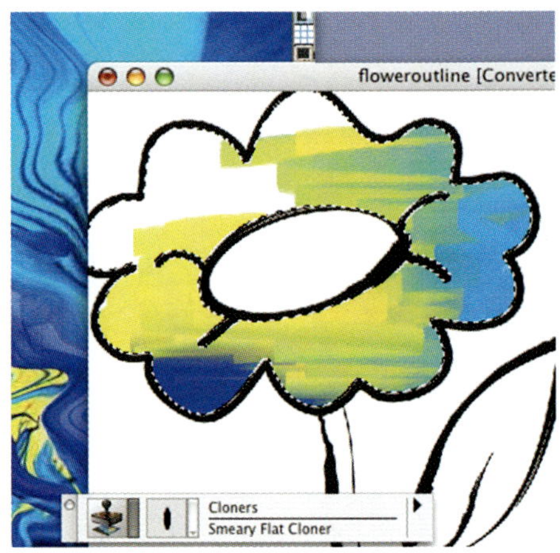

(w)

There are many, many effects and techniques available for exploration in this software, including animation, but we'll stick to these basics. Spend a fair amount of time studying the information we've just covered. Now let's move on to practicing the techniques necessary to creating an original image using this software.

Hands On Practice

1. Begin by practicing the techniques in the previous How To Basics section. Then open a new file. Save the document as a RIFF before doing anything else. Now spend time practicing brush strokes using a wide variety of Painter brushes. Do not try to make a recognizable image; just enjoy the abstract beauty of the mark.

2. Add a layer and draw on it, experimenting with a variety of hues, values, and tones using the Colors palette.

3. Next practice creating and saving selections. Load multiple selections and manipulate them by adding to and subtracting from their shape. Color inside and outside the selection with patterns, gradients, and weaves.

4. Now open a Photoshop photographic image inside Painter (perhaps one of yours from the previous section or from the CD). Create a clone, selecting a variety of clone brushes to render the image.

When you have completed some practice techniques, it will be time to apply them to an original image.

Warming Up

Reference a drawing or painting you have done in another class and re-create a section of it using the Painter brushes. This is your opportunity to experiment with the rich variety possible by limiting yourself to just this section of Painter. The example in **Figure 5-25** is rich and varied in technique, while the concept is to present a world record in tattoos. The airbrush (along with research and imagination) was the primary tool used by multimedia designer Dan Kurowski to create this piece for his student portfolio. He began by practicing with and learning the potential of the brush palettes.

Select two related images to open in Painter. Use one as the primary file. Choose File>Clone; choose Select All and delete; turn on tracing paper; and begin to paint. Paint with a variety of cloning brushes. Choose File>Clone Source to change images and create a painterly collage of the two original related images.

In The Studio

Now is your opportunity to use what you have learned in this chapter to create a portfolio piece.

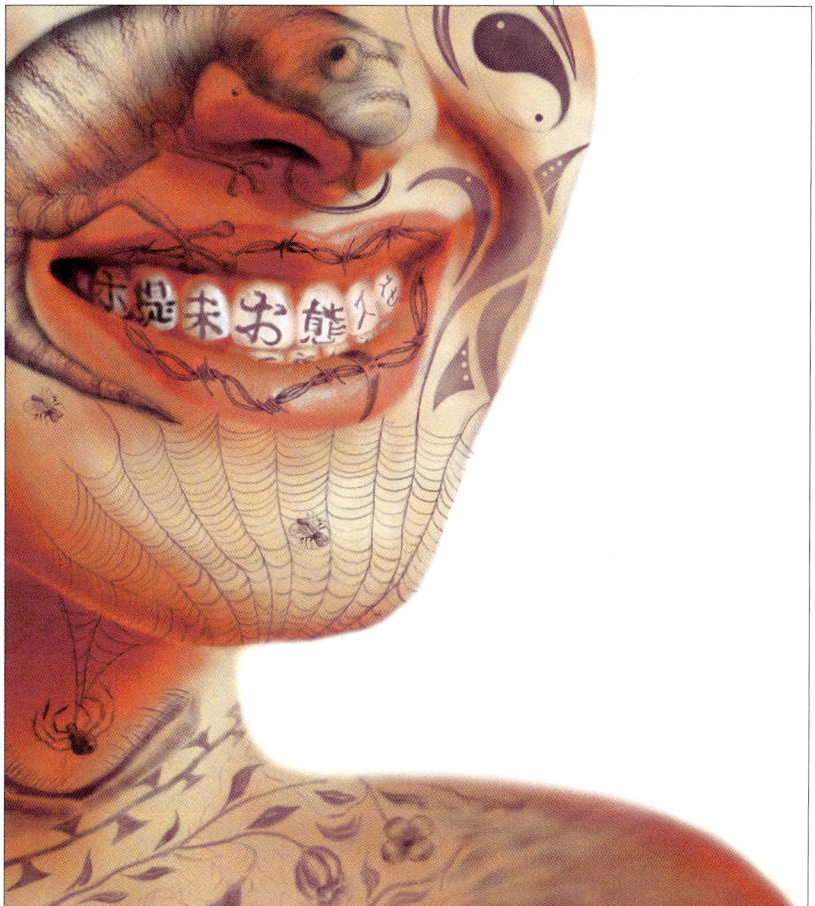

◆ **5-25** *Dan Kurowski.* Guinness Record (Most Tattoos, 5,473). *2002. Inkjet print on paper. 17" × 11". This project was suggested by Richard Wilde's book* Visual Literacy.
Courtesy of the artist.

Using Painter, create four seasonal illustrations for a calendar. Plan to use Painter for these, but feel free to incorporate other software or traditional media as well. Begin with thumbnail sketches and visual research. Good ideas can be found throughout art and design history as well as in contemporary artwork. Periodicals such as *Communication Arts, Print,* and *Step-By-Step Graphics* show what other graphic designers and illustrators are creating. Study magazines such as *ARTnews* and *Art in America* for fine art. Craft-specific magazines also showcase excellent work in those fields.

Link your four images through concept, design, and technique. **Figure 5-26** shows a student portfolio solution that shows mastery of all three categories. Tiffany Dorner-Jones created an integrated series of twelve images to reflect the changing seasons. Her statement follows. Plan to create a similar statement to present at your critique.

"This series, while on the surface is a collection illustrating the twelve months, is perhaps more importantly about rediscovery. Each illustration invites the

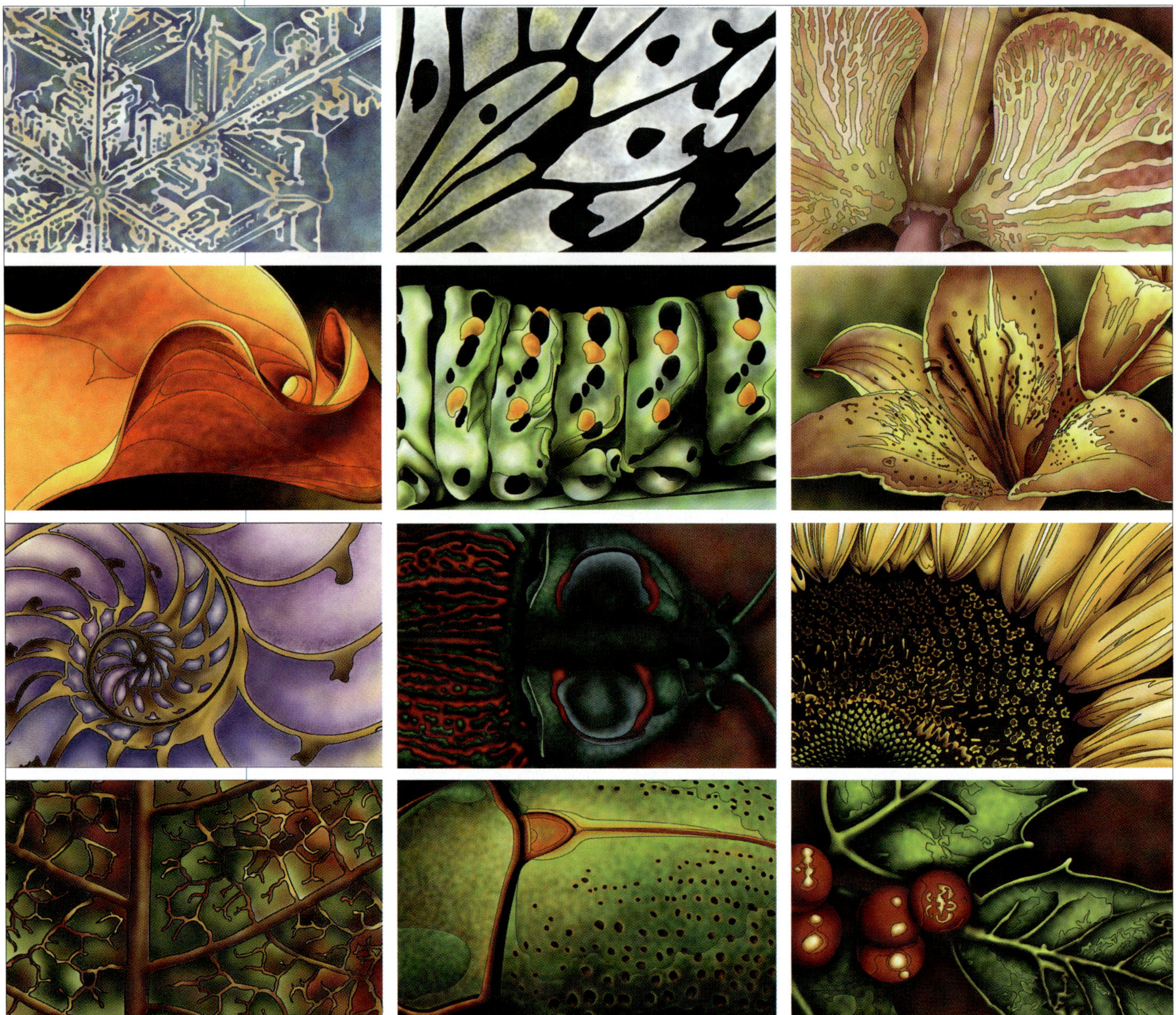

◆ **5-26** *Tiffany Dorner-Jones.* Calendar Series. *2004. Created in Illustrator and Painter. Each image appears on a separate calendar page.*
Courtesy of the artist.

viewer to reconsider a familiar aspect of nature, focusing on the shape, color, and inherent design of the subject.

"Each image began with a line drawing created in Adobe Illustrator, which provided a visual and structural framework for the piece. The Illustrator document was then placed into Corel Painter, where selections were converted into layer masks, allowing the image to be painted in defined, easily edited sections. Painter's pressure-sensitive brushes allowed colors to be layered and mixed on the canvas, creating a complex color palette and added dimension."

SUMMARY CRITIQUE

As you look at your finished piece, ask the following questions: Do repetition and continuation tie the four separate seasons of your artwork together? What is the underlying design concept? Are there any design techniques or concepts in your solution that were influenced by pre-computer art and design history? How did you achieve your effects with the software? Analyze your work in

Gallery Profile

Joan Truckenbrod is a Professor in Art and Technology Studies at The School of the Art Institute of Chicago. She is a pioneer in digital imaging and exhibits her computer artwork internationally. She began her work with computer graphics and video paint systems in the mid 1970s. Her early work included experiments with image transfer to fabrics, as shown in **Figure 5-27**, titled *Electronic Patchwork*. First, she wrote programs to generate a series of abstract, patterned images. Not wanting to place these on a piece of static paper, she chose fabric. It was subject to air movements and light effects, thus suiting her aesthetic purpose. Her explorations with available paint system technologies have continued to the present, as can be seen in Figure 5-5 (see page 105), where she digitally creates environments incorporating her own photography.

Recently, Truckenbrod's conceptual creations have become more three-dimensional, incorporating sound and movement. **Figure 5-28**, titled *Spirit Sites*, has a video of salmon jumping and struggling upstream to spawn, passing over images of people. This video is projected into an empty handmade model house, suspended from the ceiling of the gallery, with the video imagery spilling onto the wall behind it. The video washes over photographs mounted behind small window frames on the back wall of the gallery. The sound of the rushing water accompanies these visuals. **Figure 5-29**, titled *Quantum Realities 1*, is also a video installation. The sound of rushing water, accompanied by flickering light, joins the video of salmon, projected onto an actual pool of water. Pebbles surround the water. Professor Truckenbrod states, "*My current work is inspired by the ritual of body painting in indigenous cultures, with the reflection of firelight in a ceremonial dance revealing the meaning of these symbols. In the shadows of the firelight, mystical forces from other realms of experience peer out. In this video installation the spirit of the underwater world is summoned up by the power of the salmon in their transformative journey.*"

terms of icon, symbol, and index. Reference the statement at the end of the Painter section as well as the statement in Joan Truckenbrod's Artist Profile to build comments on your own work.

MOVING ON

The next chapter covers intermediate techniques in Illustrator. If you are doing raster graphics first, followed by vector software, return to the section of Chapter 3 that introduces vectors. Chapter 6 will continue to discuss Gestalt unit-forming principles.

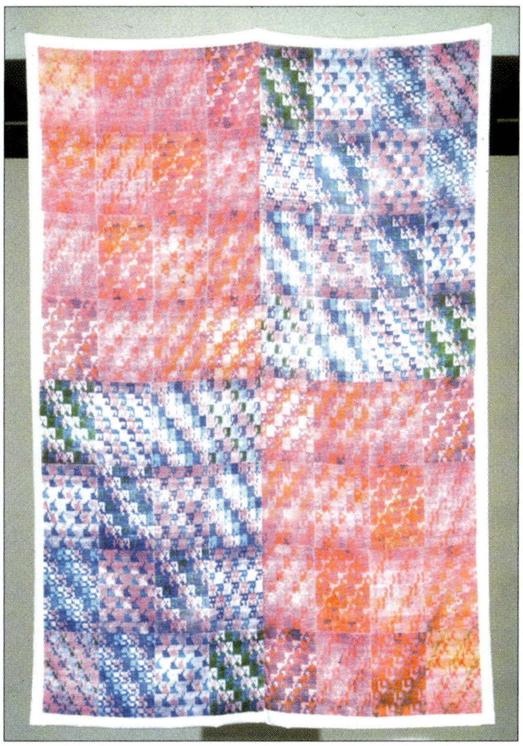

5-27 *Joan Truckenbrod.* Electronic Patchwork.*1978. Computer images with heat transfer color xerography on fiber, 84" × 60".*
Courtesy of the artist.

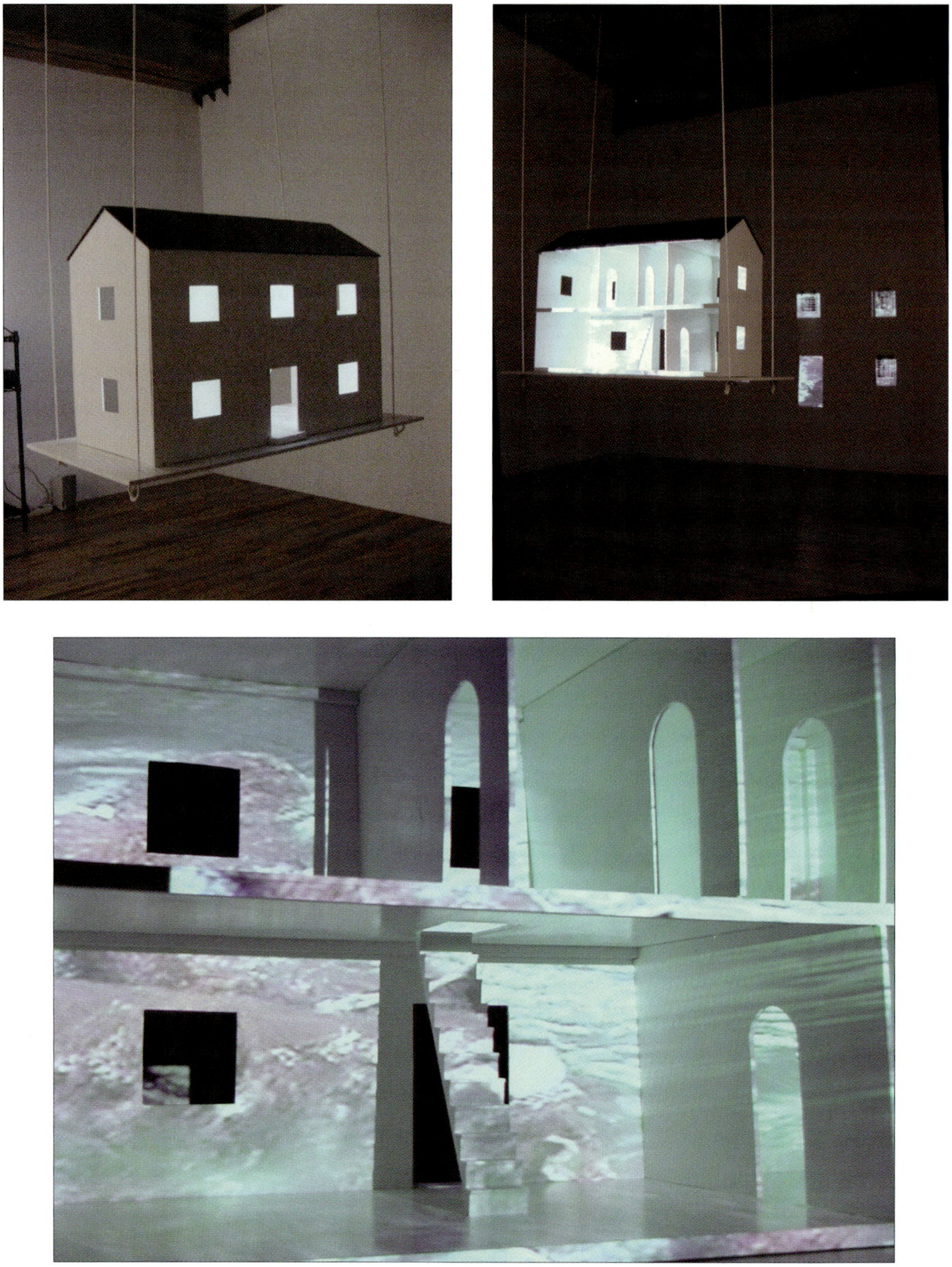

◆ **5-28** *Joan Truckenbrod.* Spirit Site. *2002. Multimedia installation. Video projection, model house, sound, window frames on walls with photographic images. The model house is 25 inches high by 20 inches deep by 48 inches wide. It is mounted on pillars at eye level in the gallery. The installation occupies an area 12 feet by 16 feet.*
Courtesy of the artist.

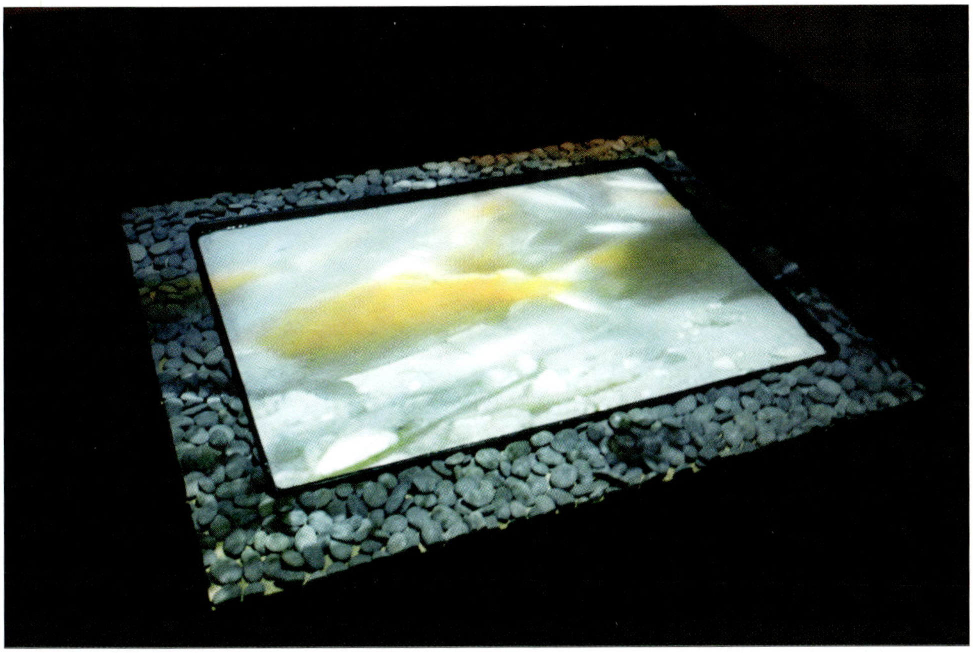

◆ **5-29** *Joan Truckenbrod.* Quantum Realities 1. *2002. Multimedia installation 38" × 54" × 3". The pool of water in this video installation creates a visual and emotional resonance for the video imagery projected into it. River pebbles surround the pond.*
Courtesy of the artist.

TERMINOLOGY

CHAPTER 6

See Glossary for definitions

- Closure
- Focal Point
- Eye Direction
- Graphics Tablet
- Blend Tool
- Pathfinder
- Mesh Gradient
- Patterns
- Vector Masking
- Similarity
- Proximity
- Continuation
- Closure
- Figure/Ground

6 Intermediate Vector Graphics

Vector graphics are used in a great variety of creative applications. They are clear, crisply articulated images that can be resized without loss of detail. Because vector programs are strongly shape-based, artists using vector graphics often focus on design principles of repetition and variation, figure/ground relationships, continuation, **closure**, **focal point**, and **eye direction**. This chapter introduces the latter three design principles: closure, focal point, and eye direction. **Figure 6-1** is a professional illustration created in Adobe Illustrator that makes good use of these principles (see page 134). Vector programs such as Illustrator and Freehand provide a high level of precision and control over artwork. You'll learn more about mastering Illustrator software in this chapter.

Applying the Vector Image

Vector graphics are used in a wide range of digital illustrations, from technical and scientific to advertising and editorial creations. Almost all typographic applications are also done in vector programs. The companies that produce this software now include a significant focus on creating

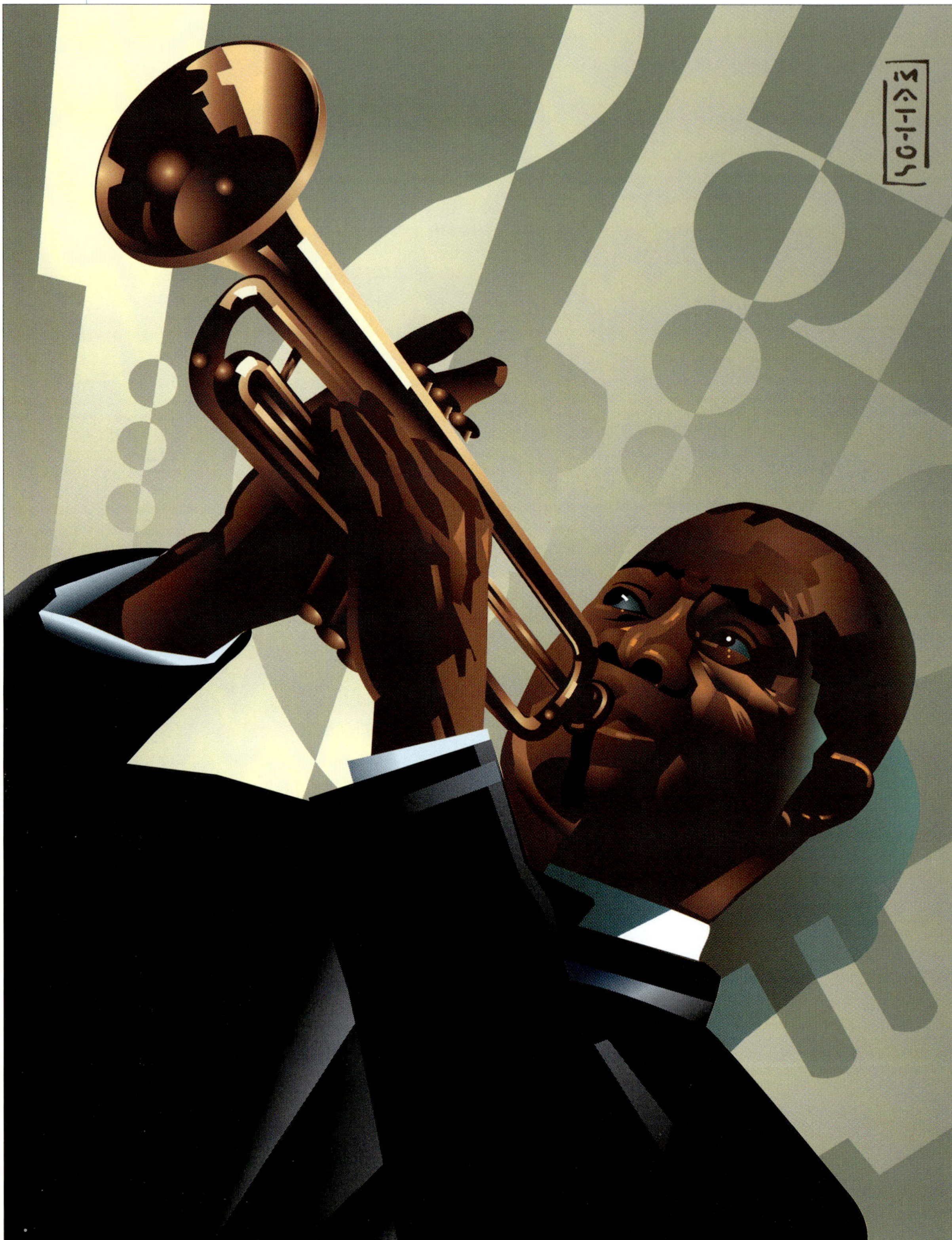

◆ **6-1** *John Mattos.* Portrait for the Baltimore Sun. *Digital illustration created in Illustrator.* Courtesy of the artist.

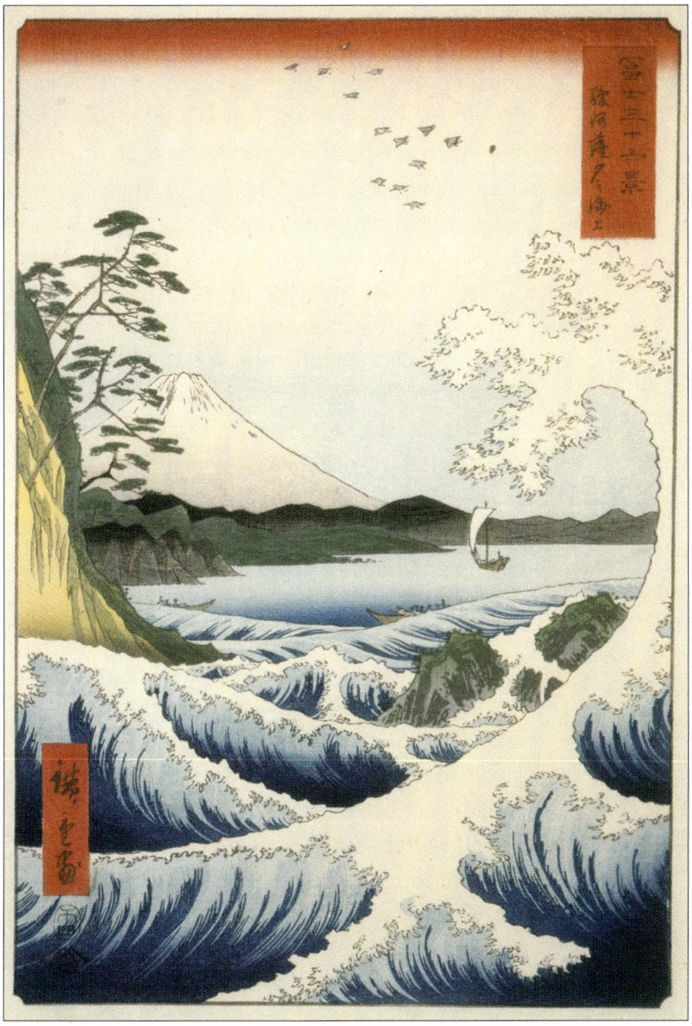

◆ **6-2** *Utagawa Hiroshige (Japanese, 1797–1858).* The Sea off Satta in Suruga Province. *1858. Color woodcut.*
The Elvehjem Museum of Art, University of Wisconsin-Madison. Bequest of John H. Van Vleck, 1980.

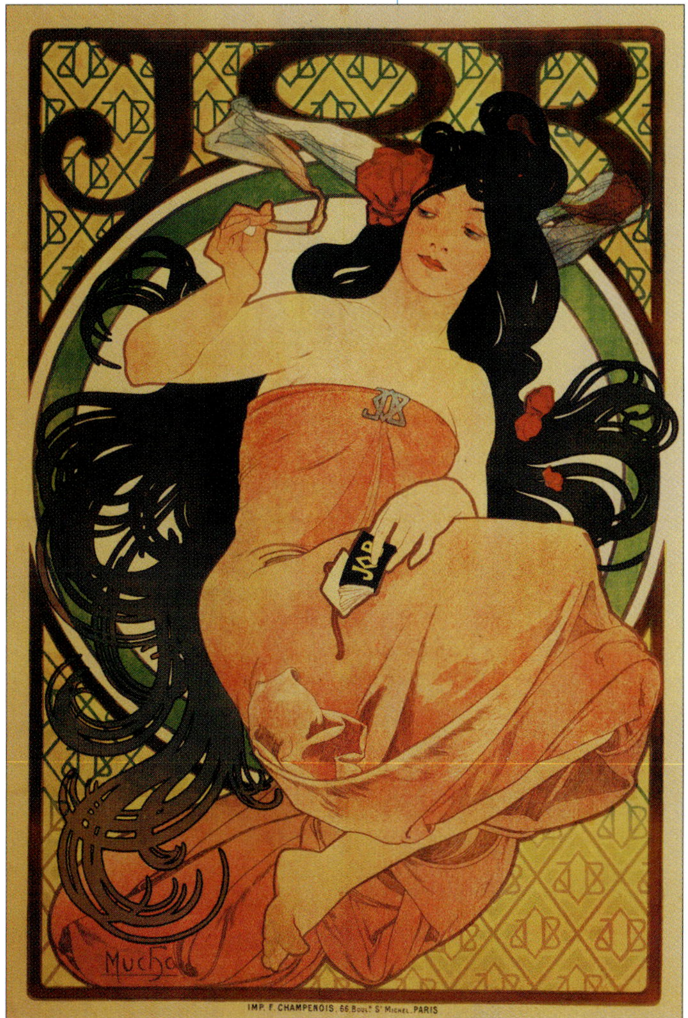

◆ **6-3a** *Alphonse Mucha.* JOB. *1898. Lithographic poster.*
Digital image © The Museum of Modern Art/Licensed by Scala/Art Resource, NY.

elements for web graphics. This makes it easier to create small files with elaborate web buttons and animations. Chapter 7 will discuss web graphics and the importance of file structure.

To enrich your own solutions to visual problems, you can look to the wide array of contemporary illustrators and designers who use these programs. But also look at the vast array of work in the history of art and design that was originally created by hand but could now be created in vectors. The Japanese color woodcut from 1858 in **Figure 6-2** is a good example. So is the wonderful illustration by Alphonse Mucha created during the Art Nouveau period (**Fig. 6-3a**). Both of these artworks use clearly defined shapes in their composition. This kind of shape creation is very readily created in vector graphic programs, as you learned in Chapter 3. We will be learning more about methods to design shapes in this chapter. Figures 6-2 and 6-3a also make a good point about the relevance of art historical images to contemporary digital design. Remember that the artists mentioned throughout this chapter are references for further visual research.

Applying Design Principles

The Japanese woodcut in Figure 6-2 uses the large foreground wave to frame the composition, bringing the eye up its long sweep, finally pointing to the distant mountain. The placement of the birds echoes the foam on the wave. There is a very thoughtful, well-implemented use of eye direction in this image.

Alphonse Mucha's JOB (a cigarette paper product) in Figure 6-3a is an excellent example of an advertising illustration that incorporates a number of design principles to make a coherent and integrated whole. First, look for a repetition of shapes. The JOB symbol is found in the background and in the clasp on the woman's dress. The circular shapes in the hair repeat the large background circle.

The principles of eye direction and focal point are used in a very direct fashion to bring attention to the product. Although eye direction usually describes how the eye is directed between various shapes, in this case the image of the eye itself plays an important part. The woman is looking at the cigarette, while the smoke from it draws us back to her eyes. The circle in the background draws a line between the eyes and the product.

Continuation also plays an important role in this artwork (see Visual Perception, page 142). The large background circle suggests a continuation through the central figure's eyes. The folds in the gown line up with and help to continue the circle, while the position of the leg also reinforces the circle. Finally, *closure* is a design principle that occurs when the eye completes a line or curve in order to form a familiar shape. It also can be applied when we have closure with a concept, as in "Now I understand." In this artwork, we visually close the circle around the woman.

Although this artwork is an image of a beautiful woman and a cigarette product, it is also a very fine application of abstract design elements and principles. These same design elements and principles can be successfully applied in contemporary digital imaging.

Illustrator John Mattos applied a number of design principles in the creation of the dynamic, digitally generated artwork in Figure 6-1 (see page 134). The line of the horn crosses the decorative background lines, creating a dynamic tension. All lines radiate from the figure, placing him at the center of the viewer's attention. The mouth on the horn becomes a focal point. There are repeated shapes in the circles in the background, and in the two fingers echoed by the two shapes behind the head. Finally, this artwork is united by close attention to color treatment. It includes a strong value contrast between light and dark, and a subtle, toned down blue/green that complements the orange facial tones.

How can vector tools help in the creation of such well-designed work? We need to study, practice, and master additional software techniques, then apply those techniques with an eye for incorporating the design principles just discussed.

Figure 6-3b by Chris Eichman incorporates many of the techniques we will discuss in this chapter. This figure also shows his design process, beginning with a poster, shown at the top center, by Alphonse Mucha (see Fig. 6-3a). Eichman selected this work because he admired the design qualities of eye direction and focal point. He pencil-sketched *his* version, changing the design concept into a wine label for his student portfolio. Collaged photographs were then collected and assembled in Photoshop. This work was then re-created using Illustrator tools, as shown on the left. The final artwork on the right was colorized using a complementary palette of red and green, incorporating linear and radial gradients.

Creative Imaging in Illustrator

Keep in mind that the tutorial and help menu packaged with the full version of Adobe Illustrator gives an excellent in-depth introduction to all the software techniques. **Figure 6-4** shows how to access that menu. Work your way through the opening chapters of the tutorial. Be certain you've mastered the vector techniques described thus far in this textbook. The following section summarizes the intermediate techniques in Illustrator and their potential applications. Remember that the procedures of working in Freehand and Illustrator are very similar. Although this book focuses on Illustrator software, the techniques covered

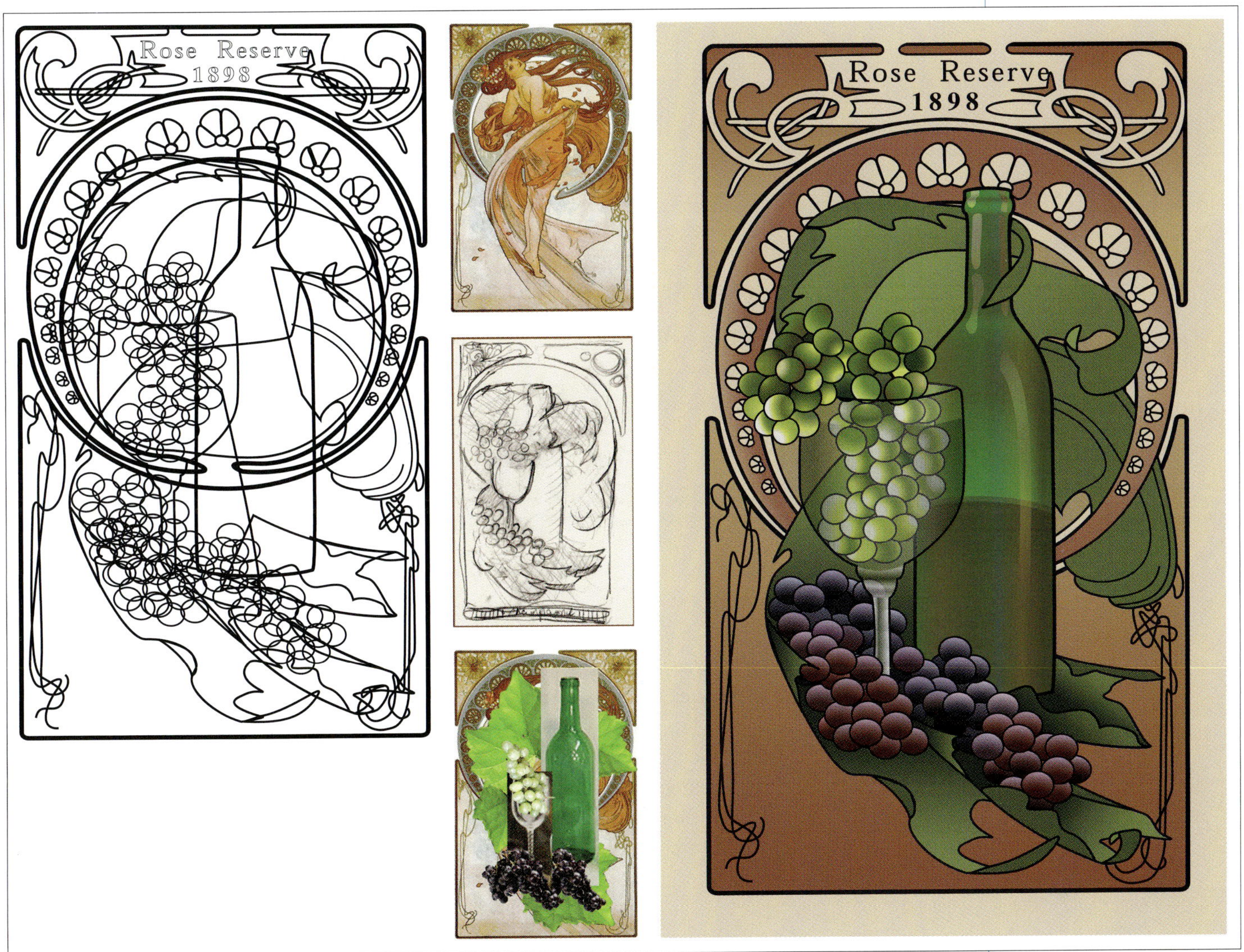

6-3b *Chris Eichman.* Wine Label Stages. *2003. Illustrator file.*
Courtesy of the artist.

here will make you familiar with the structure of any vector graphics program.

Until now, we have assumed that you are working with a mouse in your vector graphics program. Another very useful tool for drawing is the **graphics tablet**. The toolbox options remain the same, but the quality of drawing is different with an electronic pen on a graphics tablet. The tablet has a grid embedded in it that translates your pen marks to the digital file. You may find that

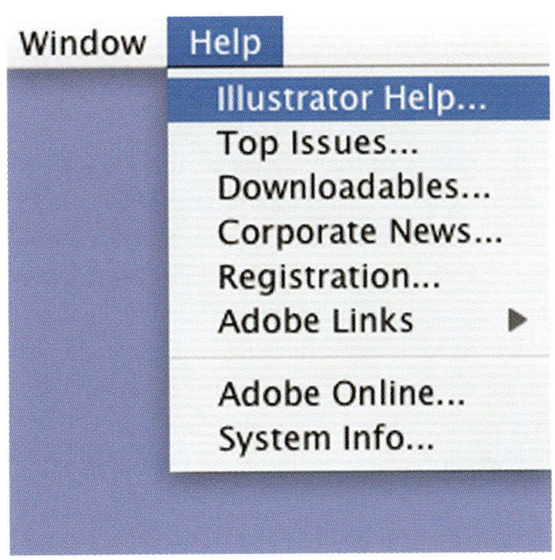

6-4 *Accessing the tutorial and help menu packaged with Illustrator.*

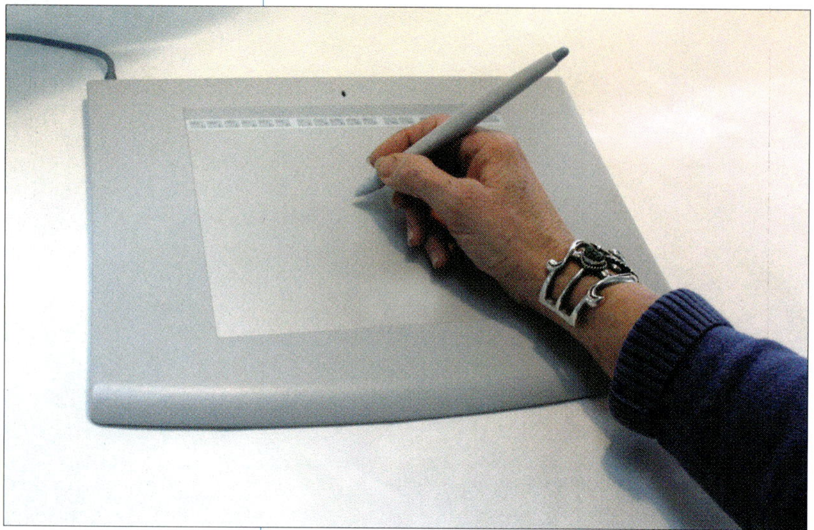

◆ **6-5** *The graphics tablet can help create a fluid, dynamic stroke.*

◆ **6-6 [a–f]** *The Pen tool can be used to trace a photograph with careful attention to control of anchor points.*

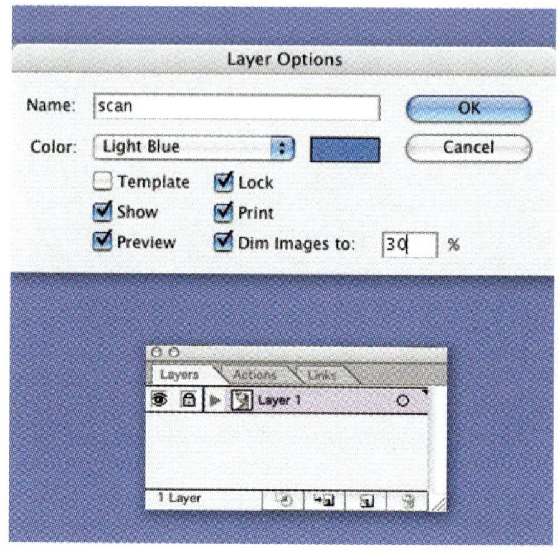

(a)

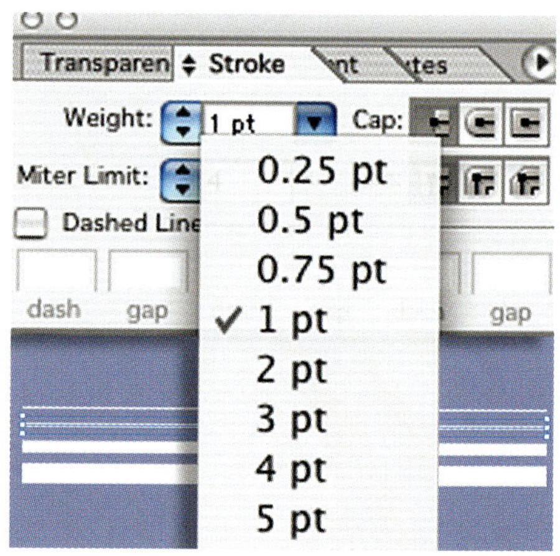

(b)

a–n: Adobe product screen shots reprinted with permission from Adobe Systems Incorporated

the freehand tool in Illustrator is most useful when using a graphics tablet. **Figures 6-5** shows a photograph of a pen and tablet in use. Now let's begin a series of continuing technical instructions in this software package. Remember that the purpose of this text is to provide you the basics of software operation within a context of art and design principles.

How To Basics

Study the techniques shown in **Figures 6-6a–n** to gain a better working knowledge of Illustrator. You'll have an opportunity to practice these new techniques in the next Hands On Practice section.

We will start with *Importing and Working with Scans.* If you choose to use a hand-cut photo collage or your original drawing reference as your beginning document, create the scan and File>Place it in a new Illustrator file. Double clicking on this layer allows you to choose to dim this photo reference, as shown in Figure 6-6a. You can then lock that layer and create a new layer on top to draw and trace upon.

The *Pen* tool can be used to trace your photo reference. As you know from previous chapters, pen tools also work well for direct drawing techniques. Careful attention to the use of the pen tools can lead to the creation of a rich and finely tuned image. Fine-tune the stroke width by clicking on Window>Show Stroke>Choose Weight (Fig. 6-6b). Choosing various brushes makes an array of effects possible (Fig. 6-6c). Holding down the pen tool icon shows several options (Fig. 6-6d). There are pen tools to add a point, subtract a point, and convert to a corner point. Combining the use of these tools with dragging on the anchor point handles gives complete control of the vector outline (Fig. 6-6e). It takes a while to master this technique, so plan to practice it. As you know from Chapter 3, closed shapes can be filled with solids or gradients or patterns (Fig. 6-6f).

The *Auto Trace* tool is located beneath the **Blend tool.** It allows you to trace a raster reference placed in

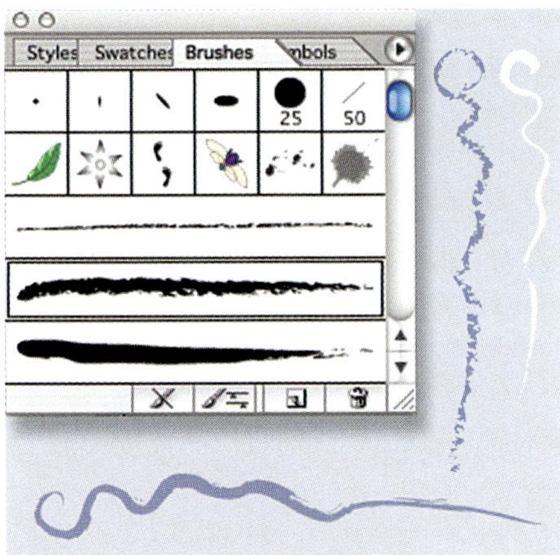

(c)

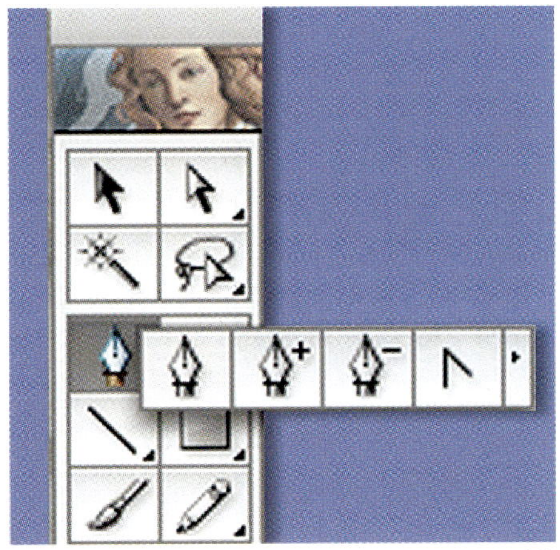

(d)

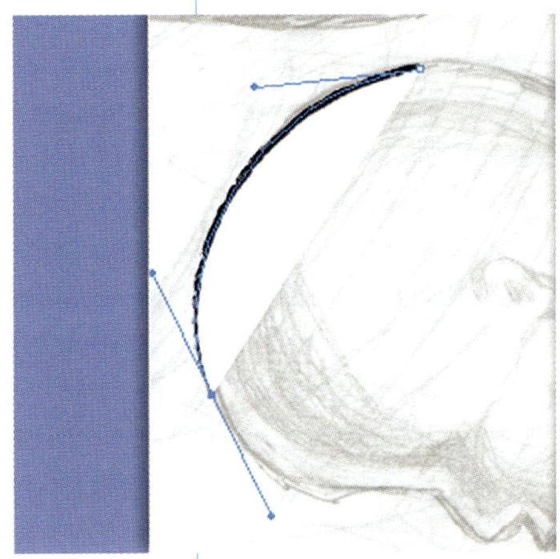

(e)

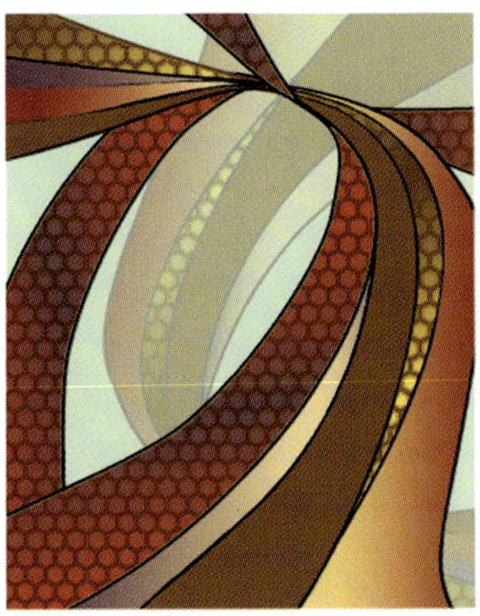

(f)

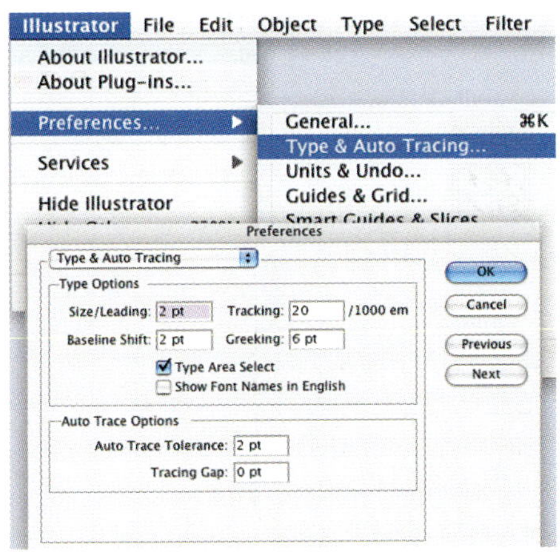

(g)

6-6g *The Auto Trace tool is beneath the Blend tool. Set the number of anchor points in Preferences.*

Illustrator. Setting the tolerance that determines the density of anchor points is done in Illustrator>Preferences>Type and the Auto Tracing menu (Fig. 6-6g).

The Photoshop command *Export Paths to Illustrator* (see Chapter 5) creates an Adobe Illustrator file that can be opened inside Illustrator. It appears as a blank, unstroked, and unfilled path that you are free to select and manipulate, as shown in Figure 6-6h.

Vector Typography allows a variety of effects in combinations of type and image. Choose the Type tool from the toolbox. Click on the screen and type a word. There are three ways to select and make changes to it. Depress the mouse and drag backward before releasing to select the type you want to alter. Or position the pointer at the baseline of the word, and click to select it. The third method is to use the black arrow key to draw a selection box around the word. After using any of these methods, you can then change the type style and treatment, or choose a new

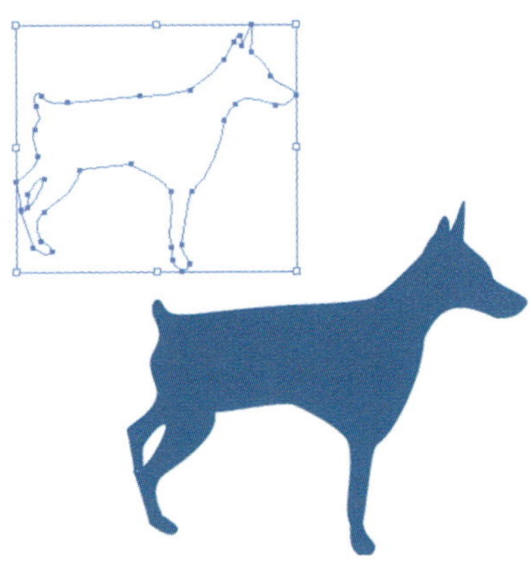

(h)

6-6h *Importing a path from Photoshop to Illustrator.*

color from the pull down menu (Fig. 6-6i). Check the options under Object>Transform and try them out. Underneath the Type tool in the toolbox are a variety of options for alignment (Fig. 6-6j).

◆ **6-6 [i–j]** *Working with vector typography.*

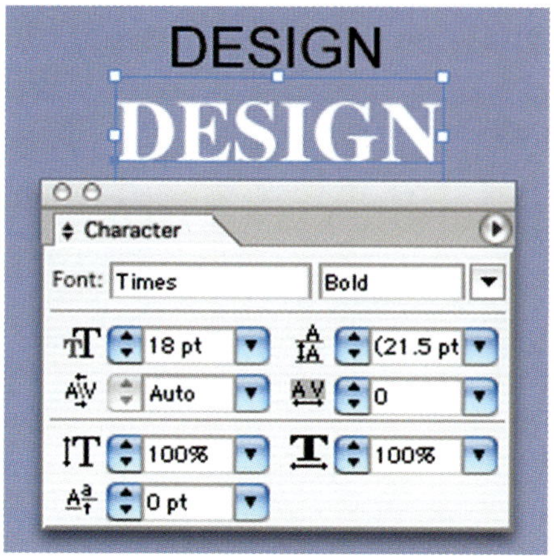

(i)

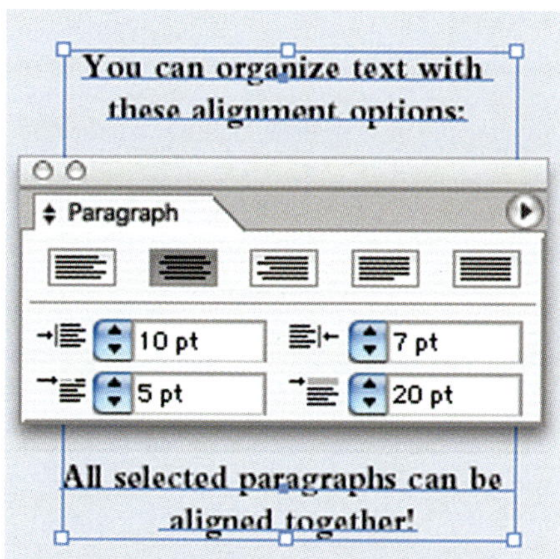

(j)

The *Area Type* tool is used to fit type inside a shape, as shown in Figure 6-6k. Use this when creating a layout inside Illustrator, to establish your text boxes and column structure. Begin by creating a shape with no color in the stroke or fill. Click with the Type tool inside the shape and start to type. The *Vertical Type* tool creates type inside a rectangle on a vertical orientation.

◆ **6-6 [k–m]** *Options for arrangement of typography found under the Type tool.*

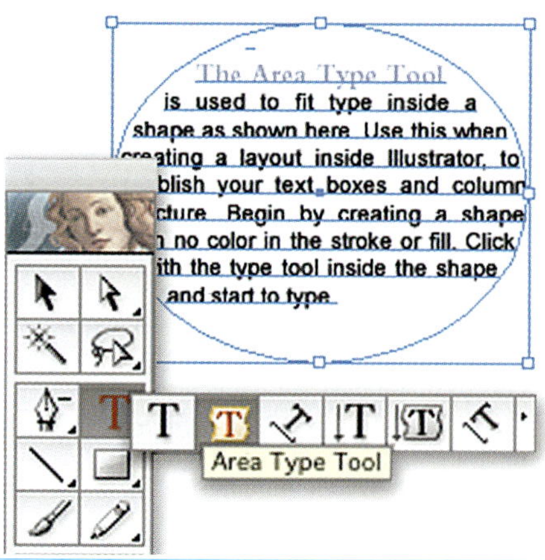

(k)

To change the size or shape of a text rectangle, select the Direct Selection white arrow. Position the pointer on the edge of the text box you want to adjust, without selecting any type baselines. Click and drag the edge or corner of the text rectangle (Fig. 6-6l).

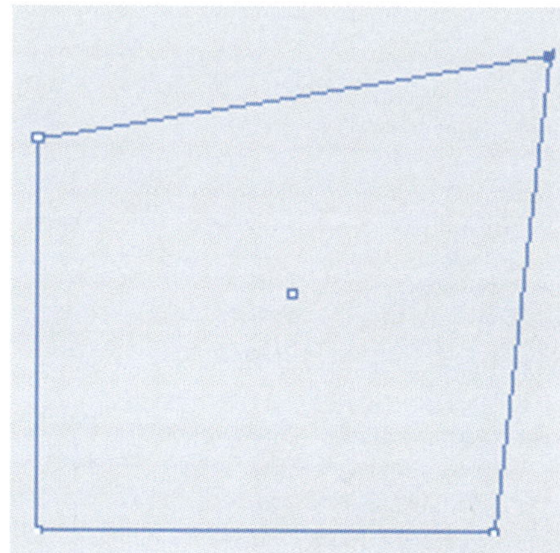

(l)

The *Type on a Path* tool lets you draw a shape or free-form line (usually without color in stroke or fill), then click on that line to keystroke typographic shapes and curves, as shown in Figure 6-6m.

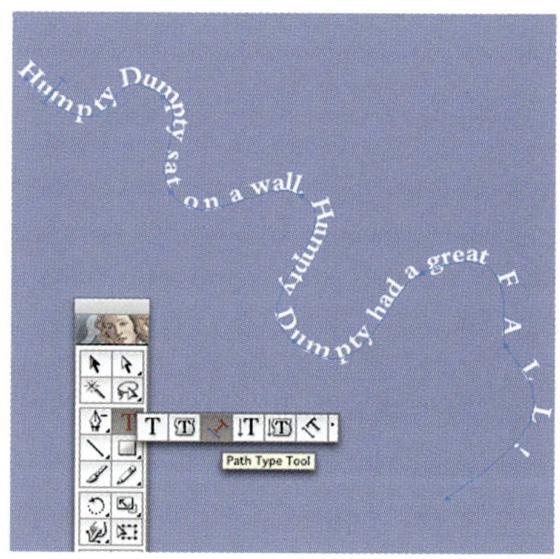

(m)

The ***Pathfinder*** palette can be used to modify shapes based on the intersection of overlapping objects. With the black selection arrow, select two objects to modify. These can be drawn shapes or type changed to outline shapes (Type>Create Outline). Choose Window>Show Pathfinder, and click on a

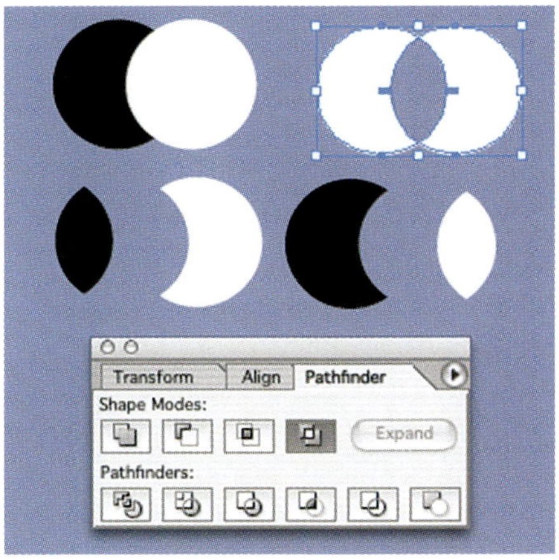

(n)

6-6n *Using the Pathfinder palette.*

Pathfinder command. Figure 6-6n shows some of these effects:

Unite traces the outline of all selected objects as if they were a single object.
Intersect traces the outline of all overlapping shapes in any two selected objects.
Exclude traces all nonoverlapping areas of selected objects and makes the overlap transparent when an even number of objects are selected.
Minus Front subtracts the front objects from the back.
Minus Back subtracts the back objects from the front object.
Divide will divide a piece of artwork into its filled areas that are undivided by line segments.
Trim removes the hidden part of an overlapped object.
Merge combines overlapped objects.
Crop deletes all parts of the artwork that fall outside the boundary of the topmost object.
Outline divides an object into its edges and is used for prepress techniques.

Now we have finished the reading and lecture materials that give a background in the intermediate vector techniques.

We'll go on to create these effects. But first take a moment to look at **Figure 6-7**. Matt Morris Cook created this lyrical, sensual, typographic piece that uses the Type on a Path tool to describe the shape of the imported photograph. **Figure 6-8** shows a cut and paste, overlapping typographic texture with a powerful message about design today. These typographic illustrations show some of the creative imaging possible with type.

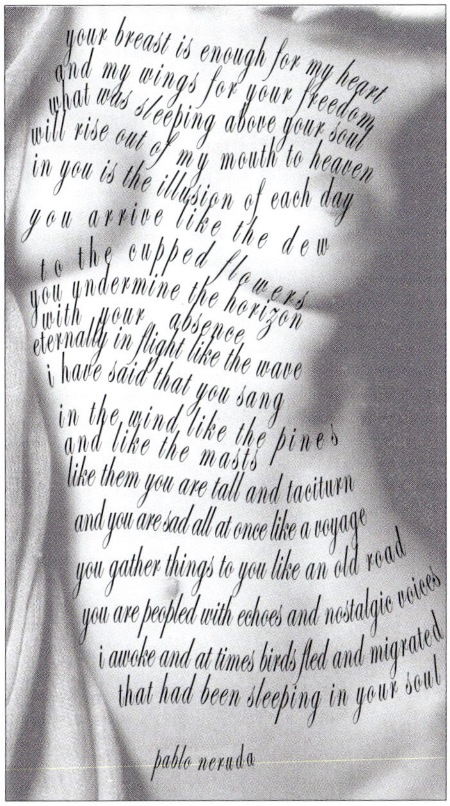

6-7 *Matt Morris Cook.* Neruda. *2003.* Courtesy of the artist.

The Type on a Path tool follows the body form with poetry in this student portfolio piece.

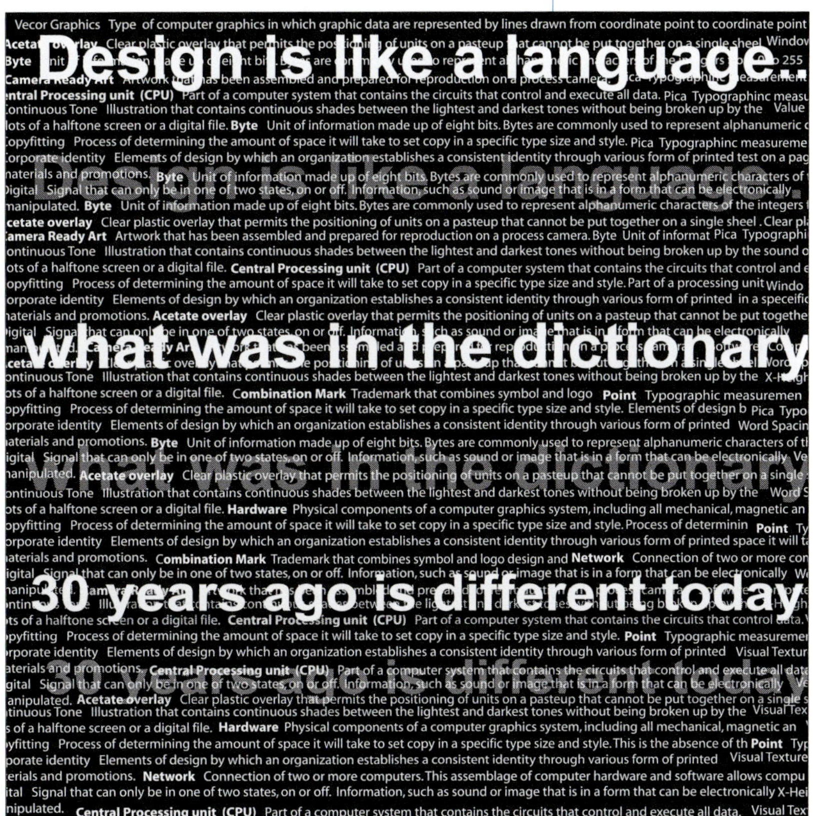

6-8 *The Area Type tool is used in this typographic illustration that uses a quotation from the designer Keiko Hayashi.*

Visual Perception

There are a variety of design principles that help make a coherent whole of a visual image. We have discussed several of them in previous chapters. Now let's consider continuation, eye direction, and focal point.

The principle of continuation states that the viewer's eye will follow along a line or curve. The eye and brain will continue along an adjoining line, drawing an invisible connection. When the eye is carried smoothly into the line or curve of an adjoining object, continuation has occurred. Shapes that form a harmonious relationship with adjoining shapes please the eye.

Alphonse Mucha's JOB poster in Figure 6-3a (see page 135) makes excellent use of this principle and is discussed in the previous text. Continuation helps to make a whole and pleasing visual Gestalt of any 2-D image, whether it is an illustration, a painting, a logo, or a page layout. Continuation is a fundamental principle of successful art and design structure. (See page 149 on Gestalt Principles.)

Eye direction is the path the design sets up for the eye to follow. In Figure 6-1 (see page 134), the mouth on the horn becomes the focal point, with several lines radiating from it. The focal point is where the eye is primarily drawn. A focal point can also be a strongly different element of value, color, or shape. It is the first area that attracts attention and encourages the viewer to look further. If at first glance, our eye is drawn equally to several areas, either the design is poor, or the design concept is an overall symmetrical pattern. A focal point can be set up in many ways. The eye can be drawn to it through a skillful use of continuation.

Hands On Practice

Stop reading now and practice tracing a scan or just drawing with the pen tools. Incorporate a word or phrase into the artwork. As you create the file, look for similarities between type and image, and use continuation to tie the placement of the text to the image. **Figure 6-9** shows a student's solution to this problem. Keith Kurtz used a moth scan (some scans are included on the **CD** for your use) and locked the scan. Then he opened a new layer and traced the scan with Illustrator pen tools, filling the closed shapes with solid colors and gradients. He could have chosen to use the Auto Trace tool. He converted his typography to outline, using the Type>Create Outlines command, and then treated the resulting shapes with color fills. He also did a fairly advanced process by using the pen tools to move the points of his typography to join with the moth.

Practice using the Pathfinder tool on a set of overlapping type and image combinations. The Exclude command produces good results.

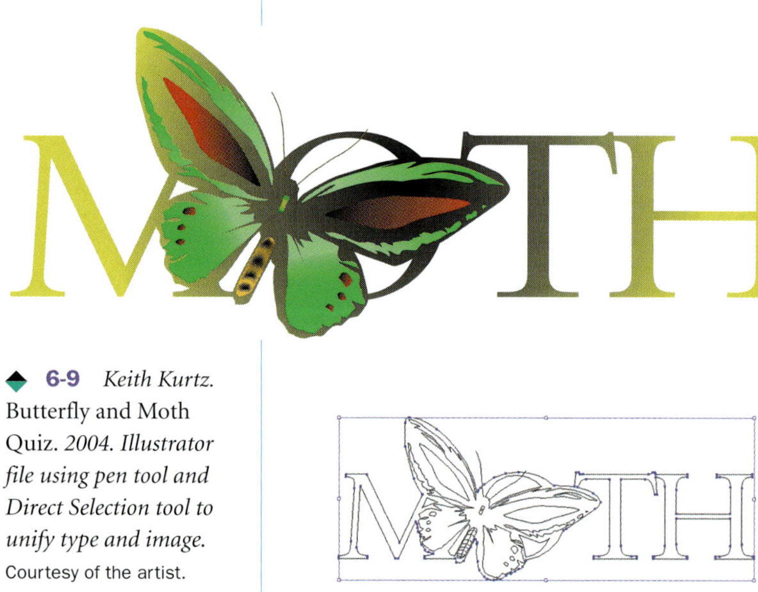

(a) (b)

◆ **6-9** *Keith Kurtz.* Butterfly and Moth Quiz. *2004. Illustrator file using pen tool and Direct Selection tool to unify type and image.* Courtesy of the artist.

More How To Basics

When you are working with filters, gradient meshes, blends, and other effects presented here, you are working at an intermediate level in Illustrator. **Figures 6-10a–f** accompany instruction in filters and styles. As always with software effects, the challenge is not only to learn how to use them, but to think of how to use them successfully and creatively.

Applying Filters will vary depending upon whether your object is raster or vector. Vector shapes can be altered with several options under Filter. Choose Effect in the pull down menu and experiment with *convert to shape* through *warp* for another array of possible variations (Figs. 6-10a–b).

Open *Window>Styles* and *Window>Style Libraries>Fills*. Select a vector shape you've created and click on a style to apply to it, as shown in Figure 6-10c. The Appearances window gives you data about that style effect. You can edit it by clicking on an attrib-

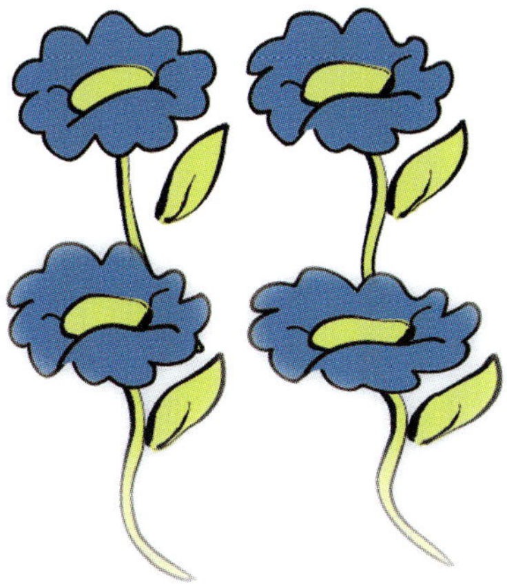

a–f: Adobe product screen shots reprinted with permission from Adobe Systems Incorporated

(a)

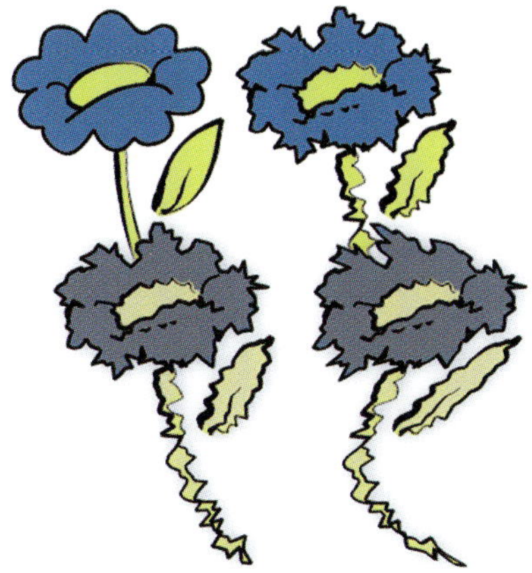

(b)

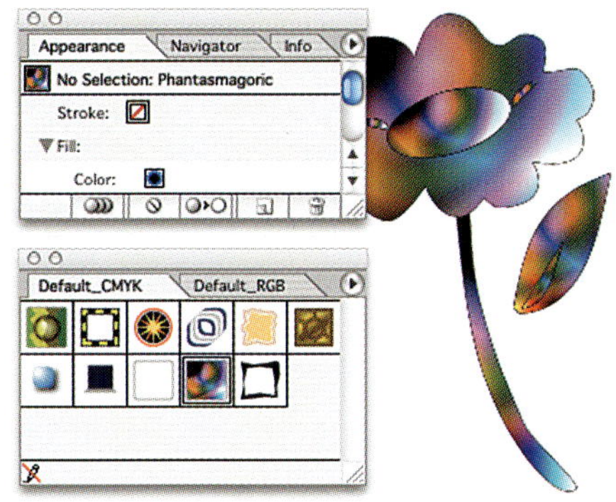

(c)

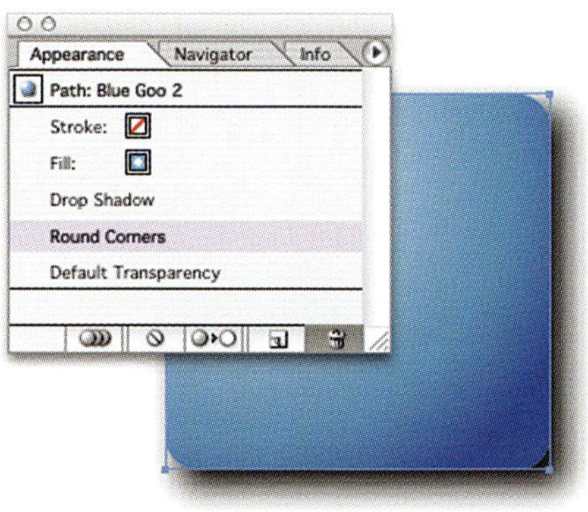

(d)

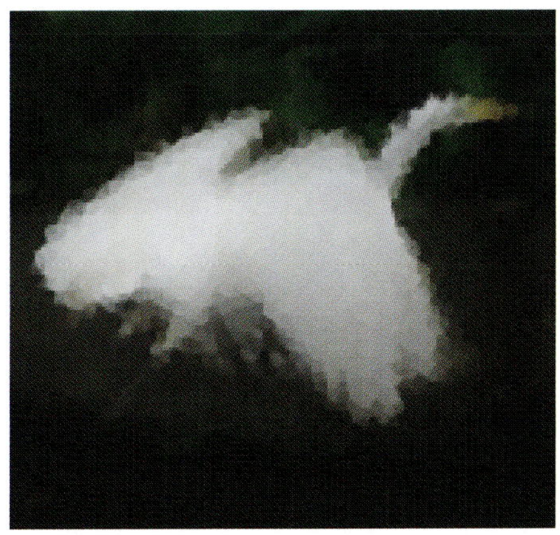

(e)

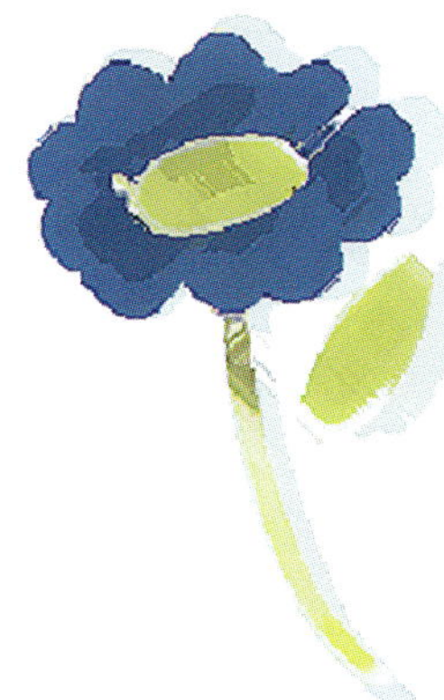

(f)

◆ **6-10 [a–f]** *Working with filters and styles provides a wide array of effects.*

ute and clicking on the trash to delete it. Choose and make a shape from the shape toolbox. Select it and apply the Style>Blue Goo effect and use the Appearances window to eliminate the rounded corners (Fig. 6-10d).

A *bitmapped* imported raster scan has some different filters that can be used on it. Fig 6-10e shows a Filter>Pixelate>Crystallize. These effects can also be added on top of one another for further variations. When selected in the Filter pull down menu, most filters will present a pop up window with an array of settings to investigate. Filter>Distort, pen and ink, and stylize are available anytime. Figure 6-10f shows some of these effects.

More How To Basics

Figures 6-11a–k show the process of working with more complex gradient effects and introduce patterns and symbols. When you open a Window for each of these effects, be sure to look along the bottom of that window to select your options. Figure 6-11a shows the Swatches window with patterns active.

The **Mesh Gradient** is a powerful tool, capable of creating wonderfully soft and realistic color effects.

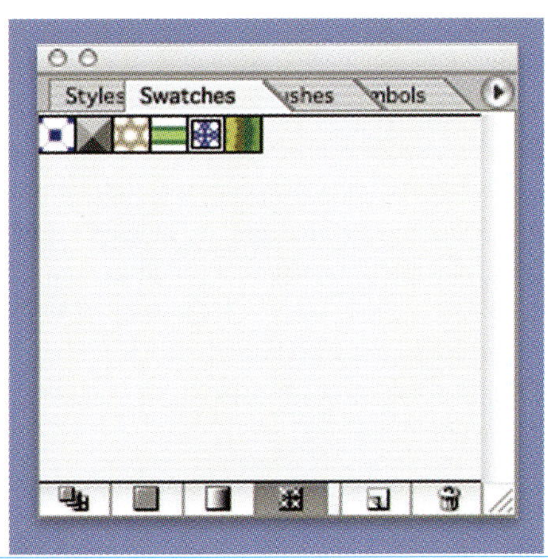

a–l: Adobe product screen shots reprinted with permission from Adobe Systems Incorporated

(a)

◆ **6-11a** *Specify your effect using the icons at the bottom of the window.*

◆ **6-11b** *Comparing radial gradient (left) and mesh gradient (right).*

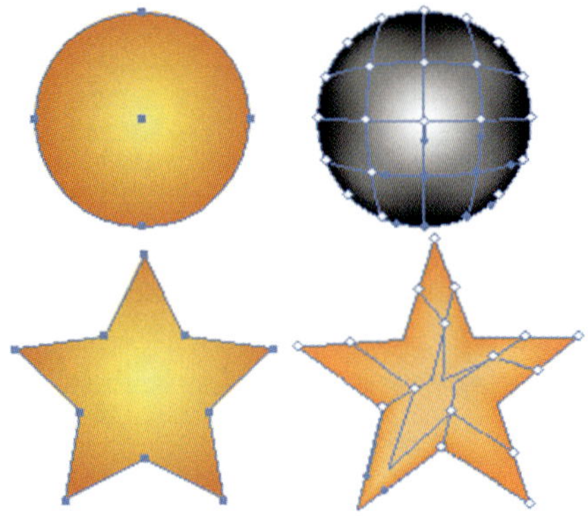

(b)

These gradients can be manipulated for very detailed shifts in color. Whereas the gradient fill creates a smooth color gradation across an object, the gradient mesh tool transforms an object into a complex mesh of color that can flow in different directions. It can be precisely adjusted and manipulated, placing a color at each intersection of the mesh. Figure 6-11b shows different gradient effects that we'll examine.

To create a mesh gradient, select a solid filled object. Choose Object>Create Gradient Mesh. This mesh is constructed on a grid. In the pop up window, enter the number of horizontal rows of mesh lines in the *Rows* text box. Then enter the number of vertical columns of mesh lines in the *Columns* text box (Fig. 6-11c). Select the direction of the highlight from the Appearance pop up menu; usually center is the most pleasing. Select the percentage of highlight, with 100 percent being brightest white.

◆ **6-11 [c–f]** *Creating a gradient mesh.*

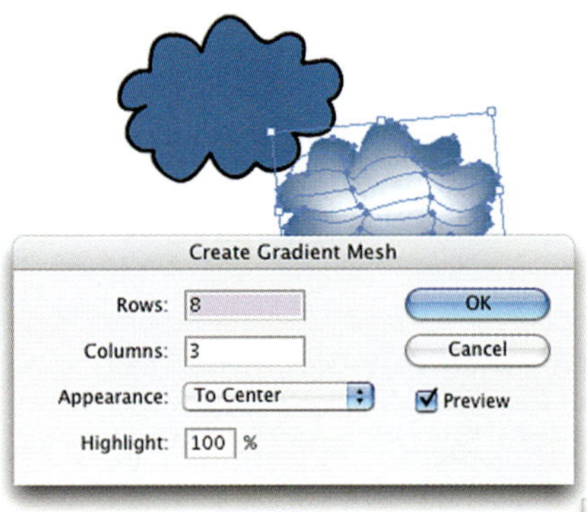

(c)

To add or delete mesh points and mesh lines, select the Mesh tool. Anchor points can be added to your object by clicking on a line or a space. To delete a mesh point and its lines, use the keyboard to Alt-Click (Windows) or Option-Click (Mac OS) directly on the mesh point, as shown in Figure 6-11d.

To edit a mesh point, select the Gradient Mesh tool and click on a mesh point. Direction lines appear that you can drag to edit the mesh point just as you

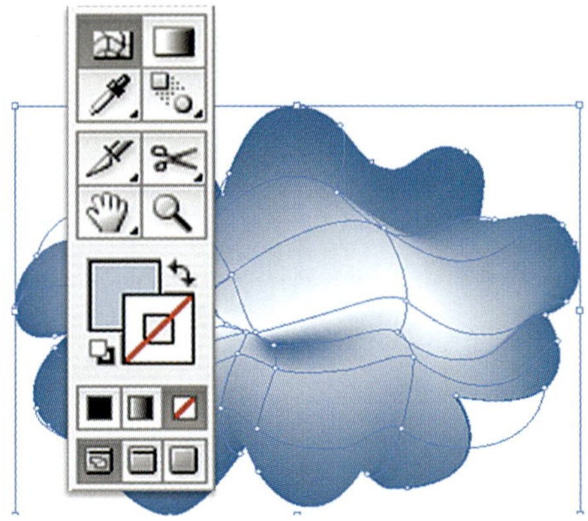

(d)

would edit an anchor point. You can use the Direct Selection tool to edit the mesh points just as you edit anchor points. Figure 6-11e shows this editing process.

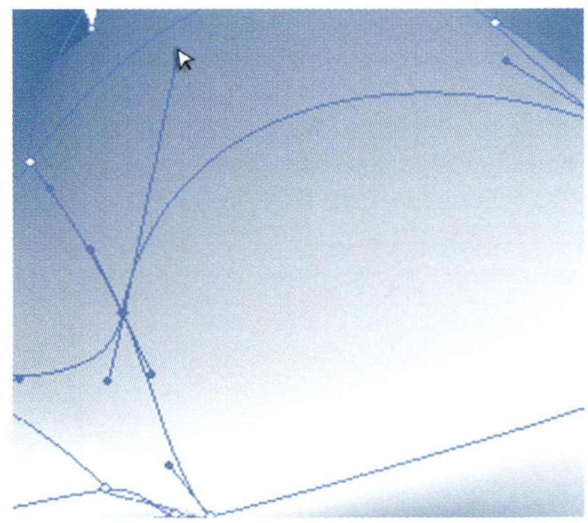

(e)

Colors are added by dragging and dropping or by using the Paint Bucket tool. When you click on a mesh point, the point and surrounding areas are colored with the current fill color. When you click a mesh patch, all four points surrounding the area are colored. You can change the shape of the colored areas by editing the mesh points (Fig. 6-11f).

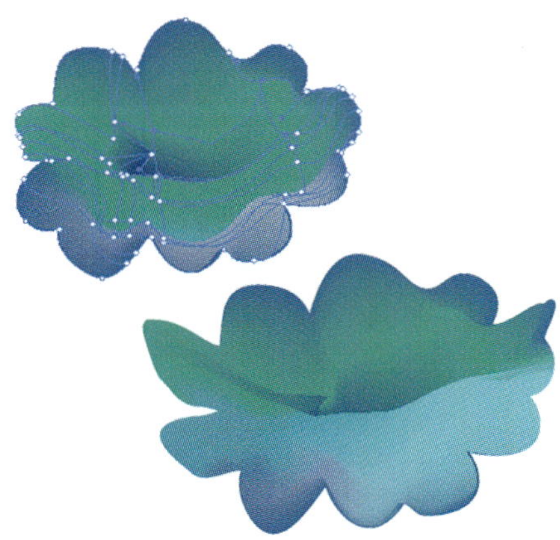

(f)

The *Blend* tool is located on the toolbox in the same box as the Mesh Gradient. You can create blends of colors and shapes between objects using this tool. You may select the beginning and ending shape or color, and ask Illustrator to create the intermediate steps. You can edit blends that you created by moving, resizing, shading, and re-contouring objects. However, you *cannot* blend between gradient mesh objects.

To create a blend with the Blend tool, first select the tool. Then click objects to blend in sequential order. Click the Blend tool again when ready to start a new blend, as shown in Figure 6-11g. You can also generate a blend with the Make Blend command. First select the objects to blend, then choose Object>Blends>Make. To unmake a blend, select the blend with any selection tool, and choose Object>Blends>Release (Fig. 6-11h).

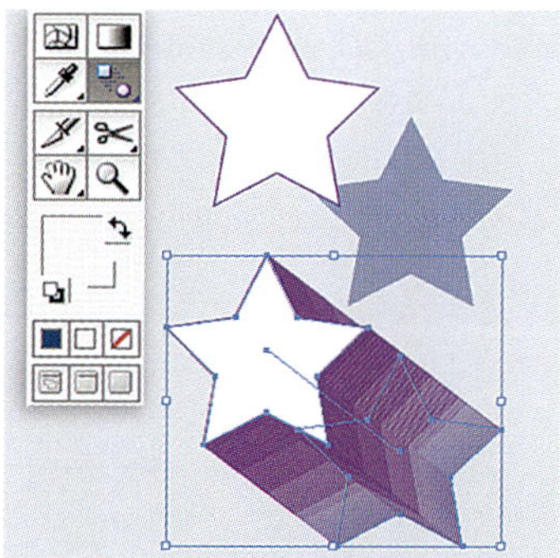
(g)

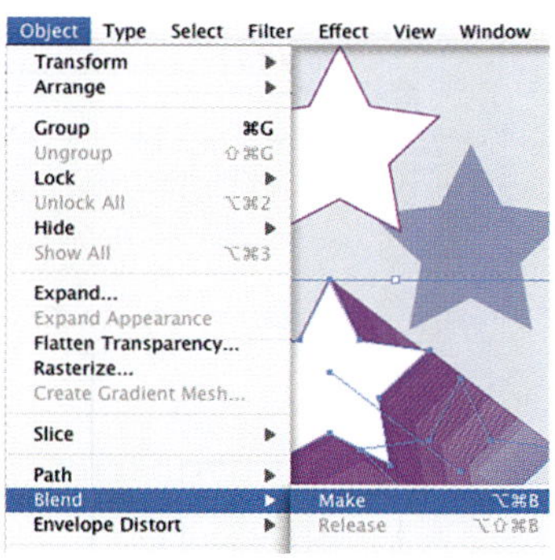

(h)

◆ **6-11 [g–h]** *Working with the blend tool.*

Patterns can be applied to a path using brush tools, or applied to a shape. You can create personalized pattern tiles and save them in the swatches palette, just as you save color swatches and gradients. To make a pattern, start by creating artwork that you want to use as a pattern tile. Choose Window>Show Swatches, and drag the artwork to the swatches palette. This process is shown in Figure 6-11i. When

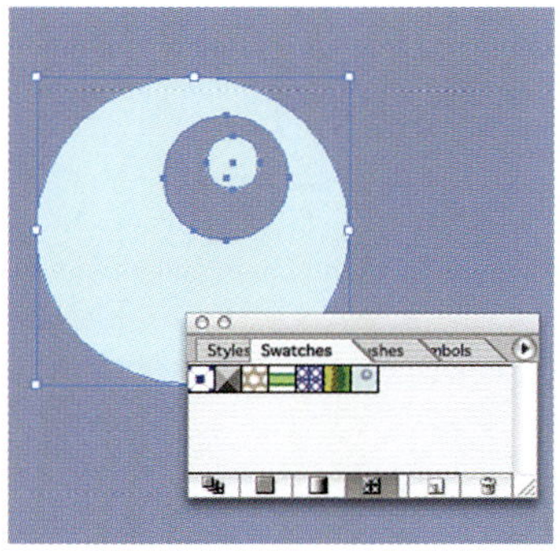

(i)

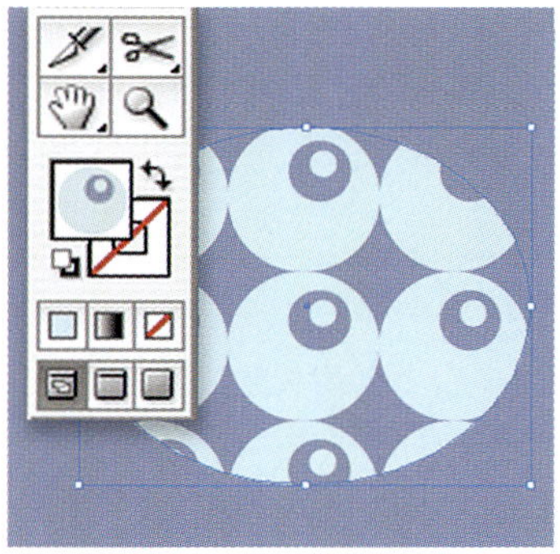
(j)

◆ **6-11 [i–j]** *Creating a pattern swatch.*

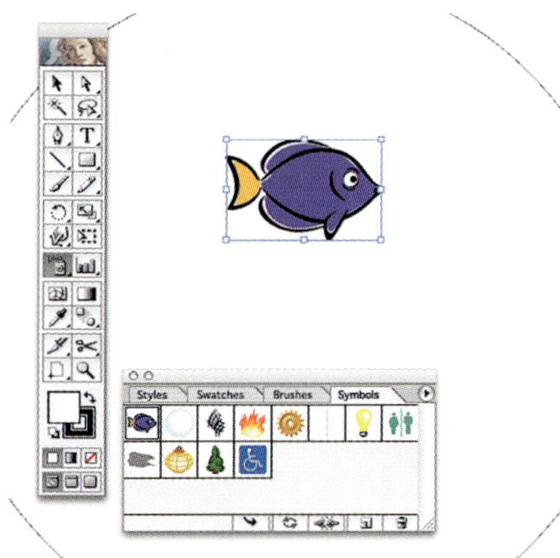

(k)

◆ **6-11k** *Using the Symbol Sprayer tool.*

creating the artwork, keep detail simple and group objects that are painted with the same color. To apply the pattern, select an object and select the desired pattern in the swatches palette (Fig. 6-11j). You can apply the pattern to stroke or fill. Be sure to select which effect you want.

Figure 6-11k shows the process of creating and applying symbols. Select a symbol from the Symbols window. Now apply it by selecting the Symbol Sprayer tool located in the toolbox. Double clicking on this tool gives a pop up window with options to control symbol attributes.

Now we have completed another How To Basics section introducing intermediate techniques. This section is intended for lecture and study. Once you are reasonably familiar with this material, try practicing these techniques.

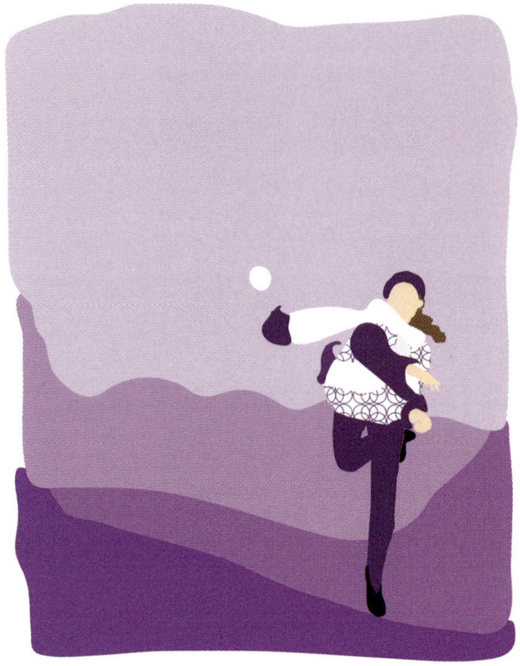

◆ **6-11l** *Carla Cannistra.* Winter. *2003. Illustrator file.*
Courtesy of the artist.

Hands On Practice

Practice all the techniques presented in the How To Basics above, including creating mesh gradients and blends, and working with patterns and symbols. Apply all of these to simple geometric and organic shapes. After you complete this practice, continue with the next How To Basics. **Figure 6-11l** shows an image created by Carla Cannistra for her student portfolio by generating a pattern and applying it to shapes traced from a family photo. She generates eye direction with the visual path between the figure and the ball, and the scarf connecting them. See her Portfolio Profile on the accompanying **CD,** and examine her process.

◆ **6-12a** *David McLimans.* Sketchbook cover. *2003. Collage with found papers, 6 3/4" × 10 1/4".*
Courtesy of the artist.

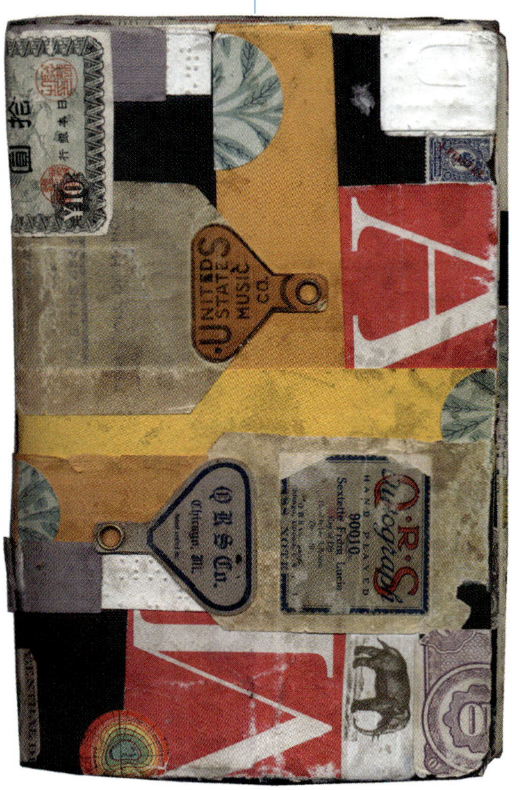

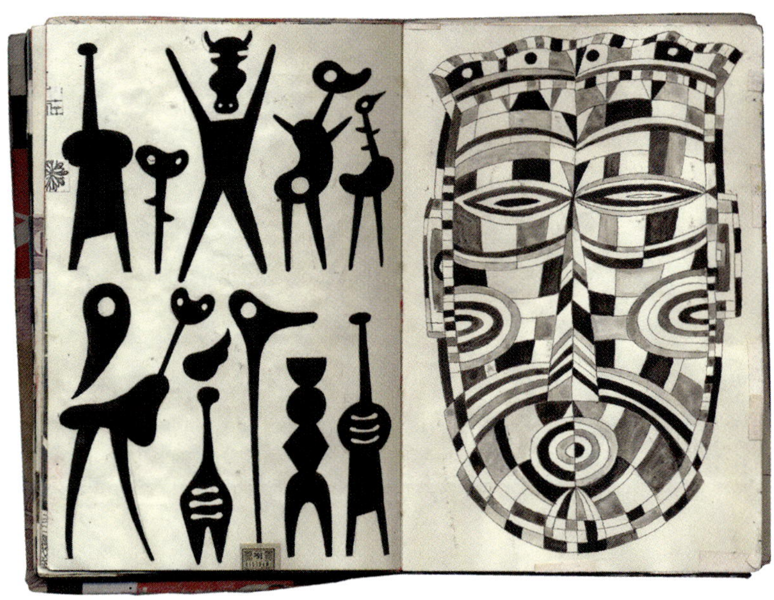

◆ **6-12b** *David McLimans.* Sketchbook interior spread. *2003. Pen and ink, 13" × 10".*
Courtesy of the artist.

Gallery Profile

David McLimans (1948—) is a contemporary freelance illustrator. He earned an MFA and began his career in illustration after working for a time as a graphic designer. His work has appeared in many national publications, including the *Washington Post*, *AIGA* (the journal of the American Institute of Graphic Arts), *Time*, the *New York Times*, the *Progressive*, the *Atlantic Monthly*, and *Harper's*. He currently lives and works in Madison, Wisconsin. McLimans has won numerous awards for his editorial illustration, including an Award of Excellence from the Society for News and a Certificate of Excellence from *Print* magazine.

The sketchbook cover and interior pages shown in **Figures 6-12a–b** demonstrate the creative, generative process behind the solutions McLimans develops for his clients and for his own artwork. He says, "Sketchbooks are for free play and experimentation. With no constraints, spontaneous and unexpected ideas develop." His drawings and illustrations utilize a strong sense of figure/ground, as shown in **Figure 6-13**. This black-and-white illustration for a *Newark (N.J.) Star Ledger* section cover accompanied an article on preserving wildlands. It was created in pen and ink. **Figure 6-14** is a hand-cut collage that illustrated an article for the *Washington Post* "Outlook" section on "Digging Up Dirt" on politicians. There is a close tie between the concept discussed in the article and the illustration. Concept and design principles unite in this illustrator's work. The shovel becomes the head of a politician in this visual metaphor. McLimans says "Concepts are the impetus for my editorial illustrations. Design is the underlying structure for making images. Figure ground is used to merge shapes and symbols. Color rhythm and scale are employed to create dynamic movement. Simple, formal relationships bring the composition together."

The computer is a handy but not indispensable studio tool for this artist. His artwork is created by hand. It may then be scanned and color corrected, final "tweaking" applied before the file is sent to the client as an email attachment. Photoshop and Illustrator are the two programs that he uses in this process.

McLimans also has a strong interest in fine art. He carves sculptural figures that become part of his "family," as shown in **Figure 6-15**. *Wheel Head* is a combination of wood, newspaper collage, and found object. Influences from Analytic Cubism and Dadaism can be found in this work. "For replenishing the body, mind, spirit and soul, I return to nature. I cleanse my eyes."

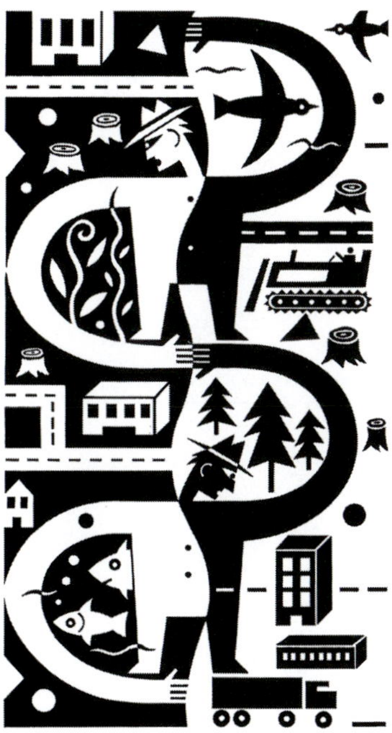

6-13 *David McLimans.* Newark (N.J.) Star Ledger *(section cover). 1998. Pen and ink, 6 1/2" × 12".*
Courtesy of the artist.

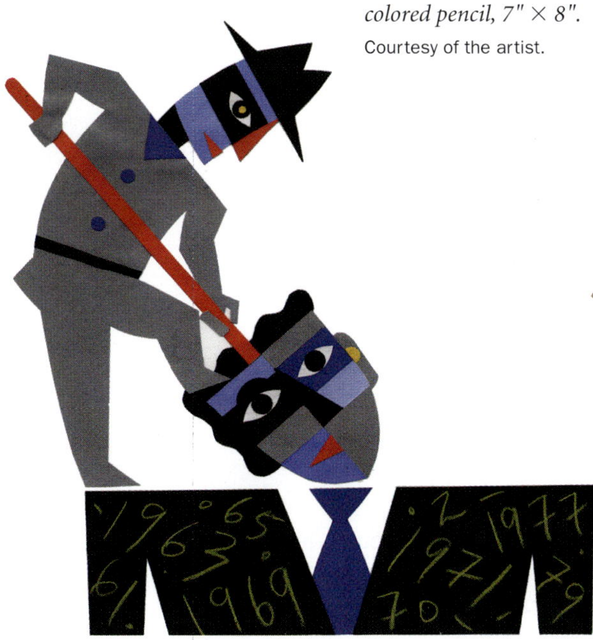

6-14 *David McLimans.* Digging Up Dirt. *2000.* Washington Post *"Outlook" (section cover). Cut paper and colored pencil, 7" × 8".*
Courtesy of the artist.

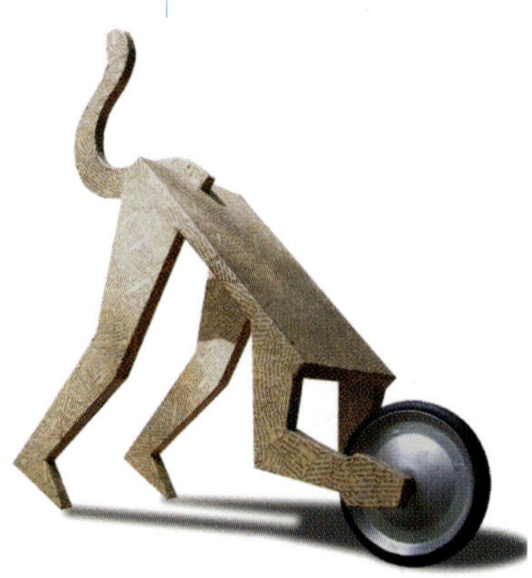

6-15 *David McLimans.* Wheel Head. *1995. Newspaper collage over wood and found object, 16 1/2" h. × 5 1/2" w. × 21" l.*
Courtesy of the artist.

How To Basics

Figures 6-16a–d present the **vector masking** function in Illustrator. *Masking* allows you to crop an image, creating a mattelike effect. It can also be used to create interesting window effects that frame the image layers beneath the mask.

To crop unwanted areas from an image edge, create a geometric or organic cropping shape without ink in the stroke or fill. If you want to mask only the items in a single layer, make the mask the top object in that layer, select it, lock all the other layers, Select All, and Select Object>Clipping Mask>Make, as shown in Figure 6-16a.

For more complex masking, with the mask selected, also select only the objects in lower layers that you want to be affected by the mask. Now select Object>Clipping Mask>Make. The resulting effect is shown in Figure 6-16b.

◆ **6-16 [a–d]** *Working with clipping masks.*

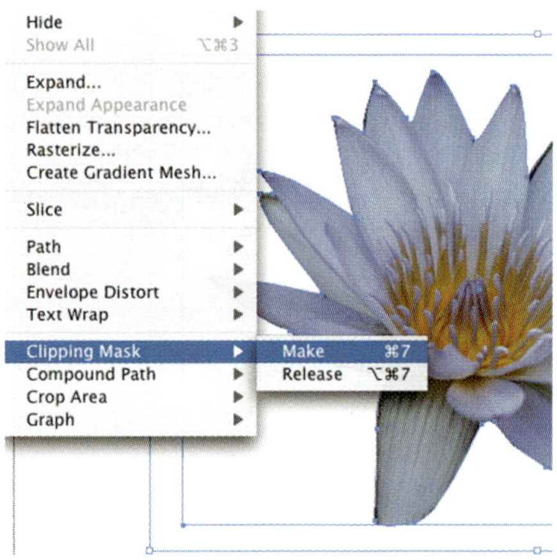

a–d: Adobe product screen shot(s) reprinted with permission from Adobe Systems Incorporated

(a)

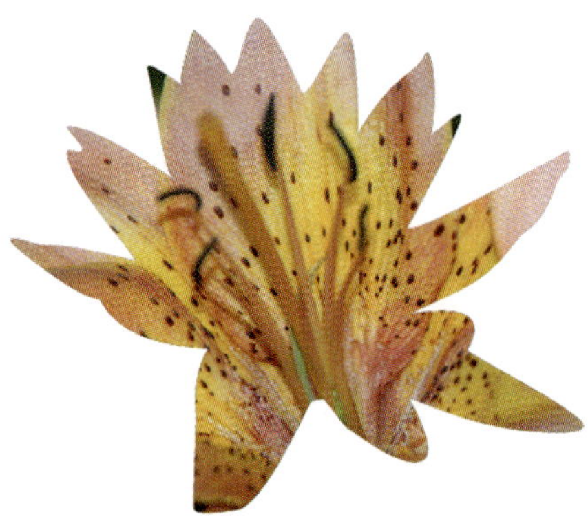

(b)

Integrating Raster and Vector. There are a variety of methods that allow you to include Illustrator (or Freehand) Paths into other programs. These paths define the boundary of an image when it's placed in other programs. Painter lets you import paths as stencil-like "friskets" that allow you to apply painting effects to only a specific path area. Use Illustrator's Pathfinder merge filter before importing paths into Painter to eliminate path overlaps.

To place your Illustrator image into a page layout program such as QuarkXPress, save it as an EPS file to be placed in Quark. The EPS file can be relied upon to preserve transparency settings and clipping masks. To export an Illustrator file to Photoshop, choose File> Export, then select Photoshop as a file type. In Photoshop, go to File>Open and select this file.

Clipping Path. There are also methods allowing you to import files from a raster program into a vector file, without an accompanying white background. First, create a selection in Photoshop, using the magic wand tool or other selection methods. Convert the selection into a clipping path by choosing Path>Make Work Path>Save Path. File>Save Paths to Illustrator. This process is shown in Figure 6-16c. In Illustrator choose File>Open to place the outline clipping path. You won't see anything until you Select>Select All and fill it with the desired fill and stroke color (Fig. 6-16d).

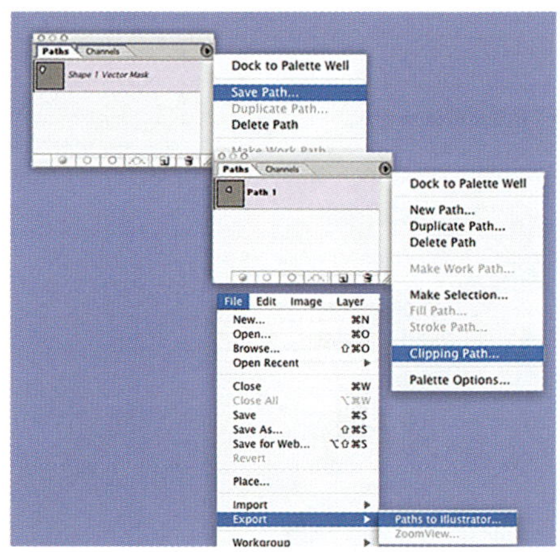

(c)

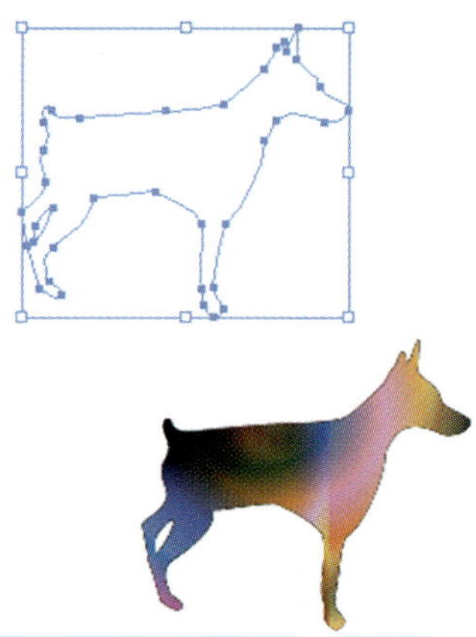

(d)

Again, now that we have covered an introduction to the techniques, let's apply them. While practicing these software processes, keep design principles in mind.

Hands On Practice

Practice all the masking techniques presented in the How To Basics above, including making a "matte" effect on your artwork based on the techniques introduced in the previous How To Basics. Also practice creative masking by making a shape to cover and redefine the edges of your artwork.

Experiment with clipping paths in Photoshop. This will be easier if you have been integrating the Photoshop software along with the Illustrator instruction. Make a selection around one of the solid color background CD images, and convert the selection to a clipping path inside Photoshop. Import it to Illustrator, as described above. Select and colorize.

Focus On Concept

This chapter discusses design principles in artwork from design history, art history, and contemporary illustration. What is the relevance of visual design principles throughout art and design history? A very clear example can be found in Figure 6-3b (see page 137). Can you find a favorite artwork that uses these principles? Look for repetition and variation, analyze the use of color, and search for continuation, eye direction, and focal point. Plan to present these in class and explain your choice.

Is there a difference in the aesthetic intent from 1900 to today? What is it? Think about previous discussions about modernism and postmodernism. Also consider the influence of our tools on what we make. What are the similarities throughout this period?

Gestalt Principles

By now you are familiar with the unit-forming principles behind Gestalt design. However, let's review them as a group before beginning the next Studio assignment, which will ask you to combine your newly acquired software skills with your design skills.

An artist and designer works not simply with lines on paper, or pixels in a digital file, but with the structure of visual perception itself. In 1890, German psychologist Christian von Ehrenfels published an essay called "On Gestalt Qualities." Ehrenfels suggested that the whole is more than the sum of its parts. The parts interact to form a new whole, and our perception of an object is affected by the objects around it. This led to the development of the Gestalt unit-forming principles, which describe how we perceive, organize, and interpret visual data.

These Gestalt perceptual principles help you to understand and utilize the way the eye, brain, and digital image interact. The principle of similarity states that when we see things that are similar, we naturally group them. As discussed earlier, **similarity** occurs when we see similar shapes, locations, sizes, colors, angles, or values. Grouping by similarity in spatial location is called **proximity**, or nearness. The principle of **continuation** occurs when the eye is carried along a line or a curve into that of another object. **Closure** occurs when the eye completes a line or curve to form a shape. The principle of **figure/ground** states that the eye and mind must separate an object (figure) from its surroundings (ground). This can be done several ways, because some visual designs have a more dynamic figure/ground relationship, while others are stable.

These Gestalt relationships in art and design are intended to help you give form to a strong concept. In the optimum design, there is an integral relationship between form and concept.

Warming Up

This is your opportunity to practice some of the design principles and the software techniques introduced in this chapter. The work created in the Warming Up sessions can be among the best you will do.

Select an object that interests you. If you're on a campus, maybe something from the Theater Department's prop department will be attractive; otherwise, look at Goodwill, in the attic, or at an antique store. Photograph or draw the object. Now put the digitized photograph or scanned drawing into Illustrator and render it with Illustrator pen tools. Remember to create shapes, not lines, and fill those shapes with colors, gradients, patterns, and blends, as desired. Keep an eye on the Gestalt design properties of your image. Be sure to include a background that has a particular shape and color. Consider incorporating the use of shadows and light source to generate visual interest.

Finally, you are asked to integrate many of the techniques in this chapter to create the following portfolio assignment.

IN THE STUDIO

Create a stamp design for the current postal rate. It should include the cost, the letters "USA," and a brief identifying word or phrase. **Figures 6-17a–b** are a related student design.

Select from the following topics:

An artist or art period that you appreciate and enjoy.
A stamp reflecting your state or country's identity.

The size may vary but you should be able to read it at approximately $1^1/_4" \times 1^1/_4"$. In the final class presentation, include a large version of the stamp design, around $5" \times 5"$, along with small versions in two different color schemes.

Begin with thumbnails and sketches. Incorporate repetition, interesting figure/ground relationship, and a carefully planned color scheme. Use the basic 2-D design principles of continuation, and establish a definite eye direction and focal point. Stop by your local post office for a little visual research. Many fine designs are available for a few cents. Remember that a clean, simple design is often the best answer. Don't assume that more is better.

Plan to scan your sketches or photo collages, or draw directly in Illustrator when beginning the actual piece. This is a full-color design. Identify a color scheme (analogous, complementary, triadic, split complementary) and stick with it. Include colors that are toned down, not just high saturation. Be sensitive to value range. Execute this design in RGB or PANTONE spot colors and incorporate a mask. As you work on this piece, look often at the image at actual size and do occasional print proofs. Now create two more versions of your finished design using a different color scheme.

Figure 6-18 is Casey Swanson's solution to this problem. It shows the outline of the state of Wisconsin used as a mask. It is placed over an assembly of images associated with the state. The artwork began with a cut-and-paste collage of photographs in Photoshop. (It could also have been created as a hand-

6-17 [a–b] *A series of stamps created for a student portfolio based on the theme of endangered species. The stamps were printed as 8" × 10" documents as well as in traditional stamp size.*

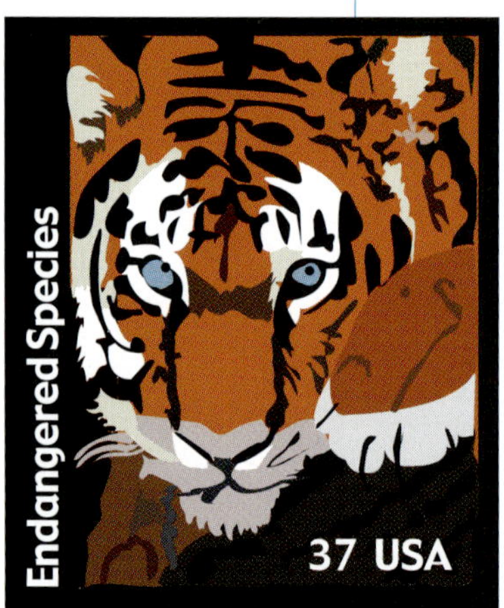

(a)

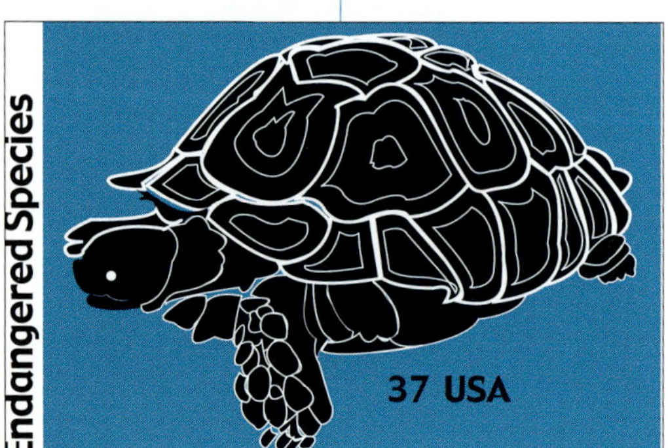

(b)

6-18 *Casey Swanson.* Wisconsin Stamp. *2003. Illustrator file.*
Courtesy of the artist.

A mask is applied to this Illustrator file, achieving the outlined effect.

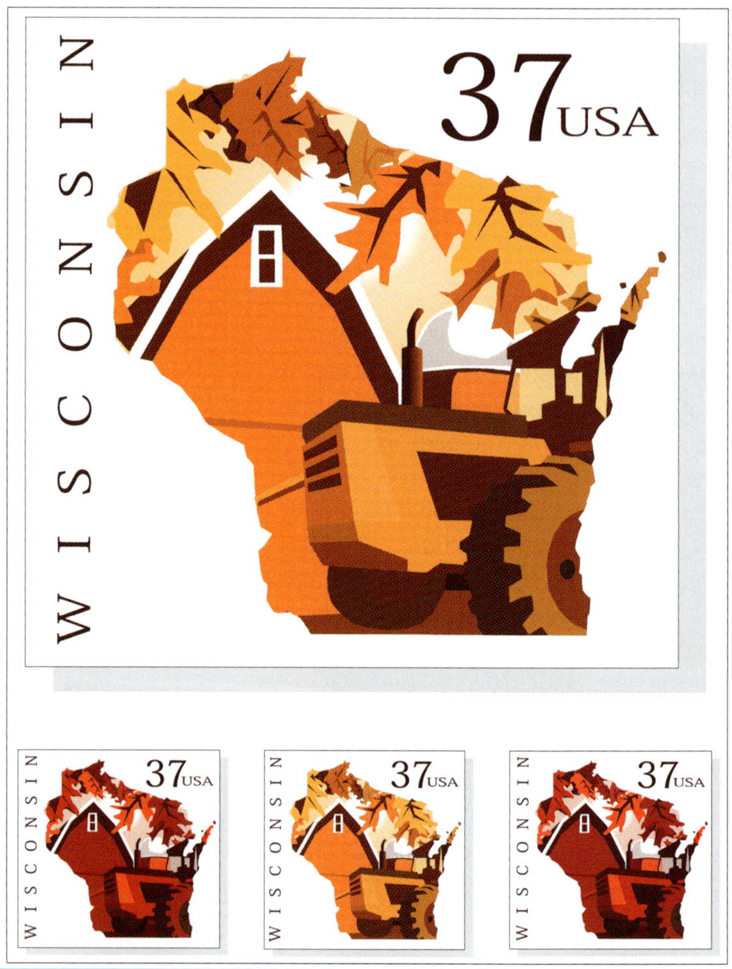

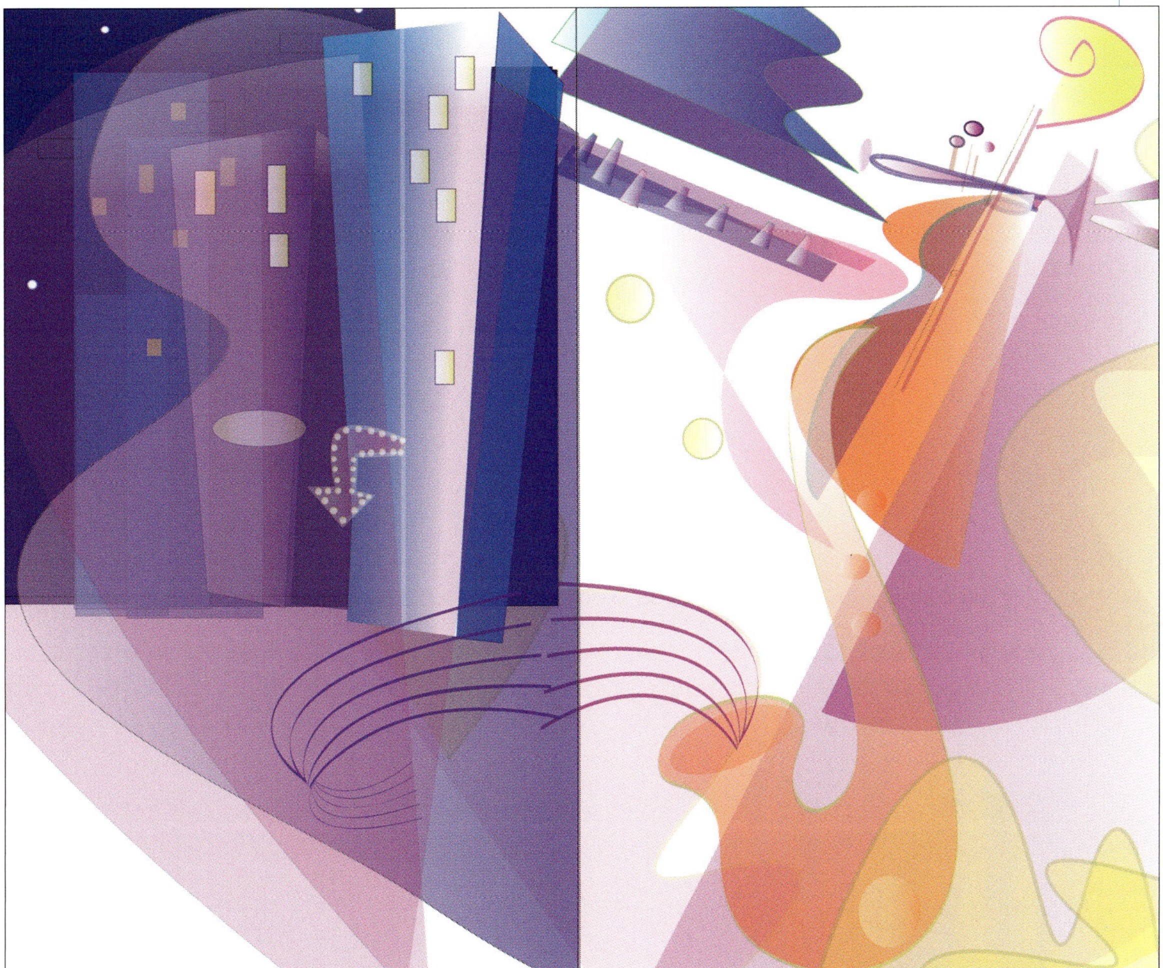

◆ **6-19** *Melissa Ramsey. Two related posters. Ink jet prints. 24" × 20" each.*

This artwork created in Illustrator pursues the theme of jazz music. It shows what is possible in vector graphics and may inspire you to future investigation.
Courtesy of the artist.

cut, scanned collage.) The resized and assembled images were then placed into Illustrator. The photo layer was locked, and a series of new layers were created to hold the drawing. The final layer was the mask drawn in the shape of the state. **Figure 6-19** shows a mastery of design and software.

SUMMARY CRITIQUE

In the final critique on your work, be prepared to discuss the following questions. What design principles did you incorporate in this artwork? Especially point out how you considered and incorporated eye direction, focal point, continuation, and/or closure. Be prepared to look for and discuss these principles in other students' work. For example, select the best example of continuation in all the work shown. Explain why you chose it. Describe your visual decision-making process. Why did you select the image and topic you are working with? Is there a conceptual dimension that you are addressing through symbol or metaphor? What works in your design and what doesn't? How might you improve the piece? What software techniques did you use? Is there anything you would like additional instruction and explanation on?

MOVING ON

The next chapter introduces the structure of web design. It will discuss what is similar and what is different between web- and print-based digital design. You will be asked to create pages for a website, using software you already know.
As we progress from chapter to chapter, you'll be asked to build and apply your skills in all three areas of technique, concept, and composition.

TERMINOLOGY

CHAPTER 7

See Glossary for definitions

World Wide Web
TCP/IP
Interactivity
New Media
Time-based
HTML
URL
Download Time
ISDN
DSL
AOL
Interlaced GIF
Progressive JPEG
Default
Website
Link
Rollover

7 Web Design

Until now, we have been studying computer graphics as a print form, rather than as something viewed in its final form on a monitor. There are many design and aesthetic similarities between print graphics and web graphics, but much of the excitement and the challenge lie in their differences. This chapter can be used as a tool to learn about design issues in creating for the web and to practice critiquing and scripting a website. Many students will find the aesthetic and communication design structure introduced in this chapter useful for a later full course in web design.

An Introduction

The **World Wide Web** (WWW) has quickly become one of the most powerful and innovative tools for designers today, with tremendous potential for text- and image-based applications. Let us spend a little time covering some historical background of the global network of computers called the Internet.

Gallery Profile

Jessica Helfand (1960—) works with William Drenttel at their studio JH/WD where they do editorial and **New Media** design for clients such as Netscape, the Yale Law School, Lingua Franca, and The Museum of Modern Art. The Asterisk Project, created for the Cooper-Hewitt, National Design Museum, presents a design exploratory for the National Design Awards. (See the address on the accompanying **CD**.)

Helfand is currently on the graphic design faculty at the Yale School of Art, and was formerly an adjunct assistant professor at New York University's Interactive Telecommunications program. She is the author of several books on graphic design and cultural criticism, including *Reinventing the Wheel* and *Paul Rand: American Modernist*.

Helfand's web projects show how it is possible to establish identity, design a clear navigational interface, and bring a unified visual interest to a site. The JH/WD studio design for the Cooper-Hewitt is shown in several screen captures in **Figures 7-1**, **7-2**, **7-3**, and **7-4** that demonstrate the clear communication structure of this important site.

At the JH/WD website (see the address on the accompanying **CD**) are several important statements about the design philosophy of this studio:

"We love finding new ways of looking at old things."
"We hate seeing design flounder as a superfluous cosmetic device."
"We love it when the written word extends a visual idea."
"We love thinking in **time-based** and interactive media."

What's your take on JH/WD's design philosophy? Which statements reflect the postmodern approach to design and how?

Origins

The growth of computer science as an academic discipline in the 1960s and 1970s fostered the rapid growth of the Net. There are many names associated with Internet development, but the original concept is often attributed to J. C. R. Licklider of the Massachusetts Institute of Technology (MIT). In 1962, he presented his "Galactic Network" concept. In spirit, it was much like the Internet of today. MIT researcher Lawrence Roberts took this concept to heart when he went to work for the U.S. Department of Defense Advanced Research Projects Agency. He put together the plan for ARPANET (Advanced Research Projects Agency NETwork), publishing it in 1967.

In 1969, the U.S. Department of Defense (DOD) commissioned ARPANET to research a communication and command network that could link the separate computer networks of the DOD and the military contractors and universities performing military research. There were many steps along the way and numerous contributors. The network at this time was used only to share access to the world's few supercomputers, but universities and corporations would soon be eager to join.

In 1974, collaborating with Vinton Cerf, Bob Kahn developed a packet-switching protocol that came to be called Transmission Control Protocol/Internet Protocol (**TCP/IP**) that is now used throughout the Internet. TCP/IP is a software protocol that permits computer networks to communicate. Military funding helped create this standard, and the Defense Department's adoption of it in 1980 for its own operations gave TCP/IP a crucial boost. Again, it was a research group at MIT that demonstrated how a compact and simple version of TCP could run on desktop computers.

In 1990, Tim Berners-Lee started work on a hypertext browser/editor. He made up "Worldwide Web" as a name for the program, which he created on a NeXT computer. A graduate of Oxford University, England, Tim now holds a chair at the Laboratory for Computer Science and Artificial Intelligence Lab at MIT. He directs the World Wide Web Consortium, an open forum of companies and organizations with the mission of evolving the protocols and standards associated with the web to their full potential.

By 1996, over 30 million people were using the Internet. Now Yahoo! alone has 300 million global users. Currently over 56 percent of the sites are in English, followed by German at 8 percent,

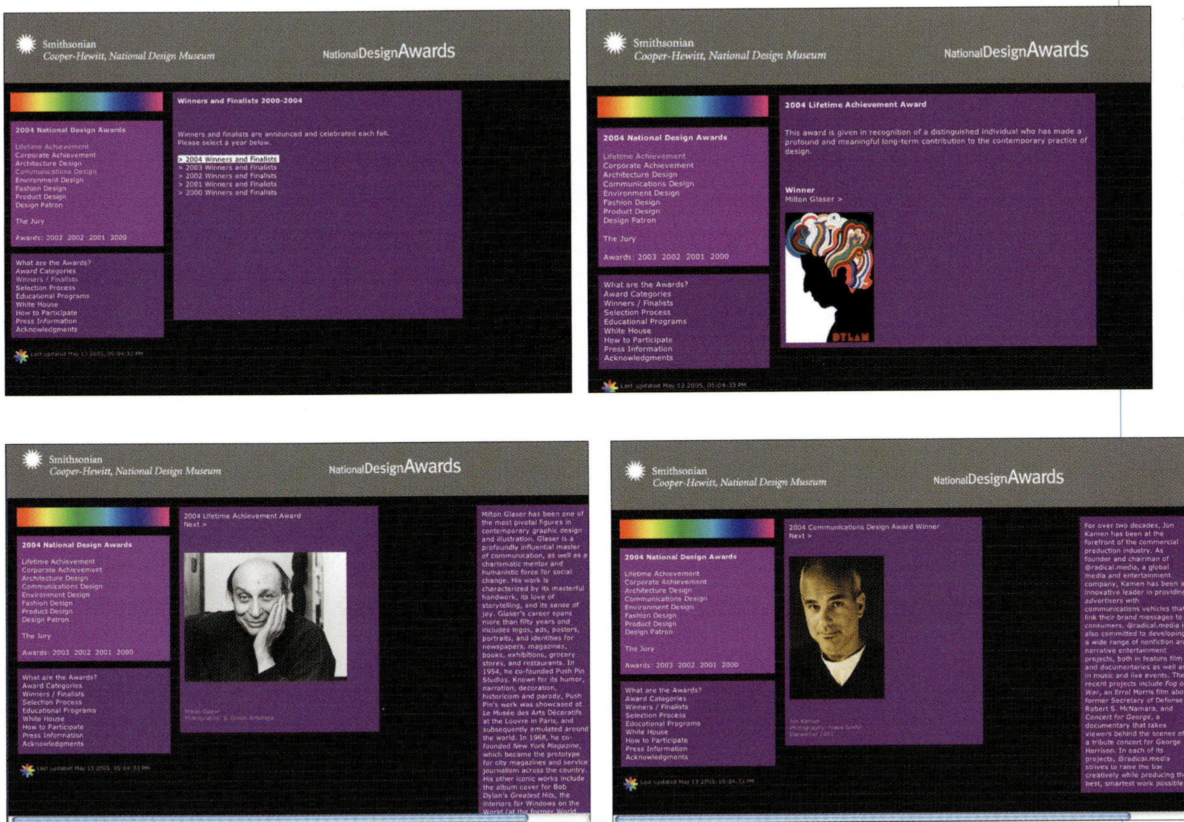

7-1, 7-2, 7-3, 7-4 *Cooper-Hewitt National Design Museum website pages. Design by Jessica Helfand and William Drenttel.* Courtesy of the Cooper-Hewitt National Design Museum.

according to the Wikipedia free web encyclopedia. The highest Internet traffic is in North America, followed by Europe, then South America. The web is widely used in classrooms, offices, and homes, tying us in a new global communications network. It is continuing to grow and evolve. Where has it gone since its origins? Easier access, much more data availability, faster downloads, and greater **interactivity** and animated movement are among the more recent developments. A clear communication structure continues to be a vital ingredient of successful website design, as demonstrated in the site for the Cooper-Hewitt, National Design Museum illustrated in Figures 7-1 through 7-4.

New Media

Contemporary web design is a form of New Media that takes us beyond the print realm of text and image and has the power to incorporate additional sensory data. Human perception is a blend of sensory input from sight, sound, touch, and smell, all shaped by memory. Increasingly, New Media incorporate the senses of the human body, including sound and movement. *New Media* is a general term for the use of computer- or electronic-based technology, often interactive. It includes such things as websites, DVD and CD-ROM technology, virtual reality, digital cameras, and even telephones. The term is used in relation to "old" print media forms that are static representations of text and graphics.

The nature of the web is unique among these categories of interactive media. It is a nonlinear, interactive medium without geographic boundaries. Web data can be delivered simultaneously around the world, freed from the physical restraints of traditional static media.

As the web allows ease of international exchange, our communication and design media become a shared, worldwide experience. This

Focus On Concept

How is the computer a tool like any other throughout history?

How does it present ways of seeing and shaping reality that are significantly different from those of the past?

What are the constants we bring to the use of new technology?

What is truly *new* about the New Media that cannot be duplicated by any other media?

How has your personal experience with the web affected you?

new medium is vitally linked to the actualization of Canadian theorist and media philosopher Marshall McLuhan's 1964 concept of a "global village." Going beyond what McLuhan was writing about in the television era, we now can share a communications link with one another and can quickly "speak" with friends, colleagues, businesses, and museums around the world. This is the basis of a global communications network that McLuhan called a contemporary village. Everyone with web access has a huge, common data bank of knowledge available for research.

Design theorist and educator Katherine McCoy is an influential contemporary voice exploring the impact of the web on our culture. On her website, Higher Ground (see the accompanying **CD**), she states:

> Designers can use other, sensual dimensions beyond vision and hearing. Sight and sound are contemplative senses that deliver somewhat distanced, abstracted and more cerebral stimuli, which tend to be more mediated. The contact senses of touch, taste, smell are more primal and less culturally mediated. They evidence some sort of hardwired link to memory. Smell, in particular, is a powerful mnemonic trigger that releases rich spontaneous associations from past experience. Emerging media technologies promise to deliver kinesthetic body sensations that design can harness.

This statement encourages us to think about what new developments may happen that engage our senses. Currently the web and other forms of New Media communicate with sight and sound, but in the future we may have the ability to involve more of our physical senses.

Now let's take a look at some very practical considerations regarding web design.

How Does the Web Work?

Internet design is typically created by designers with a combination of website design software capable of invisibly writing **HTML** code. This is sometimes referred to as WYSIWYG (What You See Is What You Get). Engineers and technicians will usually write their own code. The most powerful code-editing software for designers includes Macromedia Dreamweaver and Adobe GoLive. The graphic content for a site is produced in a variety of programs, including Adobe Photoshop for images, with ImageReady and Macromedia Flash for animation. Illustrator and Freehand are also used to produce graphics for the web. QuickTime video content can be generated with a variety of tools, including Apple iMovie and Adobe Premiere, while Painter has a video/web animation component, and Macromedia Director Shockwave makes files for online viewing. Ideally, the web designer should be familiar with a wide array of software. Familiarity with Photoshop is essential.

An Internet browser lets the user "browse," or scroll through, the World Wide Web. It is a tool used to read and display the files found on computers hooked to the web. When an address is typed into a browser, like Netscape Navigator or Internet Explorer, the user's computer sends a request over the Internet for a specific **URL** (Uniform Resource Locator) address. The file is downloaded over the Internet to the user's computer. The web browser displays the file.

The URL is the address entered at the top of the browser window to access a particular site. This URL consists of three parts. First is the Protocol, written as http://. The protocol is the communications language the URL uses. Second is the domain name, listed as www.server.com. The domain name is the server where the desired file is located. The third item in a web address is the pathname, written as folder/filename.ext. The pathname is a particular file in a site.

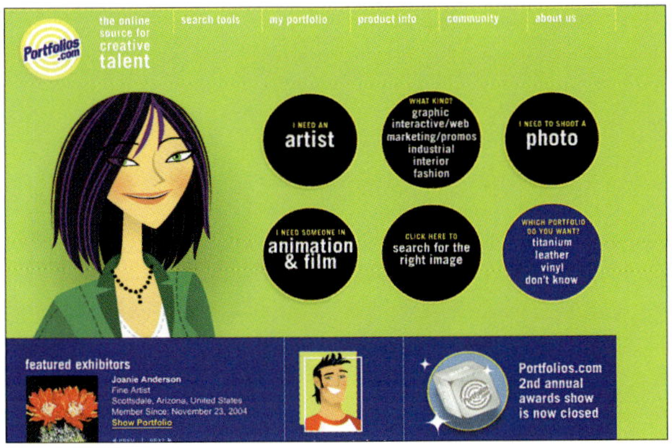

(a)

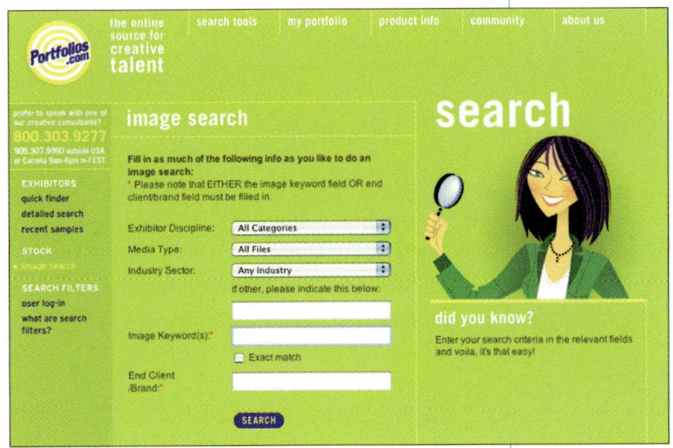

(b)

a–b: © Copyright 2004 Portfolios.com

◆ **7-5a, 7-5b** *Two pages from the website for http://www.portfolios.com.* Courtesy of www.portfolios.com.

For example, http://www.portfolios.com takes you to a site for viewing artists' and designers' portfolios, while http://www.portfolios.com/search/search.html#quick-browse takes you to a particular page in that site for a quick browse of their offerings. **Figures 7-5a–b** show this site.

Browsers often need additional software plug-ins to display media such as QuickTime video or Flash animations. If necessary, these can usually be downloaded from the software manufacturers' websites. Another option is to create two versions of a site, giving users a chance when they first log onto a site (typing the URL address) to choose a non-Flash alternative path. We have covered how the web works; now let's take a look at how a web designer works.

Methodology

There is more to website graphics than just creating the files. Some research is required in the beginning. See **Figure 7-6** for a diagram of the research and design stages. Because a website is interactive and nonlinear, and made up of several pages, some planning is required about the information flow. The following steps describe this process:

a. Begin any print or web publication by examining the message and the audience.
b. Familiarize yourself with the competition and/or leaders in the field.
c. Research, analyze, and synthesize the available resources.
d. Organize the content. In web design, that means develop a flowchart for content. **Figure 7-7a** shows a typical student flowchart for a portfolio site.
e. Design the visuals, developing a look and feel tied by a common visual/conceptual theme. We've

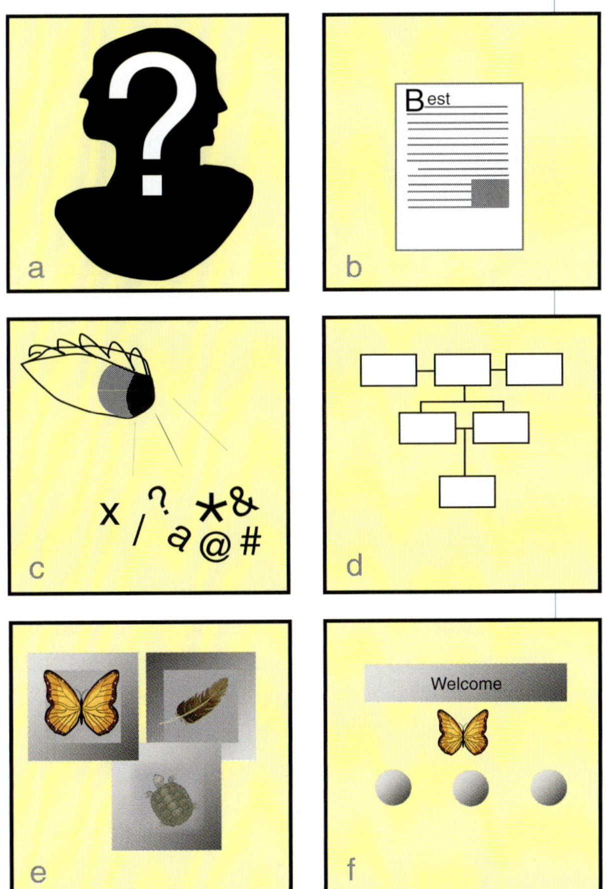

◆ **7-6** *A diagram of the research and design stages of website design.*

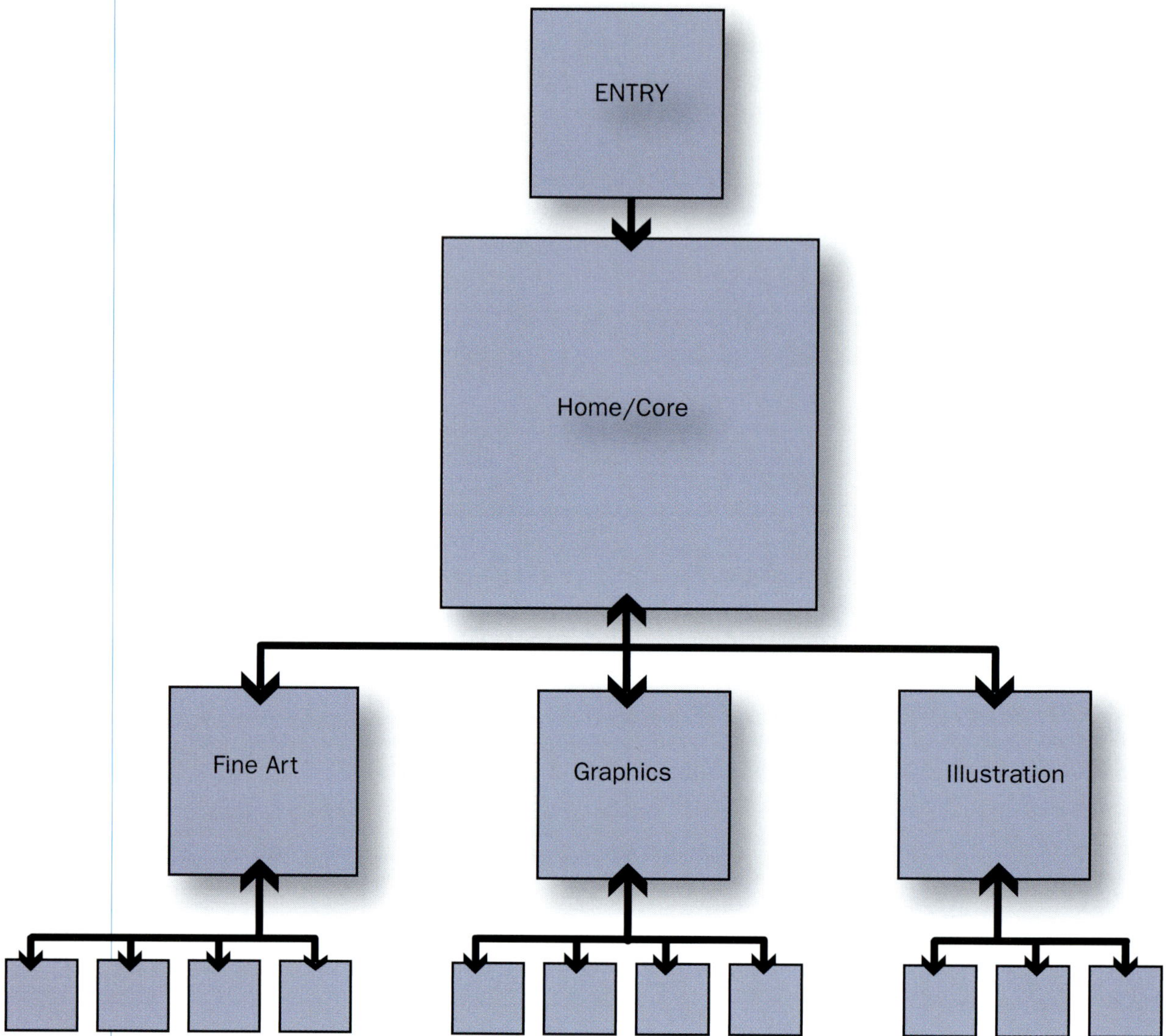

7-7a *A suggested student flowchart for a portfolio site.*

discussed this process in the previous chapters on print design.

f. The final step is to produce the website.

Design and Production

Now we will examine the similarities and differences between print and web design. Everything you have learned in this class and other art and design classes will help you create an aesthetically successful page design. But site design introduces some new elements to incorporate, including interactivity.

Similarities to Print A book or magazine presents information in a sequence of pages, as does a website. All of these pages should be tied together with a similar visual treatment, such as a uniform grid, consistent choice of font, and alignment of typography. Look for repetition in the typographic treatment. It should be justified throughout or ragged right throughout. If there are special sections that require a different treatment, keep those sections uniform.

A successful publication in the art and design field, whether online, in print for graphic design, or in an artist's series, often incorporates a visual and conceptual theme that unites the parts. Consistency in placement and treatment of items, such as page numbers and navigation bars or buttons, is important. Remember that color sets a mood and communicates a message, whatever your method of output. Each section of a website or a print publication can be color-coded. **Figure 7-7b** shows three pages of an artist's personal website that are united in color, structure, and visual theme.

The 20th century has produced excellent examples of graphic design. A study of basic design principles applied to the field of graphic design/communication shows a number of visual principles that seem to cross cultures and decades.

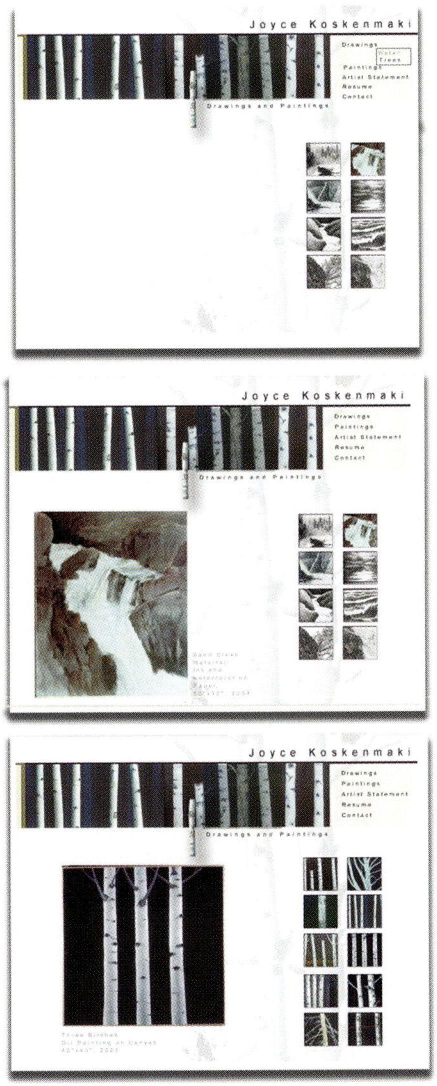

◆ **7-7b** *Artist Joyce Koskenmaki's website is unified in color, structure, and visual theme.*
Courtesy of the artist.

The Gestalt unit-forming principles of visual perception are a base for the design of web graphics as well as print media. Repetition and variation, rhythm, continuation, and figure/ground treatment are fundamental to the design of any publication. All cultures deal with these visual foundations. Today, however, as we communicate with web pages around the world, it is more important than ever that we have effective visual language skills that can be understood by a diverse audience.

Unlike a print publication, a web designer often cannot predict the cultural background of visitors to a site. Although currently the majority of web traffic is written in English, with an audience in North America and Europe, there is also a sizable audience in very diverse corners of the world. This broadens the challenge for the web designer. What other things are distinct about designing for the web?

Differences between Web and Print How does the web differ from print graphics? The answer is complex, involving conceptual and practical issues that need some examination. A painting, a photograph, or an illustration presents a singular unit of information. A book or magazine presents visual and written information in a linear format. None of these is time based because they do not take time to load like web graphics, and they do not take time to move across a screen. For example, music is a time-based medium, while painting is not. But isn't a book time based? Yes, to a degree. The pages of a book sequence from front to back. The structure of a book's information flow is one directional, and this flow is reasonably simple to create. However, information on the web is nonlinear and highly interactive. **Figure 7-8** shows a page in a student web portfolio with multiple choices on its home/core page. Several buttons (stones) are available to take the visitor to various locations in the site. The home page is usually the beginning page of your site where visitors are given choices about how to proceed. For example, do they want to view your resume, or see your art portfolio first?

The information flow in a site is often complex and should be diagrammed before creating the site. Create a map or flowchart, as shown in

7-8 *Pages from Leah Shea's web portfolio show her use of a consistent, unifying style as well as highly interactive buttons and links.*
Courtesy of the artist.

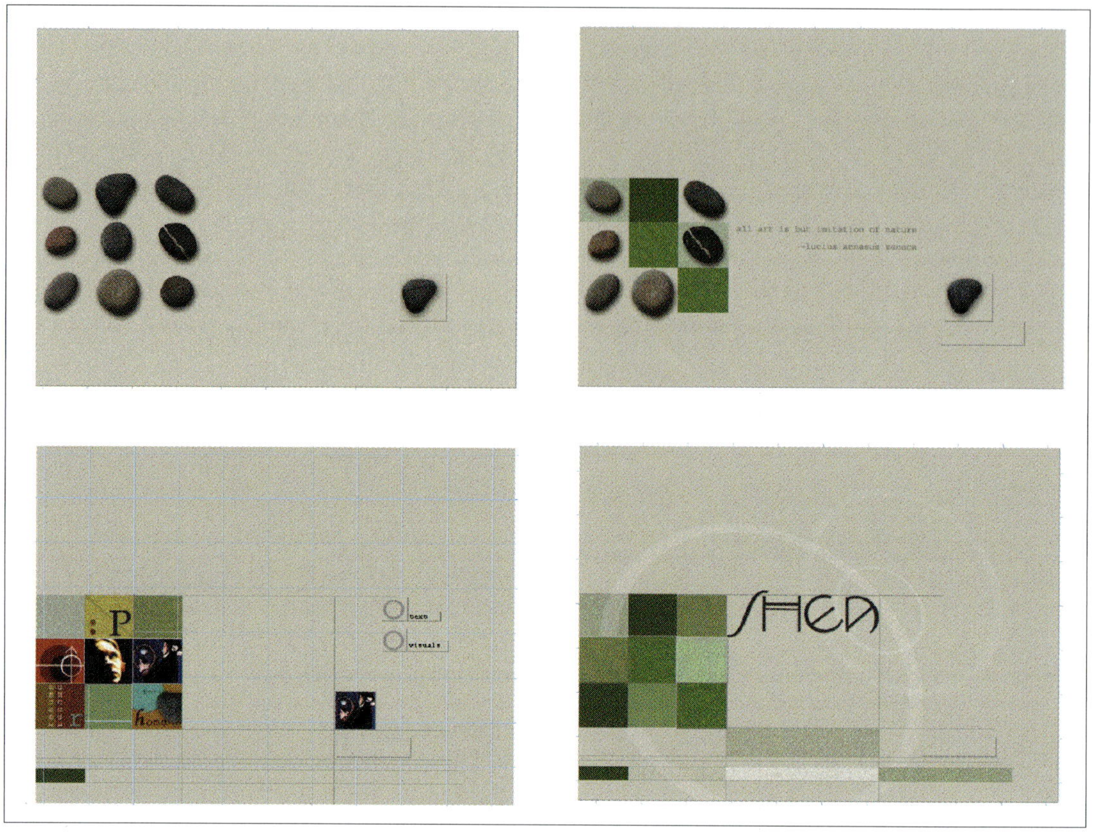

Figure 7-9, of where each button will take the visitor. How will visitors get back to where the links are? It is possible to get stuck out on a limb in a website with no links back into the information flow, causing a viewer to end the session. A successful flow leaves the viewer only a click or two from the home/core page at any time. This can mean putting a small button icon on most pages that is linked to your home page.

Time, motion, and sound are important components of web design. Students of web design will want to learn the aesthetic sensibilities and the production skills necessary to create animation and sound files that communicate the intended message. All design communicates a message, but it may not have the intended and desired effect if the designer is not careful and well prepared.

Web design has unique production considerations. The dpi (dots per inch, or resolution) of image scans, availability of fonts, appropriateness of file formats and sizes, the color gamuts of RGB (red, green, blue) versus CMYK (cyan, magenta, yellow, black) must all be learned anew for their application to web graphics. Consider the ephemeral quality of the online experience with its varied user environment versus the concrete reality of the canvas or the printed page. How is the web more ephemeral?

Fine artwork can be viewed on a gallery or museum wall. Printed graphic design can be reread any time, and its format retains the same paper, font, and layout size. In web design, the fonts, image size, and even color can vary depending upon the viewer's equipment. This is a very important difference. Factors that affect the way a page is seen include the monitor resolution and the web browser preference settings, and display differences between the Macintosh and PC-based environments. Although the majority of designers work on a Mac, the majority of web users are on a PC-compatible system. Always view your site on both platforms to be sure it "reads" correctly.

Download time is also an important issue affecting outcomes in web design, a factor that does

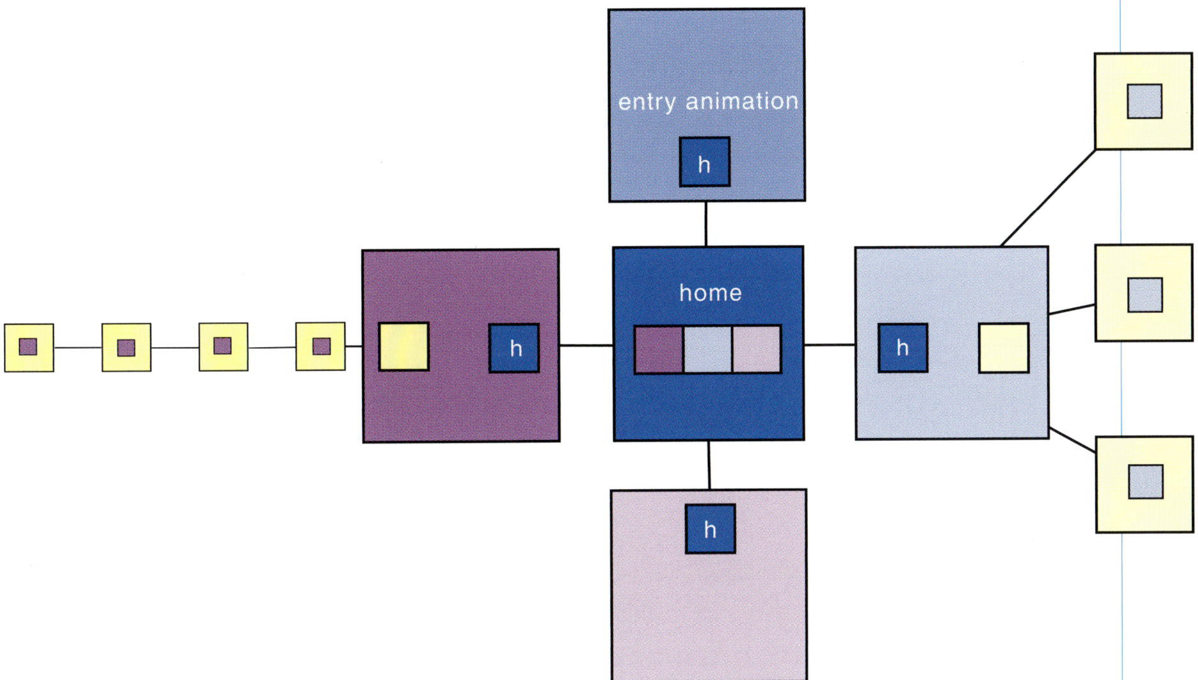

not exist in print graphics. File size is calculated in bytes. As you will remember from Chapter 2, there are eight bits in a byte, and 1,024 bytes in a kilobyte, or 1K. The smaller your file, the more quickly it will download to the viewer. A 50K file will take around fifteen seconds to download on an individual user's 56K modem. Cable, **ISDN** (Integrated Services Digital Network), **DSL** (Digital Subscriber Line), and Satellite are broadband Internet hookups that provide a much faster download capacity than a phone line. Download times are increasingly fast, especially in the United States, but it is always wise to keep an eye on the size of your file.

The web is a "picky" medium, and it's vital to understand its rules in order to reach the audience with the intended message. If you don't create your images, pages, and site exactly right, they won't be viewable. For example, naming conventions (what you name your files) must be understood and rigidly adhered to in web graphics. Just as when printed pieces are sent to press or fine art pieces are sent for exhibition, when the website is mounted on line, all elements must be prepared to function and communicate the most effectively. Now we will discuss how to build your site correctly.

What Are the Rules?

The preceding section discussed the aesthetics and uniqueness of the web environment. As in other chapters, now we'll focus on technique and equipment, followed by an introduction to using software to create web graphics.

Naming Your Files Filenames use different conventions and restrictions depending on the operating system (PC Windows, Mac OS, UNIX). A server computer that hosts and mounts your site may run an operating system different from yours. For example, Charter and **AOL** (America On Line) are servers that have their own computer equipment. Therefore, you will want to name your files so that they can be correctly read on the server computer.

When creating and naming pages and graphics, use filenames that are no longer than eight characters, followed by a three- or four-character extension. Do not use spaces or other special symbols; use only lowercase letters and numbers. A web page should have an html extension: report.htm or resume.html. Name your first page index.html, or default.html. Check with your web provider about which to use before creating the

7-9 *A flowchart plans where each button will take the visitor within a website. On this chart, an entry animation leads to the home page, where three buttons can be clicked. These three locations have buttons leading back to the home location as well as buttons leading on.*

site. Name the graphics and GIF animation assets with eight or fewer characters, followed by the extension .jpg or .gif, as shown in **Figure 7-10**.

Keep all files related to your site in one folder, with sections grouped together either by folders or by naming conventions like pic1.jpg, pic2.jpg, pic3.jpg. The html pages are usually kept in one folder, while the assets or images are in another.

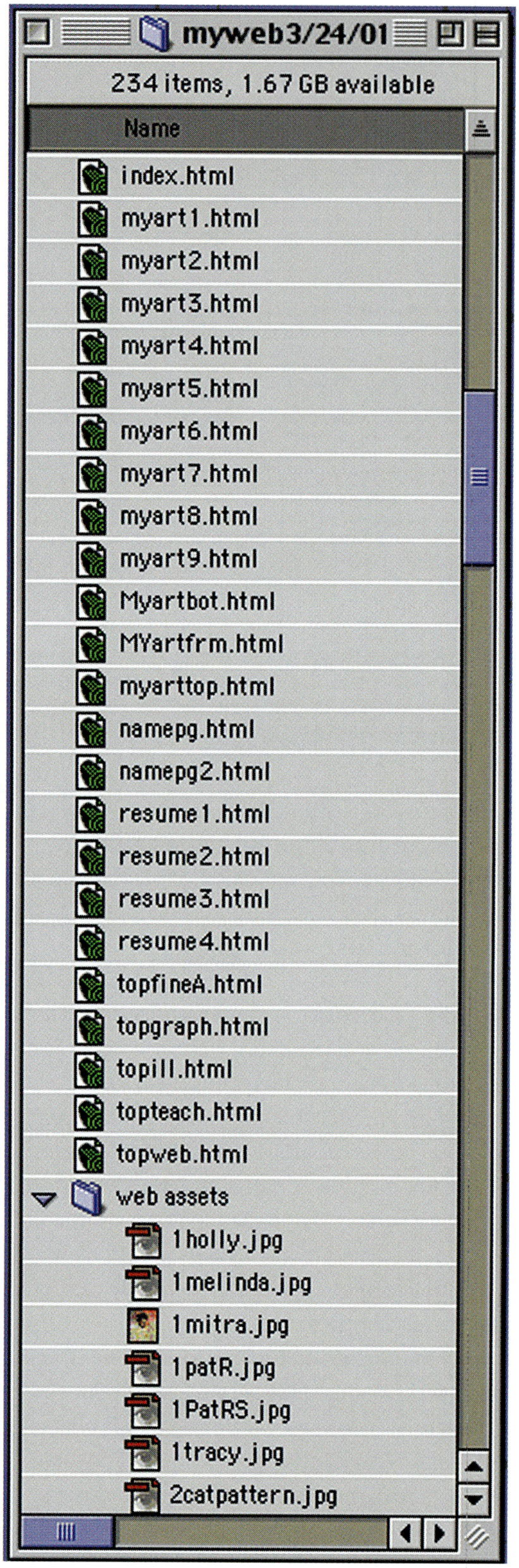

◆ **7-10** *A website is comprised of HTML pages and JPEG or GIF assets (images) on those pages.*

Resolution Prepare final web files at 72 ppi (pixels per inch). Often the best results come from scanning or otherwise preparing images at a larger resolution and reducing the file later. A file with all its layers intact is not flattened. You will need to flatten the web file, but keep an unflattened, high-resolution version of your image files, so you can go back and make all changes on the original. This ensures the best-quality final image. **Figure 7-11** shows the Photoshop Save For Web option in various resolutions of JPEG and GIF file formats. Remember to never resave a JPEG over itself because it throws away data each time (lossy format).

File Size How long will a visitor to your site be willing to wait? A good rule of thumb is to expect the average viewer's patience to be exhausted after several seconds. Try it yourself and measure your patience on various sites. We're becoming more and more demanding in our expectations for rapid delivery. Keep graphics as small and concise as possible to avoid long download times and frustrated users. Flat, solid areas of color reduce a file's size considerably. If you are choosing to use gradients, top-to-bottom creates a smaller file size than right-to-left gradients. Reuse graphics on your site because downloaded graphics are cached or held in memory, eliminating the need to download a graphic again. **Interlaced GIF** and **progressive JPEG** images will begin to load instantly and gradually achieve full clarity. Interlaced GIF is a GIF image that is gradually displayed in a web browser, showing increasingly detailed versions of the entire image until all the data has finished downloading. Progressive JPEG allows an image to be gradually displayed in a web browser, until all the data has finished downloading. Although this is similar to inter-

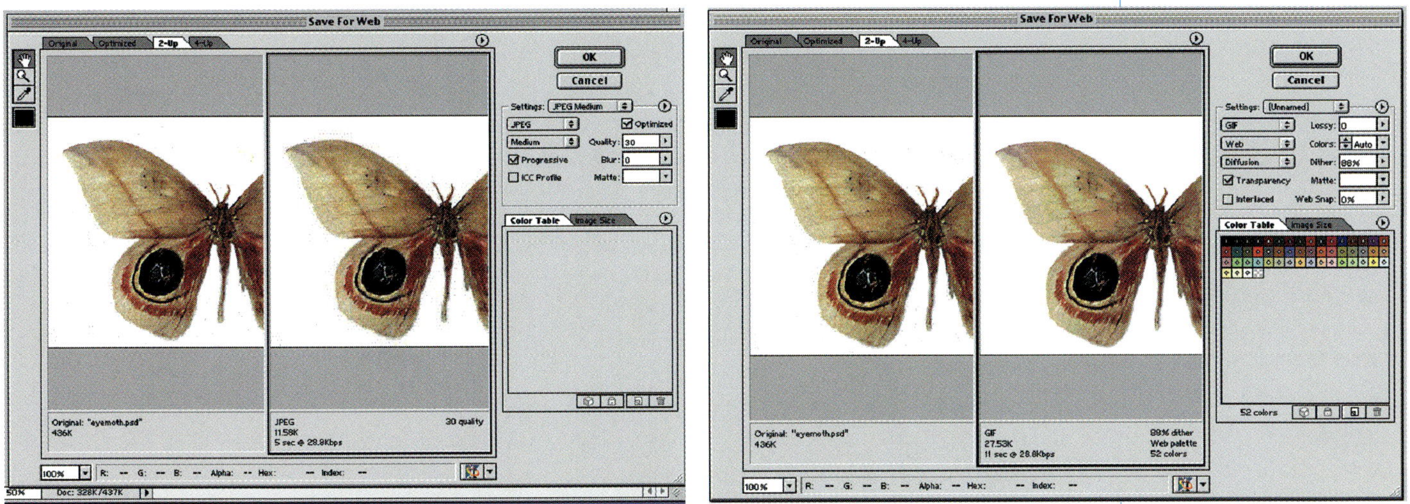

◆ **7-11** *The Photoshop Save For Web option.*

Adobe product screen shots reprinted with permission from Adobe Systems Incorporated

laced GIF images, progressive JPEG images can retain the high quality of 24-bit color. This immediate appearance of the start of an image can satisfy a viewer and keep him or her at the site until the full image is viewable. Text file sizes are the smallest kind of data, followed by visuals, then video, sound, and finally interactive animation with Flash and Director Shockwave files.

Monitor Size For a conservative size, guaranteed to reach most users, some websites keep important elements, text, and graphics within a 640 × 480 pixel area. Although most people have a larger monitor, they often surf the web with more than one window open. If that size is simply too restrictive for you as a designer, an 800 x 600 display space is usually safe. Designers often create their images on a 1600 x 1200 display, but not all viewers will be using a similarly sized monitor. To check the approximate way your file will look on various monitors, on the Macintosh, go to Chooser>Monitors>Resolutions; on the PC, right click on the desktop and go to Properties>Settings. Web authoring programs will also tell you information about your file.

Macromedia Dreamweaver is an excellent and widely used web design software package. We will use it for some sample pages in this chapter. **Figure 7-12** shows the Dreamweaver desktop environment, including the bottom of its window containing information on the file's download speed based on your Internet connection as well as monitor size viewing options.

File Formats As you remember from Chapter 2 file format tells the computer what kind of file it is dealing with. The web accepts GIF and JPEG. These are both compressed file formats, producing graphics with smaller file sizes. The GIF file format is used for images featuring type and flat

◆ **7-12** *The Dreamweaver desktop environment.*

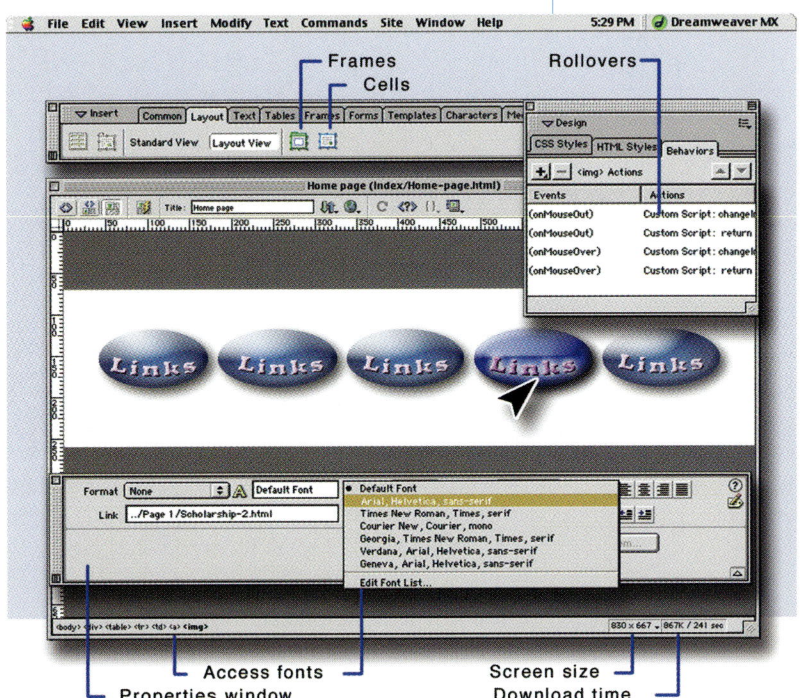

Courtesy Macromedia, Inc.

color images. It is a lossless file format that compresses graphics without eliminating detail and is designed for 8-bit (256 colors or less) graphics. You can reduce file size and improve loading time by saving solid color graphics as a GIF, as shown in **Figure 7-13**, utilizing Illustrator's Save for Web option.

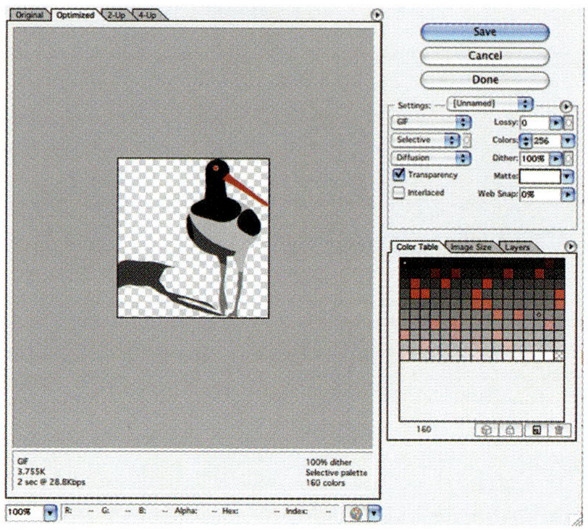

Courtesy Macromedia, Inc.

◆ **7-13** *Saving solid color graphics as a GIF from Illustrator's Save for Web option.*

Use JPEG for gradients or photographic images. Complex graphics with photo-based imagery reproduce better as JPEG. It is a lossy file format designed for displaying 24-bit true color. It does not support transparency, but can display a larger, more photo-like image with less data, making for smaller files and faster downloads. PNGs (Portable Network Graphics) are also a compressed, lossless file format. Not all browsers support PNGs, but one of their advantages is 256 levels of transparency.

Web Color Converting files to the RGB color palette is the final image production step. Because web files are viewed on monitors, they need to be saved in the monitor's red/green/blue method of displaying color. Changing an image from RGB to Indexed Color reduces an image's color usage from RGB's 16.8 million colors to a smaller palette of 256 colors. **Figure 7-14** shows converting an RGB to an indexed color palette. When you choose to index an image, you don't have to use all 256 colors. If your image only requires twenty colors, you can limit the palette to that number, making the file size smaller, and a quicker load.

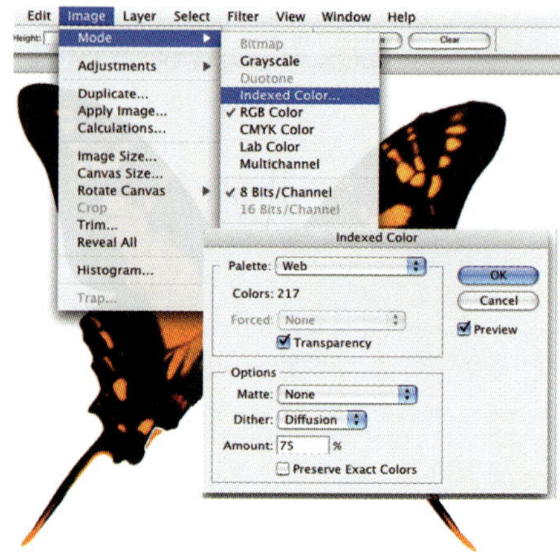

Adobe product screen shot reprinted with permission from Adobe Systems Incorporated

◆ **7-14** *Converting from RGB to Indexed Color.*

There are a number of smaller color palettes to choose from. The 216 web-safe colors, the 256-color Mac and Windows systems palettes, or custom palettes such as Adaptive are available. Using web-safe colors from a 216 web-safe color table, as shown in **Figure 7-15**, produces an 8-bit file. Many programs have "Save For Web" options that help the user through a pop up window of choices to specify the format and color table, and look at file size and probable download time.

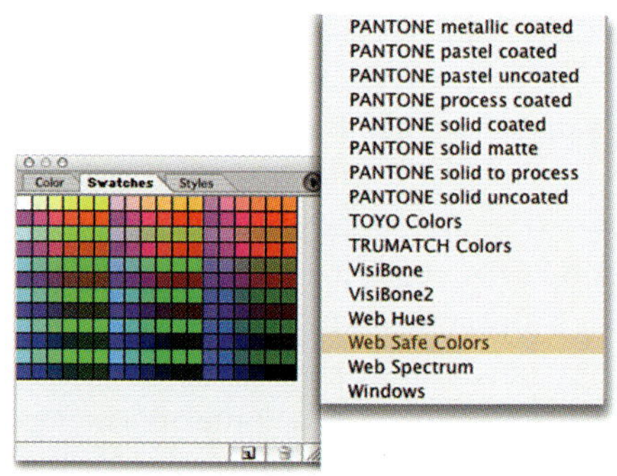

Adobe product screen shots reprinted with permission from Adobe Systems Incorporated

◆ **7-15** *The Photoshop Color Swatches window can be set to Web Safe Colors.*

How do you decide when to use the web-safe or the Adaptive palette? If the graphic contains photographic imagery and some flat color elements filled with web-safe colors, choose an Adaptive palette (**Fig. 7-16**). It is made up of colors most appropriate for the particular image. Re-rendering an image with a limited number of colors produces a pixilated effect called *dither-*

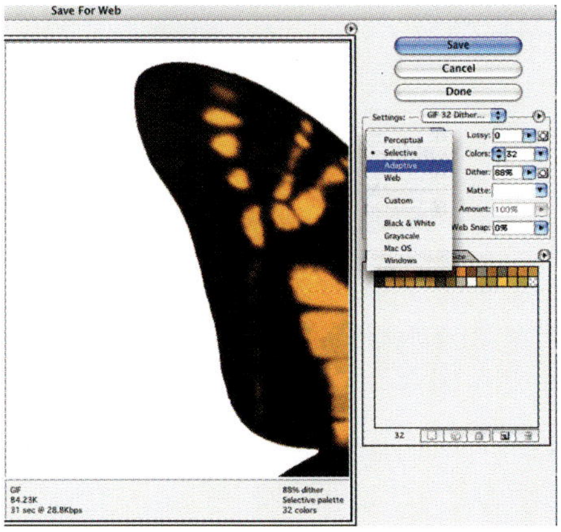

Adobe product screen shots reprinted with permission from Adobe Systems Incorporated

◆ **7-16** *Choosing an Adaptive Palette reduces colors to those most appropriate for particular images.*

Visual Perception

A website communicates visually as much as or more than it does by word. There are many visual elements, ranging from the layout of the page to the images on it. A good site design has the following eight characteristics:

a. An appealing entry page or "tunnel" that attracts viewers.
b. A clear navigational structure.
c. Elements (links and assets) that always work.
d. An integrated design with possible use of metaphor or symbol.
e. Good use of design basics.
f. An acceptable download time.
g. An appropriate message for an identified audience.
h. Compatibility with the user's monitor.

ing. It is noticeable in solid flat color areas. Choosing colors from the reduced web-safe palette as often as possible when creating flat color graphics helps reduce dithering. When composing solid background it is advisable to use web-safe color. You can open a browser-safe swatch palette in most graphics programs and choose your colors only from that swatch.

Text In the basic HTML, which is the structural foundation of web graphics, there are three types of fonts always available, including Times on Windows or Helvetica on the Mac. Courier on both systems is generally used for columns and tables because it has a fixed width. These are the **default** fonts that will be installed on all systems. Using a typeface not installed on a user's system will mean that typeface is displayed in one of the default fonts. There are, of course, ways to get around these limitations. The text can be transformed into a graphic image in programs like Photoshop, Illustrator (Convert to Outlines), or Freehand. This also works with print graphics if you do not want to or cannot send the font along with the file. However, on the web, converting type to image graphics increases file size and makes indexing by search engines difficult. Stick with text when possible.

Cascading Style Sheets (CSS) embed instructions in the page that include basic formatting like leading and letterspacing information. This avoids an awkward reformatting of your layout on the user's monitor. Most web software packages include CSS. They also allow you to specify your choice of default font, if the user's computer does not have your original choice.

Now that we have discussed how the web behaves, let's take a look at its various elements.

Web Components

As we have learned, there are elements that are part of the web environment that are not available in print. These elements include linked interactivity and the optional inclusion of sound and movement. The nature of the web's dissemination is also very different from that of print graphics. The next section will cover these topics.

Pages and Sites

A **website** is composed of separate, linked pages. The site must be mounted on a server if it is to be viewed anywhere but from a disk. This is a brief but important distinction. You can build your images, animations (assets), or layout in a software program and load them in your web program onto pages. These pages filled with elements or assets become your site.

Interactivity

A **link** (also known as a *hyperlink*) is an interactive part of a document. Every link contains the web address for the page that the link refers to.

This web address is called the page's URL (Uniform Resource Locator). Clicking a link can take you to another part of the same web page, or to other web pages on your hard disk, or to a location on a remote computer. These links are often created as graphic buttons, but are also

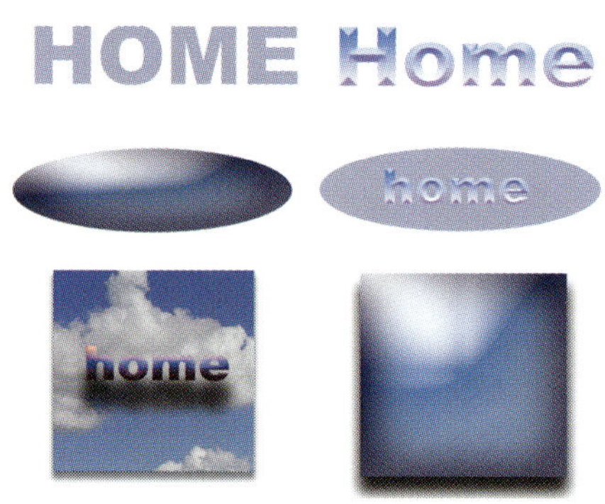

Courtesy Macromedia, Inc.

◆ **7-17** *Graphic buttons that can be used as links are often created in Photoshop, then placed in Dreamweaver.*

designed as clickable text or as part of an image map. **Figure 7-17** shows three buttons created in Photoshop.

To create a link in Dreamweaver, select a word or button. This button may have been created in Photoshop or in Dreamweaver. Click in the Link field of the Properties palette and type in a complete URL, or pick one of your other pages from the pop up menu. **Figure 7-18** shows how to establish a link location.

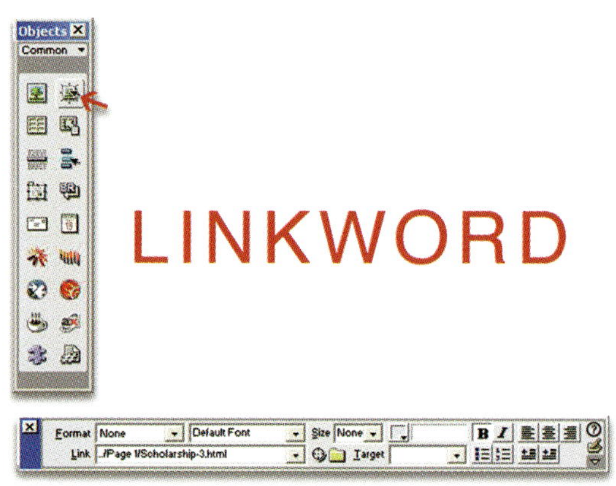

Courtesy Macromedia, Inc.

◆ **7-18** *How to establish a link location.*

A **rollover** button changes as the mouse passes over it. Rollovers use a second graphic to replace the first. You will need to create both graphics and use the software rollover function to select the first image. Then specify which image replaces it. **Figure 7-19** shows the creation of a rollover.

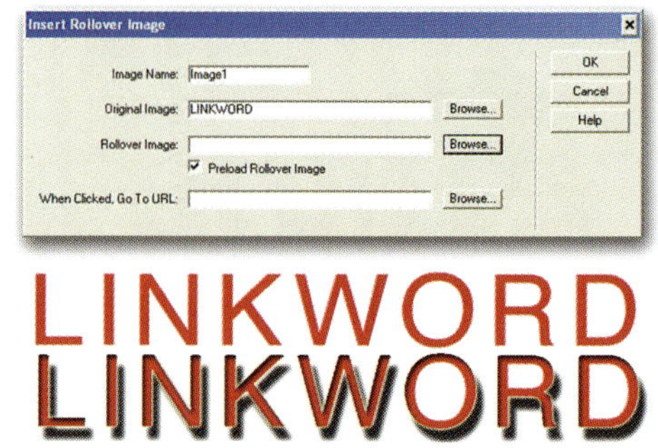

Courtesy Macromedia, Inc.

◆ **7-19** *The creation of a rollover.*

Tables and Frames

Tables allow for the precise alignment of layout elements into columns and rows. They keep data from jumping around when the window is resized. Think of tables as similar to the underlying grid that provides structure to a print publication design. If a table width is set to 100 percent of the window size, it will flow to fit the user's monitor.

Frames are very different from tables although they look similar. **Figures 7-20a–d** show a home site by Planet Propaganda, a Madison, WI, design firm that makes use of frames. It also makes good use of a design structure that incorporates repetition and variation. A frame splits the page into sections. Typically, there may be one stationary frameset on the left side that has links that call varying content into the frame on the right side. Frames are also often placed across the top of a layout. Each frame is actually a separate web page. Frames are a device for controlling the presentation and flow of information.

Animation and Sound

GIF files can be used to create animations. Adobe's ImageReady comes packaged with Photoshop and is an excellent program for creating small animations. **Figure 7-21** shows the ImageReady desktop environment. We'll learn how to create animations using ImageReady in Chapter 8.

Flash is the top program on the web capable of generating sophisticated motion that downloads quickly as well as producing richly interactive

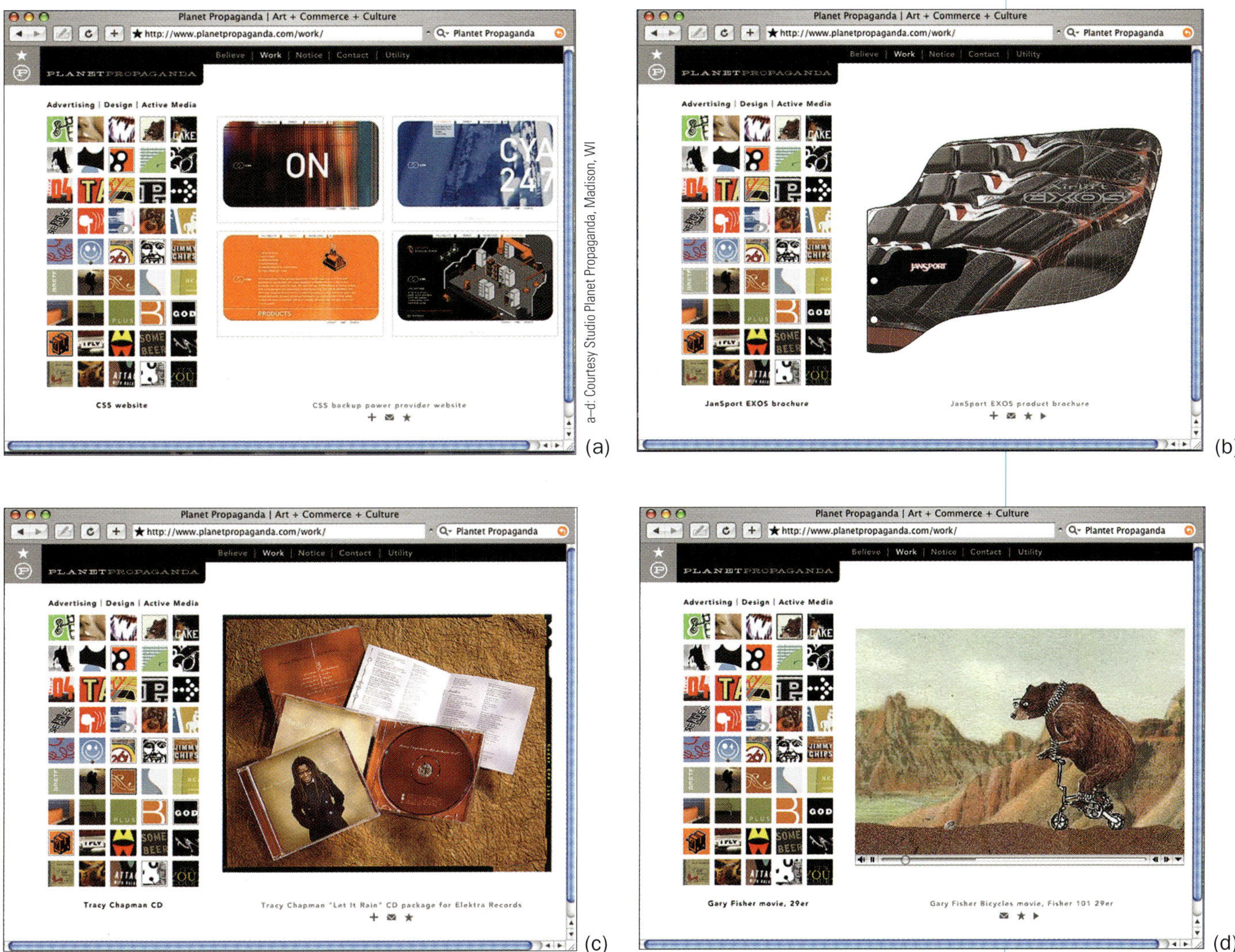

(a) (b) (c) (d)

a–d: Courtesy Studio Planet Propaganda, Madison, WI

7-20 [a–d] *The home page for Planet Propaganda.* Courtesy of the studio.

7-21 *A GIF animation with its several stages is ready to be inserted in a website.*

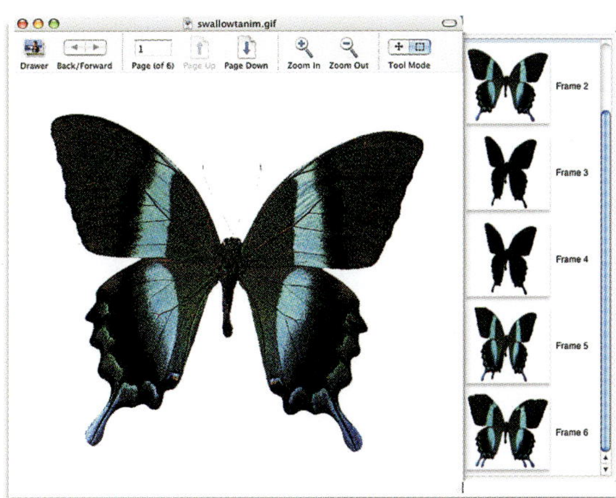

Adobe product screen shot reprinted with permission from Adobe Systems Incorporated

sites. **Figure 7-22** consists of stills from a Flash interactive file in which an animated image and a connected song play as each of the three buttons is clicked. To create such a file, you will need a separate program to generate a sound file. We'll learn the elements of using Flash in Chapter 8.

SoundEdit Pro is a very accessible program for inputting, manipulating, or generating sound that can be used on the web. Sound files are often compressed for quicker download time, sacrificing some tonal quality. Speech works at 11 kilohertz, while music should be saved at 22 kHz.

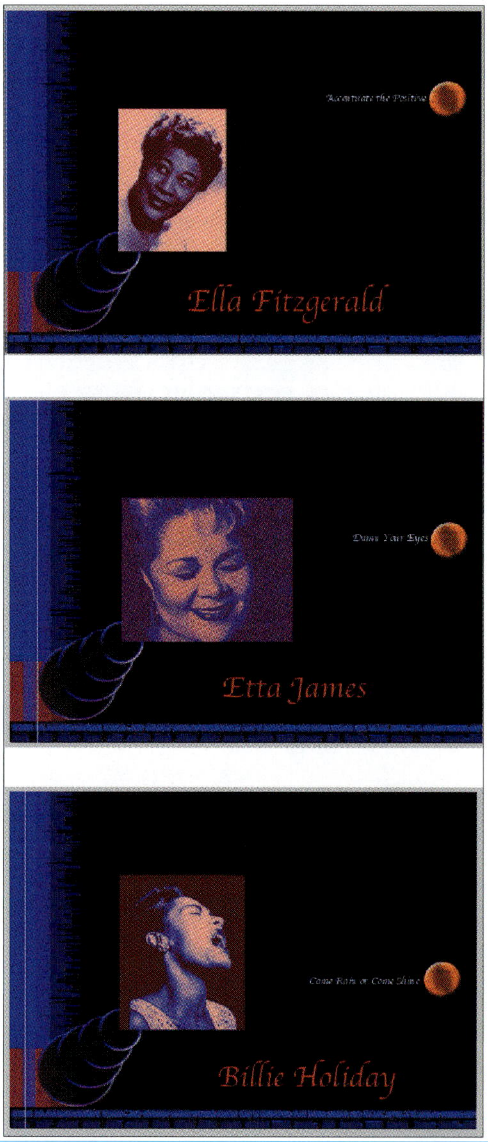

Courtesy Macromedia, Inc.

7-22 *Dawn Disch created this Flash interactive file that incorporates sound and animation for her student portfolio.*

Video

Apple QuickTime operates on both the Mac and PC-compatible platforms. Its file extension is (.mov). Windows Media Player (.avi) works only with the Windows operating system. A relatively low frame rate such as twelve frames per second (fps) and a small window size help video to deliver smoothly over the web. Several animations on the accompanying **CD** are saved as QuickTime files.

Web Publishing

There are a great variety of online services for web publishing. Many Internet service providers grant access to the web, email, and free space for a website. America Online or CompuServe are familiar to most. The majority of college campuses provide a limited amount of free space for student web pages.

Another place to examine is http://www.geocities.com. It is a free location to publish your website. Like commercial television, it runs advertisements to turn a profit, so be prepared to have ads running along with your pages. But it gives excellent practice in troubleshooting and mounting a site.

The web is a postmodern format, full of layered information. Its values may encompass modernism's rational, ordered organization of information, but the structure of the web is by nature a mix of stratified data. We've discussed these terms throughout the previous chapters. They apply not only to print design but also to web and multimedia design.

Hands On Practice

Select an existing website to critique. Remember that when critiquing a print- or web-based creation, you need to be looking at issues specific to that medium.

- Consider the overall complexity of the site. How many JPEGs, GIFs, animations, or tables are there?
- How complete is the research on the site's topic?
- How successful is the visual/conceptual theme?

- How is that theme established?
- Is there a clear logic to the navigational structure?
- Are the files error free?
- Does the image fit the intended screen size well?
- How would this information look and function in print?

Create four additional pages in Photoshop that would logically fit with, or improve upon, the site in content and visual treatment. This assignment asks that you evaluate a site by the criteria we have discussed earlier in the chapter. When you show your pages in class, be sure to present the site you have chosen, and your critique of it.

Warming Up

Refer to the methodology discussed earlier in this chapter to plan and design about six pages for a hypothetical website. The topic is "design history," and you are to research and prepare a short web presentation on an artist or a designer presented in this text or approved by your instructor. Gather and prepare several images for the web. The Internet is a good research tool to locate images and information for this assignment, as is the library and the sites on the accompanying **CD.** Your pages can be assembled in Photoshop. Write a brief amount of copy. Be sure to create buttons intended to act as links between pages. Print these pages for presentation.

If you have enough time to spend on this assignment, either now or in a later class, the Photoshop pages can be inserted in a web program.

In The Studio

If you feel you are ready to build an actual site, create a professional site for yourself. Sketch a map of your navigational structure. Build the buttons and images in Photoshop. Assemble these elements and your text in Netscape's Composer, or in a professional web design program like Dreamweaver, ready to mount on line. Include active links and tables. View this site on the monitor for final critique. Both Composer and Dreamweaver come with tutorials. Finally, consider using Geocities or another site to actually post your design on the Internet. Look at the site in both Netscape Composer and Internet Explorer. And view it on a Mac and a PC-compatible platform to determine its success.

MOVING ON

The final chapter will discuss multimedia design. Multimedia design has several characteristics in common with web design because its pages are nonlinear and interactive, and usually combine sound with movement. Again, the final chapter can be read solely as an introduction to the design considerations inherent in this medium. However, if you want to experiment with animation or multimedia programs, there are step-by-step instructions to assist you.

TERMINOLOGY

CHAPTER 8

See Glossary for definitions

Multimedia
Motion Graphics
Interactivity
Animation
4-D (Four-Dimensional)
Holography
Keyframes
Inbetweener
Stage
Panels
Symbol
Instance
Library
Movie Clip
Layers
Frames
Movie
Shape Tweening
Motion Tweening

8 Multimedia Design

Any medium that includes a combination of graphics, moving images, sound, video, and animation is considered **multimedia** design. It is sometimes called **motion graphics**, or New Media, and it may include some aspect of **interactivity**. As the web and other forms of interactive design continue to grow, designers become increasingly involved not just with creating an object but also with structuring an interactive communication event with the user. This chapter will look at the ways interactivity and motion are created, and will introduce the basics of using ImageReady and Flash, which are used to generate movement on the web. Many complex software packages are used in multimedia, including 3-D animation, sometimes integrating film and video effects. It is good to have an overview of this New Media, regardless of whether you choose to master the varied software at this point in your academic career.

Interactivity

Interactivity is part of our daily lives. We respond to and interact with other people using all our available senses. That interaction has always taken place through some form of visual, aural, or written communication. Multimedia design takes our innate capacity for interaction and builds on it, using a variety of new technologies. Files can be output on CD-ROM and DVD or the web to deliver a multimedia package with an interactive interface. The user controls his or her progress along the navigation path on the web, in video games, and in other venues such as information kiosks in airports, museums, and various public spaces. The web is a very powerful form of interactive multimedia with an incredible reach. **Figure 8-1** uses movement to give a colorful sense of excitement and action. This promo, created by the design studio Planet Propaganda, presents

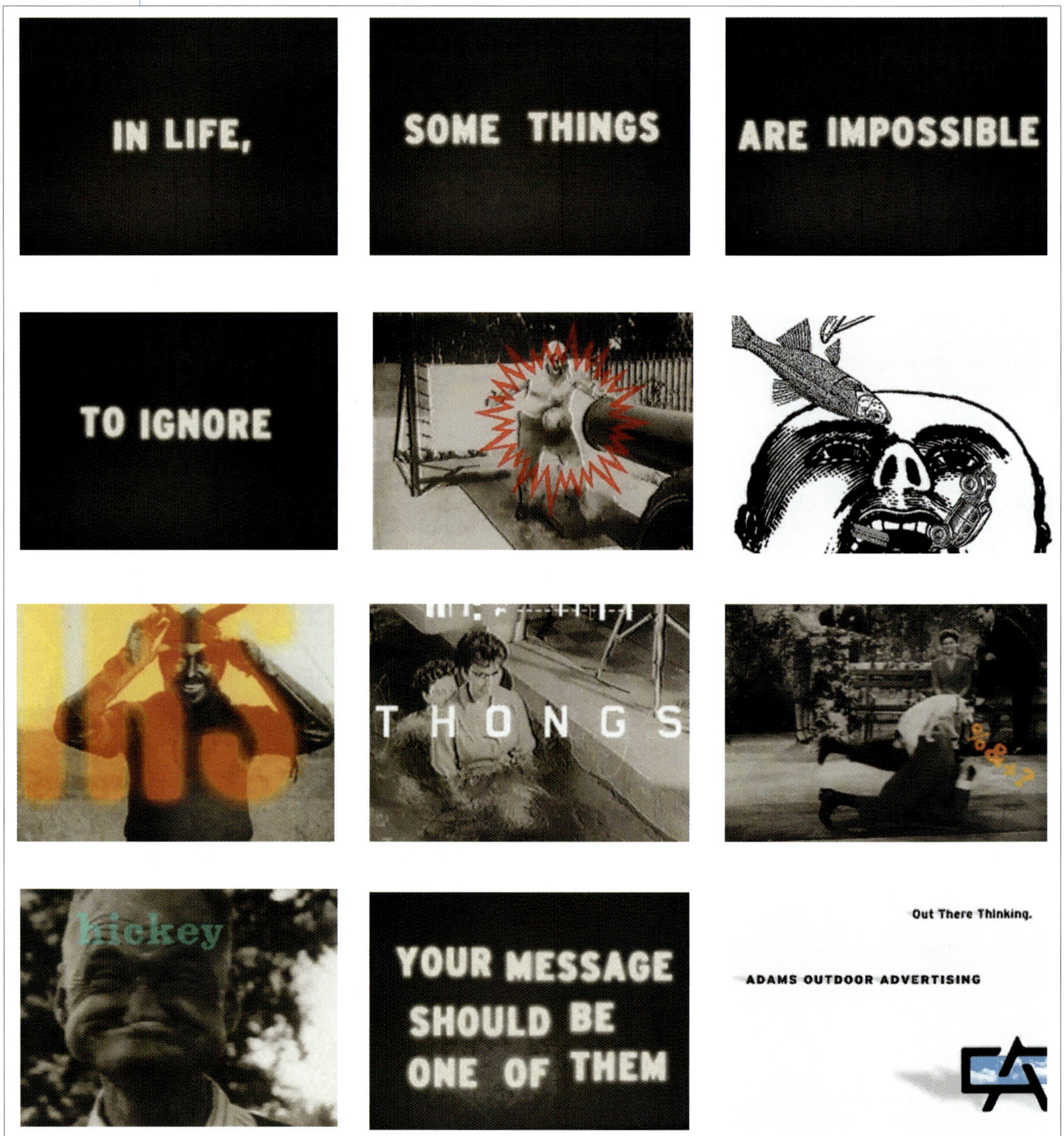

8-1 *Planet Propaganda design studio. Consumer website.* Courtesy of Planet Propaganda, Madison, WI.

its client, Adams Outdoor Advertising, in an animation that is truly "impossible to ignore."

Television is another form of multimedia that is present in virtually every home. Incorporating all the components of multimedia, television is not interactive in nature. Many of its elements are digitally created, but it is still delivered by primarily an analog signal. Meanwhile, it presents a wide array of computer graphics career opportunities for the designer with its advertising, news graphics, title sequences, and more. **Figure 8-2** shows a title **animation** created by StudioVerb for HBO's Sunday Night Series. A series of animated panels become a movie screen

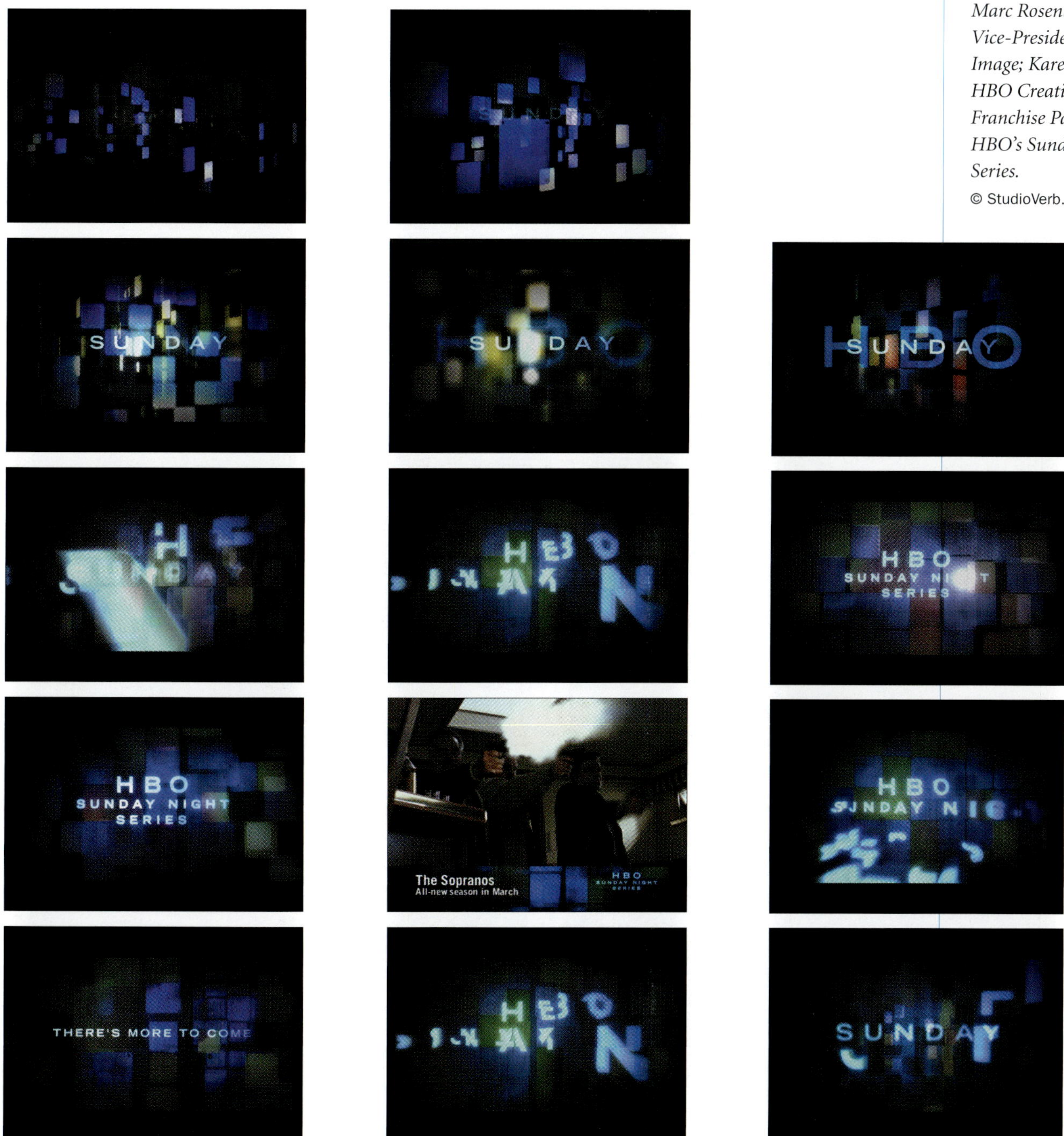

◆ 8-2 *StudioVerb, studio; Greg Duncan, creative director; Bill Bergeron, producer; Marc Rosenberg, HBO Vice-President of Brand Image; Karen Sands, HBO Creative Director. Franchise Package for HBO's Sunday Night Series.*

playing film imagery. Much of this animation was created using a program called Cinema 4D and finished in Adobe After Effects.

Multimedia designers may be fine artists, musicians, filmmakers, animators, writers, illustrators, or graphic designers. These people often work together to produce a finished multimedia piece. Multimedia art and design are created with the user in mind, and designers need to ask several questions before they begin. Who is the audience, what is the message, and where and how will this production be received? Will the audience be a home computer user or an institution with a single, powerful station? Will the product be viewed in a gallery setting or a performance venue? Increasingly, consumers are becoming accustomed to viewing amazingly complex animated effects and are even creating powerful visuals themselves on home computers. **Figure 8-3** shows a multimedia production created for a live musical performance. It incorporates still and animated still photography with video footage. The intent was to convey a feeling of motion and transit in an urban environment. Graphic Havoc created the piece for the world tour of recording artist Wamdue Project, for Strictly Rhythm Records. Now that we've seen some of the creative effects possible with multimedia, let's look at how some of these effects are achieved.

How Does Multimedia Work?

In addition to creating for the web, multimedia can be saved to DVD or CD, or it can be output for film or TV. In these venues, the viewer sees the document as created by the designer, not a re-creation on a distant monitor as happens on

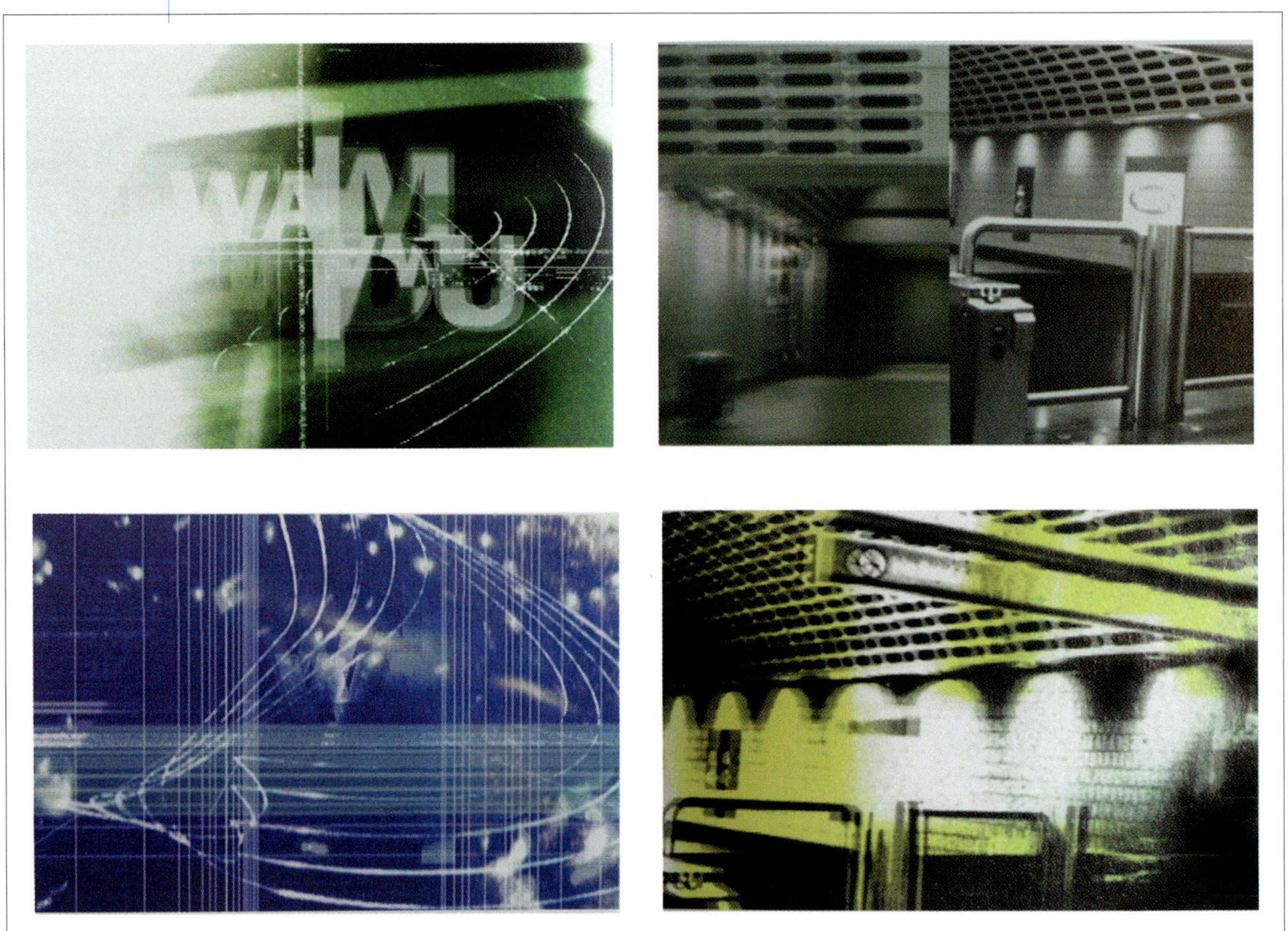

◆ **8-3** *Graphic Havoc avisualagency, studio. Video projection for a concert tour by Wamdue Project.*
© Graphic Havoc avisual-agency.

the web. Another benefit is that a DVD can deliver full uncompressed-quality audio and video. The choice of fonts is nearly infinite, and the graphics need not be compressed into JPEG and GIF files. Remember that compressed files take less memory, but also often result in a loss of quality. Because CD-ROM and DVD drives do vary in speed, a file created to work on the newest and fastest drives may not work smoothly on older ones. This is a mild challenge, compared to the web. In many ways, nonweb multimedia creations are more like desktop publishing. The outcome can be produced and delivered within set standards without the loss of control found in web delivery.

Compared with print images, multimedia still calls for a sound grasp of basic 2-D design principles. It is a layout environment, incorporating text and image. But it also calls for a **4-D** sensibility that pays attention to the choreography of movement across space and time. And it helps to have a conductor's sense of timing as sound is integrated with that movement. How are multimedia designs created?

Methodology

In the previous chapter on web design, we talked about its methodology. This included examining the message and the audience and researching the competition. Similar steps are involved in multimedia design production (**Fig. 8-4**).

1. Begin any multimedia production by examining the message and the audience, and by considering the final output venue. Will it be the web, DVD, film, or TV?
2. Familiarize yourself with the leaders in the field, and set high standards for yourself.

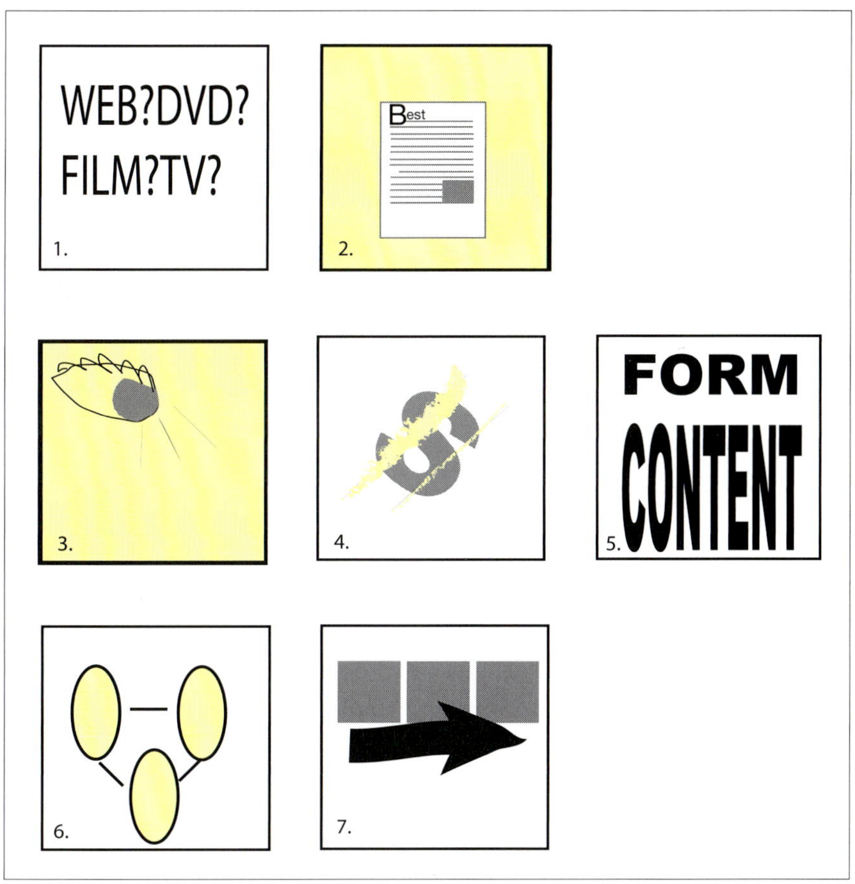

◆ **8-4** *The steps in multimedia design production range from examining the audience and message to producing the design.*

3. Research and evaluate the available visual and sound-based resources.
4. If there is a budget, keep an eye on it as the project progresses.
5. Design the visual and conceptual theme, remembering that form and content should be related. This is a single step, but a big topic!
6. Organize the content, developing a structure for the flow of information. If the piece is interactive, this structural diagram is especially complex and important.
7. Produce the multimedia piece, using appropriate software tools.

Design and Production

If you are working alone, you will need many skills to create a multimedia production. This is often true of students producing a portfolio piece, unless you work in a production group. When working as a freelancer, you may want to develop a resource list of photographers, musicians, or sound designers and animators to call upon. If you are working for an in-house client, all the necessary resources may be available around you.

It is good to know the basics of what various programs can do and how they function as you become acquainted with the field of computer graphics. That way you'll have a better idea of where you want to focus your advanced-level efforts. Now we will start to look at specific software that can create movement.

Authoring Software

Many kinds of software are used in multimedia productions, and this part of the chapter introduces some of them. Movement is a vital part of multimedia, and since you now have some familiarity with the web from Chapter 7, let's examine two programs that can generate animation for the web. This software has a very different interface than print software, but again it is true that once you learn one program, understanding the others comes more easily.

Animation

Animation is an illusion of movement that is created by quickly presenting a sequence of still images. Disney Studios and other early film animators used hand-drawn images. The primary drawings that established movement were **keyframes**. These were connected by a series of finely varied in-between drawings that connected the keyframe action. **"Inbetweeners"** were the artists who drew all these connecting frames. Motion pictures themselves are a series of still photographic frames that are moved quickly through a film projector to give the illusion of movement. If you put a few images together in sequence, the result is a short animation. If you put millions of images together, you have a movie. People sometimes call *animation* the sequencing of drawn, painted, and constructed images, while *motion graphics* refers to the process of photographic manipulation and sequencing of images. Others use the terms interchangeably.

More and more images and animations are being constructed for the web. Photoshop and its accompanying program ImageReady are packaged together and are capable of producing high-quality GIF animations for the web. GIF animations do not need a special plug-in on the user's computer in order to be viewed. They can be displayed in any web browser. Like all animations, GIFs are created from a series of gradually altered

Visual Perception

Visual rhythm refers to how the elements in a design move the viewer's eye through the composition. Rhythm is one of the terms that we use to critique a 2-D design. Traditionally, in 2-D design, we are talking about a single image, such as a painting or a poster or a print of a computer art piece. Rhythm is also an important factor in layout design with multiple pages. In 2-D compositions, we try to establish a visual rhythm throughout a piece, like a meter in a musical score.

In new modes of digital design, the rhythm we are talking about has expanded. It includes actual movement that directs a viewer's eye through a 4-D, time-based composition that we can now call an unfolding event.

The relationship between time and space is part of the new visual rhythm. In a 4-D environment, objects move and events take place across a space, within a "space of time." The animation stills throughout this chapter show the rhythm and eye direction that unfold throughout time.

images, shown one after the other to simulate movement.

Figure 8-5 shows the ImageReady desktop along with the Photoshop layers that contain the original still images. One of the advantages of this animation program is that if you own Photoshop, you own ImageReady. It is included on the accompanying CD as an animation. When you reach the Hands On Practice section of this chapter, you may want to consider using ImageReady or GifBuilder to construct your first animation. Again, a powerful help menu for ImageReady is located in Help>ImageReady, where you can scroll through the contents or search for a specific topic.

Focus On Concept

Interaction is as old as the human race. We interact with one another through conversation. We interact with books as we read and visualize the story in our mind. The quality of the interaction is always what matters. Is it inspiring, boring, redundant? Does it allow us to move at an effective speed? Does it carry a message or an activity that captivates our imagination?

New Media tools structure an interactive communication event with the user in a new way, but the quality of the interaction still depends both on the relationship between user and communicator and on the quality of the visual communications event. The communication interface continues to change with the development of new tools for the web, DVDs, entertainment, virtual reality games, and fine art.

Where will the future take us? What new forms of interactivity will be developed? Will there be a role for **holography**? Will these new forms of computer graphics isolate us as individuals or nation-states—or bring us together? Consider communication theorist Marshall McLuhan's "global village," mentioned in the opening chapter. He believes our new tools join us as never before.

◆ **8-5** *The ImageReady desktop and a sample animation are shown in this illustration by Chris Eichman.*

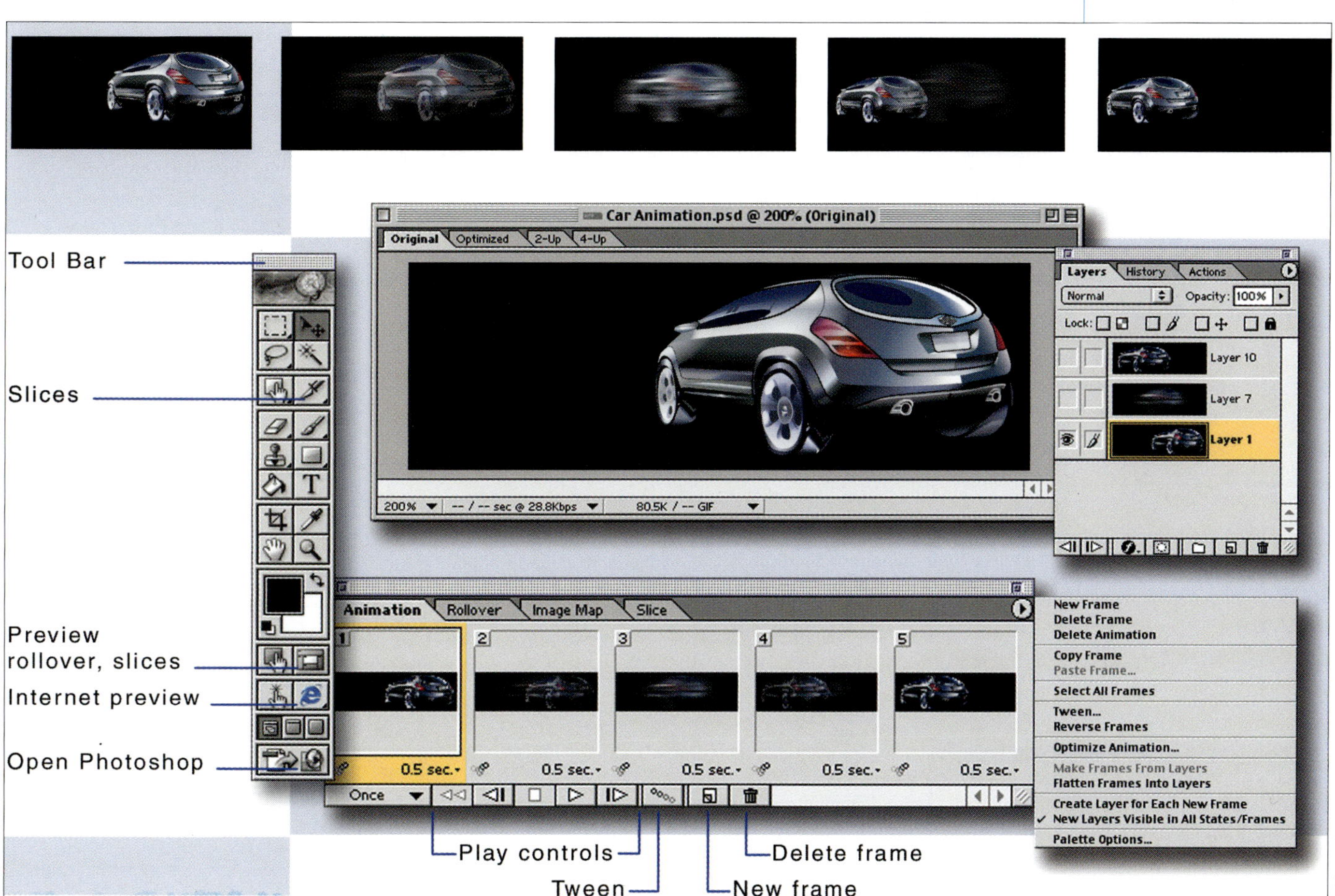

How To Basics

These steps discuss the process of creating an animation in ImageReady.

Begin by creating the various still frames, or cells, in Photoshop, each on its own layer. Make sure that each image is slightly different from the previous one (Fig. 8-6a).

When the cells are completed, open the file in ImageReady, using the Edit in ImageReady command at the bottom of the toolbox (Fig. 8-6b).

If necessary, select Make Frames from Layers in the animation pop up palette. This palette is opened from the window menu at the top of the screen. Each layer becomes a single animation frame (Fig. 8-6c). The triangle arrow at the top of the palette shows the many options available in dealing with frames.

Use the drop-down menu beneath the animation frames to set a loop or limited number of replays. Each frame can be set for the number of seconds of viewing time by clicking on "0 sec" beneath the frame. Use the Forward, Reverse, and Stop commands to view the animation as you develop it (Fig. 8-6d). Other options beneath the animation window include a Make a New Page command and a Tweening command (Fig. 8-6e).

The tabs above the animation window allow you to create cells specifically for a rollover button or other interactive area created as an image map or a slice using ImageReady software (Fig. 8-6f).

The Optimization settings at the top of the image window let you alter the file's attributes, such as color and dither (Fig. 8-6g).

Preview the animation on a web page by choosing Preview in Default Browser in the ImageReady toolbar. If you are satisfied, go to File>Save Optimized As. View ImageReady animations in the Chapter 8 section on the accompanying **CD.**

◆ **8-6 [a–g]** *The process of creating an animation in ImageReady.*

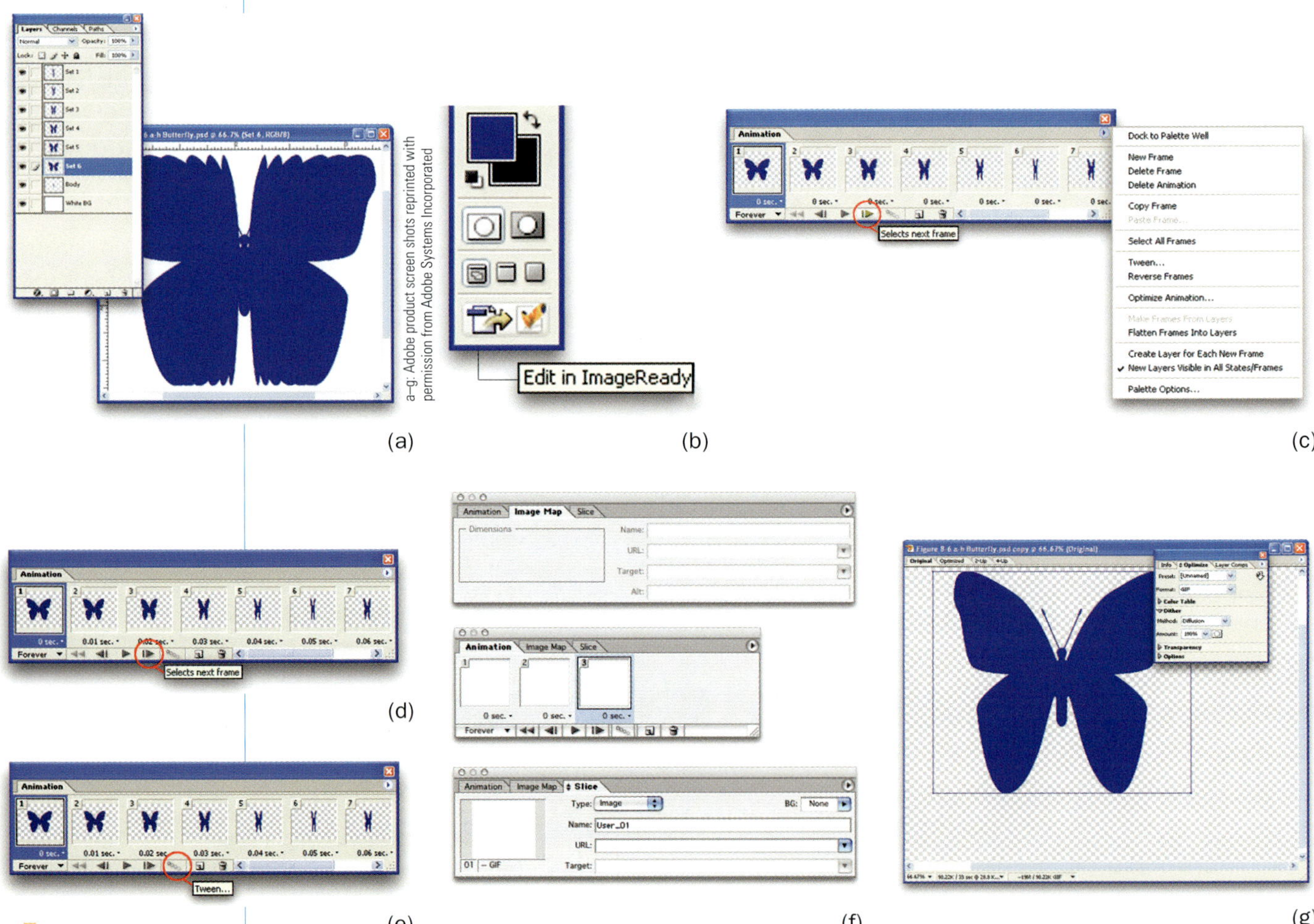

a–g: Adobe product screen shots reprinted with permission from Adobe Systems Incorporated

Animation Packages

Other powerful animation packages designed for web graphics include LiveMotion, Fireworks, and Flash. If you are looking for a quick learning curve, GifBuilder is a small, free, effective animation program. **Figure 8-7a** shows some stills from an animation built with this program. QuickMorph is another small but effective animation tool. Animations for the web are sometimes not terribly complex, using primarily 2-D effects. Web banners and small animated GIFs are forms of web advertising that these small programs can create. Dreamweaver itself has considerable animation capability, as shown in the butterfly animation in **Figure 8-7b**, which is an interactive opening sequence in a website.

Macromedia's Flash is perhaps the most powerful and widely used animation program on the web. For that reason, we will look at it a little more closely. **Figure 8-8** shows the Flash desktop. You may or may not want to take time to investigate it fully at this point in your study. It's a complex program, but it's a powerful and exciting tool that supports both tweening and interactivity. A Flash player lets you view Flash files without owning the program. The Flash player download is located at http://www.macromedia.com.

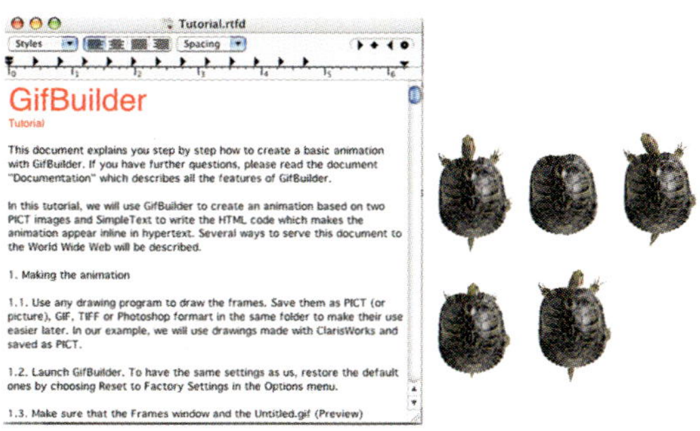

GifBuilder by Yves Piquet

◆ **8-7a** *GifBuilder windows and sample animation.*

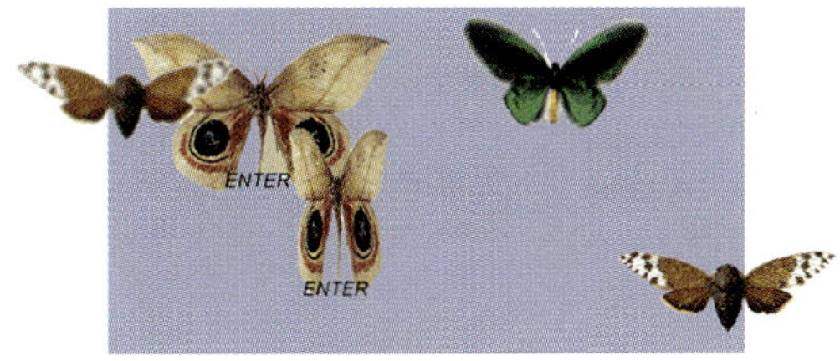

Courtesy Macromedia, Inc.

◆ **8-7b** *This animation begins to move when clicked. It was constructed in Dreamweaver.*

How To Basics

We'll begin by examining the new terms that the Flash software introduces. Learning the Flash language is the first step to understanding how the program works.

The **stage** is the area where you place content and create interactive events and animations. The Flash work area is the gray area surrounding the stage that you can work on but the viewer cannot see. **Panels** contain controls for the Flash functions and allow you to modify content. A **symbol** is a reusable graphic, animation, or button. An **instance** is an individual occurrence of a symbol on the stage. The **library** contains files you have created and stored (or clip art). A **movie clip** is a mini movie that can be inserted in a layer. **Layers** can be stacked within a

◆ **8-8** *The Flash desktop.*

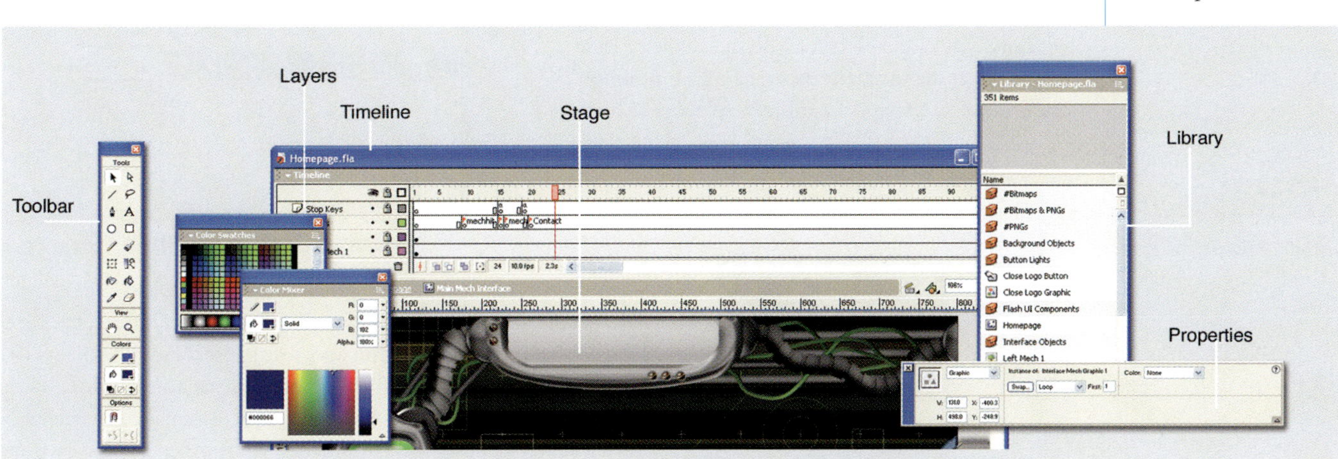

Courtesy Macromedia, Inc.

scene's timeline. These units are responsible for the illusion of time in an animation. **Frames** are individual moments within a timeline layer. *Static frames* repeat the content of the previous frame, while *keyframes* are where content is originally placed or changed. A **movie** is an organization of animated sequences composed of a number of scenes.

Animation is the vital part of this program. Animation is achieved through frame-by-frame drawing of a series of gradually varied keyframes (time consuming) or by tweening where Flash interpolates between keyframes. There are two kinds of tweening in Flash. **Shape tweening** morphs objects. Don't use this for text, symbols, or groups unless you "Break Apart" first. **Motion tweening** is used for groups, symbols, and text.

Imported Files Flash accepts GIF, JPEG, AI, EPS, PICT, PNG, and QuickTime file formats that can be imported into a Flash movie. Its audio format is .aiff, and sound is easy to incorporate. Designers sometimes create their files in Adobe Illustrator before bringing them into Flash for animation because Illustrator offers better image creation tools. However, we will assume that we are going to create everything inside Flash itself.

Creating a Basic Flash Animation

Figures 8-9a–s show the step-by-step process of creating a simple animation.

You will start with the *drawing* and *painting* functions.

Begin drawing and painting using the tool palette. The line, rectangle, and oval tools work the same as in other graphics programs. Stroke and fill commands are at the bottom of the toolbox, as are options related to the selected tool (Fig. 8-9a). Create a rectangle, selecting blue as the fill color. Use the arrow or lasso tool to select the rectangle by dragging a bounding box around it. A shape may also be selected by double clicking with the arrow tool. When selected, the shape is filled with a cross-hatch pattern.

◆ **8-9 [a–s]** *The step-by-step process of working in Flash.*

a–s: Courtesy Macromedia, Inc.

(a)

Select the rectangle and go to the scaling modifier at the bottom right of the tool palette to resize the rectangle to fill the top third of the window (Fig. 8-9b).

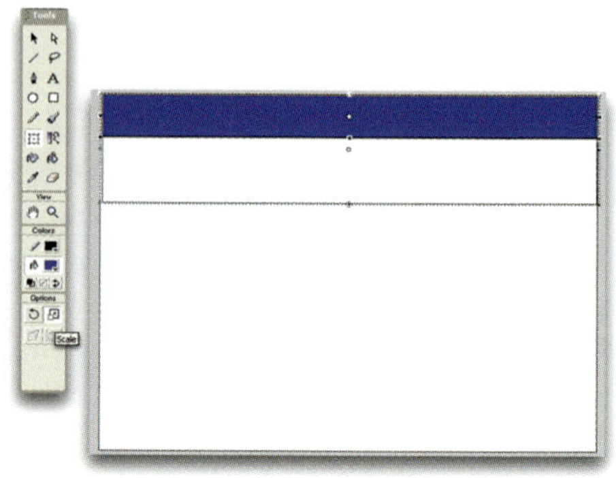

(b)

Next we'll work with layers. Flash layers work like other programs you have studied. Think of them as transparent sheets stacked on top of one another. Layers are viewed in the Timeline (Fig. 8-9c). They are used to edit artwork on one layer without affecting artwork on others. They are also used to organize animation. Selecting artwork on the stage also selects the layer it is on, and vice versa. The layer selected in the Timeline window is active. As in other graphics programs dragging layers above and beneath one another changes their stacking order and the overlapping of the artwork on the stage. Naming, locking, and hiding layers are the same as in other programs you have studied.

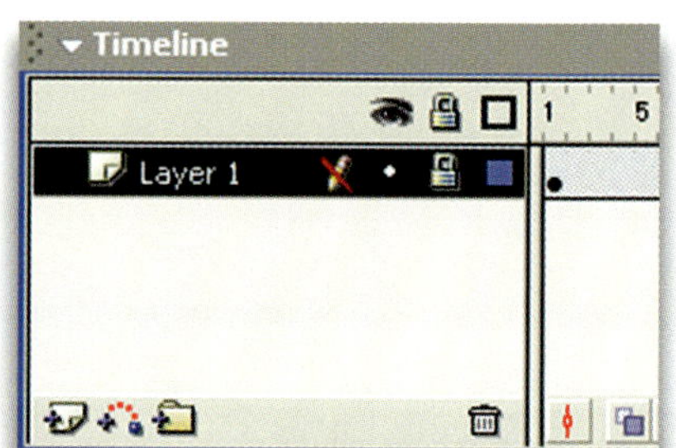

(c)

In the timeline, click on frame 30 of layer 1. Go to the Insert menu and select Insert Frame. This sets a duration of thirty frames for the animation. Click under the lock icon for layer 1 to make sure the background stays untouched while other objects are transformed (Fig. 8-9d).

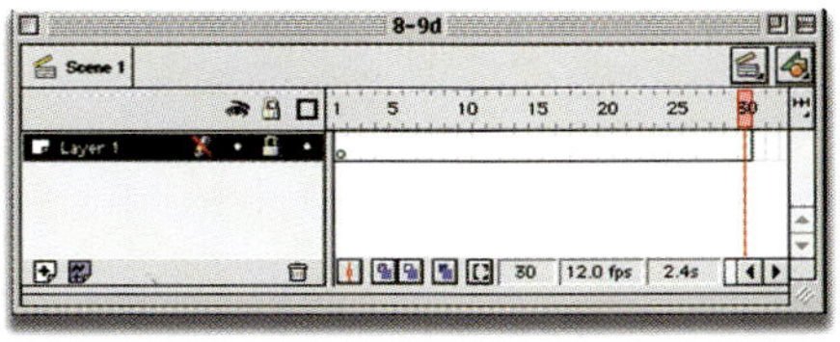

(d)

To import an image onto its own layer, go to Insert/ Layer to create a new layer on top of the background. Go to File/Import, select an appropriate file, and then "import" (Mac) or "open" (PC) (Fig. 8-9e). You can also pull images onto the stage from the library palette (Fig. 8-9f). You can practice this now, but we will create our own image next and make it a symbol so it can be repeated. The Libraries menu shows the Flash collection of graphics, buttons, and movie clips. Window> Library shows your current movie library.

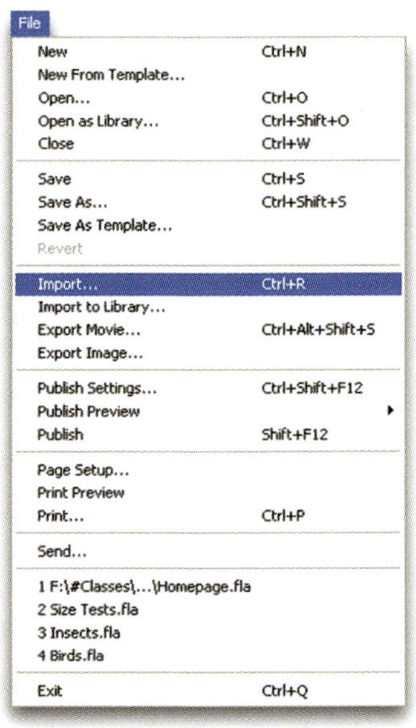

(e)

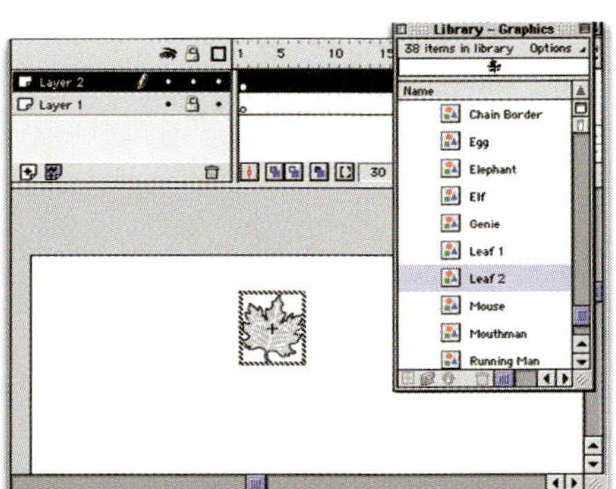

(f)

If you use the same element more than once, make it a symbol for convenience and to save file size and playback speed. A symbol needs to be downloaded to a browser only the first time. Remember that a symbol can be a reusable image, animation, or button.

1. Go to Insert>Layer to create a new layer.

2. Use the painting and drawing tools to make a star (Fig. 8-9g). The pencil tool allows you to choose between straight and smooth lines in the tool modifiers at the bottom of the toolbox. (Don't worry about making a perfect star.) The ink bottle tool controls line quality. Once a shape or line is selected you can use any available modifiers to change it. Single clicking on a line selects a line segment, while double clicking selects the entire segment. Clicking on the interior of a shape selects the fill.

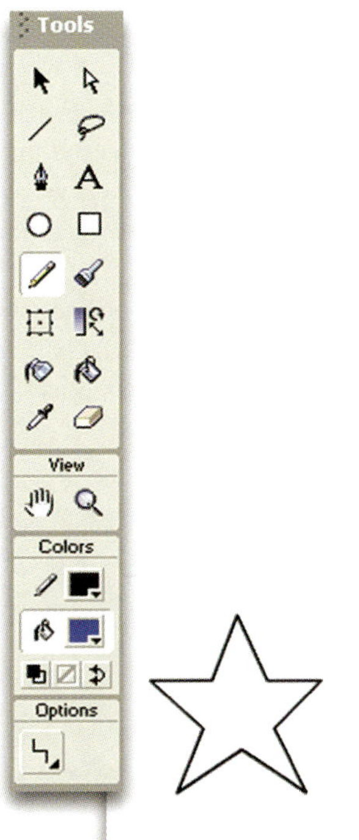

(g)

3. Use the arrow tool to draw a bounding box around the star (or double click it) and go to Insert/Convert to Symbol. Name it "star" in the Symbol Properties box and click "OK" (Fig. 8-9h). The star on stage is now an instance of the symbol. Flash stores symbols in the library. You're saving this as a graphic, not as a button or a movie clip.

4. Select Window>Library and select "star" from the library and drag a few copies onto the canvas, over the blue rectangle (Fig. 8-9i). You can select and modify

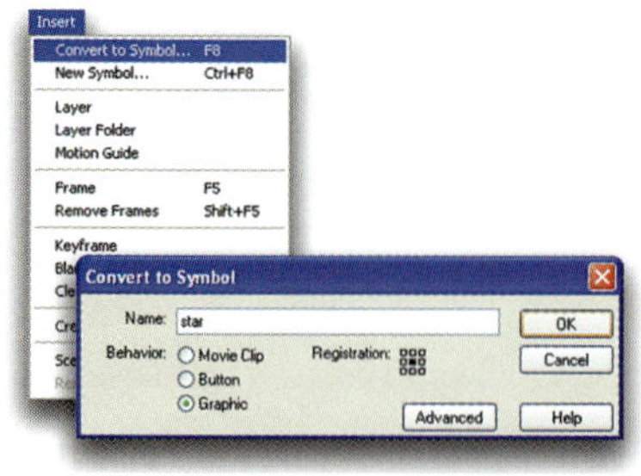

(h)

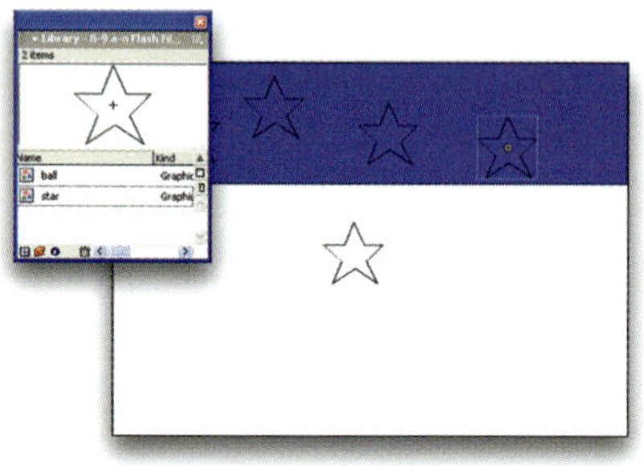

(i)

each of these without affecting the other instances. Try Modify>Instance to change the color. If you didn't put a fill color in the star, you can't modify the color. Next modify the scale on a few stars by choosing the arrow tool and selecting the scale modifier at the bottom of the toolbox. The rotate modifier is right beside it (Fig. 8-9j). Handles appear on the shape. Use these to change the size. Drag a corner handle to resize proportionately. Edit>Edit Symbols lets you change the symbol and all its instances.

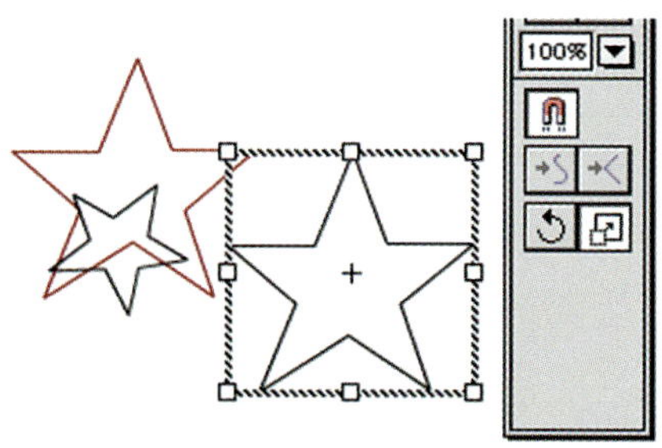

(j)

5. When the same-colored shapes are created on a layer, Flash connects them. Different overlapping colors form separate shape segments when moved apart. Figure 8-9k shows same colors connecting on the left and different colors separating on the right. You can prevent both segmenting and connecting by grouping lines and shapes before overlapping them. Use the arrow tool to select the shapes and choose Modify> Group (Fig. 8-9l).

Animating a symbol is the next thing you'll learn. A symbol can be animated and saved to use as needed. Go to Insert>New Symbol (Fig. 8-9m). Name it

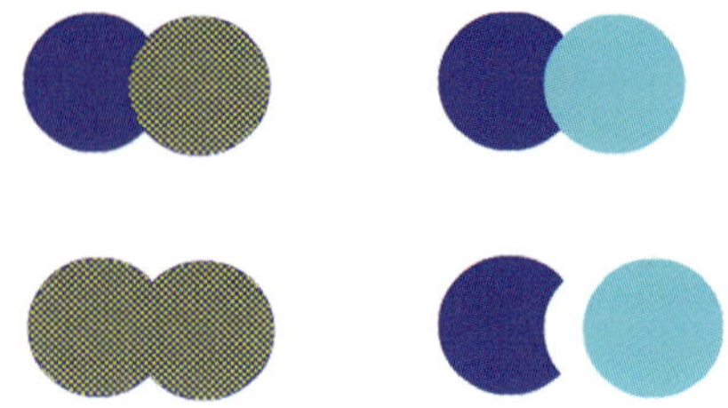

(k)

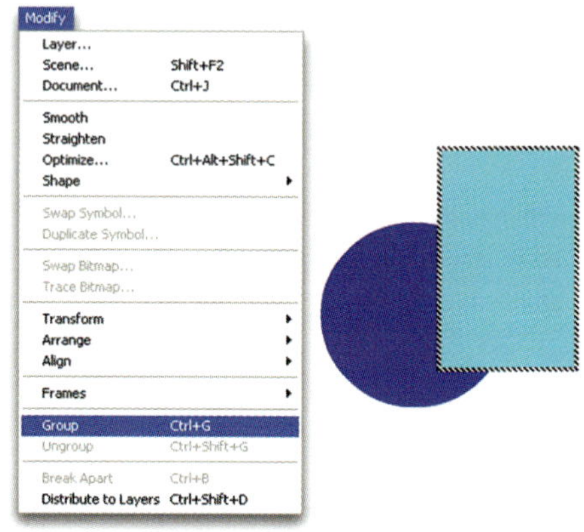

(l)

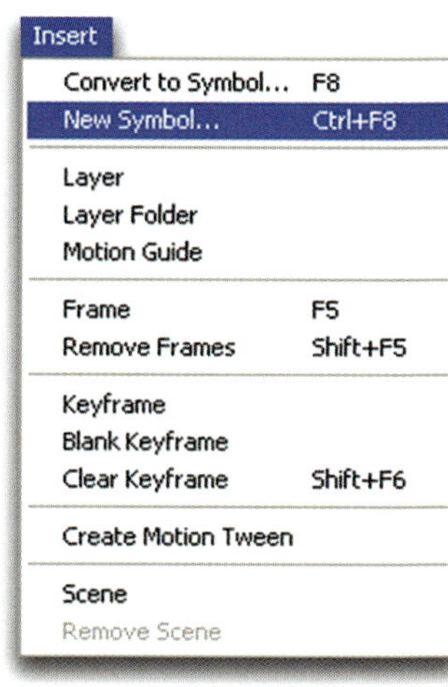

(m)

"Ball," and select Graphic and click OK. This takes you directly to symbol-editing mode. Use the painting and drawing tools to create a beach ball. Use View>Grid to help your alignment. Put a pattern on the ball using the painting tools. Figure 8-9n shows the color palette accessed at the bottom of the toolbox. It also shows the Window>Color Palette that allows you to choose from solid colors or the gradients shown along the bottom. The Alpha number controls transparency. This palette can be used anytime for either stroke or fill colors. The linear or radial color gradient is manipulated the same as in other programs you've studied.

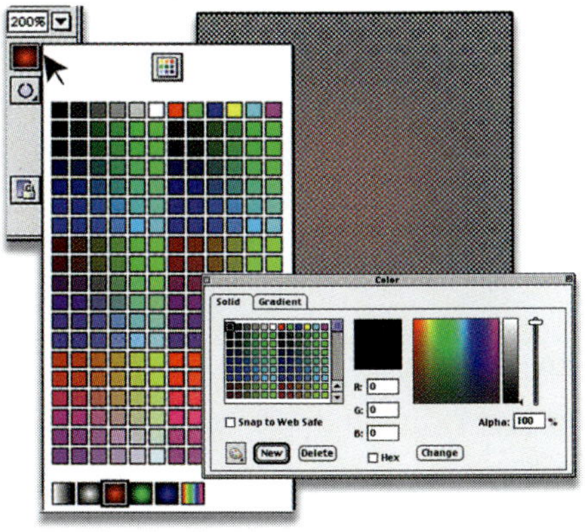

(n)

Select all the ball's visual components and Modify>Group them. Click on frame 20 of the ball layer in the timeline. Go to the Insert menu and select Insert>Keyframe. Select frame 1 and press Command F (Mac) or Control F (PC) to open the Frame Properties window (Fig. 8-9o).

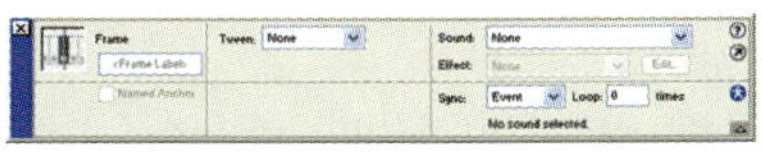

(o)

Select Motion>Tweening in the resulting dialog box. On the Rotate pop up menu select clockwise (CW). Enter "1" on the times field and press "OK." Press Enter or choose Control>Play to see the animation (Fig. 8-9p). Go to Edit>Edit Movie to exit the symbol-editing mode you've been in. You now have an animated symbol to use in your movie. In the current movie it has a clockwise rotation for 20 frames. The event is not set to repeat. Now delete the ball on your layer, or turn the eye off and lock the layer. We're going to do a more complex animation.

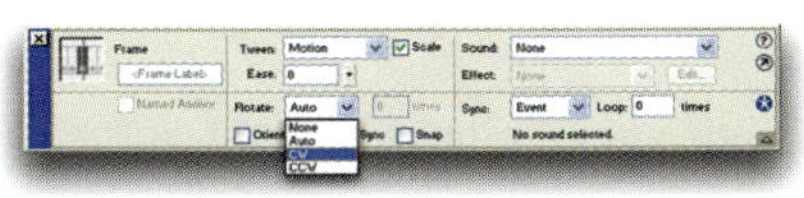

(p)

Now let's look more closely at *tweening*. It is a technique for creating movement and change in a movie. A keyframe is a frame where you specify changes in the animation. In tweened animation you can create keyframes at various points in the timeline while Flash creates the inbetween frames. Click on a frame and use the Insert>Keyframe command to create one. Keyframes in the timeline appear as black circles in a frame, but a keyframe for a layer with no graphics is hollow (Fig. 8-9q)

If you want the ball to roll across the bottom of your screen, select Insert Layer, and use Modify>Layer to name it "Beach Ball." Click the timeline of the beach ball layer on frame 5 and insert a keyframe.

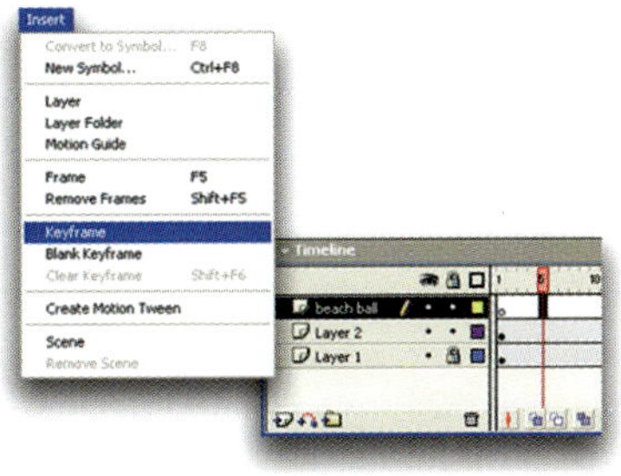

(q)

Open the Library window, select the ball, and drag a copy to the canvas. Place it on the bottom left side of the canvas, in the gray work area outside the stage (Fig. 8-9r).

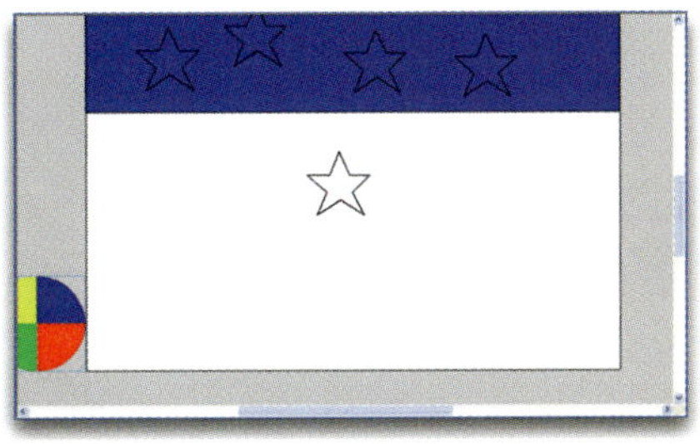

(r)

Click the timeline of the beach ball layer on frame 30 and insert a keyframe. Drag a copy of the beach ball to this position. In the timeline, select the keyframe that you created in frame 5 of the beach ball layer and open the Frame Options window (Command or Control F). Choose Tweening>Motion (Fig. 8-9s). Press Enter to see the animation. Now try to make the ball bounce by setting a new keyframe position in the top middle of the stage. With the keyframe selected, drag the ball to the new position. Play the movie.

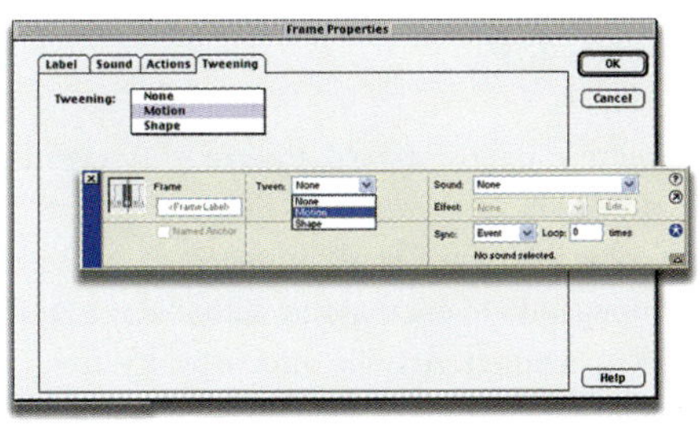

(s)

Let's clarify what you've done and what Flash will automatically do for you. To make the ball bounce use the arrow tool to select the ball. Choose Insert>Create Motion Tween. In the ball layer, a dotted line appears to indicate an incomplete motion tween. (Using this approach, the ball automatically becomes a symbol in the library if it is not already one.) When you are creating a motion tween, the image you tween must be a symbol or a group. Select a frame in the timeline and then drag the ball across to the top center.

Flash inserts the keyframe automatically. Choose Control>Rewind and Control>Play to test the movie.

These techniques can be explored to create a variety of animated effects. The accompanying CD shows two versions of the animation just discussed. *Buttons, Interactivity,* and *Sound* are also basic components of a Flash movie. You can learn these properties very effectively with the help menu and the tutorial that comes packaged with the program. The tutorial interface is shown in **Figure 8-10**.

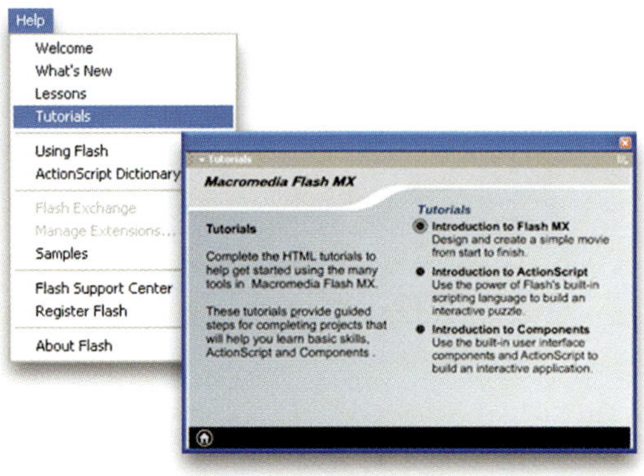

Courtesy Macromedia, Inc.

8-10 *The tutorial package that comes with Flash is very complete and interactive.*

Hands On Practice

Choose one of the programs described above and *plan* a brief animation of your choice that will be built in that program. Begin the planning stages with a storyboard of keyframe stills, created either by hand or in a software program. The objective of this assignment is to focus on "a plan of action" and write a visual script.

Warming Up

Now animate your storyboard. **Figure 8-11**, created in ImageReady, is an example of this assignment. **Figure 8-12** is a series of Flash animations created by Planet Propaganda to correspond with client Artville's clip art print catalogs. Artville offers royalty-free stock imagery.

Now that we have completed the Hands On Practice and Warming Up, we'll conclude with a brief examination of 3-D multimedia and animation in the advertising and entertainment industries.

Advertising and Entertainment

Animation has come a long way since its beginnings at the midpoint of the 20th century. It has applications in a great variety of fields, including education, medicine, entertainment, and advertising.

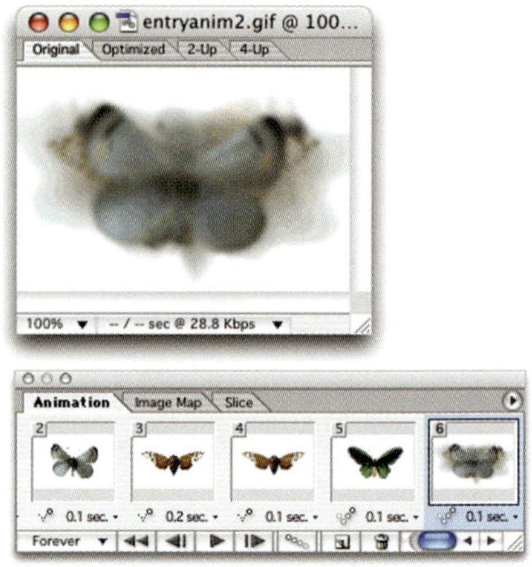

8-11 *An animation created in ImageReady. You can use your images or those on the accompanying CD to experiment with this program.*

Advertising and entertainment are making wide use of animation. **Figure 8-13** shows stills from a brief 3-D animation created by Seth VandeLeest as part of his portfolio. This desktop animation makes use of 3-D animation, varied points of view, and a rhythmic choreography that pays attention to issues of space and timing. Effects such as these are created in the advertising and entertainment industries with a wide variety of advanced software. See the animated version on the accompanying **CD**.

Video Editing

Shooting video can be done straight in the camera and used for home movies with minor editing, or it can be edited and added into web and CD or DVD interactive creations. Whatever the final intent, begin with a digital video camcorder and a fast computer with lots of storage. Plan to feed your video into an editing system. The software choice can vary widely. Macintosh's iMovie is simple, effective, and available on all new Macs. Final Cut Pro is a high-end editing program available to personal computer users. The software program Adobe Premiere is available for the PC and has been in use for quite a while by artists, graphic designers, and communications professionals.

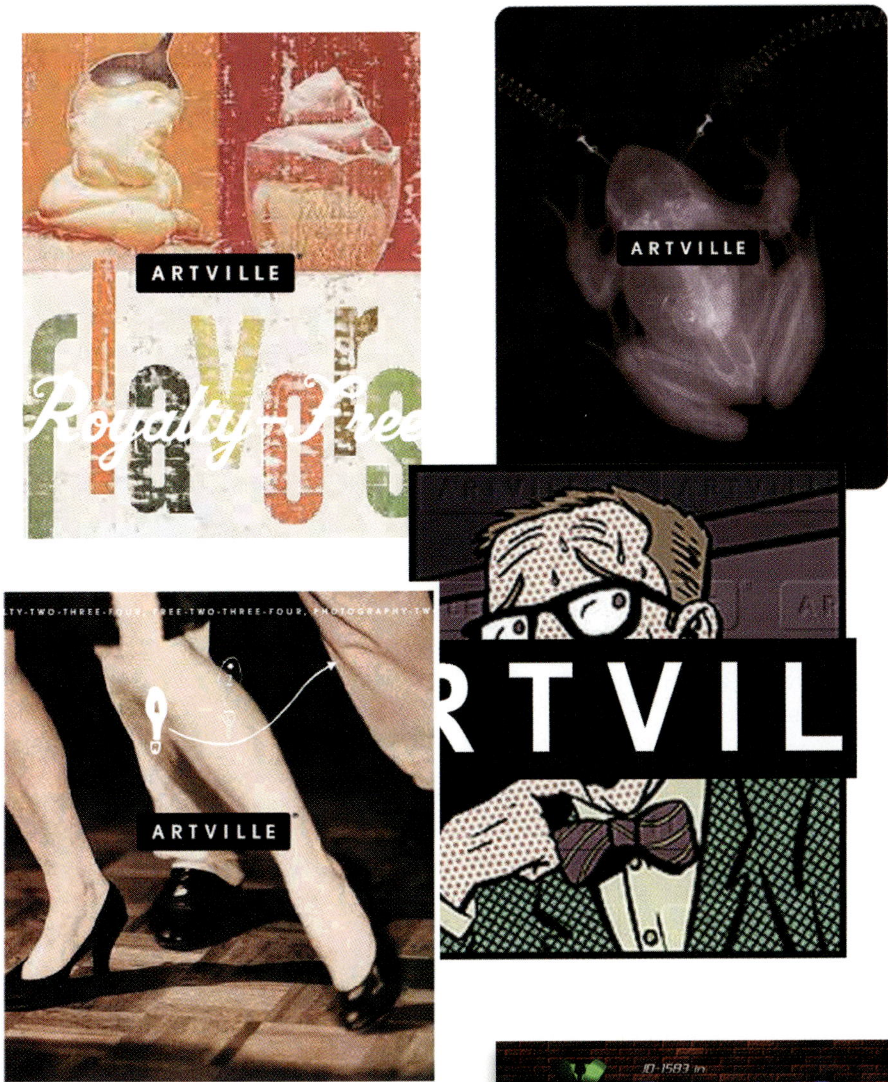

◆ **8-12** *Planet Propaganda, studio; Kevin Wade, Ben Hirby, Dan Ibarra, Martha Graettinger, Corey Szopinski, Brian Wilson, designers.* Artville. *Consumer website.*

Courtesy of Planet Propaganda, Madison, WI.

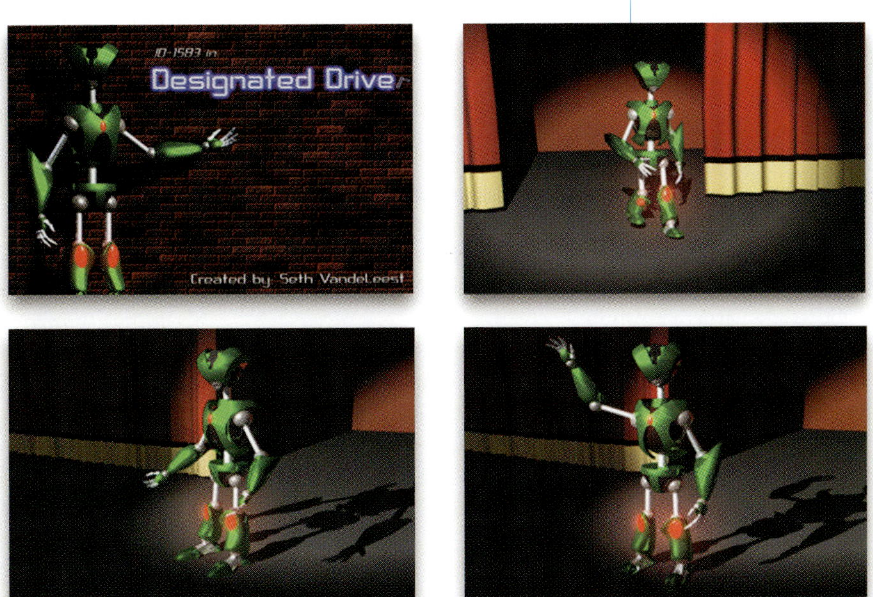

◆ **8-13** *Seth VandeLeest.* Character Animation. *Maya software. 2005.*

Courtesy of the artist.

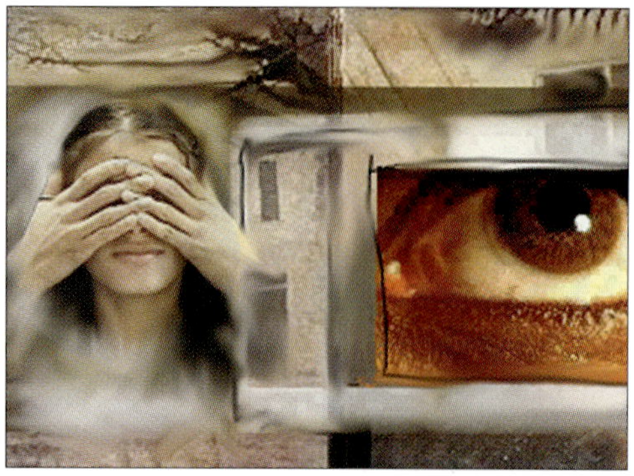

◆ **8-14** *Coleen Deck.* Search Twice. *2001. Video animation created in Adobe After Effects.*
Courtesy of the artist.

Adobe After Effects is an industry standard program for producing broadcast-quality composite digital video. It feels like an empowered Photoshop, only with video capabilities. Graphics, video, and sound can be imported, placed, collaged, and layered. **Figure 8-14** shows an After Effects collage by artist/educator Coleen Deck that resembles a Photoshop collage in still form, but it is animated. Special effect filters can be applied to the video clips for a wide array of purposes. This creation can be exported to QuickTime, to Windows Media Player, or to a professional video postproduction system. Used to create title sequences for TV and multimedia presentations, the program is not interactive.

In The Studio

Choose a program from this chapter to build one of the following assignments. This gives you an opportunity to practice your skill with a new software program, while showing your abilities at conceptualizing and scripting. Remember to consider both how your shapes move through space and their rhythmic quality.

A Public Service Announcement

Use the steps described at the beginning of the chapter under Methodology to plan and create a brief multimedia animation. This animation should be capable of mounting on the web *or* running on a CD. It need not be interactive. Choose a topic of importance to you and prepare a fifteen-second announcement dealing with something you care about, for example, drunk driving or environmental or literacy issues.

A Personal Narrative

Your second choice is to build a personal narrative. Use the steps described at the beginning of the chapter under Methodology (see pages 175–176) to plan and create a multimedia animation. This animation should have interactive buttons, and you can choose whether to build it for the web or burn it onto a CD. Tell a personal story of no more than 30 seconds in duration.

Gallery Profile

Nam June Paik (1932—) is an international artist whose video-based artwork began as part of the Fluxus movement (see Chapter 1). Paik's work has had a profound influence on the media culture of the late 20th and early 21st centuries. He redefined video as an artist's medium.

Paik was born in Korea and later moved to Japan where he graduated from the University of Tokyo with studies in both the history of art and the history of music. He first incorporated TV monitors in his work for a Fluxus exhibition in 1963. His first solo exhibition in the United States, "Electronic Art," was in 1965 in New York City. His electronic artwork continued to develop throughout the next decades, with the development of multi-monitor installations. In 1982, he was given a retrospective at the Whitney Museum of American Art, New York City, and in 1988, he constructed *The More the Better*, an installation of 1,003 monitors for the Olympic Games at Seoul. In 1998, he received the Kyoto Award.

His retrospective at the Guggenheim Museum in Bilbao, Spain, in 2001 showed the breadth and depth of his lifelong involvement with time-based concepts. His television and video installations, performances, and collaborations, combined with the impact of his teaching and writing, have expanded the definition of art into New Media culture. His recent investigations with New Media installations include laser technology, smoke, and water.

Paik lives and works in New York City (part of the year), and teaches at Staatliche Kunstakademie in Düsseldorf. **Figures 8-15** and **8-16** show his multiple-monitor installations and sculptural constructions.

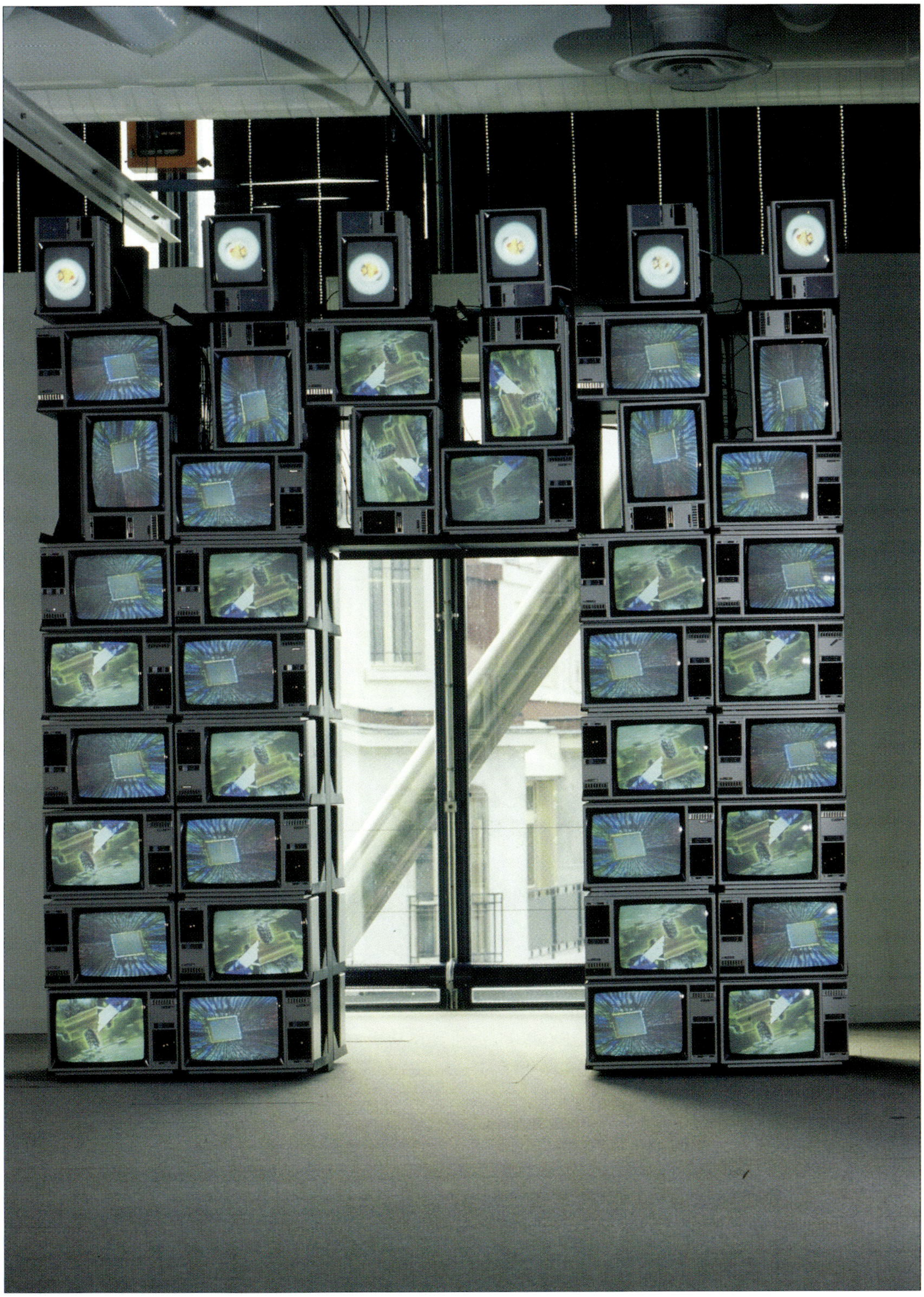

8-15 *Nam June Paik.* Arc Double Face. *1985. Three-channel video installation.* Musée National d'Art Moderne, Centre Georges Pompidou, Paris, France/ CNAC/MNAM/Dist. Réunion des. Musées Nationaux/ Art Resource, NY.

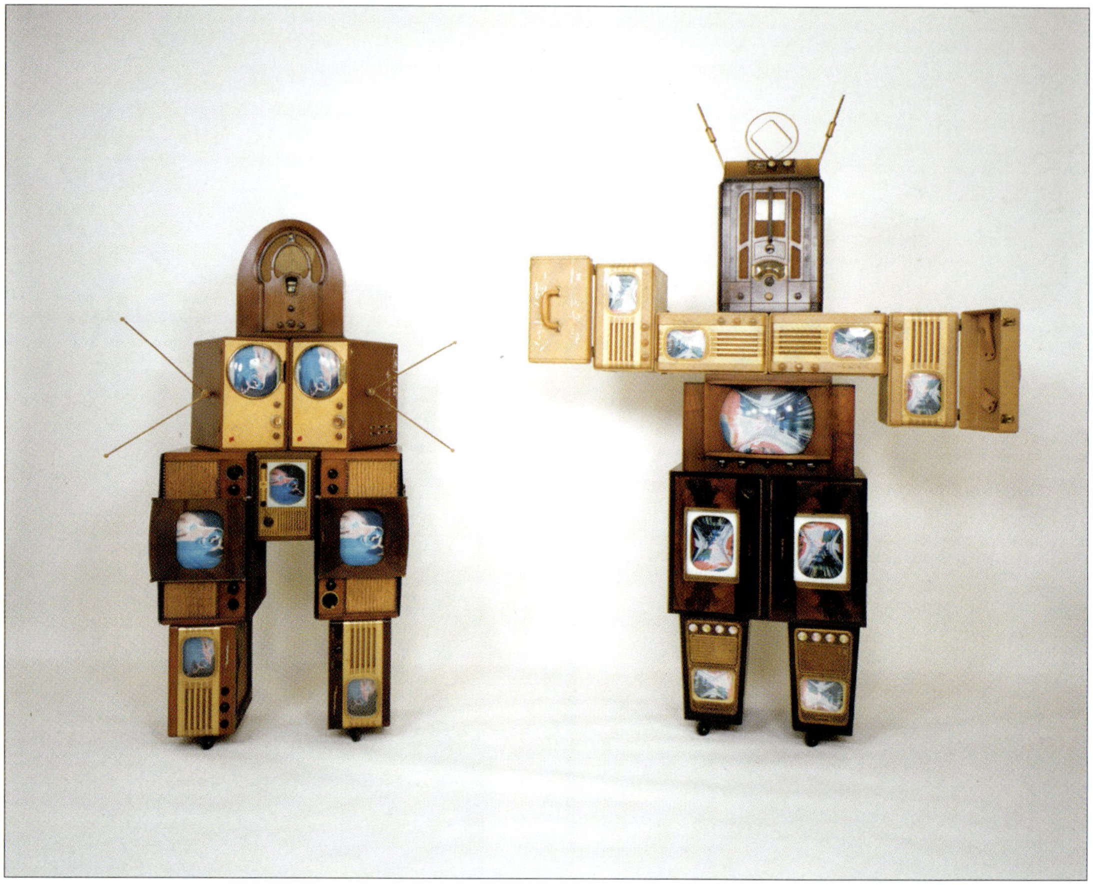

8-16 *Nam June Paik.* Family of Robot: Grandmother *(left) and* Family of Robot: Grandfather *(right). 1986. Single-channel video sculpture with vintage television and radio casings and monitors.*
Carl Solway Gallery, Cincinnati, OH, photo by Cal Kowal.

SUMMARY CRITIQUE

What should you look for when critiquing your own work and that of others in the class? Of course, your studio project should make good use of the software techniques available with your chosen program. Consider also how the viewer is involved with the interactive elements. Are the choices clear? How about the time element? Do things happen too quickly? Too slowly? How do the images move across the screen? Do they make good, dynamic use of the available space? Do you reach the intended viewer with the message you want to convey? What have you done right, and what would you improve, given time and expertise?

MOVING ON

Although the book is at a close, "moving on" seems the right way to conclude this text on computer graphics. The field evolves on an almost daily basis, touching both our professional and personal lives. It will be a challenge and often a delight for all of us to stay current with its rapid development. Software is increasingly both more powerful and easier to use. Computer graphics is an excellent partner to enable a creative artist's and designer's flights of imagination, and the majority of the best art and design in the early 21st century will be created with digital design.

The eye, heart, and mind of the designer combined with powerful new digital tools promise to bring enormous changes to the field of art and design.

Glossary

Additive Primaries The additive color model uses the primary colors red, green, and blue to create all other colors in light-based systems such as photography and computer monitors. The more additive colors are mixed with others, the lighter they become.

Analog An analog signal is data that is primarily linear and continuous, like long-playing records and continuous tone photographs. Analog refers to everything in the real, non-computerized world.

Analogous Color Hues that lie next to one another on the color wheel.

Analytic Cubism An early-20th-century school of painting and sculpture characterized by the reduction of natural images, often into fractured geometric planes, structured from multiple perspectives on a single picture plane.

Animation The art or process of simulating movement based on a sequence of images.

AOL America Online.

Bauhaus A school of design in Germany from 1919–1933 whose faculty encouraged the use of techniques and materials from industrial sources. The Bauhaus school affected graphic design with its emphasis on the elements and principles of design. *Form follows function* is a phrase that describes the Bauhaus interest in how the form of an object (its dimensional appearance) should be descriptive of how the object is used.

Binary A numbering system that has only two possible digits, 0 and 1. In computers, the "on" or "off" command at the code level is represented by a "0" or a "1." Binary code is written with a string of 0 and 1 instructions.

Bit A binary digit that is the smallest unit of computer memory. It is expressed as either a 0 or a 1 representing on or off, something or nothing.

Bitmap Mode Font or image comprised of dots (pixels) as distinct from an object-based image, characterized by jagged edges, also known as a raster image. *See* Raster Graphics.

Bitmapped Graphics A bitmap is a "map" that describes the location and "on" and "off" state of the bits that comprise an image. Bitmapped graphics are made up of bits and are edited by modifying individual pixels.

Blend Tool In Illustrator, the Blend tool creates a smooth flow between the color and shape of multiple objects.

Byte A grouping of eight bits (0s and 1s). It is possible to rearrange 8 bits in only 256 ways, and so a byte can represent any of 1 to 256 different values per pixel.

Calibration To align or adjust to needs or to a standard. To calibrate is to adjust a monitor to your needs or so that an image appears the same on different monitors.

Camera Obscura To experience a camera obscura, go into a very dark room on a bright day. Make a small hole in a window cover and look at the opposite wall. The world outside the window will appear upside down on the wall. Light travels in a straight line and when some of the rays reflected from a bright subject pass through a small hole in thin material, they do not scatter but cross and reform as an upside-down image on a flat surface held parallel to the hole. This effect can be observed in a room or captured in a small box. The small box, called a pinhole camera, can have photographic paper placed on the back wall.

Cartesian Coordinates A geometry system that uses numbers to locate points on a grid plane. A line is then drawn between two or more points to create a graphic.

Channels Channels store information in grayscale images. Each channel can store data for a different color or mask in an image. *See* Masking.

Clipping Path A Bezier outline that defines which areas of an image should be transparent or "clipped." Using a Path tool, a clipping path creates straight and curved lines around a shape. When exported as an EPS format, a file containing a clipping path can be imported into a layout in any shape that has been created. This avoids the white rectangle around imported images.

Cloning Cloning creates a copy of part or all of an image that can then be applied elsewhere.

Closure When the eye completes a line or curve in order to form a familiar shape.

Collage An artistic composition made up of an assembly of diverse elements.

Color The way in which an object reflects or refracts light.

Color Gamut The gamut is the set of possible colors within a color system that can be displayed or printed. No one system can reproduce all possible colors in the spectrum.

Color Models A color model is the specific color system used to display and print images. Common models include HSB (hue, saturation, brightness), CMYK (cyan, magenta, yellow, black), and RGB (red, green, blue).

Color Scheme A selection of colors to be used in a composition.

Color Theory Color is produced when light strikes an object and reflects back in your eyes. This element of art has three properties:

Hue is the name of a color (e.g., red, yellow, blue).

Intensity is the purity and strength of a color (e.g., bright red or dull red).

Value is the lightness or darkness of a color.

Color theory is a set of principles used to create harmonious color combinations.

Color Wheel A representation of the color spectrum in the form of a wheel.

Complementary Hues that are opposite one another on the color wheel.

Computer Graphics The general "umbrella" term that refers to the entire field of hardware and software that evolved in the 20th century, enabling us to create a visual image on the computer.

Continuation When the eye is carried smoothly into the line or curve of another object.

Dada An artistic and literary movement from the post–World War I period that produced anti-art based on the irrational, the absurd, the nihilistic, and the nonsensical.

Default The preliminary hardware or software settings before they are changed by the user.

Depth Cueing Depth cueing is used by the computer to render 3-D effects such as haze and distance. It can generate the visual effect that objects farther away from the viewer get less clear with increasing distance.

Digital A digital signal can be in only one of two states, either on or off. These discrete units of information can be accessed and manipulated as separate, distinct entities.

Diptych A two-panel artwork.

Download Time The time necessary to access a web page or image. *See* World Wide Web.

DSL Digital Subscriber Line. A generic name for digital lines that are provided by telephone companies to their local subscribers and that carry data at high speeds.

Duotone The combination of two halftone reproductions with different color and tonal ranges made from the same single-color original.

Eye Direction The way the eye is drawn through a two-dimensional composition.

Figure/Ground The fundamental law of visual perception that makes it possible to discern objects as separate from their surrounding. There are three types of figure/ground relationships:

Stable figure/ground is an unambiguous relationship between an object and its background.

Reversible figure/ground is a relationship in which it is likely that the figure and ground can be focused on equally.

Ambiguous figure/ground is a relationship in which the main object is made up of many objects that can be focused on individually.

File Formats Refer to the way a program arranges data for storage and display. The format by which the image is stored on the disk determines which programs can open, read, and edit that image, as well as the amount of storage space it takes up. Common file formats for bitmapped images are TIFF and JPEG, while EPS is often used to store an object-oriented file.

Fluxus The word *fluxus* means "a flow." Fluxus originated in 1962 and developed mainly in North America, Japan, and Europe. It aimed at the liberation of art from any specific language or specific media. The movement's radically untraditional works included the video art of Nam June Paik, the performance art of Josef Beuys, and the music of John Cage.

Focal Point The point of a design with the most impact and, therefore, the starting point visually.

4-D (Four-Dimensional) Time, space, and movement comprise the fourth dimension. Computers increased the exploration of space and time in art and design.

Frames Frames are the core of a Flash animation. They are the stills that generate animation. The default setting for Flash is 12 frames per second, a good setting for the web.

Gestalt A physical, biological, psychological, or symbolic configuration or pattern of elements so unified as a whole that its properties cannot be described as a simple summation of its parts.

Gigabyte A unit of computer memory that has approximately 1,000 (1,024) megabytes.

Gradient The smooth transition from one color or tone to another.

Graphics Tablet A digital pad using a stylus for input to a computer.

Grayscale Mode The mode utilized to allow smooth black to white transitions and to recreate black-and-white photographs.

Halftone Pertaining to plates, processes, or the pictures made by them in which gradation of tone in the photograph is reproduced by a graduated system of dots. These dots are usually nearly invisible to the unaided eye and are produced by the placement of a screen between the camera and the subject.

Hardware The physical components of a computer graphics system, including all mechanical, magnetic, and electronic parts.

Hidden Line Elimination In computer graphics, leaving out the part of an object that is partially hidden by another object.

Holography A method of producing a three-dimensional image of an object by recording on a photographic plate or film the pattern of interference formed by a split laser beam. The pattern is then illuminated either with a laser or with ordinary light.

HSB Hue, saturation, and brightness is a color model based on light transmission of an image or a computer monitor.

HTML Hypertext Markup Language. A text-based page language used for documents to be viewed with web browsers. *See* World Wide Web.

Hue The attribute of color associated with a dominant spectrum wavelength. One of the three properties of color and the name by which we identify a color.

Illuminated Manuscript Illuminated manuscripts are a particular type of book. "Illuminated" refers to a type of illustration, while "manuscript" refers to the text, which is written by hand. Illuminated manuscripts were generally created no later than the Renaissance and were written and painted entirely by hand.

Inbetweener An individual artist who creates the images between keyframes in an animation.

Indexed Color Mode An image mode using a maximum of 256 colors where a smaller data file is needed. A look-up table (index) is used to assign the nearest color to replace one not in the index.

Instance Each copy of a symbol in Flash that is used in a movie is an *instance* of that symbol.

Interactivity The dialogue between a user and a website or between a computer and a user that allows the user to influence content.

Interlaced GIF A Graphic Interchange Format image presentation in which the image is revealed in increasing detail as it is downloaded from a web page.

International Style An influential modernist style that began in Europe and the United States in the 1920s and 1930s and lasted several decades. It was characterized chiefly by unadorned geometric forms in architecture and the grid system in graphic design.

Interpolation A computer process used to estimate unknown values. For example, when a raster image is enlarged, interpolation will make estimates to fill in the missing pixels. It is by nature an inexact process.

Iris Print A high-definition, archival printing process.

ISDN Integrated services digital network. A set of communications standards allowing a single wire or optical fiber to carry voice, digital network services, and video. ISDN is intended to eventually replace the telephone system.

Keyframe A single animation frame in which information is stored as a reference for subsequent in-between frames.

Layers A level to which you can assign an element of a design you are working on.

Library Flash provides a "library" container for storing objects that can appear in several movies.

Link Highlighted text that takes a user to another location or page.

Lossy A method of file compression that loses information each time an image is saved. JPEG is an example. This is the opposite of lossless compression.

Masking Isolating or protecting part of an image while applying filters or other changes. When you select part of an image, the area that is not selected is "masked," or protected from editing.

Megabyte A unit of computer memory that has approximately 1,000 (1,024) kilobytes (K).

Mesh Gradient In Illustrator, the mesh gradient can be used to create a complex color shift across an object or objects.

Metaphor A figure of speech or a visual in which a word, a phrase, or an image that ordinarily designates one thing is used to designate another, thus making an implicit comparison, as in "*All the world's a stage*" (Shakespeare).

Mezzotint A method of reproducing an image in tones rather than lines; traditionally used in intaglio.

Modernism Modern art refers to an approach to art in which it was no longer important to literally represent a subject. The invention of photography had made this function of art less important. Instead, artists started experimenting with new ways of seeing, often moving toward abstraction.

Monochromatic Use of a single hue in varying values.

Motion Graphics Another term for computerized animation, involving the process of photographic manipulation and sequencing of images.

Motion Tweening *See* Tweening.

Moveable Type Each character of typography is created on an individual form, thus allowing the characters to be placed in a variety of sequences before being inked and printed.

Movie Clip Flash provides two kinds of animated symbols—graphic symbols and movie clips. A Flash movie clip symbol is like a film loop. It runs on its own time line.

Multimedia The combination of communications media, such as text, graphics, sound, and motion, into an integrated presentation usually utilizing computers.

New Media The term *new media* is often used to describe digital presentations that can combine various forms of communication, such as visuals, sound, motion graphics, or interactivity. It refers to computer or electronic media, rather than print-based media.

Object-oriented Graphics A software technology that uses vectors to define graphics by drawing lines between points. The quality of the line between each point is determined by the resolution of the output device.

Opacity The degree to which an object is "see through." The Transparency palette in Illustrator allows you to control the opacity of an object or a color.

Paint Systems A combination of software and hardware that allows the artist/designer to create freehand drawings. The images are stored as bitmaps and can easily be edited.

Pathfinder Palette The Illustrator Pathfinder palette is used to access filters for combining paths and shape mode commands, which create and modify compound shapes.

Pattern Swatch The Illustrator Swatch tool palette contains sample colors, tints, gradients, and patterns. You may add your own selections as well.

Patterns Can be selected from a palette and used to fill a shape or line.

Photogram An image produced without a camera by placing an object on photosensitive paper and exposing it to light.

Photomontage The technique of making a picture by assembling pieces of photographs. This is often done in combination with other nonphotographic collage materials.

Physiological Characteristic of the normal functioning of an organism. Physiology is the study of the mechanical, physical, and biochemical functions of living organisms.

Pixel Indivisible picture elements that are the smallest element of a computer image that can be individually accessed and manipulated.

Postmodernism Of or relating to art, architecture, or literature that reacts against earlier modernist principles. This is sometimes achieved by reintroducing traditional or classical elements of style or by carrying modernist styles or practices to extremes.

Primary Colors The three basic colors from which all other colors can be made. Light-based primaries—red, green, and blue—are called *additive primaries* because when added together they produce white light. Pigment-based primary colors of the traditional color wheel are red, blue, and yellow. The *subtractive primaries* of process printing are cyan, magenta, and yellow.

Progressive JPEG A JPEG image presentation in which the image is revealed in increasing detail as it is downloaded from a web page.

Proof Prints A print taken at various stages from inkjet printers, imagesetters, offset presses, etc., to check the progress and accuracy of the work.

Proximity Visually grouping by similarity in spatial location.

Quadtone A halftone image printed with four colors.

RAM Random-access memory into which an application's code is loaded while you work with it. The amount of memory available in RAM is important because both the operating system and applications require more and more memory.

Raster Graphics Graphics that are created from rows of pixels.

Renaissance The humanistic revival of classical art, architecture, literature, and learning that originated in Italy in the 14th century and later spread throughout Europe. The period of this revival, roughly the 14th through the 16th centuries, marks the transition from medieval to modern times.

Resolution Resolution refers to the fineness or sharpness of a screen display or computer-generated printed piece based on the number of pixels per inch in an image.

Rollover The rapid substitution of other images when the mouse pointer is dragged over the original image in a web page.

ROM Read-only memory that cannot be written to.

Rough A design layout plan that comes after preliminary thumbnails and is usually executed in half or full size.

Saturation A variation in color from gray (no color) through pastel shades to pure color with no gray while the brightness remains the same.

Semiotics The theory and study of signs and symbols, especially as elements of language or other visual systems of communication.

Silver Print A black-and-white, chemical-based photographic process using silver nitrate.

Similarity and Variety The repetition and variation of unit-forming elements such as shape, angle, color, texture, and size.

Simultaneous Contrast The effect a color has on another when placed adjacent to it.

Software The programs installed on the computer.

Split Complementary A color adjacent to the complement of another color.

Spot Color A special color mixed for a particular print need, as opposed to a standard process color.

Stage The actual area in which your Flash movie is displayed.

Subtractive Primaries The subtractive color system uses the primary colors cyan, magenta, yellow, and black to produce all colors in ink-based printing. Black is technically unnecessary but is used to reduce ink costs.

Surrealism The art of producing incongruous imagery by unusual juxtapositions and combinations.

Symbol The term for any kind of Flash graphic item stored in a library, including sounds and bitmaps.

Synesthesia The effect of one sense evoking another, for example, musical tones evoking a sense of color.

Synthetic Cubism The later phase of Cubism (1913–1920s) during which paintings were composed of fewer and simpler forms and often incorporated collage.

TCP/IP Transmission Control Protocol (ensures that data bits are received in the order sent)/Internet Protocol address (identifies the unique Internet address for a specific computer or server).

Thumbnail A first-stage, miniature plan for a design.

Time-based Media Any data that changes meaningfully with respect to time. Typically, this is a wide array of visual or sound-based media.

Triadic Color Scheme The triadic color scheme uses three colors equally spaced around the color wheel.

Triptych A three-panel artwork.

Tritone A halftone image printed with three colors; often the second and third colors are yellow and magenta to produce a sepia-toned image.

Tweening An interpolation technique by which an animation program generates extra frames between the keyframes that the user has created.

URL Uniform Resource Locator. A unique web address for each document on the web.

Value Lightness or darkness of a color when related to a tone of gray.

Vector Graphics The opposite of bitmapped and raster graphics, vector files are made up of lines and curves based on the mathematical structure of Cartesian coordinates. They do not lose clarity when enlarged.

Visual Language The ability to recognize and understand ideas conveyed through visible images.

Visual Perception A dynamic exchange between the eye and the brain's interpretation of visual data.

Wavelength The distance between one peak or crest of a wave of light and the next peak or crest.

Web Browser A software package that enables a user to display and interact with documents hosted on the web.

Web Color Color system using a maximum of 216 colors to ensure the image can be handled by any browser accessing the web page.

Website An Internet location at which data or images can be accessed using a browser.

Wire Frame Drawing A three-dimensional structure displayed by showing lines for each of its edges without representing surfaces or lighting.

World Wide Web (WWW) An Internet information server consisting of sites and files accessible by a browser; the largest networked collection of linked documents.

Selected Bibliography

See the Webliography Links on the Accompanying CD.

Chapter 1

A New History for a New Medium

Aynsley, Jeremy. *A Century of Graphic Design.* Hauppauge, N.Y.: Barron's, 2001.

Bayer, Herbert, et al., eds. *Bauhaus 1919–1928.* New York: The Museum of Modern Art, 1938.

Boswell, Peter, and Maria Makela. *The Photomontages of Hannah Höch.* Minneapolis, Minn.: Walker Art Center, 1997.

Friedman, Mildred, and Joseph Giovannini, eds. *Graphic Design in America: A Visual Language History.* New York: Abrams, 1989.

Gomez, Edward. *New Design: Tokyo.* Gloucester, Mass.: Rockport Publishers, 1999.

Goodman, Cynthia. *Digital Visions, Computers and Art.* New York: Abrams, 1987.

Green, Oliver. *Underground Art.* London: Studio Vista, 1990.

Greiman, April. *Hybrid Imagery. The Fusion of Technology and Graphic Design.* New York: Watson-Guptill, 1990.

Heller, Steven, and Elinor Pettit. *Graphic Design Time Line.* New York: Allworth Press, 2000.

Heller, Steven, and Seymour Chwast. *Graphic Styles from Victorian to Post-Modern.* New York: Abrams, 1994.

Meggs, Philip. *A History of Graphic Design.* New York: Van Nostrand Reinhold, 1998.

Müller-Brockmann, Josef. *A History of Visual Communication.* New York: Hastings House, 1971.

Schwartz, Lillian. *The Computer Artist's Handbook: Concepts, Techniques and Applications.* New York: Norton, 1992.

Varnedoe, Kirk, and Adam Gopnik. *High and Low: Modern Art and Popular Culture.* New York: The Museum of Modern Art, 1991.

Wheeler, Daniel. *Art since Mid-Century, 1945 to the Present.* New York: Vendome Press, 1991.

Wrede, Stuart. *The Modern Poster.* New York: The Museum of Modern Art, 1988.

Chapter 2

Old Tools, New Tools

Bloomer, Carolyn M. *Principles of Visual Perception.* New York: Van Nostrand Reinhold, 1976.

Botello, Chris. *Adobe Illustrator CS.* Boston, Mass.: Thomson Learning, 2005.

Goodman, Nelson. *Languages of Art.* Indianapolis: Bobbs-Merrill, 1968.

Gregory, R. L. *The Intelligent Eye.* New York: McGraw-Hill, 1970.

Kepes, Gyorgy. *Language of Vision.* Chicago: Paul Theobald, 1969.

Kerlow, Isaac V., and Judson Rosebush. *Computer Graphics for Artists and Designers.* New York: Van Nostrand Reinhold, 1994.

Miller-Clark, Denise. *Within This Garden: Photographs by Ruth Thorne-Thomsen.* Chicago: The Museum of Contemporary Photography, Columbia College, 1993.

Vaizey, Marina. *The Artist as Photographer.* New York: Holt, Rinehart and Winston, 1982.

Wilson, Stephen. *Using Computers to Create Art.* Englewood Cliffs, N.J.: Prentice Hall, 1986.

Chapter 3

Digital Imaging

Arntson, Amy. *Graphic Design Basics.* Belmont, Calif.: Wadsworth/Thomson Learning, 2003.

Bennett, James Gordon. *Design Fundamentals for New Media.* Clifton Park, N.Y.: Thomson Delmar Learning, 2005.

Buchanan, Margolin. *Discovering Design.* Chicago: University of Chicago Press, 1995.

Campbell, Alastair. *The Designer's Lexicon.* San Francisco: Chronicle Books, 2000.

Gordon, Bob and Maggie. *The Complete Guide to Digital Graphic Design.* New York: Watson-Guptill, 2002.

Greiman, April. *Hybrid Imagery: The Fusion of Technology and Graphic Design.* New York: Watson-Guptill, 1990.

Supon Design Group. *International Women in Design.* New York: Madison Square Press, 1993.

Chapter 4

Mastering Color

Albers, Josef. *Interaction of Color.* New Haven, Conn.: Yale University Press, 1972.

Delamare, Francois, and Bernard Guineau. *Colors: The Story of Dyes and Pigments.* New York: Abrams, 2000.

Itten, Johannes. *The Art of Color.* New York: Van Nostrand Reinhold, 1974.

Lacey, Joel. *The Complete Guide to Digital Imaging.* New York: Watson-Guptill, 2001.

Pring, Roger, and Alastair Campbell. *WWW.Color.* New York: Watson-Guptill, 2000.

Wong, Wucius, and Benjamin Wong. *Visual Design on the Computer.* 2nd ed. New York: Norton, 2001.

Zelanski, Paul, and Mary Pat Fisher. *Color.* Englewood Cliffs, N.J.: Prentice Hall, 1989.

Chapter 5

Intermediate Raster Graphics

Adobe Creative Team. *Adobe Photoshop CS Classroom in a Book.* Indianapolis: Adobe Press, 2004.

Dayton, Linnea, and Jack David. *The Photoshop CS Wow! Book.* Berkeley, Calif.: Peachpit Press, 2004.

Georges, Gregory. *50 Fast Photoshop CS Techniques.* Hoboken, N.J.: Wiley, 2004.

McClelland, Deke. *Photoshop CS Bible.* New York: Wiley, 2004.

Heiting, Manfred. *Icons: Man Ray.* Köln, Germany: Taschen, 2001.

Threinen-Pendarvis, Cher. *The Painter 8 Wow! Book.* Berkeley, Calif.: Peachpit Press, 2003.

Weinmann, Elaine, and Peter Lourekas. *Photoshop 7 for Windows and Macintosh: Visual QuickStart Guide.* Berkeley, Calif.: Peachpit Press, 2004.

Chapter 6

Intermediate Vector Graphics

Alspach, Ted, and Jennifer Alspach. *Illustrator CS Bible.* Hoboken, N.J.: Wiley, 2003.

Seo, Hyun Sook, and Sae Nan Chong. *Mastering Artistic Design, Illustrator 10.* Cincinnati, Ohio: Muska and Lipman, 2002.

Steuer, Sharon. *The Adobe Illustrator CS WOW! Book.* Berkeley, Calif.: Peachpit Press, 2003.

Sutton, Jeremy. *Painter 8 Creativity: Digital Artist's Handbook.* Burlington, Mass.: Focal Press, 2003.

Weinmann, Elaine, and Peter Lourekas. *Illustrator 10 for Windows and Macintosh: Visual QuickStart Guide.* Berkeley, Calif.: Peachpit Press, 2004.

Chapter 7

Web Design

Burgoyne, Patrick, and Liz Faber. *The New Internet Design Project Reloaded.* New York: Universe Publishing, 1999.

Castro, Elizabeth. *HTML for the World Wide Web: Visual QuickStart Guide.* 4th ed. Berkeley, Calif.: Peachpit Press, 2000.

Layng, Jacqueline, and Terre Layng Rosner. *Media Design: The Practice of Communications Technologies.* Upper Saddle River, N.J.: Pearson Prentice Hall, 2004.

Niederst, Jennifer. *Web Design in a Nutshell.* Sebastopol, Calif.: O'Reilly, 1999.

Siegel, David. *Creating Killer Web Sites II.* Indianapolis: Hayden Books, 1997.

Towers, J. Tarin. *Dreamweaver for Windows and Macintosh: Visual QuickStart Guide.* Berkeley, Calif.: Peachpit Press, 2002.

Chapter 8

Multimedia Design

Cohen, Sandee. *Macromedia Fireworks MX for Windows and Macintosh: Visual QuickStart Guide.* Berkeley, Calif.: Peachpit Press, 2002.

Nyquist, John, and Robert Martin. *Director 8 and Lingo Bible.* Hoboken, N.J.: Wiley, 2000.

Reinhard, Robert. *Macromedia Flash MX 2004 Bible.* Hoboken, N.J.: Wiley, 2003.

Schaeffer, Mark, and Andre Persidsky. *Macromedia Director MX 2004 for Windows and Macintosh: Visual QuickStart Guide.* Berkeley, Calif.: Peachpit Press, 2004.

Ulrich, Katherine. *Macromedia Flash MX 2004 for Windows and Macintosh: Visual QuickStart Guide.* Berkeley, Calif.: Peachpit Press, 2004.

Underdah, Brian. *Macromedia Director MX Bible.* Hoboken, N.J.: Wiley, 2004.

Periodicals and Annuals

AIGA Graphic Design, USA. New York: Watson-Guptill Publications annual, 1980–present.

Artists' Market: Where and How to Sell Your Artwork. Cincinnati, Ohio: Writer's Digest Books.

Artnews. New York.

Ballast Quarterly Review. Roy Behrens, ed. Dysart, Iowa: Bobolink Books.

Communication Arts. Palo Alto, Calif.: Coyne & Blanchard, Inc.

Fine Print. San Francisco, California.

Graphic Artists Guild. Handbook of Pricing and Ethical Guidelines. Cincinnati, Ohio: Writer's Digest Books.

Graphis. Zurich, Switzerland: Walter Herdeg.

How. New York: R C Publications.

Print. Washington, D.C.: R C Publications.

Print Casebooks. Washington, D.C.: R C Publications.

Step-by-Step Graphics. Peoria, Ill.: Dynamic Graphics Educational Foundation (DGEF).

U&lc. New York: International Typeface Corporation.

Women in the Arts. Washington, D.C.: National Museum of Women in the Arts.

Picture Credits

Screen shots created by Tammy Roemer, Seth VandeLeest, and Amy Arntson.

Chapter 1

5: Corbis; **6**: Art Institute of Chicago. Gift of Mrs. Gilbert W. Chapman, in memory of Charles B. Goodspeed, 1948.561. © 2005 Estate of Pablo Picasso/Artists Rights Society (ARS), New York; **7**: Philadelphia Museum of Art: A. E. Gallatin Collection, 1952/© 2005 Estate of Pablo Picasso/Artists Rights Society (ARS), New York; **8**: Nationalgalerie, Staaliche Museen, Berlin/Bildarchiv Preussischer Kulturbesitz/Art Resource, NY © 2005 Artists Rights Society (ARS)/VG Bild-Kunst, Bonn; **9 (top)**: Musée National d'Art Moderne, Centre Georges Pompidou, Paris/Art Resource, NY/© 2005 Man Ray Trust/Artists Rights Society (ARS), NY/ADAGP, Paris; **9 (bottom)**: VG Bild-Kunst, Bonn. © 2005 Artists Rights Society (ARS), NY; **10**: © Artists Rights Society (ARS), NY; **11**: Albright-Knox Art Gallery, Buffalo, N.Y. Sarah Norton Goodyear Fund, 1993; **12 (top)**: Courtesy, MIT Archives; **12 (bottom)**: © Charles Csuri; **14**: © David Em; **15**: © Harold Cohen; **16**: Courtesy of the artist; **17 (left)**: © Barbara Nessim. Courtesy of the artist; **17 (right)**: Courtesy of the artist; **18**: Courtesy, Katherine McCoy; **19**: Ray Gun Publishing, Santa Monica, CA.

Chapter 2

25: Courtesy of the artist; **26**: Musée Condé, Chantilly, France/Reunion des Musées Nationaux/Art Resource, NY; **27**: Corbis; **29**: George Eastman House, Rochester, N.Y.; **31 (top)**: Courtesy George Bryson's daughter; **33**: Diagram by Tiffany Dorner-Jones; **37**: Helen Birch Bartlett Memorial Collection, The Art Institute of Chicago; **38 (top)**: Adobe product screen shot(s) reprinted with permission from Adobe Systems Incorporated; **38 (bottom)**: Courtesy of Judy Pfaff and Tandem Press; **39**: Adobe product screen shot(s) reprinted with permission from Adobe Systems Incorporated; **40 (top)**: Adobe product screen shot(s) reprinted with permission from Adobe Systems Incorporated; **40 (bottom)**: Adobe product screen shot(s) reprinted with permission from Adobe Systems Incorporated; **41 (top)**: Adobe product screen shot(s) reprinted with permission from Adobe Systems Incorporated; **41 (bottom)**: Adobe product screen shot(s) reprinted with permission from Adobe Systems Incorporated; **44**: Adobe product screen shot(s) reprinted with permission from Adobe Systems Incorporated; **45 (top)**: Adobe product screen shot(s) reprinted with permission from Adobe Systems Incorporated; **45 (bottom)**: Courtesy of April Greiman.

Chapter 3

51 (top): Illustration by Tiffany Dorner-Jones. Screen shot: Adobe product screen shot(s) reprinted with permission from Adobe Systems Incorporated; **51 (bottom)**: Adobe product screen shot(s) reprinted with permission from Adobe Systems Incorporated; **52**: Adobe product screen shot(s) reprinted with permission from Adobe Systems Incorporated; **53 (top)**: Adobe product screen shot(s) reprinted with permission from Adobe Systems Incorporated; **53 (bottom)**: Adobe product screen shot(s) reprinted with permission from Adobe Systems Incorporated; **54**: Adobe product screen shot(s) reprinted with permission from Adobe Systems Incorporated; **55**: Adobe product screen shot(s) reprinted with permission from Adobe Systems Incorporated; **56 (top)**: Adobe product screen shot(s) reprinted with permission from Adobe Systems Incorporated; **56 (bottom)**: Image courtesy of the author. Screen shots: Adobe product screen shot(s) reprinted with permission from Adobe Systems Incorporated; **57**: Thomas G. Boss Fine Books; **58**: Courtesy of the Artist; **59**: Collection Institut für Auslandsbeziehungen, Stuttgart/© 2005 Artists Rights Society (ARS)/VG Bild-Kunst, Bonn; **60 (bottom)**: Adobe product screen shot(s) reprinted with permission from Adobe Systems Incorporated; **64 (top)**: Image courtesy of the author. Screen shots: Adobe product screen shot(s) reprinted with permission from Adobe Systems Incorporated; **64 (bottom)**: Illustration by Chris Eichman. Screen shot: Adobe product screen shot(s) reprinted with permission from Adobe Systems Incorporated; **65**: Image courtesy of the author. Screen shots: Adobe product screen shot(s) reprinted with permission from Adobe Systems Incorporated; **66**: Image courtesy of the author. Screen shots: Adobe product screen shot(s) reprinted with permission from Adobe Systems Incorporated; **67**: Image courtesy of the author. Screen shots: Adobe product screen shot(s) reprinted with permission from Adobe Systems Incorporated; **68**: Adobe product screen shot(s) reprinted with permission from Adobe Systems Incorporated; **69**: Adobe product screen shot(s) reprinted with permission from Adobe Systems Incorporated; **70**: Adobe product screen shot(s) reprinted with permission from Adobe Systems Incorporated; **71**: Adobe product screen shot(s) reprinted with permission from Adobe Systems Incorporated; **73**: Banque d'Images, ADAGP/Art Resource, NY/© 2005 C. Herscovici, Brussels/Artists Rights Society (ARS), New York; **74**: The Menil Collection, Houston, Texas/© 2005 C. Herscovici, Brussels/Artists Rights Society (ARS), New York; **75 (top)**: Courtesy of the artist; **75 (bottom)**: Courtesy of the artist; **76**: Courtesy of the artist.

Chapter 4

80: Courtesy of the artist; **82 (top)**: Courtesy of the artist; **84 (top)**: San Francisco Museum of Modern Art, Gift of Mrs. Anni Albers and The Josef Albers Foundation; **84 (bottom-left)**: San Francisco Museum of Modern Art, Gift of Mr. and Mrs. William C. Janss; **84 (bottom-right)**: San Francisco Museum of Modern Art, Gift of Mrs. Anni Albers and The Josef Albers Foundation; **88 (top)**: Adobe product screen shot(s) reprinted with permission from Adobe Systems Incorporated; **88 (middle)**: Adobe product screen shot(s) reprinted with permission from Adobe Systems Incorporated; **88 (bottom)**: Adobe product screen shot(s) reprinted with permission from Adobe Systems Incorporated; **89 (left)**: Courtesy of the artist; **90 (right)**: Courtesy of the artist; **91**: Artwork by Steve Hojinski. Screen shots: Adobe product screen shot(s) reprinted with permission from Adobe Systems Incorporated; **92**: Adobe product screen shot(s) reprinted with permission from Adobe Systems Incorporated; **93**: Adobe product screen shot(s) reprinted with permission from Adobe Systems Incorporated; **94**: Illustration by Chris Eichman. Screen shots: Adobe product screen shot(s) reprinted with permission from Adobe Systems Incorporated; **95 (right)**: Adobe product screen shot(s) reprinted with permission from Adobe Systems Incorporated; **96**: Adobe product screen shot(s) reprinted with permission from Adobe Systems Incorporated; **97**: Adobe product screen shot(s) reprinted with permission from Adobe Systems Incorporated; **98**: Adobe product screen shot(s) reprinted with permission from Adobe Systems Incorporated; **99 (left)**: Adobe product screen shot(s) reprinted with permission from Adobe Systems Incorporated; **99 (right)**: London Transport Museum; **101**: Courtesy of the artist.

Chapter 5

104 (top): Courtesy of the artist; **104 (middle)**: © Man Ray Trust/ADAGP–ARS/Telimage—2005. © 2005 Man Ray Trust/Artists Rights Society (ARS), NY/ADAGP, Paris; **104 (bottom)**: The Museum of Modern Art. Gift of James Thrall Soby (132.1941)/Digital Image © The Museum of Modern Art/Licensed by Scala/Art Resource, NY/© 2005 Man Ray Trust/Artists Rights Society (ARS), NY/ADAGP, Paris; **105 (top-left)**: Courtesy of anonymous collector; **105 (top-right)**: © Jerry Uelsmann; **105 (bottom-right)**: Courtesy of the artist; **106 (left)**: The Museum of Modern Art. Gift of James Thrall Soby (110.1941)/Digital image © The Museum of Modern Art/Licensed by Scala/Art Resource, NY/© 2005 Man Ray Trust/Artists Rights Society (ARS), NY/ADAGP, Paris; **106 (right)**: Courtesy of the f-5 group; **107 (top)**: Courtesy of the artist; **107 (bottom)**: Courtesy of the artist; **108**: Courtesy of the artist; **109**: Adobe product screen shot(s) reprinted with permission from Adobe Systems Incorporated; **110**: Adobe product screen shot(s) reprinted with permission from Adobe Systems Incorporated; **111**: Adobe product screen shot(s) reprinted with permission from Adobe Systems Incorporated;

112 (top-left): Adobe product screen shot(s) reprinted with permission from Adobe Systems Incorporated; **112 (bottom-left; right)**: Adobe product screen shot(s) reprinted with permission from Adobe Systems Incorporated; **113 (top-left)**: Courtesy of the artist; **113 (bottom-left; top-right)**: Adobe product screen shot(s) reprinted with permission from Adobe Systems Incorporated; **113 (bottom-right)**: Adobe product screen shot(s) reprinted with permission from Adobe Systems Incorporated; **114 (top)**: Adobe product screen shot(s) reprinted with permission from Adobe Systems Incorporated; **114 (bottom)**: Courtesy of the artist; **115**: Adobe product screen shot(s) reprinted with permission from Adobe Systems Incorporated; **116 (bottom-left)**: Courtesy of the artist; **116 (bottom-right)**: Courtesy of the artist; **117 (top)**: Courtesy of the artist; **117 (middle)**: Courtesy of the artist; **119 (bottom)**: Corel Painter; **120 (top)**: Courtesy of the artist; **120 (bottom)**: Corel Painter; **121**: Corel Painter; **122**: Corel Painter; **123**: Corel Painter; **124**: Corel Painter; **125**: Corel Painter; **126**: Corel Painter; **127**: Courtesy of the artist; **128**: Courtesy of the artist; **129**: Courtesy of the artist; **130**: Courtesy of the artist; **131**: Courtesy of the artist.

Chapter 6

135 (left): The Elvehjem Museum of Art, University of Wisconsin–Madison. Bequest of John H. Van Vleck, 1980; **135 (right)**: Digital image © The Museum of Modern Art/Licensed to Scala/Art Resource, NY; **137 (top)**: Courtesy of the artist; **138**: Adobe product screen shot(s) reprinted with permission from Adobe Systems Incorporated; **139**: Adobe product screen shot(s) reprinted with permission from Adobe Systems Incorporated; **141 (top-left)**: Adobe product screen shot(s) reprinted with permission from Adobe Systems Incorporated; **141 (top-right)**: Courtesy of the artist; **142**: Courtesy of the artist; **143 (top; middle)**: Adobe product screen shot(s) reprinted with permission from Adobe Systems Incorporated; **143 (bottom)**: Adobe product screen shot(s) reprinted with permission from Adobe Systems Incorporated; **144**: Adobe product screen shot(s) reprinted with permission from Adobe Systems Incorporated; **145**: Adobe product screen shot(s) reprinted with permission from Adobe Systems Incorporated; **146 (top)**: Courtesy of the artist; **146 (bottom-left)**: Courtesy of the artist; **146 (bottom-right)**: Courtesy of the artist; **147 (left)**: Courtesy of the artist; **147 (middle)**: Courtesy of the artist; **147 (right)**: Courtesy of the artist; **148**: Adobe product screen shot(s) reprinted with permission from Adobe Systems Incorporated; **150 (right)**: Courtesy of the artist.

Chapter 7

155: Courtesy of the Cooper-Hewitt National Design Museum, Smithsonian Institution; **157 (top)**: © Copyright 2004 Portfolios.com; **159**: Courtesy of the artist; **160**: Courtesy of the artist; **163 (top)**: Image courtesy of the author. Screen shots: Adobe product screen shot(s) reprinted with permission from Adobe Systems Incorporated; **163 (bottom)**: Courtesy Macromedia, Inc.; **164 (left)**: Courtesy Macromedia, Inc.; **164 (top-right)**: Adobe product screen shot(s) reprinted with permission from Adobe Systems Incorporated; **164 (bottom-right)**: Adobe product screen shot(s) reprinted with permission from Adobe Systems Incorporated; **165**: Adobe product screen shot(s) reprinted with permission from Adobe Systems Incorporated; **166 (top-left)**: Courtesy Macromedia, Inc.; **166 (bottom-left)**: Courtesy Macromedia, Inc.; **166 (top-right)**: Courtesy Macromedia, Inc.; **167 (top)**: Courtesy Studio Planet Propaganda, Madison, WI; **167 (bottom)**: Adobe product screen shot(s) reprinted with permission from Adobe Systems Incorporated; **168**: Courtesy Macromedia, Inc.

Chapter 8

172: Courtesy Studio Planet Propaganda, Madison, WI; **174**: © Graphic Havoc avisualagency; **177**: Art by Chris Eichman. Screen shots: Adobe product screen shot(s) reprinted with permission from Adobe Systems Incorporated;

178: Adobe product screen shot(s) reprinted with permission from Adobe Systems Incorporated; **179 (middle-left)**: GifBuilder by Yves Piquet; **179 (top-right)**: Courtesy Macromedia, Inc.; **179 (bottom)**: Courtesy Macromedia, Inc.; **180**: Courtesy Macromedia, Inc.; **181**: Courtesy Macromedia, Inc.; **182**: Courtesy Macromedia, Inc.; **183**: Courtesy Macromedia, Inc.; **184 (left)**: Courtesy Macromedia, Inc.; **185 (top)**: Courtesy Studio Planet Propaganda, Madison, WI; **185 (bottom)**: Courtesy of the artist; **186**: Art courtesy of Coleen Deck. **187**: Musée National d'Art Moderne, Centre Georges Pompidou, Paris, France/CNAC/MNAM/Dist. Réunion des Musées Nationaux/Art Resource, NY; **188**: Carl Solway Gallery, Cincinnati, OH, photo by Cal Kowal.

Index

A

Additive color model, 85
Additive primaries, 85
Adjusting gradients (Illustrator), 92–93
Advertising
  animation for, 184
Albers, Josef, 84
  Homage to the Square, 83
Alpha channel (Photoshop), 113
Ambiguous figure/ground relationship, *56,* 58, *59*
  portfolio assignment, 62
Analog data
  analog to digital conversion, 32–33
  defined, 29
Analogous color scheme, 82
Analytic Cubism, 6
Anchor points, 50–51
Animation, 173, 176–177
  for advertising and entertainment, 184
  defined, 176
  in Flash, 179–184
  language for, 179–180
  vs. motion graphics, 176
  packages for, 179
  steps for, in ImageReady, 178
Animation, web design, 166, 168
AOL, 161
Apple Computer, 13
Applying a gradient (Illustrator), 92
Applying filters (Illustrator), 142–143
Area Type tool (Illustrator), 140
Arntson, Amy E.
  7 am to 7 pm, 80
  Painterly, 119
Auto Trace tool, 138–139

B

Basic Shapes, 50
Bauhaus, 7, 9
Bayer, Herbert
  cover for *Bauhaus* Magazine, *9*
Behrens, Roy, 103
  Barbarian Seville, 107
  At a Loss for Words, 104
Bellavance, Leslie, 89, *89*
  Bellavance Wall #7, 89
  Bellavance Wall #11, 89
  Threshold, 89
Bergeron, Bill, *173*
Berners-Lee, Tim, 154
Binary data, 34
Bison cave drawing, *24*
Bit, 34
Bitmap, 34
Bitmap Mode, 86
Bitmapped graphics, 48, 62. *See also* Raster graphics
Blend tool, 138, 145
Blinn, Jim, 12
Book of Hours, 25
Braque, Georges, 6
Brightness correction, 66
Browser, 156–157
Brushes (Painter), 123–124
Bryson, Robert
  Longcase clock, 31
Byte, 34

C

Calibration, 90
Cannistra, Carla, *60*
  Calendar illustration, 82
  Winter, 146
Canvas
  setting up, 40–41
Carson, David, 18
  Mixed Messages, 20
Cartesian coordinates, 48, 50
Cascading Style Sheets, 165
Cerf, Vinton, 154
Channels, 113–114
Clipping path (Illustrator), 148
Cloning, 125–126
Closed shapes, 51–52, 54
Closure, 133, 136, 149
CMYK, 85–86
Cohen, Harold, 14
  AARON Painting, 15
Collage, 6
Color. *See also* Color, electronic
  defined, 79
  eye and brain, 80–81
  hue, 81
  intensity, 81
  light and color perception, 80
  physics of, 80
  properties of, 81–82
  psychology of, 83
  saturation, 81
  simultaneous contrast, 83–85
  synesthesia, 87
  value, 81
  warm, 83
Color, electronic
  additive color model, 85
  Bitmap Mode, 86
  calibration and printing, 90
  CMYK, 85–86

Color, electronic *(continued)*
color creation basics in Illustrator, 92–95
color creation basics in Photoshop, 95–101
color gamut, 86
color models, 85
gradient, 90–91
Grayscale Mode, 86–88
HSB, 88
Indexed Color Mode, 88
output, 88, 90
RGB, 85
spot color, 91
subtractive color model, 85
Web Color, 88
web design and, 164–165
Color Balance, 67
Color correction, 66–68
Color Balance, 67
curves function, 67
Hue/Saturation dialog, 67
variations dialog box, 68
Color gamut, 86
Color models. *See* Color, electronic
Color Palette (Photoshop), 96
Color Picker (Photoshop), 96
Color schemes, 82–83
analogous, 82
complementary, 82
monochromatic, 82
split complementary, 82–83
triadic, 82
Colors palette (Painter), 122
Color theory, 79, 81–85
additive model, 85
subtractive model, 85
Color wheel, 81
Color Window (Illustrator), 92
Complementary color scheme, 82
Computer graphics
defined, 4
desktop development, 13
early innovation in, 11–13
illustration and graphic design, 15–17
layered communication, 18–20
moving dot, 11
painting and drawing development, 13–15
realism in, 11–13
Continuation, 136, 142, 149, 159
Contrast correction, 66
Cook, Matt Morris
Neruda, 141
Copy function, 52, 54
Corel Painter. *See* Painter
Csuri, Charles, 12
Hummingbird, 12
Cubism, 6
Curved line, 53
creating, 51
Curves function, 67

D

Dada, 6–7
Daguerre, Louis-Jacques-Mandé, 27–28
Dailey, Heidi
logo, *83*
Davis, Jessica, *49*
Deck, Coleen
Search Twice, 186
Default fonts, 165
Delaroche, Paul, 104
Depth cueing, 12
Descartes, René, 49, 50
Deselecting, 52
Design principles
for raster graphics, 105–108
for vector graphics, 135–136
Desktop computer graphics
development of, 13
Digital data
analog to digital conversion, 32–33
defined, 29
elements of, 30–32
Diptych, 107
Direction selection tool, 53
Dithering, 164–165
Domain name, 156
Dorner-Jones, Tiffany, 33, 51
Calendar Series, 128
Composite Portrait, 113
Download time, 160–161
Drawing
innovative artists in, 13–15
vector graphics for, 48
Dreamweaver, 179
Drenttel, William, 154
Cooper-Hewitt National Design Museum website, *155*
DSL, 161
Duncan, Greg, *173*
Duotones, 87, 90

E

Eastman, George, 28
Ehrenfels, Christian von, 149
Eichman, Chris, *94, 119, 177*
Wine Label Stages, 137
Electromagnetic spectrum, 80
Electronic color. *See* Color, electronic
Em, David, 13–14
Transjovian Pipeline, 14
EPS (Encapsulated PostScript), 38–39
Eye direction, 133, 136, 142

F

Fenster, Diane, 24, 76
 LookListen, 25
 Phlebas the Phoenician a Fortnight Dead, 76
 Untitled (Shoes), 75
Figure/ground relationship, 47, 50, 56–62, 149, 159
 ambiguous, *56,* 58, *59*
 defined, 56
 Gestalt, 73
 reversible, *56,* 57–58
 stable, *56,* 57
File formats
 lossy, 39
 types of, 38–39
Files
 format for web design, 163–164
 naming conventions for, 39
 naming for web design, 161–162
 size of, for web design, 162–163
Fill and stroke command, 52, 54
Filters, 70
Fireworks, 179
Flash, 179
 steps for creating basic animation in, 179–184
Fluxus, 10–11
Focal point, 133, 136, 142
FOCOLTONE, 91
Fonts
 creating, 52, 55
 default, 165
 web design, 165
Form follows function, 5, 7, 10
Found objects, 6, 7, 10
4-D (Four-Dimensional), 175
Frames, web design, 166
Frames (Flash), 180
Freehand, 48

G

Gestalt, 73, 149, 159
GIF, 39
 interlaced, 162
 using in web design, 163–164
Gigabytes, 32
Gradient, 90–91
Gradient Editor (Photoshop), 96–97
Gradient effect (Photoshop), 110–111
Gradient (Illustrator), 92–93
Gradient (Painter), 125
Gradient Swatches (Illustrator), 92, 95
Gradient Tool (Photoshop), 96
Graettinger, Martha, *185*
Graphic design
 innovative artists in, 15–17
 similarities/differences between print and web design, 158–161
Graphic tablet, 137–138
Grayscale Mode, 86–88
Greiman, April, 15, 45
 Design Quarterly #133. Does It Make Sense?, 17
 Summer Programs poster, *45*
Gutenberg, Johannes, 25
 Gutenberg Bible, 27

H

Halftone, 28
Hardware, 32
Hayashi, Keiko, *141*
Helfand, Jessica, 154
 Cooper-Hewitt National Design Museum website, *155*
Hidden line elimination, 11
Hieroglyph, 24
Hirby, Ben, *185*
Hiroshige, Utagawa
 The Sea Off Satta in Suruga Province, 135
Histogram, 65–66
Höch, Hannah
 Cut with the Kitchen Knife (through the Last Beer-Swilling Cultural Epoch of the Weimar Republic), 8
 Flucht (Flight), 59
Hofmann, Andy, *63*
Hojinski, Steve
 Honda S2000, 91
Holography, 177
HSB, 88
HTML, 156
Hue, 81
Hue/Saturation dialog, 67

I

Ibarra, Dan, *185*
Illuminated manuscript, 25
Illustration
 innovative artists in, 15–17
Illustrator. *See also* Vector graphics
 applying filters, 142–143
 Area Type tool, 140
 Auto Trace tool, 138–139
 Blend tool, 145
 clipping path, 148
 color creation in, 92–95
 Export Paths to Illustrator, 139
 graphic tablet, 137–138
 importing and working with scans, 138
 integrating raster and vector, 113–114, 148
 intermediate steps/tools for vector graphics, 136–149

Illustrator *(continued)*
lines, creating, 50–51
Mesh Gradient, 143–144
Pathfinder palette, 140–141
patterns, 145
Pen tool, 138
Type on a Path, 140
as vector graphics, 48
vector masking, 148
vector typography, 139–140
ImageReady, 176–177
steps for creating animation in, 178
Inbetweeners, 176
Indexed Color Mode, 88
Instance (Flash), 179
Integrating raster and vector, 113–114
Intellectual unity, 117
Intensity, 81
Interactivity, 155
multimedia design and, 171–174
web design and, 165–166
Interlaced GIF, 162
International Style, 9–10
Internet. *See also* Web design
basics of browsing, 156–157
historical background of, 154–155
as New Media, 155–156
Internet browser, 156–157
Interpolation, 64
Iris prints, 88, 89
ISDN, 161
Ives, Frederick, 28

J

JPEG, 39
progressive, 162–163
using in web design, 163–164

K

Kahn, Bob, 154
Kandinsky, Wassily, 87
Keyframes, 176, 180
Kurowski, Dan
Guinness Record (Most Tattoos, 5,473), 127
Kurtz, Keith
Butterfly and Moth Quiz, 142

L

LaBelle, Julie
Abstract Photograph, 116
Park Bench, 117
Presence, 117
Window, 116
Lancaster, Edward
Greet the Sun, 99
Lasso tool, 42, 69
Layer Adjuster tool (Painter), 122
Layered communication
innovative artists in, 18–20
Layer masks (Photoshop), 112
Layers, 44, 70
vector graphics and, 52–53, 55
Layers (Flash), 179–180
Layers (Illustrator), 53
Layers (Painter), 121
Layers (Photoshop)
blending, 109
linking, 109–110
opacity of, 109
organizing data by, 109
rearranging layers, 109
Layers Styles (Photoshop), 110
Library (Flash), 179
Licklider, J. C. R., 154
Light
color perception and, 80
electromagnetic spectrum, 80
as wave, 80–81
white light and color, 80, *81*
Limbourg brothers
Les Très Riches Heures, 26
Link, 165–166
Linotype machine, 25
LiveMotion, 179
Lossless file format, 39
Lossy file format, 39

M

Macintosh, 13
Magic wand, 42, 69
Magritte, René, 63
La lunette d'Approche (The Field-Glass), 74
Les Valeurs Personnelles (Personal Values), 73
Marquee tool, 69
Masking (Illustrator), 148–150
Masking (Painter), 126
Masking (Photoshop), 112–115
Mattos, John, 136
Fidel of Dreams, 90
Portrait for the Baltimore Sun, 134
Maxwell, James, 80
McCoy, Katherine, 18, 156
Cranbrook recruiting poster, *19*
McCoy, Michael, 18
McLimans, David, 147
Digging Up Dirt, 147
Newark (N.J.) Star Ledger, 147
Sketchbook cover, 146
Sketchbook interior spread, 146
Wheel Head, 147
McLuhan, Marshall, 3, 20, 156

Megabytes, 32
Memory
  accessing memory, 36
  basic units of, 34
  RAM, 34–35
  ROM, 34–35
Mergenthaler, Ottmar, 25
Mesh Gradient (Illustrator), 143–144
Metaphor, 116
Mezzotint, 44
Mixer palette (Painter), 122–123
Modernism, 4–5
Monitor
  size of, and web design, 163
Monochromatic color scheme, 82
Motion graphics, 171, 176
Motion tweening (Flash), 180
Moveable type, 24–27
Movie clip (Flash), 179
Movie (Flash), 180
Moving dot display, 11
Mucha, Alphonse, 136
  JOB, 135
Muller-Brockmann, J.
  poster for Kunstgewerbemuseum, *10*
Multimedia design, 178
  advertising and entertainment, 184
  animation, 176–184
  authoring software, 176
  defined, 171
  design and production team for, 176
  Flash, 179–184
  ImageReady, 177–178
  interactivity and, 171–174
  research and design steps in, 175–176
  video editing, 184, 186
  visual rhythm and, 176
Muybridge, Eadeward
  Galloping Horse, 5

N

Naming files, 39
  for web design, 161–162
Nessim, Barbara, 15
  Call Waiting, 17
New Media, 4, 154. *See also* Multimedia design
  defined, 155
  Internet as, 155–156
Newton, Sir Isaac, 80
Niépce, Joseph, 27

O

Object-oriented graphics, 48. *See also* Vector graphics
Opacity
  of layer, 109
Opacity options, 70
O'Sullivan, Timothy
  Fort Hell, 29

P

Page, Dustin, *61*
Paik, Nam June, 10–11, 186
  Arc Double Face, 187
  Family of Robots, 188
  Piano Piece, 11
Painter, 48
  brushes, 123–124
  Canvas, 121
  cloning, 125–126
  gradient, 125
  intermediate steps/tools for raster graphics in, 118–128
  layers, 121, 122
  masking, 126
  new/existing file in, 120
  palette, 122–123
  Paper Selector, 124
  Preferences, 121
  tool box, 120–121
Painting
  innovative artists in, 13–15
Painting tools, 70
Paint systems, 13
Palette windows (Painter), 122
Panels (Flash), 179
PANTONE, 86, 91
Paper Selector (Painter), 124
Paste function, 52, 54
Pathfinder palette (Illustrator), 140–141
Patterns (Illustrator), 145
PDF, 39
Pen tool creations and Shapes (Painter), 121–122
Pen tool (Illustrator), 138
Pfaff, Judy
  Sweet Lily, 38
Photograms, 7, 28, 106
Photographic image
  analog, 29, 30
  digital, 30–32
  historic perspective on, 27–29, 104–105
Photomontage, 6–7
Photoshop. *See also* Raster graphics
  basic steps/tools for raster graphics in, 65–72
  brightness correction, 66
  channels, 113–114
  color correction, 66–68
  color creation in, 95–101
  contrast correction, 66
  Export Paths to Illustrator, 139
  gradient effects, 110–111

Photoshop *(continued)*
Histogram, 65–66
integrating raster and vector, 113–114, 148
intermediate steps/tools for raster graphics in, 109–118
layers, 109–111
masking, 111–112
as raster graphics, 48
Physiological, 83
Picasso, Pablo, 6
Daniel-Henry Kahnweiler, 6
Still Life with Violin and Fruit, 7
PICT, 39
Pictographs, 24
Pixels
defined, 31
interpolation, 64
in raster graphics, 48, 49, 62, 64
resolution and, 36
Placing scans, 53, 55–56
PNG, 164
Postmodernism, 4–5, 10
Print design
similarities/differences with web design, 158–161
Printing
calibration and, 90
Chinese invention of, 24
Linotype machine, 25
moveable type, 24–27
Progressive JPEG, 162–163
Proof prints, 36
Protocol, 156
Proximity, 149
Psychology of color, 83

Q

Quadtones, 87
Quark, 48
Quick Mask (Photoshop), 111–112
QuickMorph, 179

R

RAM, 34–35
Raster graphics, 62–77
basic tools/steps in Photoshop for, 65–72
characteristics of, 48
compared to vector graphics, 48–49
design principles for, 105–108
image correction, 65–68
image creation, 68–72
intermediate steps/tools in Corel Painter, 118–128
intermediate steps/tools in Photoshop, 109–118
as painterly approach, 48
pixels and, 48, 49, 62, 64
resizing exercise, 65
size and resolution, 64
uses of, 48
Raster image, 38
Ray, Man, 106
Champs delicieux, 9
Noir et Blanche, 104
Rayograph, 106
Rectangular selections, 44
Reed, Ethel
Miss Träumerei, 57
Renaissance, 25
Repetition, 159
Resolution
defined, 36
pixels and, 36
for print graphics, 36
raster graphics, size and, 64
screen, 36
for web design, 162
Reversible figure/ground relationship, *56,* 57–58
portfolio assignment, 58, 62
RGB, 85
Rhythm, 159
visual, 176
Roberts, Holly
Young Man Smiling, 105
Roberts, Lawrence, 154
Roemer, Tammy, *119*
Wine Calendar, 120
Rollover button, 166
ROM, 34–35
Rosenberg, Marc, *173*
Rough, 115

S

Sands, Karen, *173*
Saturation, 81
Scanner
working process of, 32–33
Scanning (Photoshop)
adjustments, 42
adjustments to scan not done in Photoshop, 40
basic steps in, 39–40
copy, paste, and filters, 43–44
creating variety, 42–44
selections, 42–43
setting up canvas, 40–41
similarity and variety assignment, 42–44
Scans
placing, 53, 55–56
Schwartz, Lillian, 14–15
Selecting, 52

Semiotics, 115
Server, 161
Seurat, Georges
  A Sunday on La Grande Jatte, 37, 39
Shape tweening (Flash), 180
Shea, Leah, *160*
Silver print, 104
Similarity, 149
Similarity and variety, 38, 39
  scanning assignment, 42–44
Simultaneous contrast, 83–85
Sketchpad, 11
Software, 32
Sound, web design and, 168
Split complementary color scheme, 82–83
Spot color, 91
  in Illustrator, 92
  in Photoshop, 96
Stable figure/ground relationship, *56,* 57
  portfolio assignment, *58*
Stage (Flash), 179
Static frame, 180
Storage
  bits and bytes, 34
Subtractive color model, 85
Subtractive primaries, 85–86
Suer, Matt, *72*
Sura, Stephanie, *63*
Surrealism, 105
Sutherland, Ivan, 11
Swanson, Casey
  calendar illustration, *101*
  Dream Narrative, 107
  Wisconsin Stamp, 147
Swatches (Illustrator), 92
Swatches palette (Photoshop), 96
Swiss design, 9–10
Symbol (Flash), 179
Symmetrical pattern, 54–55
Synesthesia, 87
Synthetic Cubism, 6
Szopinski, Corey, *172, 185*

T

Tables, web design, 166
Talbot, William Henry Fox, 28
TCP/IP, 154
Textures, 44
Thorne-Thomsen, Ruth
  Two Faces Are a Vase, 58
Thumbnail sketch, 115
TIFF (Tagged Image File Format), 38
Time-based, 154
Tingesdahl, Jorel
  Artist Portrait Series, 114
TOYO, 91
Transform, 52
Triadic color scheme, 82
Triptychs, 107–108
Tritones, 87
Truckenbrod, Joan, 15, 129
  Electronic Patchwork, 129
  Quantum Realities 1, 131
  Spirit Site, 130
  Thresholding, 16
  Veil of Secrecy, 105
TRUMATCH, 86, 91
Tweening, 12, 180
Type
  creating, 52, 55
  web design, 165
Type on a Path (Illustrator), 140

U

Uelsmann, Jerry
  Untitled (floating globe), 105
Undo, 52
URL, 156

V

Value, 81
  simultaneous contrast and, 85
VandeLeest, Seth
  Character Animation, 185
  Digital Salamander, 108
Variation, 159
Variations dialog box
  for color corrections, 68
Variety. *See* Similarity and variety
Vector graphics, 49–62
  ambiguous figure/ground relationship assignment, 62
  basic steps/tools for, 50–53, 53–56
  characteristics of, 48
  compared to raster graphics, 48–49
  design principles for, 135–136
  drawing, 48
  intermediate steps/tools in Illustrator, 136–149
  reversible figure/ground relationship assignment, 58, 62
  stable figure/ground relationship assignment, 58
  uses of, 48, 133, 135
Vector masking (Illustrator), 148
Vector Paths (Photoshop), 97–99
Vector typography (Illustrator), 139–140
Video editing, 184, 186
Visual communication tools
  analog and digital data, 30–32
  moveable type, 24–27
  photographic image, 27–29

Visual language
figure/ground relationship, 56–62
similarity and variety, 38
Visual perception, 36
Visual rhythm
multimedia design and, 176
Visual unity, 117
Vo, Anna, *72*

W

Wade, Kevin, *185*
Warm colors, 83
Wave
light as, 80–81
Wavelength, 80
Web address, 156
Web Color, 88
Web design
animation and sound, 166, 168
color and, 164–165
differences with print design and, 159–161
download time and, 160–161
file format for, 163–164
file size, 162–163
interactivity, 165–166
monitor size, 163
naming your files, 161–162
pages and sites, 165
research and design stages, 157–158
resolution, 162
rules for, 161–165
similarities to print design, 158–159
software for, 156
tables and frames, 166
text, 165
video, 168
web publishing, 168
Web publishing, 168
Website, 165
White arrow tool, 51
Wilson, Brian, *185*
Wire frame drawing, 12
World Wide Web, 153. *See also* Internet; Web design

Y

Young, Thomas, 80

Z

Zang, Xiao
Pregnancy, 62